THE 116

JAMES P. MUEHLBERGER

THE 116

THE TRUE STORY OF ABRAHAM LINCOLN'S LOST GUARD

RESEARCH ASSISTANCE BY
DEBBY LOWERY AND JUDY SWEETS

ANKERWYCKE

Cataloging-in-Publication data is on file with the Library of Congress.

ISBN: 978-1-63425-195-2

Discounts are available for books ordered in bulk. Special consideration is given to state bars, CLE programs, and other bar-related organizations. Inquire at Book Publishing, ABA Publishing, American Bar Association, 321 N. Clark Street, Chicago, Illinois 60654-7598.

www.ShopABA.org

To my heart of hearts –
Jayme, Alexandra, and Maximillian

Contents

Prologue

On April 12, 1861, America was dying. To slave owners, recently elected President Abraham Lincoln, not slavery, was the cause. Considered a sectional candidate by the South, and winning the election with only 39 percent of the popular vote, Lincoln was so despised that seven states pulled out of the Union, and more threatened to do so. Many American cities, fearing civil war, slid into an economic recession.

Years before Abraham Lincoln stepped into Ford's Theatre for the last time, he was the target of assassins. Following his election, Lincoln began receiving death threats in telegrams and letters from Southern locations. While traveling by train to Washington for his inauguration, he had narrowly escaped assassination in Baltimore. Slave owners knew that although Lincoln's term might end in four years, the impact of that term, if it resulted in the abolition of slavery, or merely arrested its westward expansion, would end the South's dominance of America's political landscape.[1]

Five weeks after Lincoln took office, on Friday, April 12, a solitary boom rang out across Charleston harbor as a Confederate shell exploded over Fort Sumter, signaling the start of the Civil War. Confederate guns forced the federal troops to surrender the next day, and the Confederate stars and bars rose over Sumter. The Sunday morning headlines screamed the news from Charleston: Fort Sumter had fallen after a two-day bombardment by Confederate cannons. The firing on the flag at Fort Sumter, the President proclaimed, "forced upon the country the distinct issue, immediate dissolution or blood."[2]

Confederate leaders realized the South was vastly outnumbered. The Confederates' best chance for success depended on a quick strike leading to sudden victory. Many believed their best chance for victory would

1

be to eliminate the one person with the courage and determination to "put the foot down firmly" if necessary—Abraham Lincoln. *New York Tribune* editor Horace Greeley said, "There was forty times the reason for shooting [Lincoln] in 1860 than there was in '65, and at least forty times as many intent on killing him or having him killed."[3]

Washington was located in the heart of Confederate country. Located miles south of the Mason-Dixon Line in slaveholding territory, the nation's capital of 34 states was a slave-owning city in Maryland. Most of its residents and government employees either owned slaves or were pro-slavery, and the city was completely surrounded by the slave states of Virginia and Maryland. With no fortifications, only a handful of loyal soldiers, and infested with Confederate spies and saboteurs, the President and the city were easy prizes for the Confederate States of America.

When news of the attack on Fort Sumter reached the capital, many of those loyal to the Union panicked. Now, with the first shot of the Civil War fired, all believed the Confederate Army was ready to make a dash at Washington. Confederates tore up large sections of the only railroad leading to Washington, burned railroad bridges, and cut tele-graph wires, severing Washington's physical and communication ties to the loyal states. Washington was isolated, and her residents began fleeing the city on foot and by horse and wagon to avoid the anticipated battle all believed was imminent. The nation's capital was surrounded, isolated, and vulnerable—and the South rang with cries of "On to Washington!"[4]

A few hours after Confederate guns began bombarding federal troops at Sumter, Confederate Secretary of War Leroy P. Walker shouted to a jubilant crowd in Montgomery, Alabama, the capital of the Confederate States of America: "No man can tell when the war this day commenced will end, but I prophesy that the flag which now flaunts the breeze here will float over the dome of the old Capitol at Washington before the first of May." Jefferson Davis's wife sent out cards inviting her friends to a May 1st reception at the White House. President Lincoln startled his cabinet by stating, "If I were [Confederate General Pierre G.T.] Beauregard, I would take Washington."[5]

War stared at Lincoln from just 800 feet away. Only the width of the Potomac River separated the United States from the newly formed Confederate States of America. In the wooded Virginia hills overlooking the river, dozens of Confederate campfires blinked like evil red eyes at the city. It was rumored the Confederate army intended to attack Washington that night, kill or imprison Lincoln, and move the Confederate capital north of the Potomac. The nation's courage—and its very existence—was about to be severely tested.

On Monday, April 15, Lincoln issued an emergency proclamation calling for 75,000 troops to crush the rebellion and protect the capital. Washington was caught between Virginia, which seceded on April 17, and Maryland, which was in upheaval and looked as if it would also secede. One question now transfixed the nation: Whose soldiers would reach Washington first? Federal troops to save it? Or the Confederate army to seize it?

For ten days, the city's fate hung by a thread. The U.S. Army numbered less than 16,000 men, and nearly all of them had been scattered by a treasonous Secretary of War on the frontier west of the Mississippi River to guard against Indians raids. The military force that remained in defense of Washington consisted mainly of loyal government clerks and the military band. The clerks had been armed, but they knew little about warfare. Washington desperately needed fighting men who could handle a gun and would stand under fire. Rumors were heard in the city's saloons and whispered on gas-lit streets that the Confederate army was marching to Washington to hang Lincoln from the nearest tree. Lincoln was without protection in a city packed with rebels who were hoping to witness a *coup d'etat*. A journalist wrote: "From the 15th to the 25th of April the nation held its breath in anxious suspense."[6]

The most intriguing mystery of the Civil War is why Confederate soldiers did not storm Washington and kill or capture Lincoln shortly after the fall of Fort Sumter. Historians have noted Washington's escape from a "near-certain Southern capture appeared a miracle, and many Northern leaders could not understand why the Confederates had not attacked the lightly defended city." Was it incredible good luck that saved Lincoln, or something else? The only force standing in the Confederates' way was James H. Lane and 115 other Westerners, who Lane called together at Lincoln's request to protect the President and the White House. Lane called his company the "Frontier Guard," and most of its soldiers camped in the White House during the first ten days of the Civil War.[7]

The story of how Jim Lane and his emergency company of soldiers protected President Lincoln during the first days of the Civil War has been virtually ignored by generations of Civil War historians, most of whom have relegated it to a footnote, perhaps because no official records of the company had been discovered. Accordingly, lost to time were the identities of these brave soldiers and a detailed account of their actions. Letters written decades after the fact by some in the company identified a few of the men, but the letters were often inconsistent, incomplete, and riddled with inaccuracies. The story of the Frontier Guard has therefore long cried out for study.

Historians have lamented that, at best, only 51 of the names of these men were known (and many of these were questionable, as many men wanted to claim, after the fact and for obvious reasons, that they had risked their lives to save Lincoln), and the adjutant general could find "no roll of this organization." Were these men merely "hotel guests," as suggested by one historian, opportunists hoping to curry favor with the President, as suggested by others, or something more fearsome to the Confederates?[8]

Lawyers are storytellers, and we piece together a narrative based on the evidence. During my 35 years as a trial lawyer, I have combed through tens of thousands of documents looking for the "smoking gun" to make my case. I have spent months, sometimes years, tracking down witnesses—many of whom did not want to be found—who might know key facts. I've used the same approach here, arranging the facts as a lawyer would in presenting a case to a jury.

Because Lane had been asked by Lincoln to form a military guard, Lane's military training and experience would have led him to elect officers and prepare a muster roll and after-action report of the company's activities. Where was it? After six years of spending my weekends sifting through records in the Kansas historical collections located in Topeka, Lawrence, Leavenworth, and Lecompton without success, I traveled to Washington, D.C. during a sabbatical to continue the search. After several weeks, I finally stumbled upon the dusty record of the Guard, buried in the Library of Congress.

On the cover of a faded, forest-green 7 x 8½-inch volume, were embossed gold letters that read: "Frontier Guard Roll & Other Proceedings." The black ink made by a quill pen on the first page was as dark as the day it dried, but some of the ink was so faded on later pages that I could barely make out the words. The paper was yellowed, and I feared some of the pages might crumble if I turned them. What I discovered was startling. I later read nearly 500 original sources, including letters, memoirs, military reports, and newspaper articles, in order to prepare the manuscript. Here, for the first time, is the story these long-lost documents tell.[9]

Why should we care about Jim Lane and his Frontier Guard? After all, this pivotal event has been washed away from national memory by the rivers of blood shed over the next four years of war. The Union victory in the Civil War was not preordained, however, and Lane and his brave band likely saved Lincoln's life, thereby changing history. Without Lane's actions there might not have been an Emancipation Proclamation, and the Civil War may have turned out quite differently.

This is the story of a moment in our young country's history when almost everything hung in the balance. As we celebrate the 150th anniversary of the guns falling silent, it is fitting that we consider the men who saved Lincoln's life and constitutional government in the United States. Confederate General Theodore B. Gates called the Confederacy's failure to capture Lincoln in the first days of the Civil War one of the "unsolved riddles of Confederate policy."[10] This book, at long last, answers the riddle.

1

The White House Is Turned into Barracks

The United States shattered in April 1861, as the Confederate states and the Union began a fight to the death in a four-year Civil War that would leave 750,000 dead. Because the South was vastly outnumbered, Confederate leaders believed the South's best chance for success depended on a quick strike leading to sudden victory—the assassination of Abraham Lincoln. The day before Lincoln's inauguration, *The New York Times* noted grimly: "Heavy bets are pending on the question of Mr. Lincoln's safety through tomorrow's exercises, and great anxiety is felt . . . ." The *Philadelphia Inquirer* reported "there are rumors afloat of difficulties tomorrow . . . and a large number of picked men, in citizens' dress, will be near Mr. Lincoln all day."[1]

Lincoln's March 4, 1861, inauguration was the first chance for many Washingtonians to see their tall Western President. Under a dark curtain of heavy clouds, somber and threatening rain, multitudes packed themselves into the blocks around the White House, flowing down wooden boardwalks and dirt streets. The crowds mingled uneasily with the hundreds of troops put in place by General Winfield Scott to guard against an attempted assassination. At 75, he was older than the Capitol building, its dome then under construction. By 1861, Scott had served for almost half a century, under 14 presidents, from Thomas Jefferson to Lincoln. Protecting Lincoln's life and the capital from the Confederates would be the last, and perhaps the greatest, challenge of his long and distinguished career.

U.S. Army marksmen peered down from rooftops and windows along Pennsylvania Avenue. Cavalry were strategically located along Lincoln's parade route. Mounted soldiers accompanied the carriage containing the tall and energetic Lincoln and the short and thickset President James Buchanan, nearly 70, who had a sorrowful expression on his aged face. The soldiers crowded so close together and around the carriage that no shot could reach Lincoln during the ride from Willard's Hotel to the Capitol, where Lincoln gave his highly anticipated inaugural speech.[2]

The Western politician was a gigantic figure of long joints and imperfect proportions: enormous forehead, long legs, huge hands, and giant feet. At 52, he was 200 pounds of muscle on a 6 foot 4 inch frame, his black suit draped over sinewy shoulders and a narrow waist. His shoulders and forearms were so strong that he could hold a heavy, double-bladed ax horizontally in one outstretched arm and hand without a quiver. His gray eyes, under bushy eyebrows, set in a leathery face, peered out from under his stovepipe hat. He was the virile figure of his campaign: the strong, independent, Western rail-splitter, and not yet the haggard, hollow-eyed figure of Civil War photographs.

Lincoln spoke from a wooden platform constructed out from the east portico of the half-finished Capitol before nearly 30,000 spectators anxious to hear his inaugural address. He sat in the front row of dignitaries along with President Buchanan, Senator Stephen A. Douglas, and U.S. Supreme Court Chief Justice Roger B. Taney. Lincoln's wife, Mary, and their three sons sat behind him. As Lincoln made his way to the front of the platform and the little table from which he was meant to speak, he stared around in amazement at the crowd. It rolled away from the platform in great banks of humanity, filling the open spaces around the Capitol to overflowing. The blowing clouds parted momentarily, and the sun shone down on the platform as he began to speak.

No advance copies of Lincoln's speech had been given to the press, and none would be passed out until the words were spoken. Lincoln's clear, high voice, trained for over 20 years in outdoor speaking venues in the West, could be heard by nearly everyone. He tried to calm Southern anxiety by promising he had no intent "to interfere with slavery in the States where it exists." He made a powerful case for continued federal authority over what he insisted was an "unbroken" Union. He closed with a lyrical assurance that "the mystic chords of memory . . . will yet swell the chorus of the Union, when again touched . . . by the better angels of our nature."[3]

At the end of Lincoln's speech, Supreme Court Chief Justice Roger Taney, a slave owner, then walked slowly to the little table and grudgingly administered the oath of office, his hands shaking very perceptibly with emotion. At the age of 83, the withered Taney was several years older than the Constitution, whose interpreter he had been for a quarter century. Four years earlier, Taney had authored the *Dred Scott* decision, in which he said African-Americans were not citizens and had "no rights which the white man was bound to respect." In taking the oath, Lincoln swore to "preserve, protect, and defend" a nation that was, for the first time in its brief history, in imminent danger of coming apart. General Scott was heard to exclaim, "Everything is going on peaceably—thank God Almighty!"[4]

The text of Lincoln's speech made its way halfway across the country almost immediately by telegraph, stopping at St. Joseph, Missouri, where the lines ended. Getting the message to San Francisco still meant doing as the ancient Romans had done, enlisting relays of dozens of riders—in this case the Pony Express—galloping nearly 2,000 miles across mountains and deserts with mail pouches strapped to their saddles. In the record time of "seven days and seventeen hours," Lincoln's speech could be read in Sacramento, California.[5]

Senator Jim Lane, representing the Union's newly-minted state of Kansas, was a frontier lawyer like Lincoln. Tall and lean, with his typically tousled hair adding another inch or so to his 6 foot frame, he had a hawklike face, seamed and bronzed by sun and wind. Prominent eyebrows overwhelmed his dark, deep-set, piercing eyes, and his face gleamed with passion and good humor. He was muscled, strong of limb, with a swelling chest. In Kansas, he typically wore a cowhide vest, a gun belt holding a revolver, black pants tucked into worn and scuffed, down-at-the-heel boots, and a black, flat-brimmed hat. Photos suggest he never made the acquaintance of a comb. One suspects he may have deliberately maintained an uncivilized look.

Lane was nearly as much of a national figure at the time as Lincoln. Lane was also a Westerner, a product of the frontier, of a primitive, rude society where he forged the emotional strengths of courage, self-reliance, and resourcefulness in the crucible of personal hardship. He developed an exaggerated style of speech and a boisterous and aggressive manner when stump-speaking out West. He had demonstrated great courage, leadership, and cunning in leading the Kansas Free State fighters to one surprising victory after another against larger armies of pro-slavery soldiers. As a result, pro-slavery men both hated and feared him.

Like Lincoln, Lane had left home, journeyed west, studied law, developed a reputation as an orator, and became an opponent of the spread of slavery. He became a national hero in the Mexican War of 1846–1847, and he achieved even greater fame as the general who successfully led Kansas freedom fighters against pro-slavery soldiers and a federal government determined to make Kansas a slave state. Eastern newspapers had dubbed him the "General Washington of Kansas." He was elected as the first United States senator from Kansas because he was the shrewdest and canniest of his rivals.[6]

After his election on April 4, Lane hurried to Washington from Lawrence, Kansas, arriving on Saturday, April 13, the day Fort Sumter fell to the Confederates. He checked into Room 12 at Willard's, a great barn of a hotel, which stood at the corner of 14th Street and Pennsylvania Avenue, within a short walk of the White House. Willard's was situated opposite the massive, stone Treasury Building, which was located between the hotel and the President's House. Close by were scores of Kansans, fresh from battles with pro-slavery men on the Kansas frontier, who were hoping to use their fighting skills in the Union Army.[7]

News of the Confederate attack on Fort Sumter raced through the city. The shouts of newsboys startled patrons emerging from theaters and saloons. At Willard's, under glittering gas lamps, the news was read in the lobby to a crowd that had suddenly gathered. The "firing on the flag" quickly produced a vociferous and "volcanic upheaval" in the North. The excitement in the North was mirrored in the South. A dispatch from South Carolina read, "The ball has opened." Threats of assassination were heard in the city's saloons, and "every breeze from the South came heavily laden with the rumors of war." An excited crowd gathered and swayed with every rumor around Willard's Hotel.[8]

Jim Lane was asked to make a speech outside the hotel to a crowd of several hundred men who had assembled on rough, cobblestoned Pennsylvania Avenue, one of the few paved streets in the city. The attack on Fort Sumter made it clear to Northerners that slave owners meant to make themselves masters of the Republic, as they were masters over their slaves. The country was coming apart, and it seemed the very survival of the government was at stake. Six years of sensational national newspaper coverage on Bleeding Kansas had made Lane a national hero to the North and a hated abolitionist to slave owners. Lane spoke from a dry-goods box in the street in front of the hotel. When he climbed up on the box, the crowd, consisting mainly of Southerners celebrating the fall of Fort Sumter, shouted, "Mob him! Hang him!" Men reached to pull him from the box to make good on their threat.[9]

Lane's eyes flashed, and his voice boomed, "Mob and be damned! I have 100 men from Kansas in this crowd, all armed, all fighting men, just from the victorious fields of Kansas! They will shoot every damned man of you who again cries, 'Mob'!" The ominous click of cocking revolvers was heard throughout the crowd and the Kansas men murmured their assent. The pro-slavery men stood deathly still, for no one seemed to know who stood next to him, and then they gradually melted away into the shadows of the half-built city.[10]

Many in the North were surprised at the suddenness with which the Confederates resorted to attacking federal troops at Fort Sumter. In Washington, there were few preparations for war, even though Southern senators and representatives were daily making threats on the floor of Congress, and then resigning and leaving to join the Confederate Congress at Montgomery, Alabama. Washington's primary man-made fortification was Fort Washington, a decrepit structure built in 1809, located seven miles away on the Potomac River and defended by a single soldier.[11]

During the Great Secession Winter of 1860–1861, as Southern states seceded, their militias seized over 20 federal military installations within their boundaries, which were typically lightly defended but held guns and arsenals that treasonous Secretary of War John B. Floyd, a secession-

ist and former governor of Virginia, had ordered shifted from arsenals in
the North to the South. In a few months, Floyd would wear the uniform
of a Confederate brigadier general. In Florida, state troops seized a federal arsenal that held one million rifle and musket cartridges and 50,000
pounds of gunpowder. In Louisiana, federal officials handed over the
U.S. Mint, with over $599,000 in gold and silver coins.[12]

At the same time, the commander of the United States Army, General
Winfield Scott, had begun calling for stronger defenses in Washington
and reinforcement of the U.S. Army's southern installations. Scott's proposals were ignored by Secretary of War Floyd. Only after Floyd was
indicted for conspiracy in December 1860, and later replaced by the pro-
Union Kentucky Democrat Joseph Holt, was any action taken on Scott's
recommendations. By then it was too late.[13]

In February 1861 the Confederates formed the Confederate States
of America. The Confederates knew that if they could quickly gain control of the nation's essentially defenseless capital, they would achieve an
important psychological, if not military, advantage. They would possess
the symbols of government—the seals, the treaties, and the treasury—
and the apparent right to control the Army and Navy. Washington could
then be declared the capital of the new Confederacy. Foreign governments might recognize the Confederacy as the legitimate government
of the United States, possibly rendering aid. Seizure of the capital by
the Confederates might also cause people in the North, who were then
undecided, to support influential New York newspaper editor Horace
Greeley's view to "let our wayward sisters go in peace."[14]

Why did not Lincoln and others in the government quickly realize
their perilous position? First, Lincoln was not inaugurated until March
4, 1861. His Washington experience was limited to a two-year term as an
Illinois congressman 12 years earlier. Since then, he had been practicing
law in Springfield, Illinois, far from the intrigues of Washington. In the
first days of Lincoln's presidency, the administration was also disorga-
nized, ill-managed, and overwhelmed by job seekers.[15]

Lincoln's new administration also had to repair the damage to the
Army, Navy, and other departments caused by the secessionists in President Buchanan's administration and Congress. Insufficient funds had
been appropriated to maintain federal forts, increase the size of the Army

to guard Washington, protect federal installations, and purchase modern weapons. Finally, few Northern leaders, including Lincoln, appreciated the hatred slave owners harbored toward those who threatened the economic system that was the source of their wealth.[16]

The Kansas men in Washington, however, had fought for six long years in Western fields of battle against these same men and knew that war was inevitable. Lane and his men had learned from hard experience that slave owners would murder to preserve their way of life. The Kansans had previously felt the weight of the federal arm supporting slavery and the Slave Code. Now a great change had taken place. Lincoln and new executive officers had been elected. Freedom, instead of slavery, had been elevated upon the American standards.

On Sunday, April 14, after Lincoln returned through wind and rain to the White House following services at the New York Avenue Presbyterian Church, he attended an all-day cabinet meeting, with General Scott in attendance. At 6 feet 4 inches and 300 pounds, Scott was one of the few men in Washington who seemed to tower over Lincoln. The cabinet members, like most Americans, wanted to hear the latest news about the U.S. soldiers who had surrendered at Fort Sumter. They learned that Confederate General Pierre G. T. Beauregard had allowed U.S. Army Major Robert Anderson, Beauregard's artillery instructor at West Point, to return north by boat with his men. Many expected Beauregard to also travel north with a Confederate army that could travel by rail from Charleston to the banks of the Potomac in three or four days. *The New York Times* reported that morning that the Confederate leaders were proposing an immediate march on Washington with an army of 20,000 men, since the Confederate army now had "nothing else to do."[17]

The men discussed the surrender of Fort Sumter, how to protect Washington, and how to raise an army to put down the rebellion. The immediacy of the danger Washington faced was the subject of a heated exchange between General Scott and Pennsylvania Republican leader Alexander Kelly McClure, who attended the meeting. Scott admitted that Beauregard "commands more men at Charleston than I command on the continent east of the frontier." Scott was adamant, however, that Washington was safe. Lincoln was silent during this exchange, staring at Scott and twirling his spectacles in his long-fingered hands. Finally, he startled those in the room when he said: "It does seem to me, General, that if I were Beauregard I would take Washington." After much discussion, the alarmed group was unanimous in support of Lincoln's intent to immediately call for volunteers, whom Scott would order to Washington's defense.[18]

Lincoln's proclamation ordered state governors to raise volunteer militias. Congress had adjourned a month before, and Lincoln had to wait until the legislators returned to appropriate funds for a larger, professional army. Until then, Washington's defense was dependent upon the ability of state governors to quickly enlist and send volunteers. Lincoln decided to call for only 75,000 troops, because arms were in short supply at the remaining federal armories and it would be difficult to arm, outfit, and feed even 75,000 men.[19]

On Monday, April 15, Lincoln delivered his handwritten proclamation by telegraph to the national newspapers, calling for troops from an alarmed North to crush the Confederates. The same newspapers that printed Lincoln's proclamation reported: "32,000 [Confederate soldiers] are being mustered for an attack on Washington." Responses from the Northern governors came back almost immediately, but Lincoln worried the responses were unrealistic in their claims as to when the men could reach Washington. Accompanying President Lincoln's call for 75,000 troops to suppress the rebellion, recruiting posters screamed, "Volunteers wanted! An attack upon Washington anticipated!" In the North, the response to Lincoln's proclamation was so overwhelming he could have raised five times that number. One speaker warned that "Old Abe of the West would soon show" the Confederates their grievous error in shooting away the flag at Fort Sumter.[20]

The response to Lincoln's proclamation in Washington, however, was tepid. Washington was a Southern city, and Lincoln's inauguration had brought only economic disaster. Real estate values had plummeted, as many Washingtonians were planning to leave for the South. The price of slaves had collapsed at the markets across the Potomac in Alexandria, Virginia, as many anticipated that Lincoln would outlaw slavery in Washington. Washington was not the gleaming capital of today. To the east of the White House, at the far end of the lone paved avenue, stood the unfinished U.S. Capitol, over which a large crane was silhouetted against the sky like a gallows. To the south of the Executive Mansion, across a stinking canal fed by the Potomac River, "rose the sad stump of the Washington Monument," abandoned for lack of funds.[21]

In April 1861, Washington was a bleak start on the grand design of the Founding Fathers. The setting among the wooded hills of the Potomac River Valley was beautiful, but the city consisted of shabby brick and wooden buildings scattered along dirt roads. In the backs of most houses stood outhouses, pigsties, cowsheds, and chicken coops. During the day, the animals and birds roamed at will, in herds and flocks, through the streets and over the fields. The roughly one dozen federal buildings stood out in the otherwise rough environs for their aspirational grandeur.[22]

It was a small town. Because of the cost of draining its marshy land, development was primarily around Pennsylvania Avenue between the Capitol and the White House. Washington Circle, three-quarters of a mile west of the White House, was considered out of town. Travelers arriving in the capital on rattling train cars at the squalid Baltimore & Ohio station at the foot of Capitol Hill (near the present-day Union Station) could immediately see both the capital's promised grandeur and its squalor. To the left was a towering mass of white marble, the unfinished Capitol dome, from which "scaffold and cranes raised their black arms." To the right was a cleared space of mud, sand, and fields with wooden sheds and huts.[23]

The low elevation caused swamps, stagnant waters, and swarms of flies and mosquitoes. Primitive sanitation made the city a foul cauldron of epidemics. Family homes used outdoor privies, the contents of which regularly flooded into surrounding yards and lots and seeped into the groundwater. Hotel toilets flushed into back lots, canals, or creeks. Up Sixteenth Street, slaves hauled cartloads of human dung, which they dumped onto a stinking field ten blocks north of the White House. Garbage collection was infrequent, and the garbage-filled canals, within a few blocks of the President's House, gave off a gut-wrenching stench in warm weather and were a breeding ground for mosquitoes and flies. Outbreaks of dysentery, malaria, and typhoid fever plagued the 63,000 residents. Diplomats from Europe considered Washington a hardship post and left their families at home.[24]

Washington in the years before the Civil War seemed like a "city of slaves and old gentlemen." Washington's slaves carried water and shoveled coal, split wood and carved stone. Slaves were building the new expansions of the Capitol, just as they had built the White House a half century earlier. Slave ownership was still legal and there were 3,200 slaves in the city. Hotels in Washington catered to wealthy Southerners traveling with their slaves. The St. Charles Hotel posted a flyer in the lobby that boasted: "Hotel has underground cells for confining slaves for safekeeping." Slave pens and auction blocks, where people were bought and sold like cattle, were located seven miles down the Potomac in Alexandria, Virginia. It was almost impossible not to be in the city and experience the sights and sounds of slavery: the crack of the whip and a scream; the clanking of chains along cobblestones; the leer of a white man at a dark-skinned woman. Auctioneers shouted above the cries and wails as families were torn apart forever.[25]

On Tuesday, April 16, a wealthy New York merchant, James Henderson, sent President Lincoln a letter in which he warned of a plot against Washington. Henderson, who had numerous business relationships with Southerners, was privy to almost unsurpassed intelligence from the South. He wrote that he had been told the Confederate Army intended to march on Washington, rendezvousing at Richmond after the fall of Fort Sumter. He added that there were over "5,000 men in Virginia, 3,000 in Maryland, and 1,000 in Washington (several hundred [in the] employee of [the] government) who are ready to assist" in the capture of the city.[26]

Lincoln was surrounded by the enemy and in the midst of traitors. Those citizens remaining in Washington were mostly Southerners waiting for their army to arrive. Traitors were everywhere. Government employees openly sported palmetto plant badges in support of South Carolina's secession and attack on Fort Sumter. Even White House servants were suspect.

One week earlier, 27-year-old Kansas Free State fighter Job B. Stockton, who had spent the last six years battling pro-slavery men on the Kansas frontier, had sent a letter to Lincoln offering to raise a company of 100 Kansas men who would have "no compunctions when ordered to fire upon a band of Rebels . . . and who were acclimated to the hardships of camp life."[27] Stockton's letter got Lincoln thinking: Would the remaining federal soldiers in Washington be willing to fire upon Virginia rebels, many of whom they knew? Lincoln called in a captain of one of the Washington companies that had made a showy appearance as his guard on his Inauguration Day, just several weeks before. He asked him, "Sir, if ordered to defend the city from armed men from Alexandria and Virginia, can you depend upon your men to fire into their faces?" The captain replied, "I fear not. They have many friends there." Lincoln dismissed him.[28]

On Wednesday morning, April 17, many longtime residents began fleeing the city, terrified of being caught in a battle when the Confederates attacked. Trains were filled to overflowing. The roads were clogged with horseback riders, and carriages and wagons heaped with household goods. The poor walked, pulling their personal possessions in handcarts. Most expected the Confederates to strike across the Potomac River at the lightly defended Long Bridge, which ran from the Virginia shoreline to half a mile southeast of the unfinished Washington Monument. From there, they could quickly storm the White House and kidnap Lincoln or hang him from one of the trees on the south lawn. General Scott could muster only 50 men to defend this critical crossing. Most of these were teenage boys and volunteer soldiers who drilled only once a month for parades. These "holiday soldiers" knew nothing of the strategy of war and defending a city from attack, and had never fired a weapon at a man, much less killed a man or seen one killed. It was doubtful they would hold up under Confederate fire when faced with the raw and bloody face of death and the screams of the wounded and dying.[29]

It required a leap of faith to believe the United States would survive the crisis. The American dream was on the brink of failure, a half-finished experiment "at risk of becoming as unrealized as the Capitol dome," as "forlorn as the abandoned obelisk." In every way—militarily, politically, diplomatically—letting Lincoln and the capital fall into the Confederates' hands would be catastrophic. It must not happen. Yet it seemed unlikely the Confederates could be tamed and forced back into the Union by raw recruits, led by an unschooled frontier lawyer as commander-in-chief. Lincoln's military experience consisted of a few weeks of service in the Illinois state militia. The Confederates, on the other hand, were led by some of the most educated and experienced military men on the continent, starting with Confederate President Jefferson F. Davis, a West Point graduate, Mexican War hero, and former U.S. Secretary of War. The pro-slavery men were confident they could easily defeat the despised "Yankee shopkeeper" soldiers. The nation held its breath in anxious suspense.[30]

The War Department received secret information that an attempt would be made to kidnap Lincoln and overthrow the government. Lincoln knew he needed to take immediate action if he hoped to save the Union and his life. He had heard about Lane's speech outside of Willard's and how Lane had backed down the pro-slavery men. Lincoln desperately needed tough, battle-tested fighters, men who would stand under fire, with disciplined minds and hands, who would not hesitate to fire at the Confederates. He sent a messenger to Jim Lane at Willard's Hotel and asked him to come to the White House at once. The two had met when Lincoln had visited Kansas 16 months earlier, and they liked and respected each other. Given the sensitivity of the information Lincoln had received, he wanted to personally tell Lane about the threats to his life and gauge Lane's reaction and recommendations.

Lane and Lincoln understood each other and had much in common. Both were born near the Ohio River—Lincoln in Kentucky, Lane in Indiana. Both were poor growing up. Both received rudimentary educations, with an age difference of only five years. Both were strong and rough when young, and favorites of the wild, rough boys of the frontier. Lincoln in the 1830s was working in a general store in Illinois; Lane was doing the same thing in Indiana. Both became lawyers and went to the legislature. Lincoln went to Congress when he was 35, Lane when he was 37. Both wanted to be senator, and both were disappointed in their home state. Both were over 6 feet—thin, wiry, frontier types. Both loved to talk, and did it well. Both were humorous and dominated conversations and meetings.

When Lane arrived at the President's House Wednesday morning, he gripped Lincoln's huge, hard hand. They met for several hours in Lincoln's second-floor office, where on that cold and rainy day a fire crackled and blazed in the white marble fireplace behind a big brass fender. Lincoln's worktable stood between two tall windows that faced the south lawn, looking out across the marshes to the jumbled blocks that surrounded the unfinished shaft of Washington's monument and the Potomac River.

Lincoln explained the situation and then told Lane: "I don't know who I can depend on." Lane replied, "I'll organize a body of men who will fire when called upon." The rebels were well known to Lane; he had fought them for six years in the Kansas Territory. Lane believed the rumored attack on the White House was a near certainty. He knew the mood of his men, some of whom had been attacked by South Carolina men in the Kansas Territory. Pro-slavery men had left blood from the friends and family members of the Kansans on the Kansas grass. Now it was time to even the score. Some of these same South Carolinians had also attacked Fort Sumter and were now threatening to kill the President, their hero, Abe Lincoln. Lane warned Lincoln: "The only trouble is they may fire whether called upon or not. Their blood is up!" The two men discussed Lincoln's concerns, the Confederates' likely actions based upon Lane's experience fighting pro-slavery soldiers in Kansas, and how the White House might be protected.[31]

Lane told Lincoln that there must be a display of force at the President's House to discourage the Confederates from attacking, as pro-slavery soldiers had shown a dislike for attacking fortified positions in Kansas. He explained that the East Room could be defended as a base of operations for his men. Lane hoped that the inexperienced Confederate soldiers would hesitate to attack entrenched, well-armed, veteran fighters.

Lincoln liked what he heard but wanted to consider the matter—garrisoning soldiers in the White House was unprecedented and might be viewed as an act of desperation by a nervous public. The next morning, Lincoln learned that Confederate troops had attacked the federal armory at Harpers Ferry, at the confluence of the Potomac and Shenandoah rivers, only 122 miles away. There were rumors that the Confederates intended to invade Washington that night. He was running out of time. He immediately sent a messenger to Lane's room at the Willard to ask Lane to gather his men and have them at the White House by sundown. The mission of Lane and his men would be to protect the President. Lane sent word to his Kansas comrades-in-arms, who were staying in hotels, boarding houses, and private homes along and near Pennsylvania Avenue, and asked them to meet him in the Willard's lobby.[32]

Willard's lobby was high-ceilinged and smelled of coal smoke. Many of the rough Kansans crowded at Willard's bar, drinking cocktails at ten cents a glass. At about one in the afternoon, Lane made a speech to the assembled men. He announced that "the traitors around Washington

are liable to assassinate our President and destroy the government buildings," and that President Lincoln had asked Lane to form a guard of loyal
citizens to protect Lincoln, the White House, and the city. Lane called
upon the gathered Kansans to join him, and they roared their assent.
Now these Westerners would fight not for freedom in Kansas, but for
constitutional government in America.[33]

Lane and the soon-to-be-elected officers of the men met in Lane's
room about two o'clock Thursday afternoon to discuss the formation
of the company, the arming of the men, and how they would guard the
President. Lane ordered Clifford Arick to act as company secretary and
create a muster roll of the men and a report of their actions. Arick had just
started working two weeks earlier as an examiner at the Patent Office. He
was to record each man's name, age, height, hair color, and residence. The
men elected Lane as captain of the company and, curiously, a German-
American immigrant, John P. Hatterscheidt, as one of the other officers.
Lane decided to call his company the "Frontier Guard."

On Thursday, April 18, the Civil War was six days old. That night,
at eight o'clock, over 60 roughly dressed Westerners, bristling with Colt
revolvers and Sharps rifles, conspicuously marched (for the benefit of
Confederate spies) with Jim Lane to the White House. Tucked into their
boots, some also carried a heavy 15-inch, razor-sharp blade, which they
called an "Arkansas toothpick." It was good for hand-fighting, cutting
a man shoulder-to-belt with one stroke, and butchering meat. John Hay
remarked it looked like the knife might easily "go through a man's head
from crown to chin as you would split an apple."[34]

Lane and his Westerners brushed by "Old Edward," the wizened Irish
doorman Edward McManus, who had served seven U.S. presidents, and
set up camp in the East Room, to the left of the front entryway into
the White House. They dumped crate after crate of Enfield rifles, sword
bayonets, and ammunition in the middle of the floor where, a year earlier, America's loveliest belles had been presented to England's Prince of
Wales. Lane expected the men might have to withstand a siege, so he
wanted plenty of ammunition on hand. The East Room was an elegant
chamber of red sofas, red-fringed draperies, and red wallpaper, carpeted
with a mammoth 3,000-pound Brussels carpet adorned with garlands of
bright flowers. It was as lavishly decorated as any railroad tycoon's parlor.

The Secretary of War handed those men who lacked them shiny new Enfield rifles, to which they attached foot-long bayonets.

Lane, clad in a sun-faded shirt and coat, slept outside Lincoln's bedroom door, with a rifle, revolver, and the naked blade of his sword across his knees. The company's number swelled to 116 over the next few days. The men guarded Lincoln for the next ten days, representing the only military force protecting the President as Confederate forces massed on the other side of the Potomac River. Who were these men in whom Abe Lincoln had so much trust he allowed them to sleep under his roof, armed to the teeth? Was Lincoln so desperate as to accept any warm-bodied man to protect him, or was he confident in the ability of these Western men? Had he known them previously? Were they mere hotel guests with guns, or fearsome fighters as claimed by Lane? In order to answer these questions, we must go back seven years earlier, to the Western frontier.

2

"The Judgment of Heaven on a Country"

S lavery was the witch at the christening of the nation. The first African slaves had been brought to Jamestown, Virginia, in 1619, a year before the Pilgrims saw Plymouth Rock. At the time of the drafting of the Constitution in 1789, slavery existed in all of the original states except one. Without actually using the word "slavery," the Constitution gave official approval to it, prescribing representation in Congress for three-fifths of a state's slaves, who were referred to in the text as "other Persons." When the Founding Fathers were crafting the Constitution, with its slavery compromises, delegate George Mason predicted that slavery was a "slow poison," which would bring the "judgment of heaven on a country," and great sins would be punished with "national calamities." Although the Founding Fathers recognized and protected slavery's existence in the Constitution, they restricted its introduction into the federal territories in the hope it would fade away.[1]

This American institution did not fade away. By 1854, slavery, now 234 years old, had matured into a problem of immense social and economic proportion. The Southern states owned nearly four *million* slaves, comprising nearly half of their population, and valued at $1.75 billion. America was the largest slaveholding country in the world, and slavery had brought the nation to a boiling point. The image presented by abolitionists—"A horrible reptile is coiled in our nation's bosom"—had nearly the power of a spell. Slavery would cause Kansas to be "born in blood and passion."[2]

As a young nation, America was "stranded halfway between its love of freedom and its accommodation of slavery," mired in policies of appeasement and compromise. In order to understand the political whirlwind that carried Abraham Lincoln to the White House and James Lane to the United States Senate, one must start with the 1820 Missouri Compromise, which was a temporary solution to the hideous curse of slavery. At that time, there were 24 states, equally divided between free and slave states. In 1820, Missouri petitioned to become the 25th state, as a slave state, but there was no free state ready for admission. This meant the balance between slave and free states would be disrupted, which was anathema to those members of Congress opposed to slavery.[3]

Kentucky Senator Henry Clay, a wealthy slave owner, conceived of the Missouri Compromise as a temporary solution to the problem by establishing that from 1820 on, all states and territories north of Missouri's southern border would prohibit slavery (except Missouri), and all states and territories south of Missouri's southern border would allow slavery. The Union would be held together, half-slave and half-free, by the legislative baling wire of the Missouri Compromise for 34 years.[4]

The passage of the Missouri Compromise set off an unprecedented movement of slave-owning settlers from Kentucky, Tennessee, North Carolina, and Virginia to Missouri. By 1854, there were over 100,000 enslaved African-Americans in Missouri, most held in bondage in the northwestern Missouri River counties of Clay, Jackson, Lafayette, Saline, Howard, and Boone. In Clay and Jackson counties, one person out of four was enslaved. These were the westernmost of a string of Missouri River counties that would become known as "Little Dixie." Most of these Missouri counties boasted a few large estates patterned after those found in Kentucky, but more common were the thousands of modest farms scattered throughout the countryside. Farmers in these counties primarily grew hemp and tobacco, like their fathers in Kentucky, Tennessee, and Virginia, but the average Missouri slaveholder owned only five slaves.[5]

Missouri River farmers forced their slaves to grow, harvest, break, and haul the hemp to river landings, where the rough fibers were sold to local rope factories, where other slaves wove the hemp into rope. The slave owners then shipped the rope down the river toward St. Louis, and then down the Mississippi to the great plantations of the Old South, where it was used by other slaves to tie up cotton bales. Clay, Jackson, and the adjoining Missouri River counties were therefore tied—economically and culturally—to the South. Many residents, however, considered the area to be neither North nor South, but part of the frontier West. The West was almost a third country, tilting the balance of power between North and South.

Life was hard on the frontier. Farmers in Clay and Jackson counties believed only slaves could provide the backbreaking labor necessary to profitably raise and harvest tobacco and hemp. Slave owners in Clay County were convinced slaves were the reason the county had become one of the most commercially successful ones in Missouri. Next to land, slaves were the single most valuable property owned by Clay County men. Free states bordering Missouri on the north (Iowa) and the east (Illinois), and the prospect of another free state to the west, represented serious enforcement problems under the fugitive slave laws for Missouri slave owners.[6]

The tenuous national legislative balance was upset by the 1854 Kansas-Nebraska Act, fathered by Abraham Lincoln's political antagonist of 20 years, U.S. Senator Stephen A. Douglas of Illinois. Douglas, a short but dominant Democrat nicknamed "Little Giant," was widely admired as one of the greatest intellects in the U.S. Senate. Douglas conceived of the law as a way to promote a transcontinental railroad from Chicago to California through the territories, and perhaps lead to his nomination for president. He had lost his first bid for the presidency in 1852, when he failed to get his party's nomination because he lacked the backing of Southern states. Douglas knew if he were ever to grab the presidential golden ring, he would have to please the Pro-Slavers and yet retain the backing of Northerners.[7]

Relentlessly logical, Douglas argued that the Constitution provided for the right of each state to be governed by its own people. Each new territory should choose its policy on slavery by a fair majority vote. The Indian territories of Kansas and Nebraska would be opened to settlers from both North and South, and the people (white males) would decide by voting whether to accept or reject slavery. With the stroke of a pen, Douglas obliterated a long-standing arrangement between North and South and reintroduced the slavery question into American politics. Douglas assumed Nebraska would follow the lead of Iowa, its free-state neighbor, and Kansas would enter as a slave state because of its proximity to slaveholding Missouri, maintaining the political balance in Congress. Douglas was wrong—Kansas would become the cradle of a fire that would spread across the country, dividing Democrats, creating the Republican Party, hastening civil war, and destroying Douglas's political ambitions.[8]

For the first time, the slaveholding status of an entire territory, a huge swath of open plains stretching west to the Continental Divide and including much of present-day Colorado, where 30 million buffalo roamed and which Andrew Jackson had set aside as permanent Indian territory, would rest in the hands of a few thousand voters. Before 1854, hundreds of people had emigrated to the West annually, jumping off at places like West Port (now Westport), Missouri. In the spring of 1854, however, even as the Kansas-Nebraska Bill was debated in Congress, the number swelled to the thousands. This new immigrant traffic, however, was going to Kansas, not California.

The country had gone mad about Kansas. The decision as to whether Kansas would be free or slave split the nation. In 1854 the Kansas issue dominated an entire session of Congress and dominated the press in cities large and small, North and South. The issues were neither simple nor trivial, extending to the meaning of freedom and good government. In looking at Kansas and its troubles, the rest of the nation sensed that it was looking into its own heart. A correspondent of the *Boston Liberator* observed that the Kansas Territory was a "far famed land," the subject of conversation all over America, and to some extent, the world.[9]

In April, the Massachusetts legislature enacted the Emigrant Aid Society bill, intended to seed Kansas with anti-slavery settlers. Slave-owning Missourians, sensing an invasion, did not wait for the Kansas-Nebraska Bill to pass. They crossed the Missouri River in spring, staked claims on land owned by Indians, organized pro-slavery associations, and then went back home for the summer. On May 22, the Kansas-Nebraska Bill passed the House of Representatives by only 13 votes. Heated exchanges on the

House floor kept Washington alive with threats and rumors of duels. Two days later, the Senate took up the bill and passed it the next day. On May 30, pro-slavery President Franklin Pierce signed the bill into law.[10]

Illinois lawyer Abraham Lincoln equated revoking the Missouri Compromise with repudiating the Declaration of Independence. "I was losing interest in politics," he wrote, when "the repeal of the Missouri Compromise aroused me again." The year 1854 became a historical fulcrum for Lincoln. Before that date, he and many other Northerners believed that "slavery was in the course of eventual extinction." Suddenly, however, slavery was given new life by the Kansas-Nebraska Act, and could conceivably reach as far west as the Pacific Ocean. The Republican Party emerged in the immediate wake of the Act, uniting diverse groups of Northerners under the explicit goal of prohibiting the spread of slavery. Lincoln left his law practice and representation of the railroads to go back into politics.[11]

The Kansas-Nebraska Act turned the Great Plains into a tinderbox as thousands of homesteaders poured into the Kansas Territory. There were no railroads to the territory, not even stagecoaches. The only way to get there was to ride a horse 260 miles across the slave state of Missouri, or take a steamboat up the Missouri River from St. Louis to Fort Leavenworth, then mount up and ride one of the rough and lonely trails. No detailed maps existed of the territory. It was a lonely, desolate place, the edge of civilization.

In May 1854, fewer than 800 white settlers lived in the Kansas Territory. In the nine months following the territory's opening, that number increased tenfold until, by the first territorial census, there were over 8,000 white settlers, with 192 slaves. The inevitable clash between free labor and slavery quickly turned violent. Neither side was willing to shrink from the bitter "competition for the virgin soil of Kansas."[12]

Slave owners in Missouri assumed the Kansas-Nebraska Act was in the nature of a compromise intended to consign Kansas to slavery and Nebraska to freedom. The northern and southern latitudes of Kansas were roughly equal to those of the slave states directly to its east—Missouri, Kentucky, and Virginia. The soil and climate of Kansas was also considered suitable for crops such as hemp. Missourians threatened: "You'll have to fight for Kansas. Kansas belongs to the South."[13]

Missouri's Democratic U.S. Senator David Atchison led the Missouri "Border Ruffians." Atchison declared that "the game must be played boldly." "If we win," Atchison promised, "we can carry slavery to the Pacific Ocean. If we fail, we lose Missouri, Arkansas, Texas, and all the territories." Kansas was not merely a contest between settlers, but a war between North and South. In 1854, the usual politics of speechmaking and handshaking along the Missouri-Kansas border was replaced by violence, raids, destruction, and murder. The fate of the new territory would be decided by bullets and blades, not ballots.[14]

In July 1854, a band of 27 anti-slavery settlers departed from Boston, Massachusetts. The men first traveled to Rochester, New York, where they met the bearded, charismatic Daniel R. Anthony, a 30-year-old native of Massachusetts, who was then living in Rochester. Anthony's Quaker father had been disciplined for marrying out of the faith. He was finally expelled from the faith for allowing his children to dance. His children, son Daniel and daughter Susan B. Anthony—the suffragette—reflected their father's independent streak. Eli Thayer, the noted Massachusetts abolitionist, had asked Anthony to lead the men to Kansas.[15]

The men traveled from Rochester to Buffalo, where they boarded a steamer, aptly named the "Plymouth Rock," to Chicago. From Chicago they rode a train to St. Louis, where they were joined by the austere, 36-year-old physician Charles R. Robinson, who was an agent for the New England Emigrant Aid Company. Robinson had earlier scouted along the Kansas River for a possible location for a town to be established by the company. In St. Louis, the men boarded the "Polar Star," a three-story, paddle-wheel steamboat, and headed west on the "Big Muddy" Missouri River, fighting the relentless current for 457 miles. The trip was slow, tedious, and took four days. Anthony and the New England men kept to themselves and were as inconspicuous as possible, since there were nearly 300 pro-slavery men on board.[16]

Anthony rested his hands on the boat rail and stared towards the shore as he listened to the rhythmic pounding and splash of the paddle wheels. He saw dark, mysterious walls of forest on either side. Huge cottonwood, hickory, ash, elm, sycamore, willow, and live oak trees towered over the water, blocking out and filtering the light close to the banks. Day after day, the heavy, old-growth forests passed slowly by, broken only now and then by a meadow or a tiny clearing. The steamboat was forced to stop at numerous landings and wood yards for fuel for its enormous boiler. The channel swung from one side of the river bed to the other, shifting with every change in the volume and velocity of the water. Often the branches of huge old trees hung over the steamboat. At other times the boat was far from the banks, moving along in bright sunlight. One day the rain fell in sheets, and Anthony could see only a few yards from the boat.

River travel was a chancy thing, and the pilot had to be a bit of a gambler and magician to do it well. The dark, strong current rapidly chewed the soil of its banks, undercutting shorelines and felling trees. The river carried debris, flowing sand, sediment, silt, clay, and mud, and was studded with whole trees that had been uprooted when a bank caved in. Snags were the most dangerous obstacles. Battered against riverbank and riverbed, drifting trees lost most of their limbs and branches. The heavy, dirt- and gravel-encrusted root ends sank to the bottom and became embedded in rapidly accumulating sand and mud. With its shaft angled toward the surface downstream, the snag lay like a lance lurking in the muddy water, ready to pierce the wooden hulls of unsuspecting steamboats coming upriver. For safety, the boats tied up to shore when darkness fell.[17]

The paddle wheeler strained its way past the prosperous ports of Boonville, Lexington, and Independence, Missouri, before gliding up to the muddy little river town of Kansas (now Kansas City). Anthony could see the two long fingers of the pier thrust into the muddy water, which was sucking around the pilings. The steamboat tied up and the New England men hurried nervously down the gangplank. The little band stayed in the town of Kansas for two days while they purchased horses, wagons, and supplies, and then left for the wild Kansas Territory.[18]

They loaded their tents, cooking utensils, and household possessions into wagons and rumbled along the twin ruts of the Santa Fe Trail, their trace chains rattling. They left all that was familiar behind, venturing into a new and frightening country, where any stranger was a potential enemy. They rode between walls of big bluestem, switch grass, and cord grass, some as tall as a rider's head. For 40 miles they followed the trail, which led to a vast sea of tall prairie grass. As the lead riders stood in their stirrups and looked to the west, they saw a black object move out of a draw and start into the plain, then another followed . . . buffalo. The men gaped at the strange, 2,000-pound shaggy monsters, with great masses of hair over their shoulders and humps, massive heads and sharply curved horns, broad flat faces, and dark beards that almost touched the grass. They rode past bones of the great beasts, bleached by sun and wind, grass growing through the rib cages.[19]

The group rode up a hill that looked like a hog's back on the southern bank of the Kaw River, crowding the bluffs beyond. They looked out in all directions over an immense rolling grass plain as far as the eye could see, a sprawling landscape indifferent to the needs and the lives of settlers. Only one log house existed in the area, built by settler Sam Wood, who greeted them, along with a local band of Delaware Indians, which gave the New England tenderfoots a welcoming shock.[20]

The men pitched their tents and built a campfire with buffalo chips. Their tiny fire was the only light in a vast world of darkness; everywhere they looked there was nothing but night. Stars shone white in the dark sky—passionless, watchful eyes looking down upon the little group. The men huddled close to their fires and peered uneasily into the darkness, the silence broken only by the howls of prairie wolves. They decided to stay and eventually named the small hamlet they began to build Lawrence, after their chief financial backer, Amos Adams Lawrence.[21]

The Kansas Territory was not like the world from which the men had come. It was a rugged, deadly place. Fear was ever present, not only of Pro-Slavers and Indians, but of hunger, thirst, and cold. When a man entered the territory, his way of life retreated 100 years from the civilization back East. The Easterners were used to homes of red brick with perfect, straight chimneys, cobblestoned streets, and constables that one could call to take care of thieves and criminals. Laws had given the Easterners security from murderers and thieves. In the Kansas Territory, there was no law except the law enforced by men with guns, and court was often held in the saddle and the sentence executed with a pistol or rope.

The newcomers found the life hard and the ways rough. The work was hard and long, from daylight to dark. The settlers built their cabins of cottonwood logs cut and dragged from along the river. Every task demanded strength, for the logs used in building the cabins were from

8 to 20 inches thick, and 20 to 30 feet in length. There was no market where the settlers could buy what they needed. Everything had to be hunted, gathered, or made by hand. Few were able to store sufficient corn or meat to last the winter. Hunting in winter was chancy: the deer were bedded down, rabbits deep in their burrows under the snow. The supply of wood to give their drafty cabins warmth was always running low, and so the settlers constantly had to brave the elements to go out and cut down and haul back more wood, and then still more. Until a well could be dug, they had to haul water by bucket from nearby creeks and the river. They had to clear ground for spring planting, move rocks into piles, and cut stumps and large roots. Survival was a continual struggle. Many were unwilling or unable to do the work it required just to survive, and quit.

The settlers also discovered that education and judgment do not always accompany one another. Some of the New Englanders were book-smart, but they did not have the experience to survive in a brutally hard land. Settlers needed to know how to start a fire, build a log cabin with a rock chimney that would draw, care for and raise livestock, shoot a rifle for food and a pistol for protection, hunt for meat, get along with native Indians, treat wounds and sickness, avoid poisonous snakes, grow corn and sweet potatoes, and know which plants were poisonous and which were edible or medicinal. Many settlers left within the first year. One of the early settlers estimated that two-thirds of his original party returned home.[22]

In accordance with certain Christian teachings, many New England men valued nonviolence and held pacifism in high regard. Back East, there had been little or no violence in their lives. While most settlers from New England were not complete pacifists, the level and type of aggression demonstrated by rough-hewn settlers from Ohio, Illinois, Indiana, Iowa, and Wisconsin often disturbed them. They soon learned, however, that if a man was drawing a gun on you in the Kansas Territory, there was not much choice but to shoot him, if you could.[23]

The Pro-Slavers were in the territory for one reason—to protect their right to own other human beings and live off the sweat and toil of those they held in bondage by brute force and threat of the whip, club, and gun. Men who believed in freedom were shot down and killed by the slave owners, who used the same violence against free-state men as they did against their slaves. About a week after arriving, Anthony and Sam Wood rode for supplies into West Port, where they stopped in a general store. Five or six armed men were lounging around the place. On the walls were posters offering $1,000 "dead or alive" for Eli Thayer, the abolitionist who had asked Anthony to lead his party into Kansas. Wood asked the men if they would try to take Thayer if they could find him. They said they would. With one hand on each of his revolvers, Wood replied, "Take me if you can." No one moved. Afterwards, Anthony, a Quaker committed to nonviolence, decided to start carrying a revolver. It was a good thing he did.[24]

If the Pro-Slavers even suspected a man was anti-slavery, that man's life was in danger. Once, as Anthony walked along the main street of Leavenworth, a new, raw, and wild frontier town, a man barked, "Whar yuh from?" "New York," answered Anthony. "One of them abolition-ist nigger lovers!" snarled the stranger. He drew his pistol and fired at Anthony, knocking his hat off. Anthony drew and fired twice, but the man escaped. Anthony was unharmed, but he decided to begin carrying *two* revolvers. He was in several gun battles and was severely wounded once. He later served in the Frontier Guard.[25]

Weapons began flooding into the Kansas Territory. These included Samuel Colt's patented revolving pistol. The most popular of these was the Colt Navy, introduced in 1851. The Navy was a .36 revolver with an almost 8-inch barrel. Colt called the revolver the "Navy" because of the scene engraved around the cylinder commemorating a battle between Texas and Mexican vessels. In 1847 Samuel Walker, a Texas Ranger, had explained to Colt that he needed a more rugged, larger-caliber weapon with stopping power. The result, the Walker Colt, was one of the most effective and deadly pieces of technology ever devised, one that would soon kill more men in combat than any sidearm since the Roman short sword. It was a small cannon. It was more than a foot long, with an enormous 9-inch barrel, and was very heavy, weighing in at 4 pounds, 9 ounces. The pistol was as deadly as a rifle up to 100 yards. The Colt revolver, sometimes called the "peacemaker," soon became the ultimate recourse to maintain order in the Territory.[26]

There were also the feared Sharps rifles. These were single-shot rifles first manufactured in 1848, renowned for their long-range accuracy. The new breech-loading Sharps rifle, which outmatched muskets in both accuracy and speed of loading, was state-of-the-art weaponry, the AK-47 of its time. It was said the Model 1852 "Slanting Breech" carbine could blow a hole through a man "big enough to allow a stagecoach to drive through." Partisans of both sides soon became walking arsenals.

Isaac Cody, the father of William F. "Buffalo Bill" Cody, was one of the first legal settlers in the Territory. He was part of an influx of Westerners into the Kansas Territory, made up mostly of rough men from frontier towns in Ohio, Illinois, Indiana, Iowa, and Wisconsin, who were anxious to get land and did not care much about slavery except they did not want it competing with their labor. Many of these Western men were crack shots and had grown up hunting meat for the table. A kill meant the family ate, so these men had learned to make every shot count.

Many of these Western settlers were cool toward the evangelistic New England settlers. They smirked under their hats at the lack of frontier common sense displayed by the "pilgrims" and "tenderfoots," who spoke differently than the Western men, who had taken on the vernacular of the frontier. Many of the New Englanders sounded like Boston Brahmins, more English than American. For their part, the New Englanders were suspicious about the Western men's dedication to the abolitionist cause and tended to consider themselves superior in education and culture to the rough-hewn Westerners, whom they saw as uncivilized, rowdy men with bad habits and low morals.[27]

Isaac Cody and his younger brother Joseph's early years were filled with the kind of adventures common to young boys living on the frontier. They spent their boyhood on the banks of the Ohio River, watching and listening to the puffing and whistling steamboats. They built forts and sang rude songs of the canebreak and cornfields. They learned to ride and shoot, throw a knife, and how to hunt and live off the country.

In April 1854 Isaac Cody, his wife, Mary, and their children, including 8-year-old William, began the month-long, bone-jarring ride to the Kansas Territory (shortened to "KT" by Western men). At Fort Leavenworth, young William first saw Indians and rode Indian ponies. On their way to the Pottawatomie Indian Reservation, the Codys crossed over a high hill. Isaac and Mary looked down into a beautiful valley and decided upon the site as their future home. In the Salt Creek Valley, Cody was joined by pro-slavery men from Missouri, some of whom brought bottles of whiskey with them, and when they had drunk the whiskey, they drove the bottles into the ground to mark their claims. The pro-slavery men called four logs tied together in a square an "improvement," which they offered as evidence of legal settlement. Some simply wrote their name and the date on a playing card and nailed it to a tree while continuing to live in Missouri. If the poll judge questioned the Missourian's qualifications to vote, a revolver or bowie knife was often presented as credentials. In some locations, the same credentials were used to prevent free-soil men from voting.[28]

Brutal and quarrelsome men poured into the territory from Missouri, most of them pro-slavery. They held meetings in the local trading post and boasted their intention to make the KT a slave state. "If I had my way, I'd hang every damned abolitionist!" trumpeted Missouri newspaper editor Benjamin Franklin Stringfellow. He proclaimed Pro-Slavers "are determined to repel this Northern invasion and make Kansas a Slave State; though our rivers should be covered with blood of their victims, and the carcasses of the abolitionists should be so numerous in the territory as to breed disease and sickness." At his urging, a mob of horsemen rode into the Salt Creek Valley, where the Cody family lived, and declared that slavery was "thereby instituted in the Territory of Kansas."[29]

There was little organized government. Wilson Shannon, the second territorial governor, lamented, "You might as well have attempted to govern hell [as govern Kansas]!" Violence was an everyday occurrence. Both sides formed guerrilla bands. On the very day that Cody moved his family to Kansas, a group of pro-slavery men met at the trading post. The result was the Salt Creek Valley Resolutions of June 10, 1854. The first provision stated: "We recognize the institution of slavery as always existing in this Territory and recommend the slaveholders introduce their property as soon as possible." The second provision read: "We afford protection to no Abolitionists as settlers of Kansas Territory."[30]

Isaac Cody saw little reason to be concerned about the resolutions; he was not an abolitionist—his main reason for riding to the territory was to make a living for his family. He had a reputation, however, as a good public speaker, and he was asked to address some of the local men. Cody candidly admitted that he opposed slavery in the territory. He was shouted down by angry Pro-Slavers, who tried to drag him from his platform. One man stabbed Isaac twice in the back with a bowie knife, puncturing his lung. The pro-slavery *Democratic Platform* newspaper of Liberty, Missouri, reported: "Mr. Cody, a noisy Abolitionist, was severely stabbed while in a dispute about a claim. Cody is severely hurt, but not enough it is feared to cause his death. The settlers on Salt Creek regret that his wound is not more dangerous."[31]

Isaac Cody improved, but his wounds continually plagued him. In early 1857 Isaac and his brother Joseph traveled to Chicago to attend a Republican convention, where they met Abe Lincoln, then a country lawyer in Springfield. Shortly after, Isaac Cody died of pneumonia, with his stab wounds as contributing factors. Joseph, who had recently arrived in the KT from Ohio, became 11-year-old William's surrogate father. Joseph Cody would soon serve in the Frontier Guard, and young William would soon become known to the world as "Buffalo Bill" Cody.[32]

Joseph Cody tried his hand at farming and then started an anti-slavery newspaper. In many ways, a newspaper could be an instrument as dangerous as a gun in the KT. In a country hungry for news, with a scarcity of reading material, the newspaper was going to be read, and people believed that whatever they read must be true or it would not be in print. Publishing an anti-slavery newspaper was a risky and life-threatening occupation. There was no sitting on the fence. This meant every KT newspaper publisher ran his newspaper with a gun on his desk. "The old Colt's horse pistol was as much the necessary equipment of an editor as his pencil and paper."[33]

Meanwhile, Missourians were burning the crops and cabins of Free State men, kidnapping them, binding them in ropes and chains, and carrying them across the ferry to Weston, Missouri, where they threw them in jail. The treatment received by William Phillips, a Leavenworth lawyer, was typical. In the spring of 1855, Phillips protested against the illegal voting of Missourians in the Territorial election. In punishment for his protest, a pro-slavery mob kidnapped William and his younger brother, Jared, from their Leavenworth homes in front of their terrified wives and carried them to nearby Weston. The Pro-Slavers shaved one side of William Phillips's head, stripped him of his clothing, and tarred and feathered him. His brother Jared, who would soon serve in the Frontier Guard, was able to escape.[34]

The mob mounted William on a rail, and carried him for a mile and a half through the streets, to the accompaniment of the rabble ringing bells and beating on pans. At the St. George Hotel, a slave was forced to auction off William to the highest bidder. When there was no bidder, the slave "sold" William for one penny. The Pro-Slavers ordered William to leave Leavenworth by sunset the next day, but he refused. He was later gunned down in the doorway of his home in front of his family by pro-slavery men.[35]

Back at his law office in Springfield, Illinois, Abe Lincoln warned:

The Missourians are within a stone's throw of the contested ground. They hold meetings, and pass resolutions, in which not the slightest allusion to voting is made. They resolve that slavery already exists in the territory; that more shall go there; that they, remaining in Missouri will protect it; and that abolitionists shall be hung, or driven away. Through all this, bowie knives and six-shooters are seen plainly enough, but never a glimpse of the ballot box. And, really, what is to be the result of this. Is it not probable that the contest will come to blows, and bloodshed?

Lincoln's prose was prophetic. The Kansas-Nebraska Act would result in a Midwestern bloodbath over whether Kansas would become the western edge of bondage.[36]

3

Bloody Kansas

It was December, but the warm southern air lingered. In tiny Lawrence, farmers mixed their sweat with the heavy black soil of the Kansas River Valley as they built circular earthworks and rifle pits. Jim Lane designed the earthworks to break the force of any mass attack, divide the enemy, and subject them to crossfire from the rifle pits. Occasionally one of the workmen stopped digging and leaned against the handle of his shovel, peering out to the faded brown hills to the southwest of the settlement on the Kansas River. He had a crude cabin in the hills, where his family lived and where every gust of cold wind was felt through the chinks in their log walls. He should be home making his cabin tight against the winter's coming. There would be cold, snow, and hunger before the spring brought life to the land again. The short December days would soon end, and with them, the last opportunity to prepare.

Thoughts like these were common among the men, who had come to Lawrence to fight, not dig trenches. Only the occasional rumble of cannon fire, which came from the camp of the enemy southeast of Lawrence, kept them digging. A tall, lean figure in a military cloak sensed their dark mood as he passed among them. He tried joking with the men but was met by frowns and grumbles: "We should be at home fixin' up for winter, instead of foolin' our time away here."[1]

The man in the military cloak sprang to the top of a newly created earthwork and began to speak, and nearly anyone in the Kansas Territory recognized the force and power of Jim Lane's voice. Men who heard Lane never forgot. This impromptu speech among the trenches of Lawrence in December 1855 was vividly remembered in later years by many. Marcus J. Parrott, a 27-year-old lieutenant colonel in the militia under Lane's command, and Turner Sampson, a tough horseman and a major in Lane's militia, likely witnessed the speech, as did 19-year-old George Washington Smith, Jr., a sergeant major in Lane's militia, and the tall, lanky Thomas D. Bancroft, a recent arrival from Ohio.[2]

Lane paced back and forth on the fortification, his deep-set black eyes flashing and voice booming that any man who would desert Lawrence until the villainous invaders had left the territory was a coward; anyone who stayed was a hero. His small audience grew larger as word spread that he was speaking. He soon threw his cloak on the ground. His hat fell next, revealing long, dark, unruly hair, as the men cheered his words of blood and thunder, spiked with profane references to the pro-slavery "hell hounds." When Lane finished, the men were in a frenzy, yelling and cheering for him to lead them into battle.[3]

If one visits Lecompton, Kansas, today, a marker can be seen pointing to "Constitution Hall," built by pro-slavery forces to be the capital of a slave state, a capital that was never built. Kansas, a slave state? Is that possible? But for Jim Lane, it was nearly a fact. He was a figure of titanic accomplishments. He was Kansas's most influential citizen in the 1850s and '60s. A powerful and charismatic speaker, he was called the "General Washington of Kansas," the "Liberator of Kansas," and the "King of Kansas." Lane was both the general of the revolutionary Free State fighters and the politician who wrote the resolutions and drafted the Free State Constitution. He led the Free State men in battles to make Kansas free against the pro-slavery invaders from South Carolina, Missouri, Georgia, Alabama, Louisiana, and Mississippi, who were supported by the power of the federal government.

Lane had a commanding presence, towering over 6 feet, in a day when most men stood about 5 feet 6 inches, with a powerful voice and a mesmerizing speaking ability. He was born in 1814 in the southern Indiana frontier town of Lawrenceburg, located on the banks of the Ohio River 23 miles below Cincinnati. His father, Amos Lane, was a lawyer, famous orator, and politician, representing Indiana in the U.S. House of Representatives. Lane's mother was a schoolteacher who taught her son in a one-room school. He floated down the Ohio River in flatboats as a youth, hauling freight and goods up and down the river to New Orleans with the tough flatboat brawlers. He then decided to study law and become a lawyer. He married a granddaughter of Revolutionary War General Arthur St. Clair and built a successful law practice, using his innate charisma and speaking ability to his advantage in winning cases and trials.

In the spring of 1846, the United States declared war on Mexico. President Polk made a requisition upon Indiana for three regiments of volunteers. Thirty-two-year-old Jim Lane organized and equipped a company in his home county, and the men elected him captain. He was soon promoted to colonel and led his men into northern Mexico under General Zachary Taylor. At the February 1847 Battle of Buena Vista, Lane commanded 600 men in outnumbered volunteer regiments, most of them fighting for the first time, in successful battles against thousands of Mexican troops under the command of General Antonio Lopez de Santa Anna. Lane became a national war hero by successfully leading his infantry in repeatedly repulsing the charges of a much larger force of Mexican cavalry. The Americans suffered between 600 and 700 casualties, while Mexican losses were about 3,000 killed and wounded.[4]

Lane was a master at using the terrain to his advantage and maximizing limited resources—he commanded the Third Regiment Indiana Volunteers, who were outnumbered almost 4 to 1 and yet never retreated. Lane's men were thereafter referred to as the "Steadfast Third." The Battle of Buena Vista, at which 15,000 well-disciplined Mexican troops, with ample artillery, were defeated by 4,500 ragged American volunteers, was General Zachary Taylor's greatest victory of the war and helped him win election as president of the United States in 1848.[5]

Lane returned as a national war hero to Indiana, where he was elected lieutenant governor. He was then elected to the U.S. House of Representatives. After receiving strong petitions from his constituents in southern Indiana (which was south of the Mason-Dixon Line), he voted for the Kansas-Nebraska Act, which he later called one of the biggest mistakes of his life. Perhaps in an effort to obtain a Senate seat, Lane decided to move his young family to the Kansas Territory.[6]

Arriving in Lawrence on April 22, 1855, Lane and his family were some of the earlier settlers in the territory, as recorded in the *Free State* newspaper under the caption "Distinguished Arrival": "Col. James H. Lane, late member of Congress from Indiana, arrived with his family [wife, Mary, and four children]. . . . He is comfortably ensconced in a log cabin, and will likely remain permanently with us." Unfortunately, Lane's young daughter, Anna, died shortly after the family's arrival. Lane buried the girl a short distance from his humble pioneer cabin. Around the little grave Lane built a wooden fence.[7]

When Lane threw his life and reputation into the Kansas conflict, the people of Kansas were a handful of unorganized men, with hostile Indians on the west and hostile slave-owning Missourians on the east. The fate of the new territory was hanging in the balance between slavery and freedom. In Missouri, the powerful political machinery of Senator David Rice Atchison was dictating policy in Kansas, and from Washington the greater power of President Franklin Pierce's administration was aiding the pro-slavery forces. The first territorial election for a delegate to Congress in November 1854 resulted in a pro-slavery victory, although it was tainted by illegal voting from Missouri. In Leavenworth alone, over 1,200 Missourians, armed with revolvers and bowie knives, took over the polls, voted, and prevented anti-slavery men from voting.[8]

One month before Lane's arrival, mobs from Missouri invaded Kansas and ran off over 2,000 registered voters and elected a pro-slavery legislature with 6,000 fraudulent votes. In one widely reported account, a visitor to the Kansas Territorial Legislature was asked if he inquired for the member from Fort Scott, Kansas Territory. His reply was, "Fort Scott! Hell no, I wish to see the member from Lafayette County, Missouri." The fraudulent voting also resulted in the election of a pro-slavery congressman. The anti-slavery men labeled the elected men as the "Bogus Legislature" and ignored its laws.[9]

The Bogus Legislature adopted Missouri's draconian Slave Code for the territory, legalizing slavery and outlawing anti-slavery speech with the threat of imprisonment and death, outraging free-soil supporters in the North. Merely stating that slavery did not legally exist in the territory called for a penalty of not less than two years in prison; harboring or feeding a runaway slave would result in death. The Pro-Slavers along the border began calling themselves the "Law and Order Party" and denounced the Free State men as "criminals" for criticizing slavery and the laws establishing it in the territory. Abe Lincoln wrote in private correspondence: "That Kansas will form a slave constitution and, with it, will ask to be admitted into the Union, I take to be an already settled question."[10]

The summer of 1855 saw the first incident involving considerable numbers of anti-slavery men confronting pro-slavery men in Lawrence, Kansas. In March, 27-year-old William W. Ross, his wife, and family members started for Kansas from the small town of Milwaukee, Wisconsin, in a Conestoga wagon. Accompanying Ross was a free African-American man, employed as a teamster. As they rolled through Missouri, Ross had to several times fight off Missourians who tried to kidnap the teamster under the pretense that he was an escaped slave (but most likely because they could sell him for over $1,000, which was more money than most of them had ever seen).[11]

In Lawrence, the Missourians made more attempts to take the man. Finally, an armed pro-slavery mob tried to kidnap him, when about 50 Free State men armed with Sharps rifles rallied to Ross's side, despite death threats and violence against them by the Pro-Slavers. One of the leaders of the Missourians may have been Jake Herd, who was a "holy terror, violent, quick and deadly with a revolver, fearless and daring, who would risk his life to capture a Negro." Ross later served in the Frontier Guard.[12]

A few months later, some of those same anti-slavery men, including Ross, rode to the September 1855 Free State Convention at the newly staked town of Big Springs, a four-cabin trading post and camping ground on the California Trail 11 miles east of Topeka. A crude hotel was hastily built, and a shaded platform and seating was provided for the expected 100 or so delegates. Nearly 400 men rode in, however, most of whom camped on the open prairie. They brought with them ropes, picket pins, and blanket rolls. They drove their picket pins deep into the sod, put their horses on picket ropes, and let them graze. They then bunched a few sticks, some shredded bark and twigs, and built coffee-making fires.

Most of the men also came heavily armed with revolvers and rifles knowing that the Kansas Territory was filled with violent Pro-Slavers.

Many of the Western men also took care of livestock, which was prey to wolves, cougars, coyotes, and thieves. And then there were hostile Plains Indians, rattlesnakes, copperheads, and water moccasins. In this country nobody went unarmed from sunup to sundown. The cloakroom of the hotel soon began to resemble an arsenal.[13]

Jim Lane was appointed chairman of the committee and asked to craft the Free State Party platform, an important document in the annals of Kansas. It asserted the party was to be devoted to excluding slavery and securing a free constitution for Kansas. The platform consolidated the various anti-slavery groups into a unified Free State party. For Lane, who had arrived just six months earlier, it meant the beginning of his leadership in Kansas politics until his death 11 years later. Lane was outraged by the atrocities committed by the Pro-Slavers, and he grew to believe that asking them to be reasonable about slavery was like asking a tiger to take up grazing with sheep. It was against their nature. Lane and his men boasted that they had "a new code of laws" for the territory, called "Sharps Revised Statutes," referring to their Sharps rifles.[14]

The next month, on October 23, 1855, a group of Free State men rode to Topeka, a ferry crossing on the Oregon Trail, to discuss and draft a Free State constitution. Topeka was a small settlement 20 miles west of Lawrence on the Kansas River. The prairie grass had barely been trodden down, but Topeka was already an ambitious little town that boasted a two-story stone building called Constitution Hall, where the sessions of the conventions were held.

Lane was elected chairman of the Topeka Free State convention and charged with organizing a Free State government. In taking the chair, Lane said: "You have met, gentlemen, on no ordinary occasion—to accomplish no ordinary purpose. You are the first legal representatives Kansas has ever had. Your work is to give birth to a government—your labor is to add another state to our Union." He expressed his wish that they "be imbued with the caution of Washington and the justice of Franklin." The Free State movement was now an insurrection, as there was already in the territory an official (pro-slavery) state government and legislature 20 miles away in Lecompton.[15]

Mirror governments now existed in the territory—two governors, two legislatures, and two constitution halls. Because of his Mexican War fame and experience, Lane quickly became the military leader of the Free State men located in and around Lawrence, the Free State fortress 35 miles outside of the organized United States. Lawrence was an insurrectionist city, an island in the wilderness, surrounded by hatred, with an illegal militia of freedom fighters led by Lane—and it was about to witness a dress rehearsal for the Civil War.

In November 1855, a pro-slavery settler murdered a Free State man, allegedly over a land dispute. The pro-slavery sheriff of Douglas County investigated the crime and, with a logic all his own, arrested another Free State man, Jacob Branson, whose only offense was his friendship with the deceased. Some of the Free State men became alarmed, fearing that Branson would be murdered to prevent him from testifying. On the night of November 26, 15 Free State men confronted the sheriff, Samuel J. Jones, and rescued Branson at gunpoint. One of the rescuers was 28-year-old Samuel F. Tappan, from Manchester, Massachusetts, who had traveled to Lawrence the year before in the group led by Dan Anthony. Tappan later served in the Frontier Guard. The enraged sheriff sent a message to his pro-slavery friends in Westport, Missouri, requesting 300 men to help recapture his escaped prisoner. Several of the rescuers, including Tappan, lived in Lawrence. They feared a mob of Missourians would use the rescue as an excuse to wipe Lawrence off the map.

The next day, pro-slavery men attacked the federal arsenal at Liberty, Missouri, and stole a large supply of arms and ammunition. They drove two wagonloads of weapons to Platte City, where they gave them to the pro-slavery militia for an attack on Lawrence. Over 1,000 heavily-armed Missourians rode into the Kansas Territory and made their camp along the Wakarusa River just a couple of miles south of Lawrence, near the village of Franklin.[16]

The alarmed leadership of the Lawrence Free State men asked Lane to serve as the general of the Free State Militia in Lawrence and to protect the town. Lane used his Mexican-American war experience to organize the men into an effective fighting force. Much depended upon Lane's leadership. Men, particularly Western men, did not follow cowards. When a man went into danger, he wanted to be sure that his leader would stand with him. Lane sent this dispatch: "We want every Free-State man at Lawrence immediately." He soon had 600 men enrolled in the militia under his command.

Lane ordered that every raw-sawed clapboard house in town be converted into barracks for the men. He oversaw the construction of an earthen and rock-walled fort on Oread Hill, overlooking the southern trail leading into town. He ordered that logs, tarred black, be placed in the fort's portals, to look like cannon from below.[17]

At night, Free State men held lanterns so that the digging of earthwork defenses at the town's entrances could continue. Built in circles, these fortifications stood 5 feet high, 3 feet wide at the top, and 100 feet in diameter. Lane's soldiers built four or five of these fortifications, connected by trenches and rifle pits, from which the defenders could safely direct crossfire at attackers. The fortifications were separated by a space wide enough for only one horseman to come through at a time. A classic defensive measure—the same one the Spartans had used to hold off the far larger Persian army so the Greeks could escape destruction. Since his opponent had far greater numbers, Lane wanted to make it as difficult as possible for them to employ those numbers to their advantage. He also started a propaganda campaign, exaggerating the number of his troops and reporting his men could defend the town against 1,000 armed foes.[18]

From the top of the Free State Hotel, the Free State headquarters, an American flag with 31 stars flapped in the breeze. Three stories below, on the pockmarked ground called Massachusetts Street, a primitive band started to play. Hundreds of men took their places, and the sharp commands of General Lane could be heard up and down the street. The soldiers marched side by side, up and down the rutted road past piles of sand, blocks of limestone, and two-story buildings yet to be completed. Lane told the men that the pro-slavery men would likely attack that night. "They will come," he said, "yelling and screaming, as if hell had broken loose, and all its devils were upon you. Keep cool. Be ready for them. Victory will be yours." But Missouri had also sent many troops to the Mexican War, and these Mexican War veterans within the pro-slavery ranks knew of Lane's military skill and feared to engage him in battle. Stories of Lane's skills and victories were shared around the campfire at night and quickly spread throughout the pro-slavery army.

The Pro-Slavers delayed their attack while they tried to determine the number of Lane's troops and the extent of his fortifications.[19]

On December 7, Kansas Territorial Governor Shannon rode from Lecompton to Lawrence to try to defuse the situation. As the territorial governor, Shannon was not under any obligation to the voters in the Territory; his commitment was to President James Buchanan, who had appointed him. Shannon met with Lane, the leader of the Western faction of the Free State men, and Dr. Charles Robinson, the leader of the New England group. Robinson was a cool, calculating man who had a medical degree but who was not comfortable on a field of battle. When faced with violence, he did not have the experience to fight and defend himself, or others. There was also a natural tension and rivalry between the aggressive, fiery Lane and the remote, cool Robinson. Robinson may also have been jealous of Lane's popularity with the Free State men and distrustful of Lane, since he had voted for the Kansas-Nebraska Act.[20]

Governor Shannon demanded that Lane and Robinson order the Lawrence men to surrender their weapons. Lane refused and described the atrocities committed by the Missourians: the murders, rapes, burning of homes, and theft of horses, livestock, supplies, and food. Shannon had been hearing only from pro-slavery men since he had arrived in the Territory, and now his eyes were opened. He sent a request for federal troops from Fort Leavenworth to ride to Lawrence to protect the town. As Shannon waited for a reply, a fierce storm began threatening the town. The weather matched the governor's mood. The commandant at Fort Leavenworth replied that no federal troops would be coming to protect Lawrence unless ordered by pro-slavery President Pierce, who refused to do so.[21]

The governor could stall no longer. He met again with Lane and Robinson at the Free State Hotel and they negotiated a peace treaty. The document was short and ambiguous. It was unknown how the Missouri mob would react to it. Shannon persuaded a reluctant Lane and Robinson to ride with him to the village of Franklin to meet with the leaders of the pro-slavery army under a flag of truce.[22]

Franklin was not much more than a small scattering of cabins a few miles southeast of Lawrence. The three men were intercepted outside of Franklin by pro-slavery pickets armed with revolvers and shotguns, who escorted them to a cabin as it began to rain. Inside were 13 captains of the pro-slavery army. Overhead, the rain pounded down upon the roof, and within the stuffy warmth of the cabin, the air was thick with mingled tobacco and wood smoke, overlaid by the odor of wet clothing, drying wool, and worn leather. The wind steadily increased outside and raindrops fell down the chimney upon the blazing fire, causing it to hiss and sputter. A coal oil lamp with a reflector behind it was burning on the wall, and a lantern stood on a rough wooden table. The pro-slavery men at first were threatening and belligerent, and Lane was glad he had tucked his revolver in his waistband, under his coat. About seven o'clock that night, the pro-slavery captains reluctantly agreed to disband their forces, although Lane suspected from their smirks and whispered conversations that they intended to murder Robinson and him that night. "Come!" Lane whispered to Robinson, who followed him to the door.

After the stuffy air of the tightly closed cabin, the outside air was like wind in their lungs. But the sky was dark and lowering. "Let's make a run for it!" Lane said, swinging into the saddle. Robinson mounted his horse, his head buried in his coat collar, his hat brim pulled low over his ears. Wind gusts whipped their horses' tails against the heels of their boots and the saddle leather. They saw only darkness and heard a vast roaring of wind. The trees bent before the angry wind, which lashed at the riders.

The Missourians had promised them a horseman to guide them safely through the picket lines, but their escort soon wheeled his horse and bid them "Good evening." Lane turned toward Robinson, rain streaming from his hat brim, and shouted, "Hurry up, they mean to kill us!" They spurred their horses, changed course, and turned their galloping horses down a lesser-known wagon track to Lawrence. Lane knew from his Mexican War experiences that, when traveling in enemy territory, you should never leave on the same trail you took going in—the enemy may be lying in wait. The only sounds were the howling wind and the pounding of their horses' hooves on the frozen ground.

Suddenly, Robinson's horse stepped in a deep gully and stumbled and fell, throwing Robinson. Both the horse and rider were badly shaken. Robinson was able to remount and the two men continued down the trail to Lawrence. After what seemed an eternity, they finally saw a faint flicker of light through the rain from the windows in Lawrence and heard the challenge of their own sentry. Later that night, three half-frozen, heavily armed Missourians were captured near Lawrence. Although they denied it, it was widely believed they had lost the trail of Lane and Robinson while attempting to murder them.[23]

While the citizens of Lawrence spent the night in the relative comfort of their cabins, the makeshift tents of the Missourians could not keep out the bitter cold. The furious wind blew down tents, blew off wagon covers, and nearly blew away the large campfires built among the gnarled limbs of the old oak, walnut, and cottonwood trees in the Wakarusa River bottom. Many of the campfires had to be put out for fear that the sparks sent aloft by the wind would set tents and wagons on fire. The pro-slavery men lost many of their horses, having either been stolen by Indians or strayed during the storm.[24]

The following morning, their attempted assassination of Lane having failed, the Missourians decided they did not have the stomach to attack Lane and his entrenched soldiers, broke camp, and began their 50-mile ride to Weston, Missouri. That same day Governor Shannon returned to Lawrence, worried that the bands of marauders surrounding Lawrence might attack him. The citizens of Lawrence welcomed Shannon and wined and dined him. When Lane and Robinson were convinced the governor had reached the proper degree of good cheer, they told the governor that an enemy force might attack Lawrence at any moment. They thrust a paper in front of Shannon giving them the right to fight to defend themselves and repulse the pro-slavery force. Scarcely glancing at the document, Shannon signed it. Lane could now argue that the governor had legitimized his Free State fighters.[25]

On December 11, the soldiers at Lawrence disbanded after farewell addresses by Lane and Robinson. Robinson forgot, for the time being, his animosity toward Lane and paid tribute to him: "To the experience, skill and perseverance of the gallant General Lane all credit is due," Robinson told the soldiers, "for the thorough discipline of our forces and the complete and extensive preparations for defense, . . . his services cannot be overrated. Long may he live to wear the laurels so bravely won."[26]

Attacks by pro-slavery men on Free State men continued in towns such as Leavenworth and Atchison. In December 1855, George F. Warren was abducted in Atchison by a gang of Pro-Slavers who demanded the papers he was carrying, which included the charter for a secret Free State organization. The papers also revealed the names of other Free State men, such as William Hutchison, who was general of the organization. Warren did not want to risk these men's lives by revealing their identity, so he quickly tore them up and swallowed them. The Slavers threatened to hang him, but they ended up taking him to Lecompton, where he was held prisoner by Sheriff Jones. Even George Keller, the charismatic and popular landlord of the Leavenworth Hotel, was run out of town. Warren, Hutchison, and Keller later served in the Frontier Guard.[27]

Not even the Indians could remember a more severe winter than that of 1855-56. Those who owned thermometers watched the mercury dip to 20 below zero. Bread had to be sliced in front of a fire. Cups of water froze on the tables inside cabins, and buffalo-hide blankets and coats were the only way to keep from freezing. Outside, the ground was covered in several feet of snow. The weather was particularly hard on the enslaved African-Americans who had been brought into the territory by their owners. They were typically not as warmly dressed as their masters, fed as well, or provided a warm fireplace. Worse, their masters forced the men to spend hours working outside finding and chopping firewood, fetching water from ice-encrusted creeks and rivers, and caring for livestock.

On January 15, 1856, the Free State party held elections and elected a state legislature and a delegate to Congress. On March 4, the Free State legislature elected Lane to be senator from Kansas when the state was admitted to the Union. Lane left for Washington to present Congress with the Kansas petition to be admitted to the Union as a free state. Democratic senators refused to allow it, however, alleging that it was a forgery, and they demonized and humiliated Lane.[28]

This was a decisive turning point for Lane—he decided to abandon negotiations and talk in favor of military action. The government imposed from Washington had to be defeated.

In May, Judge Lecompte, sitting in his court in the territorial capital of Lecompton and acting at the direction of Secretary of War Jefferson Davis, convened a grand jury and brought an indictment for treason against Lane and other Free State leaders and ordered federal marshals to arrest them. Charles Robinson, Marc Parrott (an Ohioan who had arrived in the KT the year before and had raised a company of men to defend Lawrence), and other Free State leaders were arrested and jailed in Lecompton, generating sensational publicity in the North. A brave lawyer from Kentucky by the name of Charles Russell, a veteran of the Black Hawk Indian war and recent immigrant to Lafayette County, Missouri, offered to defend Robinson. Parrott and Russell would soon serve in the Frontier Guard. The North was outraged that the fraudulent, pro-slavery administration in the territory would arrest and prosecute men whose only fault was to oppose slavery and seek honest elections. Newspapers warned that the arrests would cost the Democratic Party "thousands and thousands" of votes in the next presidential election.[29]

In Missouri, pro-slavery men had placed cannons along the Missouri River and stopped and boarded steamboats heading for the Kansas Territory. They searched, disarmed, robbed, beat, and sometimes killed the men recruited by Lane and sent the bloody survivors back down the river on floating debris. They seized and shut off all food and supplies for the Free State men. Severely outnumbered, and denied reinforcements and supplies, the Free State men and their families slowly began to starve. The situation looked bleak for a free Kansas. How could the outnumbered, brave band of Free State men possibly defeat the government-supported hordes of Pro-Slavers, so fiercely determined to make Kansas a slave state?

4

The Army of the North

Jim Lane, who had been about everywhere in four or five states and territories where a man could go on a horse, created an overland trail to the Territory to reinforce the beleaguered Free State men. The trail snaked west from Illinois through Iowa, crossing the Missouri River at Nebraska City, and then south through the Nebraska Territory into Kansas. He marked the trail with piles of stones, and settlers were soon calling it "the Lane Trail." While blazing and then traveling the trail, Lane met many Free State men along the way, including anti-slavery newspapermen Phineas W. Hitchcock, Algernon Paddock, and lawyer John R. Meredith, who lived in Omaha, and Orsamus Irish, publisher of the *Peoples Press* newspaper in Nebraska City. These men later served under Lane in the Frontier Guard.[1]

At the same time, the Pro-Slavers organized armed immigration through Missouri to the Kansas Territory to kill or drive off the Free State men. In late 1855, Major Jefferson Buford, an Alabama veteran of the Black Hawk War, called for men to travel to the Kansas Territory after the winter snows thawed to begin a military campaign to make Kansas a slave state. Buford offered to pay all of the men's expenses for one year and give them forty acres of land. The *Richmond Inquirer* encouraged Virginians to move to Kansas to preserve the "interests of the South."[2]

On April 7, 1856, Buford's party of 400 men, mostly from Alabama, South Carolina, Georgia, and Virginia, left Montgomery, Alabama, for the Kansas Territory. Many of them were hired killers and cutthroats who would do whatever was needed to make Kansas a slave state. Buford told the men to use force when necessary and the law when it served them, not caring which, as long as it resulted in the breaking, or death, of the Free State men. They arrived in the Territory in late April, just before guerrilla warfare broke out.[3]

The Slavers began bullying, beating, and murdering the Free State men around Lawrence, stealing and running off livestock, burning homes, and robbing travelers. The Territory became an increasingly criminal environment, populated by gangs of highwaymen, kidnappers, and killers. The Pro-Slavers lived in a series of forts they built on the major trails near and around Lawrence, hoping to cut off all reinforcement and supplies to the town. They built and fortified the forts to defy capture by anything except artillery.[4]

On April 23, Sam Jones, the Douglas County sheriff from Lecompton, took a bullet in the back. A year earlier, he had led a group of pro-slavery Missourians into the Territory to stuff the ballot boxes. The gunman who shot Jones was never identified, and the Free State men of Lawrence disavowed the act, but the shooting gave slavers the excuse they were looking for to attack Lawrence and drive the Free State men from the Territory.

On May 21, while Lane was out of the Territory traveling back from Washington, an army of about 800 men from South Carolina, Georgia, Missouri, and Virginia, including many in Major Buford's group, marched on Lawrence. The men wore rough, red flannel shirts for uniforms and carried rifles, revolvers, and bowie knives tucked into boots worn on the outside of their trousers. Without Lane's leadership, the Free State men, led by Boston native Samuel P. Pomeroy, a short, stout, balding man who was the general agent of the New England Emigrant Aid Company, attempted a policy of nonresistance. Pomeroy turned over to the pro-slavery men all of the Free State men's arms, including a cannon, and surrendered the town. The Pro-Slavers then spent the afternoon burning and pillaging.

Before shelling the Free State Hotel with artillery, David Rice Atchison, the former U.S. senator from Missouri and leader of the pro-slavery militia, spoke to the mob: "This is the most glorious day of my life! This is the day I am a Border Ruffian! (Yells.) The United States marshal has just given you his orders and has kindly invited me to address you . . . Tear down their Free State Hotel. Sheriff Jones is Deputy Marshal. You will be amply paid as U.S. troops, besides having the opportunity of [improving] your wardrobes from the private dwellings of those infernal nigger-stealers." (Cheers)[5]

The Pro-Slavers, many of whom had stolen whiskey from the town's saloons and were now drunk, then burned the town to the ground. They robbed citizens of their money and valuables and rode away, many with pillaged vests and dress coats draped over their flannel shirts. A South Carolina battle flag, with a crimson star and the motto "Southern Rights," and a banner that proclaimed "Alabama for Kansas," fluttered in the smoke-filled breeze. They left Lawrence a ruin. Fire had gutted it, and some of the stone walls had toppled. The windows gaped like great, hollow eyes that stared upon nothing.[6]

Unarmed Patrick Henry Townsend was one of the Lawrence citizens seized by the Slavers. They beat him, robbed him of his watch and boots, and threatened to burn him alive if they ever saw him again. After the robbers and arsonists left the smoking ruins of the town, Townsend decided to join a band of fighters led by a new arrival in the territory—John Brown, a lean, gray-eyed, grim-jawed abolitionist who believed that "slaveholders had forfeited their right to live." Townsend later served in the Frontier Guard.[7]

Like some horrible chapter out of the Middle Ages, gangs of pro-slavery militia roamed the border settlements and farms, appearing out of nowhere, looting, burning, and killing, before vanishing into the dark. There was no way of knowing where or when, but suddenly they would be on the road, stepping phantom-like out of the tall grass or trees, and other men would suddenly appear all around, prodding the Free State men in the back with hard steel barrels. The KT had become a war zone.

In the primeval blackness of night on the prairie, terrified settlers were forced to sleep with rifles, revolvers, hatchets, and knives within reach of their beds. Some slept in their fields, fearing an attack on their cabins during the night. Boston headlines screamed: "Murder Rules in Kansas. The bloody plot thickens. Blood flows. Freedom reels and staggers in a death grip with slavery." During the next nine years, the Kansas/Missouri border would be the scene of the longest-lived and most brutal guerrilla warfare ever seen on American soil.[8]

Sensational nationwide newspaper coverage reported on Kansas daily to an inflamed readership. Kansas was not only a national issue but, for a period of four years, *the* national issue. The pro-slavery press described the New Englanders in the Kansas Territory as fanatics, armed with Bibles and rifles, who were not amenable to reason. Northern papers described the Pro-Slavers pouring into the territory as "demons of the night" and a "depraved, brutish race of beings." The *Lawrence Republican* pronounced that "slavery, the curse of the country, makes fiends of men. There is no crime that the pro-slavers will not commit in furthering slavery." The newspaper alleged that the Pro-Slavers would "murder helpless prisoners, tear scalps from the heads of their yet living victims, tie Free State men to trees, demand that they denounce their principles, cut off finger after finger until their hands were fingerless, and riddle [them] with bullets."[9]

Newspapers compared the Kansas struggles to the American Revolution, comparing the battles to those at Lexington, Concord, and even Thermopylae, suggesting the issues were the most important not only in history of the United States but in the history of civilization: "The great spirits of history combat by the side of the people of Kansas, breathing a divine courage. . . . [One] could see the ghostly figure of George Washington marching beside Lane's militia." Reverend Henry Ward Beecher warned in apocalyptic sermons that the battle between the Free State and pro-slavery forces in Kansas would result in "blood to the horses' bridles."[10]

On May 20, the day before the attack on Lawrence, Charles Sumner, the abolitionist U.S. senator from Massachusetts, rose in the Senate chamber to deliver a two-day impassioned speech, "The Crime against Kansas." A powerful orator, the 45-year-old Sumner had devoted his enormous energies to the destruction of what Republicans called the "Slave Power," the efforts of slave owners to continue and expand their control of the federal government to ensure the survival and expansion of slavery. In his Kansas speech, Sumner proclaimed: "Slavery now stands erect, clanking its chains on the Territory of Kansas, surrounded by the code of death." Sumner called slavery a pirate ship: "Even now the black flag of the land pirates from Missouri waves at the mast head; in their laws you hear the pirate yell and see the flashes of the pirate knife." Finally, Sumner denounced the "rape of a virgin territory," the "depraved longing for a new slave state," and "the wench" slavery. Sumner singled out South Carolina Senator Andrew P. Butler for "choosing a mistress to whom he has made his vows, and who, though ugly to others, is always lovely to him . . . I mean the harlot, Slavery." Sumner's attack touched a raw nerve among slave owners who chafed at the suggestion (often true) that they engaged in sex with their female slaves.[11]

Violence against those who criticized slavery then reached the halls of the Capitol. On May 22, the day after the sack of Lawrence, Senator Butler's cousin, Preston Brooks of South Carolina, a member of the House of Representatives, entered the Senate chamber after the Senate had adjourned and savagely beat Charles Sumner to within an inch of death. Sneaking up from behind while Senator Sumner sat working at his desk, Brooks struck again and again with a heavy, gold-tipped gutta percha cane, shattering pieces off of it with each strike, while Sumner nearly wrenched the screwed-down legs of his desk from the Senate floor in an effort to rise and defend himself from his unseen attacker.

Only after being physically restrained by others did Brooks end his attack. Sumner almost died from his injuries, which kept him away from the Senate for several years. The House voted to expel Brooks but could not amass the votes to do so. To slave owners, Brooks was a hero. South Carolina held events in his honor and reelected him to his House seat. Replacement canes were sent to Brooks from all over the South. Boasted Brooks, the "fragments of the stick are begged for as *sacred relics*."[12]

The violence from Kansas had ominously spilled over into the national legislature. Abolitionists charged that slave owners had made a mockery of the phrase "land of the free," turning it into a sneer on European lips, as slave owners continued to commit crimes and outrages every day against four million helpless men, women, and children, whom they kept in bondage, "sold like cattle, and exploited for their sexual pleasure." African-American abolitionist Frederick Douglass called for retaliation: Liberty "must either cut the throat of slavery or slavery would cut the throat of liberty."[13]

Those were probably the sentiments of Old John Brown. On May 24, after learning about the attacks on Lawrence and Senator Sumner, followers of John Brown retaliated by murdering five Pro-Slavers who had been threatening Free State men and women near Pottawatamie Creek. Several of the murdered men had been involved in recent attacks on Free State men and in court proceedings to enforce the Slave Code, by arresting Free State men for the crime of criticizing slavery. One had attempted to rape a Free State woman two days earlier, and another had threatened Free State settlers that they would soon be murdered. A pro-slavery army of over 1,000 men streamed over the border to hunt Brown and Free State men. One terrified resident wrote: "Our country is invaded by an army from Missouri . . . who plunder and burn and kill." Uncivil civil war had come to Kansas.[14]

Following his defeat in Washington seeking recognition of Kansas as a free state, Lane realized he needed to motivate and move Northern men to action if Kansas was to be free, so he toured northern cities to raise money, inflame support, and excoriate the Democrats. Lane's largest venue and greatest speech was scheduled for the courthouse square in Chicago the night of May 31—a Saturday night, when the workingmen would be free, the sailors in from the lakes, the longshoremen up from the docks, the farmers in from the field. The new Republican Party that Lane promoted was radical: the masses against the classes. Adding to the hysteria of the event, the telegraph had brought news that Pro-Slavers had just burned Lawrence, and that in Washington, a South Carolina congressman had clubbed Senator Sumner of Massachusetts almost to death. Revolution was in the air, as the crowd, singing the French Revolutionary War song "La Marseillaise," saw Jim Lane, the hero of "Bleeding Kansas," appear before them on the platform.

There were wild cheers as Lane was introduced in Stephen Douglas's hometown as the man who had renounced Douglas for the cause of liberty. Lane rose to the occasion so thrillingly that nothing but confused and hysterical reports were kept of the speech. The *Chicago Tribune* said, "Language is inadequate to describe the effect of his recital of Kansas's tale of woes—the flashing eyes, the rigid muscles, the frowning brows." What people remembered most was how, when the introductions were done, wild cheers rose and crashed and eddied around him. "He stood there," a witness reported, "mouth firm, gazing with those wondrous eyes of his into the very heart of the throng. Before he spoke the fascinating spell of his personality had seized upon the whole vast audience—and for over an hour he controlled every emotion in that great gathering."[15]

That night Lane made Chicago see Kansas as "a blackened and charred land, peopled with widows kneeling to kiss the cold white lips of husbands murdered by pro-slavery villains." He described the territory as "ravished and despoiled by butchers from Missouri." He made the German-born population of Chicago roar with rage as he told how the pro-slavery men had denied Germans citizenship in Kansas. He branded the federal administration as abettors of demons and assassins, and he held up his long bony forefinger like a tremendous exclamation point as he cried, "Before God and these people, I arraign [President] Frank Pierce as a murderer." One listener reported: "Never did I hear such a speech; every sentence like a pistol bullet; . . . not a man in the United States could have done it; and the perfect ease of it all; not a glimpse of premeditation or effort, and yet he had slept in his boots every night but two for five weeks."[16]

As he ended, pandemonium took the scene. Lane was a rebel calling for a revolution against the pro-slavery U.S. government. Gamblers threw their pistols on the stage, begging Lane to take them to Kansas and use them; sailors threw their wages onto the platform at Lane's feet, staid businessmen tossed in their wallets, newsboys cast their pennies up, women wept, men wept, the people around the platform singing, shouting. Nor was it a passing craze of a single night. The next day it was reported that $15,000 (about $400,000 today) had been pledged to raise aid for the revolutionaries in Kansas, and men were enlisting to fight the pro-slavery armies in the Kansas Territory.

Chicago was Lane's greatest speech, just as two days before in Bloomington, Illinois, it had been the moment for Lincoln's greatest speech up to that time. Lincoln had also risen to the occasion with words so fiery and forceful about the Kansas conflict that reporters allegedly forgot to take it down and this, his "lost speech," became famous. William Herndon, Lincoln's law partner at the time, described the speech as "full of fire and energy and force. . . . It was logic, it was pathos, it was . . . truth set ablaze by the divine fires of a soul maddened by the wrong; it was hard, heavy, knotty, gnarly, backed with wrath."[17]

Lincoln's speech foreshadowed what Lane said two days later in Chicago. Lincoln argued in the speech that the Kansas–Nebraska Act was

misguided and was causing bloodshed in Kansas. He criticized the Democrats and Senator Douglas for passing the law, argued it should be wiped
off the books and the Missouri Compromise restored, and demanded
that Kansas be allowed to enter the Union as a free state. Given at the
first Illinois state Republican convention, which essentially founded the
Illinois Republican Party, the speech thrust Lincoln into the national
political limelight and propelled him to a second-place finish among
United States vice presidential candidates in 1856.[18]

Lane's and Lincoln's sensational speeches in Chicago, Bloomington,
and other midland cities were vital factors in the national financing of the
fledgling Republican Party. Organized wealth and conservative powers
were against the young party. Its supporters were poor. But in the money
that orators like Lane collected for the relief of Kansas "came the sinews
for the new party." Most of the states organized Kansas committees, and
these had a central committee in Chicago, which united the workmen,
since the chief issue of the campaign was, "Kansas— shall it be free or
slave?" It was an easy matter to unite the moral and philanthropic cause
of Kansas relief with the Republican campaign. Every speech made for
Free Soil Kansas was a Republican speech.[19]

Some of the emigrants who rode from Chicago to Kansas at Lane's
urging went with bayonets. When the largest body of heavily armed men
marched overland through Iowa, down through the Nebraska Territory
and into Kansas, it was called Lane's "Army of the North." Not "settlers,"
not "emigrants," but an "army." It was the overture to the Civil War, and
Lane was their general. He sent out reports intended for the Pro-Slavers
magnifying the size and number of his men. Meanwhile, letters in the
Free State newspapers from Kansans were asking, "Where's Jim Lane?
Send him back to us. He is the only man who can save Kansas."[20]

To the Free State men who had begged for his return, and in an effort
to avoid alerting the federal authorities in Kansas of his intentions, Lane
sent the message: "Look for Captain Cook on a white horse." "Captain
Cook" was Lane's alias to avoid arrest. Lane led his men along the Lane
Trail into the Nebraska Territory. Fearing things were dire in Kansas,
Lane spurred on his horse, making one of the fastest rides in the history of the West, riding so hard that his companions—one of whom
was John Brown—fell by the wayside, unable to keep up. With Lane it

was always the unexpected, always the quick start, and then travel faster than expected. Lane rode across the Kansas border at night to avoid federal patrols, even though he was dead-and-buried tired. As he rode through the darkness, the beleaguered Free State settlers heard shouts, "Here comes Captain Cook!" They "turned to see it was Old Jim, his eyes a-fire."[21]

On July 4, a day of celebrating freedom, under orders from President Franklin Pierce and Secretary of War Jefferson Davis, U.S. Army Colonel Edwin "Bull" Sumner forcibly dispersed the Free State legislature with federal troops as it attempted to convene in Topeka, the Free State "capital." Federal troops marched down Kansas Avenue opposite Constitution Hall, where Sumner ordered the convention to disperse. Sumner's artillery crews had stationed their cannons to sweep the streets and lit their slow matches, the smoke rising lazily in the 100-degree heat. Philip Schuyler, who had been elected secretary of state of the Free State administration, challenged the military leader: "Colonel Sumner, are we to understand that the legislature is to be dispersed at the point of a bayonet?" Sumner replied, "I shall use the whole force under my command to carry out my orders." The Free State men did as Sumner ordered. Schuyler later served in the Frontier Guard.[22]

Lane needed to be aggressive and seize the initiative for the Free-Staters. A political debate was scheduled outside of Topeka to discuss the future of the territory. Lane was asked to present the Free State position. Because pro-slavery leader John Calhoun was also scheduled to speak, about half of the crowd was pro-slavery. Lane rode up on his horse, hitched it to a sapling, stood in the stirrups, hung his hat on a limb, reached his right hand under his coat, and drew out a "wicked looking revolver and cocked it." For a moment no word was spoken, only the click of revolvers among the assembled crowd broke the silence. Then Lane opened his mouth and roared: "Whom the gods would destroy they first make mad. If there is any man here that don't know me, let me say, I'm Jim Lane, and if there is any border ruffian here that would like to cover himself with glory, I pause a moment while he shoots me." No Pro-Slaver had the courage to put into practice his ardent desire for Lane's death. Lane then began to hurl epithets and curse the pro-slavery men for their evil deeds while they ground their teeth and scowled—but they remained silent. One of the Free State men wrote later: "After the first terror passed, I yelled and cheered 'till I was as full of enthusiasm as a howling dervish."[23]

The Pro-Slavers put a reward out for Lane, dead or alive, and he lived in constant danger of assassination. He had many brushes with death, some remembered, some not. One instance was reported only because it involved a future president of the United States, Chester A. Arthur. In late July and early August, Arthur, then a young man of 27, came to the Kansas Territory to consider setting up a law practice in Leavenworth. After spending a week or so in Leavenworth meeting local leaders and purchasing town lots, Arthur took a stagecoach to Lawrence, where he sought out and met the famous Jim Lane. Early one morning in August, Arthur and a business partner mounted up and rode along and near the Kansas River to Lecompton to conduct some business at the territorial land office. About halfway to Lecompton, Lane, who also had business at the land office, and Sheriff Sam Walker overtook them. The four men rode on until they were met by two riders who recognized Lane and, after "looking daggers at him" and having an animated conversation, put spurs to their horses and galloped back toward Lecompton. Lane suspected them of being scouts for the Pro-Slavers. Lane lent Arthur one of his revolvers, as Arthur was not armed, and warned him there might be shooting.

As Lane, Arthur, and the two other men reached the outskirts of Lecompton, they approached Doyle's Saloon. A large crowd of men and boys had gathered. They began shouting "There's Jim Lane! Shoot the __! Hang him!" Lane and the other men rode on, with a large group of boys following them. About 60 men stood around the land office. One of Lane's friends whispered that he would be killed if he remained. Lane quickly conducted his business and rode out of town with a couple of friends. Lane's enemies made a wiser man of him of him. He began traveling with bodyguards, one of whom was a tall, raw-boned young man with a drooping mustache and hair curling upon his shoulders, who had won recognition for his ability with firearms at shooting matches in the Territory. The youth's name was James Butler Hickok (later known as "Wild Bill" Hickok).[24]

With the arrival of Lane's "Army of the North," the summer of '56 saw small armies of pro-slavery and anti-slavery men waging bloody battles in the Kansas Territory. Riding at night to avoid federal troops, Lane set out to destroy the series of forts that Pro-Slavers had built to encircle, strangle, and starve Lawrence into submission and death. Hundreds had had no flour, meal, or meat for days; many became sick, and they feared starvation. Lane ordered the nightly camps of his soldiers be formed in tight circles, guarded by sentries, and designed to protect from attack. He was about to light a fuse that would ignite a second American Revolution.

On the night of August 12, Lane led about 80 men as they approached a fortified block house in Franklin, three miles southeast of Lawrence, where Pro-Slavers had hidden a cannon they had taken from the Free State men in Lawrence. One of the men was 33-year-old William Hutchison, who later served in the Frontier Guard. Lane told his men: "Boys, there is the enemy. They are a bad lot! They need licking! Come on!" He then quoted from the Old Testament's description of Sampson's attack on the evil Philistines: "Smite them hip and thigh . . . till they surrender." After nearly four hours of shooting, Lane's men smashed in the front door of the fort as the enemy ran out the back. The Free State soldiers captured the cannon, nearly 100 stands of arms, and a large amount of food and supplies. One Free State man died, and six were wounded.[25]

Three days later, Lane led about 400 men, including John Brown, against a superior force of pro-slavery men from Georgia who were barricaded inside Fort Saunders, a large frame house on Washington Creek, about 12 miles southwest of Lawrence. Some of his men wanted to attack immediately, but Lane resisted. To one of the more militant men in his command Lane said, "You are always wanting to kill somebody. What we want to do is to make Kansas a Free State, and kill nobody."[26]

For Lane, every battle was a lesson; in each there was something to be learned. He had studied the campaigns of Napoleon, Alexander, and Hannibal and knew the accepted modes of attack and defense. He knew what had already been done, then used variations that were his own. He seemed to have an instinctive grasp of a battle situation and the terrain. He knew how to fight and apparently had little fear of death, but he knew the necessity of preserving a smaller force and avoiding casualties by outsmarting the enemy. He often declined a frontal assault on his enemy and used his wits to attack in the least expected manner.

Lane ordered his men to collect local farmers' wagons, outfit them with boards across the back like seats, cut holes into the boards and insert pegs with bundles of straw wrapped around them, and place shirts and hats over the straw to make them look at a distance like men. He then ordered all of his cavalry and infantry, mixed in with the "straw men" in wagons, to march so they were visible to the pro-slavery men in Fort Saunders as they marched across the top of a hill overlooking the fort. As the men and wagons emerged from woods on one side of the hill, they seemed to keep coming as if there were no end to them, although in reality they were just circling around behind the hills and reappearing. Believing they were severely outnumbered, the Pro-Slavers fled during the night, leaving behind large quantities of supplies and gunpowder, which Lane's men eagerly carried away. The Free State men then burned the fort.

The next day, Lane ordered an attack against Fort Titus, a log forti-fication on a hillside about 12 miles northwest of Lawrence and a mile and a half south of Lecompton, which was commanded by Colonel Titus. Titus was the leader of the local pro-slavery militia, which had been responsible for many murders and attacks upon Free State men. Titus and his men had also driven off and stolen livestock and cattle, and destroyed Free State settlements. The fort was double walled, with slits for firing from the interior. The Free State men opened fire. After three hours of shooting, no side had the advantage until the Free State men were able to bring a cannon into position, and the men in the fort quickly surrendered. The Free-Staters killed two of the enemy, captured 20 prisoners, and then burned the fort. They suffered seven wounded, including 19-year-old George W. Smith, Jr., who was shot in the arm and chest. Twenty-seven-year-old Daniel A. Clayton was shot in the ankle and would never again walk without a limp. Smith and Clayton later served in the Frontier Guard.[27]

Lane then received reports that a large force of pro-slavery men had crossed into the Kansas Territory at what is now Johnson County and were nearing the Douglas County line. Lane immediately sent out a call for "boots and saddles" to his men, and he ordered a march toward the pro-slavery army, sending out exaggerated reports of his troop strength. The Pro-Slavers fled, fearing Lane and believing they were badly outnumbered. They later made wild claims about the number of Lane's soldiers. With each fight and near-fight with the Pro-Slavers, the Free State men drew a little closer together. They emerged from each battle a little stronger, more confident, and more tightly knit than before.[28]

In condemning Lane's attacks on the Pro-Slavers, Territorial Governor Daniel Woodson, a pro-slavery man sent to the Territory by President Pierce to replace Governor Shannon, described the Pro-Slavers at Franklin as merely "law-abiding citizens" who had "sought to enforce the territorial [pro-slavery] law." Fort Saunders was a "Georgia Colony," whose men were forced to flee from Lane's men and "take refuge in an adjoining State [Missouri]." Woodson charged that the Free State men had "robbed" the pro-slavery men of "the muskets furnished by the [U.S.] government." He warned that he would "take all the measures in my power" to stop these "lawless and insurrectionary acts" and punish Lane and his men with "the severest penalties."[29]

The stories of Lane's victories were quickly passed on down the trails from campfire to saloon to riverboat, down the Missouri River to St. Louis, and across the country. Such stories were the gossip of the Kansas Territory and the border and river towns of Missouri, where they were meat and drink to lonely men who lived by the gun. In Western lands, where most news came by word of mouth, men quickly became larger-than-life legends. The stories grew with the telling. Those Pro-Slavers who decided they had had enough returned to their homes in South Carolina, Alabama, Arkansas, and Georgia, and told exaggerated tales of the wild, some said crazed, "Old Jim." Lane's reputation as a fighter "extended to the remotest cabins" of the Arkansas-Missouri country. One contemporary recorded that, again and again, through these inaccessible regions, 200 miles from railroads and telegraphs, he had been asked by the evening fire, "Do yuh know Lane in Kansas? I reckon he must be a powerful fighter."[30]

The Pro-Slavers had not been defeated in over 230 years, and they could not understand how one man, with a ragtag bunch of followers, was able to repeatedly defeat them. And they feared what they did not understand. Beating the pro-slavery men once might have been luck, even twice—but Lane's string of victories struck fear into the Pro-Slavers. Though outnumbered, Lane had out-generaled them again and again. Pro-slavery newspapers wildly exaggerated Lane's forces and hysterically reported, "There is no doubt that Lane, at the head of 2,000 armed outlaws, is making war on the pro-slavery party, . . . destroying houses and farms, killing some, and taking others prisoners to the 'Army of the North.'" Lane's name became a terror to the Pro-Slavers. Southern newspapers called him "the Grim Chieftain." He became known as one of the "wild" men of the Kansas Territory, one of the fanatics, along with John Brown, who made the Territory bleed. The Pro-Slavers feared the idea of Jim Lane as much as they feared the man himself. It was said that Lane haunted "the dreams" of the pro-slavery men.[31]

"When it was reported that [Lane] was approaching a pro-slavery town," wrote the secretary of Kansas Territorial Governor John Geary, "a general panic and stampede was the result." By the end of the summer, the western counties of Missouri were in a state of panic. The territory and border country was alive with wild rumors of Lane's comings and goings. When false news of Lane's approach reached the border town of Weston, fire bells were rung and the town emptied as the townspeople ran to hide in nearby creek beds. There was a story in Missouri that Lane was 8 feet tall and breathed fire. They said he rode like a devil, fought like a madman, and had a sixth sense which warned of danger when no outward signs of it existed.[32]

Lane became a national figure as a result of the sensational newspaper coverage. President Pierce denounced him as a "turbulent and dangerous character" and described the Free State men as "in rebellion against the government." Lane wrote a cool, calm, discreet reply, arguing that President Buchanan's speech was "without a parallel in its falsification of history." In Springfield, Abraham Lincoln, along with most of the nation, was closely following the unfolding drama in the newspapers.[33]

But the Free State victories were short lived. On August 30, a small band of Free State fighters led by Old John Brown battled a small army of about 300 pro-slavery militia outside of Osawatomie (named for the confluence of the Osage and Pottawatomie rivers), a tiny Free State village about 60 miles southwest of Lawrence. Missourian John W. Reid led the Pro-Slavers for a predawn raid on Osawatomie. A local man, Marvin White, guided the pro-slavery army. Frederick Brown, son of John Brown, was riding from Osawatomie to Lawrence when he met up on the trail with White and a few of General Reid's scouts. Thinking them to be Free State men, Brown greeted them: "Good morning, boys. Are you going to Lawrence today?" White replied, "I know you!" He drew his revolver and blasted Brown in the chest, knocking him out of his saddle. A Free State man with Brown slapped spurs into his horses' ribs and raced back to town. He breathlessly told John Brown the terrible news about his son's brutal murder and the approach of the pro-slavery militia.

Brown swallowed his grief and quickly gathered a group of about 40 men. He initially intended to defend the town from a wooden blockhouse but, learning from his scouts that the enemy had a cannon, he decided to ride out to meet the pro-slavery force on the edge of a wooded area northeast of town, along the Marias des Cygnes River. Twenty-three-year-old James H. Holmes, who had recently arrived in the Territory from New York, was one of the men with Brown. Holmes had a fierce love of battle. He put the butt of his rifle against his shoulder and fired the first shot. He heard the *whop* of the striking bullet and saw a pro-slavery soldier fall to the ground. Holmes was so fierce and frenetic that John Brown called him "my little hornet." He was everywhere during the fight, rushing to any point in the Free State skirmish line that appeared to be faltering, as pro-slavery bullets clipped the leaves and snapped and pinged against the trees and limbs.

Brown's men held off the Pro-Slavers for almost an hour, giving the women and children in town a chance to escape. By that time, heavy gunfire had caused the battlefield and forest to be covered in gunsmoke. Brown's men, outnumbered over seven to one and out of ammunition, began to fall back to the river under intense fire. Holmes and George Partridge were among the last to leave the skirmish line, providing cover fire for the retreating Free State fighters. Holmes had lost his horse during the shooting and ran toward the river and leaped in, with bullets kicking dirt and gravel ahead of and around him. Fortunately, he was a strong swimmer and was able to make it to the other side, where he quickly climbed the steep bank and tumbled into the brush, hearing the whine of bullets, death sliding through the air above him. Holmes would soon serve in the Frontier Guard.

George Partridge was not so fortunate. He was shot dead from his horse while attempting to ride it across the river. Four other Free State men were also killed during the battle. The Free State men believed they killed several times that number of pro-slavery men. The Pro-Slavers rode into Osawatomie and looted homes and businesses before setting them afire. They dragged and lifted their dead into two wagons, with legs and arms hanging out, and filled several other wagons with stolen goods. The pro-slavery army left the town blazing brightly in the afternoon sun as they rode drinking and laughing to Leavenworth to rob and burn the Free State homes and businesses there.[34]

On September 1, about 700 men from South Carolina, Georgia, Missouri, and Alabama attacked the Free State men of Leavenworth and killed or drove out one-third of the town's population. They attacked one small home where brothers William and Jared Phillips were boarding with their wives. William Phillips had been previously tarred and feathered and then jailed in Weston, but he had refused to leave. The assassins banged on the Phillipses' door, and when William Phillips opened it, they opened fire and riddled his body with bullets. He fell in his doorway, spilling his life's blood on the ground. Jared, who was standing behind William, ducked for cover but took several bullets in his left shoulder and upper arm.[35]

The brothers' wives ran to their dead and wounded husbands, as their anguished cries could be heard throughout the neighborhood. William was lying in a pool of blood, staring with glazed and empty eyes. Jared could smell the sickly-sweet smell of blood and felt faint as he looked at his arm and shoulder. The slavery men fled, thinking that they had murdered both men.[36]

Jared had holes on both sides of his shoulder and arm where the slugs had gone through, and he was bleeding badly. The bullets had shattered Jared's left arm bone and shredded his flesh, leaving the arm useless. His coat and shirt were soaked with blood, and he was pale and drained of blood by his wounds. A doctor said the arm had to be sawed off in order to save his life. Phillips turned out to be as tough as any Cheyenne warrior, however, and the stump of his left arm, cauterized by a fireplace iron, gradually healed.

Phillips had leaned towards pacifism, but after witnessing his brother's murder and narrowly escaping death, he bought a Colt revolver, which he learned to shoot with deadly accuracy with his remaining right hand to protect himself and his wife. He began buying and selling dry goods to make a living, and he learned to drive a team of horses with his right hand only, his left shirt sleeve folded over the stump of his arm. Phillips would soon serve in the Frontier Guard.

Later that month, nearly 200 men gathered at Mount Pleasant, Iowa, then the western terminus of the Burlington Railroad, to launch an expedition to the Kansas Territory to come to the rescue of the Free State men. They traveled in 20 wagons and on numerous horses and were armed with weapons purchased with funds from the New England Emigrant Aid Company: two cannon, over 200 muskets, 36 Colt revolvers, and ten Sharps rifles. Twenty-eight-year-old Edward Daniels, the former state geologist of Wisconsin, led the men for the first part of the journey.[37]

Late on the evening of September 26, 1856, Daniels wrote his sister as the expedition was camped in Iowa "pushing rapidly towards Kansas." He wrote by campfire, sitting on the ground, leaning against a stack of guns, and using a cartridge box to write on. Daniels reasoned that all the guns must not be on the bad side. There had to be guns for the righteous, too. Men were needed to carry guns not as a threat but as a protection for themselves and others. The rest of his men were asleep and no sound was heard except for the "stamping of the horses and the measured tread of the guards as they passed." The men had elected Daniels as adjutant general of the group. They marched about 25 miles per day and hoped to be in Kansas in 12 days. Earlier that day, Daniels had made a speech to the men from atop a cannon wheel, reminding them that the fate of Kansas depended upon men like them.[38]

Shortly before reaching the Kansas border, the men received word that U.S. troops, operating at the direction of pro-slavery President Pierce, were disarming all men entering the Territory. The men buried their cannons in a cemetery in the Nebraska Territory. Shortly after, on October 10, the wagon train entered the Kansas Territory. Five hundred U.S. Dragoons, patrolling the Kansas/Nebraska territorial boundary, stopped the expedition; confiscated the rifles, revolvers, and ammunition;

and arrested the men on the grounds that they constituted a military unit. Just a month before, the latest pro-slavery territorial governor, John W. Geary, had arrived in Leavenworth and outlawed armed bands of men (at least Free State men) from the Territory in the stated effort to quell the violence but in an unstated attempt to avoid adverse publicity for the Democratic Party before the upcoming presidential election. After the men were disarmed, the soldiers released them with a warning to disband and leave the Territory or be arrested. Daniels and the expedition men rode to Lawrence, where they circled their wagons at the head of Massachusetts Street on the banks of the Kaw River and built campfires. They disbursed the next day and most of them soon returned home.[39]

At the same time, the Pro-Slavers were purging suspected Free State men from office and employment in the Territory. On September 29, 1856, pro-slavery Surveyor General John Calhoun fired Robert L. Ream from his position as chief clerk, Surveyor General's Office, for allegedly supplying Lane with maps and information on pro-slavery militia movements. Things were dire indeed for freedom in Kansas. One resident wrote, "The whole country is a perfect fog from burning houses. . . . No one can view the condition of our [Free State] men without shedding tears. Half naked, half fed, and not one cent of money . . . and their small children crying for bread."[40]

Without armed Free State reinforcements, it looked as if the pro-slavery army, backed by the United States government, had succeeded in turning Kansas into a slave state. One of the best-selling books of 1856 as much as said so in its title: *A Conquest of Kansas, by Missouri and Her Allies.*[41] From where would help come?

5

The Forty-Eighters

The Pro-Slavers had counted on their deadly attacks on Lawrence and Leavenworth and the arrest of the Free State leaders to be the final blow to the Free-Staters. Back East, however, moderate Democrats were shocked at their brutal tactics, including tens of thousands of recent German-American immigrants and voters. In 1854 alone, more than 215,000 German immigrants arrived in the United States. By the late 1850s, Germany replaced Ireland as the primary source of European immigrants, and Germans quickly became the largest foreign ethnic component in Kansas.[1]

The vast majority of the German men were refugees of the failed 1848-49 German and liberal revolutions across Europe, the so-called "Forty-Eighters," who favored guarantees of basic human rights and freedom. These were men who had risked their lives to fight for liberty against the reactionary Prussian and Hanoverian armies and the ruling aristocracies, built upon involuntary servitude in the German Confederation. They failed and were forced to flee their homeland to escape execution, torture, and imprisonment in the dungeons of Brunn and Spielberz.

Most of the German immigrants who were able to afford passage to America were better educated than the average American and possessed political and military experience. Lane quickly realized he could revive the spirit of their failed struggle for liberty in a new cause—the fight against slavery. The peasants of Europe, who were often held in involuntary servitude, lived lives little better than those of slaves. Frederick Douglass wrote: "A German only has to be a German to be utterly opposed to slavery." Lane began actively recruiting German immigrants to come to the Kansas Territory and join him in the fight.[2]

In June 1856, Lane spoke in Cincinnati, Ohio. Lane told the crowd, many of whom were German-American immigrants, the Democratic Party was the party of the aristocracy, based on slavery, like the aristocracy of Old Europe based on involuntary servitude. The Pro-Slavers had no sympathy for the working man. Lane told the crowd he appreciated the German support of the Kansas cause. He shouted, "Sons of Germany! I offer to you heartfelt thanks for the understanding and support you have offered me as the representative of the Kansas people!"[3]

The German-Americans had initially aligned themselves with the Democratic Party. One of the more influential German language newspapers in the East, the *New Yorker Staats-Zeitung*, had supported the Democratic Party and President Pierce's policies. The paper, however, reluctantly concluded: "The prosecution and the arrest of the Free State men was the greatest folly that could have been perpetrated on the part of the friends of the administration." The actions were a mockery of the Kansas-Nebraska Act.[4]

Horace Greeley and the *New York Tribune* used the admissions of these mistakes as an opportunity to remind German-American citizens that the events in the Kansas Territory were similar to the injustices they had suffered in Europe: "The enforcement undertaken in Kansas of absurd and tyrannical laws, enacted by a government of disputed legality, . . . driving Free State men out of Kansas, finds no parallel . . . except in the proceedings of some of the Austrian officials." The events in Kansas rekindled the revolutionary spirit of 1848. At the same time, the newly forming Republican Party provided a realistic alternative to the brutality of Democratic Party policies for many German-Americans.[5]

The German immigrants brought with them the concept of the *Turnverein* ("Turners"). The primary activity of the Turners was physical exercise, but it was much more than that. The father of the Turner movement was Friedrich Ludwig Jahn, who advocated the elimination of involuntary servitude and a unified Germany. He began giving nationalistic speeches pleading for freedom and fatherland. The Turner societies were ostensibly created to foster sound German bodies and liberal German minds, but they also served as a cover for those who were united in opposition to the German monarchies. The Turner societies alarmed the Prussian and Austrian governments, which ordered the dissolution of all Turner societies. The Turners' stated goal of making "the fatherland free from servitude" led to revolutions in Prussia and Austria, which caused the Prussian and Austrian authorities to persecute and imprison the Turners and the Forty-Eighters, causing them to flee their Fatherland.[6]

Charles Frederick Kob was a surgeon in East Prussia who had participated in the failed German revolution of 1848 and had emigrated to Boston. Kob and many German-Americans supported the Republican nominee John Fremont in the 1856 presidential election. After Fremont's disappointing defeat, Kob and other German-Americans embarked on a plan to organize German-Americans on a national basis to resist the tyranny of the pro-slavery administration and the anti-immigration laws. On March 6, 1857, the New England Emigrant Aid Company voted to pay for Kob to travel to Kansas to establish a German newspaper in the territory to "advocate Free State principles and direct German immigration to Kansas."[7]

March 6 was also the date of the U.S. Supreme Court decision in the *Dred Scott* case, in which seven pro-slavery justices declared that any attempt to prohibit the spread of slavery was unconstitutional. Chief Justice Roger Taney said blacks "were so far inferior that they had no rights which the white man was bound to respect, and that [all blacks] might justly and lawfully be reduced to slavery." According to Taney, any black could be enslaved or killed like cattle with impunity.[8]

Kob arrived in Lawrence in April. Based upon their experiences in Europe, he and other German immigrants believed that only arming themselves would make it possible for a free state to prevail. He explained there were many resolutions and attempted peaceful negotiations with those in power, but that had not prevented Austria and Prussia from sending armies to put down the uprising. From that, Kob concluded in his Kansas German-language newspaper: "We no longer believe in resolutions. If the Free State [men] organized volunteer [armed] companies and simply sent President Buchanan the list, the Kansas issue would be decided."[9]

The New England Emigrant Aid Company increased the shipment of Colt revolvers and Sharps rifles to the territory, which soon made the Free State men one of the best-armed forces in the country. The Sharps Model 1853 carbines were soon nicknamed "Beecher's Bibles," after noted New York clergyman and abolitionist Henry Ward Beecher. Over 900 of these cutting-edge weapons were shipped in heavy crates to Kansas marked "Bibles," and were used by the Free State men.[10]

In July 1857, at the Free State Convention in Topeka, Lane told the delegates that he hoped to live to see the day when the "brutal [Democratic] party will be broken to pieces and when, from the waters of Yellowstone on the North to the warm waves of the Gulf on the South, one large line of Free States shall rear up and form an impenetrable barrier upon which the Western waves of this curse slavery shall dash in vain." The delegates designated Lane as general of the Free State forces and authorized him to organize militia companies to protect ballot boxes in the upcoming October elections. General Lane ordered muster rolls of those who enlisted. The first well-armed company of a Kansas volunteer army was located in Leavenworth and made up of 150 German-American men. General Lane inspected the company and was impressed. The muster roll of the "Kansas Volunteers for the Protection of the Ballot Box" included all of these men.[11]

A few weeks later, Lane led a meeting of nearly 500 men in favor of a slave-free Kansas at Grasshopper Falls (today Valley Falls). The result of the convention was an "Address to the American People on the Affairs of Kansas," which demanded fair elections and warned continued out-of-state intervention "would lead to war, protracted and bloody, between Missouri and Kansas, [and] it may be extended . . . to the Atlantic Coast. A dissolved Union and broken government may be the result." Lane signed as chairman. The delegates authorized Lane to use military force to protect the ballot boxes, as the general of the Free State Militia.[12]

The delegates also proposed a slate of Free State candidates. They nominated John P. Hatterscheidt, a German immigrant from Ohio, for the state legislature. The 27-year-old, highly educated engineer and surveyor had arrived in Leavenworth from Cincinnati with his wife and son sometime during the spring of 1857. The intelligent, charismatic Hatterscheidt would play a leading role in the Free State struggles and establish a strong friendship with Abe Lincoln. He later served in the Frontier Guard.

October 5 saw the beginning of two days of voting for the territorial legislature, which was to be seated the following January. With Lane's Free State militia and the Leavenworth German-Americans out in force protecting the ballot boxes and polling places, Kansas saw relatively honest elections in Leavenworth and Lawrence, while voting fraud continued elsewhere. The same month, the delegates in Lecompton, many of them Missouri slave owners, approved a constitution that legalized slavery and applied for statehood. Kansas was now a slave state. President Buchanan endorsed the Lecompton constitution, calling on Congress to admit Kansas as a slave state. Senator Stephen Douglas, however, stunned the political world by breaking with his fellow Democrats in opposing ratification. Douglas argued that support for the Lecompton constitution would betray his doctrine of popular sovereignty, because the elections on the constitution had been fraudulent and it did not reflect the will of the Kansas people.[13]

On November 14, 1857, Lane gave an impassioned speech to an overflowing crowd in Leavenworth, which included many members of the German-American militia, in which he proclaimed the fraudulent legislature "forced upon us by a neighboring state" had made Kansas "a slave state now." He shouted, "Your fathers call upon you to rise up and preserve the name of liberty which they gave you!" He exhorted them to have the same noble spirit "our fathers" had in "their perilous times."[14]

The phrase "our fathers" carried a special resonance for Bible-reading Americans of 1857. The Scriptures mention "our father" more than 50 times. Lane argued that the secular fathers of America had opposed slavery and expected it to end, and asked his audience to carry on that noble struggle. He concluded the framers of the Lecompton constitution should be "shot down like a damned dog." Lane's speech was widely reported and probably read by Abe Lincoln, 400 miles to the east in Springfield, Illinois. Less than six months later, on May 18, 1858, Lincoln argued in his "House Divided" speech that the Lecompton constitution "should be throttled and killed as hastily and as heartily as a rabid dog."[15]

In late 1857, Lane led a company of anti-slavery troops into Johnson County in southeast Kansas in an effort to prevent Missourians from pouring over state lines and fraudulently voting there. In tiny Oxford, he learned 1,800 Missourians had registered to vote, and the resident commanding officer of the United States troops, instead of preventing the fraud, calmly tolerated it. Lane was enraged by the repeated fraudulent actions and made an impassioned speech in Lawrence. He shouted: "Don't talk to me any longer about peaceful measures. You see what Uncle Sam has done for us and what we can expect from him. Tomorrow I will go to Lecompton and attempt to persuade the legislature to establish a provisional government and declare 'war on Missouri.'"[16]

Lane's declaration that he was prepared to "declare war on Missouri" reflected his rapidly evolving radicalism and came at a time when he promoted the idea that his soldiers were "Jayhawks." The Jayhawk became the popular symbol of anti-slavery fighters. Its early history comes to light in the autobiography of a German revolutionary, August Bondi, who was one of several German-Americans who had joined John Brown's band of fighters.

Bondi described the circumstances of the Jayhawks' origin at a meeting of the anti-slavery troops of Lane, James Montgomery, and Charles R. "Doc" Jennison in southeastern Kansas in late December 1857. At Sugar Mound (Mound City), near the border of Linn and Bourbon counties, Bondi witnessed Lane's midnight appeal to the 150 volunteer soldiers. Lane asked the men to take on the role of "Jayhawks." He explained the new name as follows: "As the Irish Jayhawk with a shrill cry announces his presence to his victims, so must you notify the pro-slavery hell-hounds to clear out or vengeance will overtake them. Jayhawks, remember, 'Vengeance is mine, saith the Lord,' but we are his agents. So originated the name, Jayhawks (corrupted Jayhawkers), afterwards applied indiscriminately to Kansas troops." Bondi said, "Of all the 150 men in and around the schoolhouse that night, I am the only survivor."[17]

Lane's Old Testament rhetoric was the catalyst for an image that attained widespread use. Settlers in the area soon called the Free State fighters Jayhawks to indicate the "celerity of their movements and their habit of suddenly pouncing on their enemy." When operating in the enemy's country, like any guerrilla fighters, the Jayhawks needed to "be self-sustaining—must subsist on the enemy. Therefore, we feed ourselves at pro-slavery larders and our horses at pro-slavery corn-cribs." Kansas Jayhawks raided Missouri slave owners, freeing slaves, stealing the slave owners' horses so that pursuit was impossible, and sometimes killing. Missouri "bushwhackers" responded in kind, fighting like "tigers" against the predatory Jayhawks.[18]

Another round of Kansas territorial elections was scheduled to take place on January 4, 1858. Lane had planned to speak at a voting meeting in Atchison the Saturday before the vote. Atchison, named for former U.S. Senator David Atchison of Missouri, was a pro-slavery stronghold just a year or so previously. An influx of German immigrants and other Free State men had recently turned Atchison and Leavenworth into Free State majorities, although a strong pro-slavery minority still existed who hoped to intimidate the anti-slavery men from voting by use of threats and violence.

The Slavers viewed Lane's speech as a golden opportunity to murder him. The brother of Atchison's mayor learned of the planned assassination, however, and he sent a dispatch to the Leavenworth Free State men asking them to ride to Atchison and save Lane's life. Eleven German-Americans and nine Americans rode out of Leavenworth before daylight on a cold, blustery Saturday morning for the 25-mile ride northwest to Atchison. Henry J. Adams led the nine Americans, while John P. Hattersheidt (shortened to "Hat" by the frontiersmen) led the 11 German-Americans. The 20 men hit the trail before sunup, keeping off the skyline as much as possible to avoid ambush. So as to not arouse suspicion, the Leavenworth men decided to bring revolvers only, hidden under their greatcoats, not rifles—a decision they would soon regret.[19]

Around noon, the men arrived in the rough-looking town of Atchison. The town had three saloons, a general store, a bank, a livery stable, and a bunkhouse that called itself a hotel. They dismounted at the livery stable at the end of what the town called a main street. They rubbed down their tired horses and fed and watered them. Outside somewhere, a horse stamped and there was a clang of iron on iron. The dusty-booted and long-spurred riders then clanked noisily down the gray, warped wooden boardwalk. The rutted street was lined with hitching rails and water troughs. The windows of the gray, false-fronted buildings showed goods for sale, while others were blank and empty. The town's main street had suddenly become empty, and here and there the men glimpsed move-

ment in a darkened doorway. Adams knew Western towns well enough
to know the word was out.

The worn and polished hitch rails in front of the town's saloons were
lined with saddled horses. Inside the saloons were a group of about 50
dirty, unshaved men, most of them with uncut hair over their collars,
loaded down with rifles, revolvers, and bowie knives sticking out of boot
tops. They stood three deep at the bars, and many of them were already
drunk. The Leavenworth men went into the town's restaurant and sat at
board tables on rough wooden benches and chairs while they warmed
themselves with coffee around the glowing-red, pot-bellied stove.

Soon the Slavers began shooting their weapons into the air and loudly
threatening Lane and other Free State men. The 20 Leavenworth men
walked slowly out onto the dirt, manure-filled street, their overcoats still
concealing their revolvers, which were tucked inside their waistbands and
pockets. At the time, pistols were generally carried in a holster, on a gun
belt, or thrust into the waistband. The habit of carrying pistols on the hip
had not yet developed to any extent.

Adams, who wanted to avoid bloodshed, was unarmed and at the
front of the Leavenworth group. He saw crowds of men spew from the
doors of the saloons. As they approached, the pro-slavery mob began yelling. Adams knew that a crowd could stoke violence the way wind stokes
fire. The lead pro-slavery men swung their rifles up menacingly at the
Leavenworth men. Adams shouted that there needn't be any bloodshed,
while at the same time he kept walking toward the Missourians, knowing
that at close range his men's revolvers would be as effective as the Missourians' rifles. One big, bearded Pro-Slaver was mounted and rode ahead
of the others, his rifle resting across the pommel of his saddle. Three
other men walked alongside him, holding rifles. The rider was apparently
looking forward to shooting some of the unarmed abolitionists, before
slamming his spurs into his horse's ribs and perhaps trampling one or
two others. His men would finish off the rest as they attempted to flee.

The mounted man reined up in front of Adams, his narrow, flat-
looking eyes opaque as a rattler's, his black rifle muzzle aimed at Adams's
chest. The three pro-slavery men with him glared at the Leavenworth
men with hard, ugly stares. Adams had seen men like this before in lynch

mobs and elsewhere. They would kill as naturally as a man would slaughter a hog or shoot a steer. One of the pro-slavery men standing next to the mounted man knocked the hat off of Adams's head with the barrel of his rifle, and the pro-slavery mob behind him yelled "Kill him!"[20]

At that moment, the Leavenworth men cocked their revolvers almost in unison as they pulled the heavy guns out from under their coats, and the four pro-slavery men suddenly realized they weren't facing defenseless pacifists, but gunmen loaded down with iron. Hatterscheidt's gun butt felt good against his palm. "If they open the ball, I want the rider," one of the men growled. It looked like there would be blood in the street—only the Pro-Slavers hesitated. The faces of the rider and his soldiers turned a sickly gray. They seemed to suddenly sober, realizing how deadly the Free State men would be with revolvers at close range. The Pro Slavers weren't going to pick a fight unless the odds were all with them. Murder was one thing, a fight another. The mounted man half-turned and shouted at the rest of the men behind him to stand down.

An Atchison citizen then intervened, taking Adams by the arm and leading him to safety in an office off the street as the Leavenworth men followed slowly, keeping their eyes on the Missourians and their pistols in their fists. In the meantime, Lane's friends had gotten word to him and convinced him not to ride into Atchison. The Leavenworth men pulled out of town that afternoon without having to fire a shot. They arrived back in Leavenworth about ten o'clock that night exhausted, but thankful to be back in the arms of their relieved loved ones.[21]

January 4, 1858, was raw and blustery, the wind swirling across the Missouri River and down the rutted road through Kickapoo, Kansas. Kickapoo lay eight miles above Leavenworth, just across the ice-crusted river from Weston, Missouri, which was a pro-slavery stronghold. The town catered to pro-slavery Missouri men, who came across the ferry and liquored up in the saloons before voting as "one-day Kansans."[22]

Twenty-nine-year-old Thomas Ewing, Jr., wrapped in a greatcoat, rode slowly into town leading over 30 other similarly bundled Free State men. Ewing was the son and namesake of Thomas Ewing of Lancaster, Ohio, a former Whig senator and cabinet member. Thomas Ewing, Jr. had served as personal secretary to President Taylor while his father was

Secretary of the Interior. Thomas Jr. and his brother Hugh came to Leavenworth in 1856 to practice law and speculate in land. At the time, Leavenworth was the largest town between St. Louis and San Francisco.

Each of Ewing's riders had at least one revolver tucked into his waistband or on a gun belt under his coat, and was determined to ensure the election would be fair. The Pro-Slavers told Ewing that they had just voted for the candidates for the Lecompton legislature, and if Ewing did not like it, they would kill him. Ewing replied that Lane's militia was at a nearby telegraph office, armed and mounted, and if the Missourians harmed any of Ewing's Free State men, Lane would build the first bridge over the Missouri River with the ashes and stones of Weston. The Missourians did not know if Ewing was bluffing, but they did not attack.

Ewing remained in Kickapoo all day, watching the long line of Missourians walk into the voting office, swear to their Kansas residency, and vote (some did so several times between drinks at the saloons). When the polls were about to close, Ewing voted, number 550 on the voting sheet. Within hours of the end of the election, Ewing swore out warrants to arrest illegal Missouri voters he saw at Kickapoo.

President Pierce had appointed John Calhoun as the chief land and election officer. When Calhoun announced that over 900 votes were cast in Kickapoo, Ewing swung into action. He wired the facts and the Kickapoo voting fraud to Free State strongholds around the territory. Anger erupted, and Calhoun fled to Washington just ahead of a mob carrying ropes. Ewing began an investigation and discovered a large box of ballots under a woodpile. An entire city directory of names had been spliced onto the voting list. The fraudulent names were disregarded.[23]

The election and investigation into voting fraud, and the Free State majority votes in Leavenworth and Lawrence, finally resulted in a Free State victory. When the *Leavenworth Daily Times* reported on the "glorious victory" of the Free State Party, it devoted an article recognizing the role of the Leavenworth Germans in the victory. Editor John C. Vaughn asserted: "There was a heroic spirit in 1848 in Germany . . . And that spirit warms the blood of our German citizens here. In every contest where Free State principles had been at stake, they have been among the first to take position, whenever the peril, and among the last to leave it. All honor to such men!" Vaughn later served in the Frontier Guard.[24]

German-American immigration to Leavenworth had caused a tipping point in the Free State struggle. The day after the election, a determined group of Leavenworth Free State men, consisting of about 35 German-Americans, including John Hatterscheidt, left Leavenworth in the dark of night determined to raid the headquarters of the pro-slavery Kickapoo Rangers militia. They intended to capture the cannon that the pro-slavery men had fired at the Lawrence Free State Hotel two and a half years earlier, and which was now positioned to fire upon Free State men who might approach Kickapoo. After a three-hour march, the Leavenworth men stormed the pro-slavery blockhouse and captured the cannon, along with other weapons, and arrested one of the pro-slavery voting officials who had helped falsify the last vote.

They had accomplished a feat which the pro-slavery men had boasted not even 1,000 men could achieve. Five hundred pro-slavery men quickly gathered and approached Leavenworth. At 10 P.M., Leavenworth bells were rung, drums sounded, and within ten minutes, Hatterscheidt and 150 heavily armed German-Americans were ready to defend the city and the cannon. As soon as the Missourians saw the force assembled against them, they retreated, never to attack Leavenworth again. The Free State capture of the "Kickapoo cannon" created wild excitement and was widely reported throughout the nation.[25]

Two months later, in March 1858, Lane was elected president of the Leavenworth Constitutional Convention, which overturned the Lecompton constitution. The U.S. Congress, however, still dominated by pro-slavery Democrats, refused to ratify the document.

Meanwhile, John Hatterscheidt emerged as a valuable ally of Lane's and a prominent leader of Leavenworth's German community. He was elected to the Territorial assembly and was a leader of Leavenworth's Turner Society. Leavenworth July 4th activities took place in the northwest part of the city, called "Little Cincinnati," where the largest concentration of Germans resided. The highlight of the festivities was Hatterscheidt's "brilliant" speech, in which he described how the Turners were the first to take up arms against the oppressors in Europe. They emigrated because they loved liberty more than their ties to their own country. The Turners were now ready to exert themselves for the "Republican institutions in America."[26]

Up to this point, Kansas was too focused on its own crisis to assume a serious role in national politics. Now the Kansas Territory began to transition from Free State politics to the Republican Party. Hatterscheidt and others began to focus their attention and efforts on achieving a Republican victory in the 1860 presidential election.[27]

Jim Lane finally had time to devote himself to his chosen profession and earn some money for his young family. In the spring of 1858, Lane formed a law partnership with James Christian in Lawrence. Lane quickly became a legendary trial lawyer in the territory. In one case, Lane was hired to defend two hog thieves. The prosecuting attorney believed the defendants would plead guilty, given the overwhelming testimony against them. It was then rumored that Lane would defend the thieves against their pro-slavery accusers. People packed the courtroom to watch.

The prosecutor produced his witnesses and the evidence was undisputed. Lane asked no questions but said the court was bound to take judicial notice of two facts: "One, I hold in my hand a copy of the poll list, showing that these men [the accusers] voted at Lawrence, and now swear they lived in Missouri. Men that would stuff the ballot boxes, overrun elections and drive voters from the polls ought to be thankful that they are not hung." He added, "Another point of which the court must take judicial notice is this pretended offense was committed on an Indian reserve, which is not part of the territory of Kansas, and over which the court has no jurisdiction." The audience was so inflamed that the accusers fled the courtroom for their lives. The judge declared Lane's clients to be innocent.[28]

On June 3, 1858, Lane had a deadly shootout with a neighbor that would challenge his leadership in the territory—and his legacy. Lane and the other man, Gaius Jenkins, had a long-standing feud over their property rights and access to a well near Lane's log cabin home. Jenkins was a Free State man, but from the Charles Robinson-New England faction that generally opposed Lane.

While Lane had been away in 1856 pleading the Free State cause before the Democratic-controlled Congress in Washington, Jenkins had moved into Lane's log house and plowed up and cultivated the land around the cabin, including the land on which Lane's daughter was buried, so that no trace of the grave remained. Lane broke down in tears when he discovered his daughter's grave had been lost or destroyed. Lane was a loving and affectionate father, passionately fond of his children. Other Free State men talked Lane out of retaliating against Jenkins, explaining that perhaps Jenkins had not known of the grave. Jenkins had also voluntarily vacated the cabin when Lane returned, although he still disputed Lane's rights to the nearby well.[29]

Sworn testimony later established that Jenkins had been drinking heavily with several anti-Lane men the day of the shooting, including former Sheriff Jones, who had allowed the pro-slavery men to sack Lawrence two years earlier. Jenkins was known to have an impulsive, violent temper when under the influence of liquor. Jenkins, his nephew, and two other men then walked up to the fence surrounding Lane's property armed with Sharps rifles, revolvers, and an ax. Lane came out of his cabin unarmed and met the men at the fence, telling them they were free to use the well for water, but they would have to come through the gate. The men refused, and one of them began chopping down Lane's fence and the others threatened to kill Lane. Lane strode back to his cabin and returned with a rifle loaded with birdshot. The men rushed toward Lane and one of them shot him in the leg. Lane then fired a load of birdshot at Jenkins, killing him. Jenkins's nephew later admitted that the men intended to kill Lane.[30]

The request for water may have even been a subterfuge for Jenkins's actions, as there was a well on Mt. Oread available to him and more accessible than Lane's well. Coincidentally, Sheriff Jones arrived at the scene immediately after the shooting and encouraged the men to hang Lane, who was now unarmed, and under the guns of the three men who had accompanied Jenkins. Charles Robinson also called for Lane to be lynched. Others in the gathering crowd suggested that if there was to be a lynching, Sheriff Jones should be the one to get his neck stretched for allowing the pro-slavery men to burn and pillage Lawrence two years earlier.[31]

Lane was tried in the national press as well as a local court. The pro-slavery press vilified him and argued that Jenkins's death proved that Lane was a deranged murderer. Tom Ewing was Lane's defense attorney. The testimony Ewing obtained at Lane's preliminary hearing a few weeks later established a clear case of self-defense, however, and Judge Joseph

Wilson agreed. Wilson was well respected both for his knowledge of the law and his honesty. He had previously been the acting land commissioner under Democratic and pro-slavery President James Buchanan, and was retained by President Lincoln as well. He was not a man who let friendship or politics influence his decisions.[32]

Judge Wilson's decision that Lane was innocent of murder and had acted in self-defense mattered little to Lane's opponents, however, who demonized Lane by claiming he was an unstable, bloodthirsty murderer of a man whose only fault had been to stop for a drink at Lane's well. A contemporary observer of the efforts to demonize Lane concluded they proved the axiom: "Falsehood will travel a mile while truth is getting on its boots."[33]

At about the same time, on June 16, 1858, Abe Lincoln, the Republican candidate for the Senate in Illinois, gave his "House Divided" speech in Springfield, Illinois, in which he declared that the former and current presidents of the United States (Franklin Pierce and James Buchanan); the chief justice of the Supreme Court (Roger Taney); and the architect of the Kansas-Nebraska Act (Stephen Douglas) were conspiring against the United States in their quest to nationalize slavery and extend it to every state and territory. These powerful statesmen were at the head of a "political dynasty" that Lincoln called the "Slave Power." The speech was subversive, powerful, and breathtaking. One of those in attendance was David M. Kelsey, a delegate from DeKalb County and a member of the Illinois House of Representatives. Kelsey later served in the Frontier Guard.[34]

On July 22, 1858, the *Chicago Daily Times* suggested, "Let Mr. [Stephen] Douglas and Mr. Lincoln agree to canvass the state together, in the old western style." Lincoln seized upon the idea two days later and issued a formal challenge, to which Douglas agreed. At the time, United States senators were elected by state legislatures, and so Lincoln and Douglas were trying for their respective parties to win control of the Illinois legislature. The seven debates were held in different Illinois congressional districts and focused on the subject of slavery and the recent experiences in the Kansas territory. Because he was so angry with Lincoln for accusing him of conspiring with the Slave Power, a week before the debates

began, Douglas even challenged Lincoln to a fistfight. The excited reporting of these debates took the place of Kansas itself in the national media.
Kansas was the ghost of Banquo at the feast, however—the specter that
could not be exorcised, the embarrassment that could be neither forgotten nor forgiven.[35]

6

Gold Fever

Shortly after the Lincoln-Douglas debates, journalists began sensational reporting of a major gold strike in the far western part of the Kansas Territory, which stretched to the Continental Divide. In the spring of 1859, Henry Villard of the *Cincinnati Daily Commercial* and Horace Greeley of the *New York Tribune* traveled to the Rocky Mountains to investigate the gold strike along Cherry Creek, in the mountains near Denver City. They reported that men were making a fortune sluicing for gold. Surely, this was the legendary gold that Spaniard Francisco Coronado had sought and that had continued to tantalize explorers afterwards. The stories were legion: mountain Indians so wealthy their arrows were dipped in gold; rivulets in the river where the water "rolled down gold dust."[1]

Frontier imaginations, fanned by these and other tales, were ignited by the news of "color" so precisely located. Young frontier horseman and hunter Edward M. McCook, from New Lisbon, Ohio, yearned for adventure and fortune. He read the articles and decided to join the stampede of adventurers heading for Denver City. The 25-year-old bachelor, sporting a thick black mustache and long sideburns, followed the trail of his cousin Daniel McCook, who had gone west the previous fall to Leavenworth to practice law with Thomas Ewing, Jr. and William Tecumseh Sherman. Daniel had written to Edward about the opportunities and the dangers in the new Kansas Territory.[2]

McCook traveled by boat down the Ohio River beyond the Mississippi, the great river that divided the country in two. He then traveled by a paddle-wheeled steamboat up the muddy Missouri River and disembarked at the levee at Leavenworth, Kansas Territory. In Leavenworth, McCook purchased the best horse he could find. He knew that the only protection he would have crossing the wild prairie was a quick eye, the ability to shoot straight, and a fast horse with staying power. He was likely armed with a Colt revolver and rifle.

Early in the morning, he saddled up and rode out to the prairie on the outskirts of Leavenworth to meet a group of other prospectors and adventurers, many of whom were traveling in monstrous Conestoga wagons pulled by eight to 12 oxen. The lead yoke was typically a pair of Longhorns, as they would cross rivers and go through rough country where barnyard bovines hesitated to tread. The drivers were as rough and wild-looking as their teams.[3]

Clothing and food filled up much of the wagon. Skillets, axes, saws, and mining equipment were also necessary. For each man, the wagon carried about 50 pounds of bacon, 25 pounds of pilot bread, 5 pounds of salt, a pound of sugar, one-half bushel of dried beans, and several pounds of coffee. The drivers strapped pairs of 10-gallon barrels of water to each side of their wagons.[4]

From far ahead came the long, familiar call, "Ro-l-l-l-l out! Roll 'em o-o-over!" Whips cracked and the wagons started. McCook watched the lead oxen move out, a step, and then another step, in a slow, swaying, rhythmical movement, the covered wagons rumbling behind. Horses were faster than oxen, so McCook and the other riders rode ahead of the wagons, scouting the trail. They rode west into a land of buffalo and Indians. Behind them, the rising sun threw their long shadows before them. The journey required riding through 600 miles of unsettled Indian territory, land most of them knew only from hearsay.

The men followed the twin tracks along the Pikes Peak trail, where earlier freighters' wagons and pack trains had cut deep into the prairie sod. Shortly after leaving Leavenworth, McCook found himself in a vast sea of grass, where only roving herds of buffalo and antelope grazed. McCook looked out onto the windswept plains, grass growing where once had been an ancient sea. It was bleak, lonely, and harsh. As the men rode toward the setting sun, huge flocks of birds flew up and glided away. They heard the prairie wind and, at night, the prairie wolves.

McCook was in the biggest country he had ever seen. Everything was immense. The great cloudless sky, the rolling sea of grass. The sun was so bright that he could tolerate it only by pulling the brim of his hat down over his squinting eyes. He saw few trees except for cottonwoods along the occasional stream. There were no sounds but the rumble of the wagons and rattle of the trace chains, the swish of horses' feet through the grass, the creak of saddle leather, and the occasional jingle of a spur. The men kept a sharp and watchful eye out for Comanche warriors, who wore black buffalo headdresses and rode unchallenged across the territory.

At days' end, as McCook rode slowly forward into the Western sun, the sky turned blood-red and bathed the grasses in crimson. The men circled the wagons and built a campfire, a lonely gleam on the great, vast plain. Firelight flickered on the flanks of horses and reflected from polished leather. Their meals were a chunk of beef and scoops of beans, or bacon and beans. McCook felt the wind off the prairie in his face and he smelled frying bacon and wood smoke from the freshly built fire. The coffee pot, blackened and beat-up, stood in the coals on flat rocks. McCook fell asleep to the sound of howling wolves and coyotes.

At dawn he rolled out of his blankets, sat up, and put on his hat. He then shook out his boots and tugged them on. He buckled his gun belt, stamped to settle his feet into his boots, and after some coffee and biscuits, saddled up, loading his gear as quietly as possible.

In the afternoon, the air was hot and still. McCook liked the movement of his horse, the feel of it between his knees, and the creak of saddle leather. He saw his first herd of buffalo grazing some miles off. A herd of several hundred made their way down the valley of a small creek toward the Solomon River. One of the men in the party leveled a rifle and fired at one of the bulls but missed, causing the herd to rumble off over the horizon. Later, the riders crested a hill and saw off in the distance a massive heard of thousands of buffalo, which darkened the prairie for miles. There were gray wolves lurking about the outskirts of the herd, waiting for an unlucky calf to stray.[5]

McCook saw a little group of Cheyenne or Kiowa warriors riding in a loose bunch roughly 100 yards away, crossing McCook's trail. They were fine-looking men with feathers in their hair, and they were riding without their women and children, which meant they were hunting or raiding. Most were armed with lances, but at least one had a rifle. From the lance of the lead warrior hung strips of bloody flesh and hair. Scalps. The Cheyenne, Kiowa, and other Plains Indians were fierce warriors, veterans of many battles, who respected courage and strength. They did not fear the white man but welcomed them, because the white men brought horses, food, and weapons they could take from them.

Two summers before, 300 U.S. cavalry troops from Fort Leavenworth had fought a battle against roughly an equal number of Cheyenne warriors in about the same location. Men on both sides died. The Delaware Indians scouting for the cavalry scalped the dead Cheyenne, and the cavalry burned a nearby Cheyenne village of tents of buffalo hides, injuring and killing women and children, causing the Cheyenne to seek revenge and attack settlers along the Kansas Territory trails. McCook had never seen such warriors—proud, confident, and capable of violent battle—and it was their land that they were riding through. McCook and the other settlers took turns keeping watch at night, paying as much attention to guarding their horses as themselves.[6]

The frontier provided its own kind of education and training ground, where each day an examination was given and failure could mean death. McCook learned that the innocent distance that lay before him was broken by hollows, folded hills, and gnarled ravines that could hide an enemy, but it seemed an even, unbroken expanse from atop his horse. He learned patience, and to not make any unnecessary movements when riding. Movement attracts the eye and draws attention. Only those with common sense and toughness survived on the trail. Fools died young.[7]

The men told time by the sun and directions by the fall of shadows. After 20 days of riding, in the mornings, the air was fresher. There was also a faint chill in the air, a sign the riders were getting higher. They had reached the western High Plains. The long grasses gave way to shorter grasses and gently rolling hills. The riders saw their first antelope and brought one down with a rifle shot. The meat was tender and delicate. Later, far off, a jagged line of mountains reared up in the western sky, the greatest mountains they had ever seen.

James H. Lane

"That he loved Kansas, and that Kansans loved him, is undeniable."

Emporia News, July 14, 1866

Image courtesy of the Kansas State Historical Society

Lane's Fort on Mount Oread, near Lawrence, Kansas Territory, 1856

Harper's Weekly, June 6, 1857

Image courtesy of the Kansas State Historical Society

Free State Cannon and the Men who Fired It At Fort Titus
(man on the right is thought to be John Brown's son, Owen)

Photographed by John Bowles, Sept. 1856 in Lawrence, KT

Photo courtesy of the Kansas State Historical Society

**Daniel R. Anthony in the
Kansas Territory**

Photo courtesy of the Kansas State Historical Society

Abraham Lincoln May 16, 1861

Photo courtesy of the Library of Congress

Crowd Gathered before the East Portico of the Unfinished Capitol to Glimpse Lincoln's Inauguration, March 4, 1861

Photo courtesy of the Library of Congress

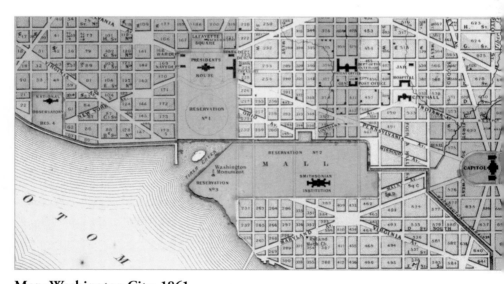

Map: Washington City, 1861

Photo courtesy of the Library of Congress

Bivouac of Gen. Lane's Command in the East Room of the White House

Illustration by Adam Rohe

Scabbard and Sword Given to Lane at the White House in April 1861

Watkins Community Museum, Lawrence, Kansas

Photo courtesy of the Watkins Community Museum

Frontier Guard on South Lawn of the White House, April, 1861

Photo courtesy of the Library of Congress

U.S. Senator James H. Lane, April, 1861

Photo courtesy of the United States Army Heritage and Education Center

Frontier Guard Member and Maj. General Thomas Ewing, Jr.

Photo courtesy of the Library of Congress

Frontier Guard Member and Maj. Daniel McCook, Sr. Paymaster, U.S. Volunteers, with his Henry rifle, 1863

Photo courtesy of the Ohio Historical Society

**Frontier Guard Member and
Brigadier Gen. Edward McCook**

Photo courtesy of the Library of Congress

**Frontier Guard Member and
Col. Samuel F. Tappan**

Wearing Sword Presented to him
by Col. Kit Carson of the
First New Mexico Volunteers

Photo courtesy of History Colorado

**Frontier Guard Member and
Lt. Col. Daniel R. Anthony,
Seventh Kansas Calvary**

Photo courtesy of Charles O'Rear

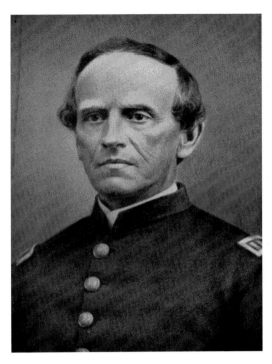

**Frontier Guard Member and
Capt. Chester Thomas, Sr.**

Photo courtesy of the Kansas State Historical Society

**Frontier Guard Member
and Col. Edward Daniels**

Photo courtesy of Hathi Trust

**Frontier Guard Member and Capt. Samuel W. Greer,
Fifteenth Regiment, Kansas Calvary,** *center*

Photo courtesy of James Albert Ling

**Frontier Guard Member and Col.
George Lea Febiger**

Photo courtesy of the United States Army
Heritage and Education Center

**Frontier Guard Member and Lt.
George Washington Smith, Jr.**

Reynolds J. Burt Photograph Collection

Photo courtesy of the United States Army
Heritage and Education Center

Frontier Guard Member and Maj. George B. Way

Photo courtesy of the United States Army Heritage and Education Center

Frontier Guard Member and Capt. Guido Ilges

Photo courtesy of Michael J. McAfee

Treasury Guards remained on duty throughout the war.

The unfinished Washington Monument in background. Seven members of the Frontier Guard served as Treasury Guards.

Photo courtesy of the Library of Congress

**Frontier Guard Member and
U.S. Rep. Sidney Clarke**
Photo courtesy of the Library of Congress

**Frontier Guard Member and
U.S. Rep. Marcus J. Parrott**
Photo courtesy of the Library of Congress

Frontier Guard Member and Sec. of the New Mexico Territory, James H. Holmes

Photo courtesy of the Kansas State Historical Society

Frontier Guard Member and Col. George Lea Febiger in his quarters at Fort Union, Indian Territory, in the 1880s

Photo courtesy of Bjarne Fibiger

Riding further, they could see the gleam of snow on the peaks and pine-clad ridges. In the morning there was fog on the ground, and sometimes it was noon before McCook began to feel warmth in the air. They saw scattered pine trees. Soon, he could see through the trees to the plains below. This was a part of the front range, the face of the Rockies looking eastward toward the wide, wide plains that ran all the way to the Mississippi, and beyond. They gradually ascended into higher country, where their horses' hoofs clattered on the rock under the thin soil. The mountain air made McCook want to inhale deeply, as if it was cold, clear water. He saw the ridges turn to flame as the sun slid down the sky.[8]

Finally, about 30 days after leaving Fort Leavenworth, his bones and muscles weary of riding, McCook arrived in the village of Denver City. He saw scattered stone huts, some ramshackle shacks of dirty canvas and planks, and farther along a frame building or two and a log house built with cedar cut on the mountainside. There were tent gambling houses and saloons, where a rough plank on the top of two barrels served as a crude bar. Whiskey was served in tin cups drawn from a barrel. Mules and horses were tied to brush or trees; others were picketed.

Here and there a wagon was drawn up and all the spaces between were crowded with men in every possible costume—coonskin caps, beaver hats, silk hats, old army hats and caps, sombreros, fringed buckskin, army jackets, and bear coats. There were all sorts of men—gamblers, prospectors, trappers, adventurers, drifters, and criminals. Some of the men had worked the California gold strike of 1848-49; others were rebounding from failed strikes elsewhere. Most of them were looking for something easy, something to find or steal. There were thieves and murderers, backshooters, and knife men who would stick a knife in your ribs for what was in your pockets. Because of sensational newspaper articles, several hundred prospectors were riding in daily by the time McCook arrived. A few men became wealthy, but there were not enough workable claims. Most lost everything; some were killed by white men, others by Indians.

It was hard work standing in icy streams, panning for the elusive gold. Even for the men who found gold, they still had to get it off the mountain while defending themselves against claim jumpers, robbers, and murderers. They bought mules or horses to carry the gold, but thieves and murderers guessed their purpose. The prospectors also needed help to get the gold down, but the help was often greedy, and some would murder for gold. Miners are gamblers by nature, and fortune could be fickle. Card cheats stole much of what the miners were able to get out of ground. The successful miners soon discovered that gold was easier found than kept.

McCook quickly grew to love the mountains. In the fall, frost turned the leaves, and the mountainsides were splashed with the gold of aspen. The aspens were a river of gold flowing down the mountain and spilling down its sides. The leaves fell in the breeze, dropping like a shower of golden coins, only this gold was there for everyone to have—they had only to look. McCook decided to make the mountains his home. He mined for gold and battled the Indians, who were fighting to hold onto their ancestral hunting grounds. He fought fierce Arapahoe and Kiowa warriors and still kept his hair. And he would soon serve in the Frontier Guard.[9]

At about the same time as McCook rode west toward Cherry Creek, the Leavenworth & Pikes Peak Express Company, the predecessor to the Pony Express, made its first ride from Westport, Missouri, to Denver, Kansas Territory. Riding for the Express was difficult, dangerous work. Newspaper advertisements for the company stated: "Wanted: Young, skinny, wiry fellows. Must be expert riders, willing to risk death daily. Orphans preferred." About 80 riders were hired. Samuel L. Hartman was one of them. Born in Vermont, Hartman had come West as a child. Sam was a crack shot and skilled rider who had spent two years as an Express messenger and guard along the Missouri River and the Kansas Territory river towns. He had survived several shoot-outs with would-be robbers and murderers. He would also soon become a soldier in the Frontier Guard.[10]

During the spring of 1859, 24-year-old Job B. Stockton also caught the Pike's Peak gold-rush fever and rode from Leavenworth to the far west of the Kansas Territory. He settled in Denver City and tried his hand at mining. He soon became discouraged, and before winter began to set in, he returned to Leavenworth in time to hear Abe Lincoln's speeches there. Stockton would soon serve in the Frontier Guard. Lincoln had no way of knowing it at the time, but the men he met during his Kansas campaign would save his life 16 months later.[11]

7

Lincoln Looks West

Abe Lincoln is considered a "Man of the West" largely due to his rough-and-tumble, log-cabin upbringing. The three states in which Lincoln was raised—Kentucky, Indiana, and Illinois—were considered part of the West when Lincoln lived there. One observer in New Salem, Illinois, where Lincoln lived during his 20s, described lanky Abe "as ruff [sic] a specimen of humanity as could be found." But Lincoln was also intrigued with the peoples and lands beyond the Mississippi. He ultimately envisioned a Union extending from sea to shining sea.[1]

In 1859 Lincoln was keenly interested in the far western territory of Kansas. Opposition to the Kansas-Nebraska Act had boosted his profile and made many consider the rail-splitter as presidential timber. The divisive issue of slavery, often considered an exclusively North-South problem, was also a problem of the West. From the mid-to-late 1850s, the political battleground over slavery was centered on the frontier. For the good of Bleeding Kansas and the nation, Lincoln opposed the spread of slavery to the West. As reflected in his debates with Illinois Senator Stephen Douglas, Lincoln was determined to make slavery's western trajectory hit a deadend on the Kansas/Missouri border, a stand that would help propel him to the White House in 1861. Lincoln's vision of the country also drew him to the West, where he envisioned railroad lines crisscrossing the Great Plains.[2]

In 1859, Lincoln made two trips across the Mississippi to deliver speeches and improve his viability as a presidential candidate. A nine-day journey in August took him to Iowa, where he spoke at Council Bluffs and discussed with engineer Grenville Dodge (who, as chief engineer, later helped construct the transcontinental railroad) the best routes west for a transcontinental railroad. Lincoln reportedly told Dodge, "There is nothing more important for the nation at this time than the building of a railroad to the Pacific Coast." Lincoln's second trip, also for nine days, took him through Missouri into the Kansas Territory.[3]

It is not well known that Lincoln spent eight days touring and giving six speeches in Kansas in 1859, just 11 months before his improbable election as the 16th president of the United States. The bypassing of this notable chapter in Kansas history and in Lincoln's life by historians is perhaps understandable. Just a year earlier, Lincoln had waged a war of words with Stephen Douglas in their great Illinois debates during Lincoln's failed run for the Illinois U.S. Senate seat. Two months later, the Western politician delivered his historic speech and appeal at the Cooper Union to the Eastern elite in New York City, which ignited his meteoric rise to the presidency. Lincoln's Kansas tour, sandwiched between these historic events, has been largely overlooked.[4]

But Lincoln's December 1859 visit to Kansas was critical for two largely unrecognized reasons. First, Lincoln tested and refined the speech he would give two months later at Cooper Union in New York City, which introduced Lincoln to Eastern voters and politicians. Second, Lincoln met and inspired many of the men who saved his life 16 months later.

In 1859 Lincoln had yet to prove himself as a national leader, yet alone show signs of true greatness. Before he became a monument, before his murder made him a secular saint, he was a frontier lawyer who defended cases both worthy and questionable. He was a stranger to those in the East and mostly thought of by those in the West as a self-educated lawyer who had lost his bid to unseat Senator Stephen Douglas, although he had earned some notoriety as a debater on slavery.

In February 1859, Mark Delahay, a Leavenworth lawyer who knew Lincoln when they were lawyers in Illinois and whose wife, Louisiana Hanks, was related to Lincoln's mother, Nancy Hanks, invited Lincoln to attend the May 1859 Kansas Republican Convention, at which the delegates drafted the platform for the newly forming Kansas Republican Party (which replaced the Free State party). Lincoln declined, concerned about losing time from his law practice and the extra distance involved in traveling to the event at Osawatomie. At Lincoln's urging, however, the Kansas Republican Party adopted an anti-slavery platform.[5]

Delahay, undeterred by Lincoln's refusal to attend the convention and being a savvy politician, thought the time was right for Lincoln to run for the presidency, and he wrote Lincoln again on November 14 and 15, encouraging him to come to Leavenworth, meet the Kansas Republicans, help them beat the Democrats in the December 6 Kansas Territorial election, and perhaps secure the Kansas delegates' votes at the May 1860 Republican Presidential Convention. In his letters, Delahay mentioned that Kansas newspapermen Jeff Dugger and Walter Ross could be counted upon to support Lincoln in the upcoming election. Delahay, Dugger, and Ross later served in the Frontier Guard.

The tenacious Jeff Dugger was well known to Lincoln. Dugger was originally from Illinois, but he had moved to Leavenworth with his young wife in 1856. The couple was forced to return to Illinois in 1857 as a result of threats upon their lives by pro-slavery men. Dugger met Lincoln, and the two lawyers partnered to represent a client in a lawsuit in March 1859, just nine months before Lincoln's visit to Kansas. Dugger had then moved back to Leavenworth and joined Mark Delahay to form a small law firm. He also became editor of the *Kansas Daily State Register,* an anti-slavery newspaper. Dugger was also corresponding with Lincoln, telling him that the Republicans in Kansas were "wide awake" and encouraging Lincoln to come to Kansas.[6]

Walter Ross was a newspaper editor who had nearly been killed by pro-slavery men during their attempt to kidnap an African-American teamster who worked for him. In December 1859, Ross was publishing the *Kansas State Record* newspaper at Topeka.[7]

Delahay also enclosed a letter signed by 53 Leavenworth leaders, merchants, and businessmen asking Lincoln, as a "Man of the Great West," to "respond to this call of your Kansas friends" to visit Kansas. At least eight of the signatories of the letter would soon serve in the Frontier Guard. In addition to Jim Lane, Mark Delahay, and Jeff Dugger, they included Henry Adams, David Gordon, Merritt Insley, John Jenkins, and Daniel Anthony. A popular and gifted leader, Henry Adams was a 33-year-old lawyer who had come to Leavenworth four years earlier and was elected as the city's first Free State mayor. Next to Charles Robinson, he would soon receive the most votes to become the first governor of the state. Tough, 27-year-old David Gordon had nearly been killed a year earlier by pro-slavery men. Gordon was Leavenworth's auditor. Merritt Insley was the 29-year-old, hard-bitten owner of Leavenworth's leading hotel, the Mansion House. John Jenkins was a recent transplant from Virginia. The 23-year-old was an attorney in Lawrence, who soon became a clerk for the Kansas legislature and, later, governor of Colorado.[8]

How was Lincoln able to inspire men he met in Kansas to travel halfway across the country on over 1,000 miles of primitive roads and railroads to come to his aid 16 months later? His words and actions in Kansas provide the answer. Lincoln's November 1859 reply to Delahay's invitation showed not only his willingness to come, but his appreciation to the Free State Kansans for their perseverance in a shared cause:

> My Friends in Kansas: It has long been an eager desire of my heart to visit you and your noble land. Old acquaintances assure me that by coming to you at this time I may possibly render a slight service to your country and our common cause. When duty calls I ever strive to obey. Not without detriment to my interests, I therefore waive all personal considerations and gladly place myself at the disposal of the friends of Freedom in Kansas, to whom I feel, in common with my countrymen, an eternal debt of gratitude.[9]

In his letter Lincoln inspired the Leavenworth men with his emphasis on duty and personal sacrifice for the cause of freedom. He persuades with his use of the rhetorical device of alliteration, the repetition of consonant sounds to bring out the beauty of rhythm and make words echo: "slight service," "country and our common cause," "friends of Freedom," and "common with my countrymen." He chose his words with a lawyer's precision and a poet's sense of rhythm.[10]

Lincoln was a gifted, self-taught reader and writer who worked tirelessly on his craft. With no broadcasting, his words reached large audiences only by print. His speeches (and many letters like the above) were reported in the newspapers, and he composed them with that in mind. Many frontiersmen could not read, so those that could often read newspapers and letters aloud to their illiterate friends. Accordingly, Lincoln generally spoke for the reader of the printed page. He said, "I write by ear. When I have my thoughts put on paper, I read it aloud, and if it sounds right, I let it pass." If you read the letter aloud, you will hear what many Leavenworth men heard who later served in the Frontier Guard.[11]

One month earlier, Lincoln had received and accepted his first major invitation to speak in the heart of the vote-rich East in New York City at the Cooper Union. He knew he would be heard there by important people and his speech would be covered extensively by the Eastern press. Lincoln's political life depended on his speech in New York, so he decided to test and refine the speech in Kansas. After all, Kansans had lived out the issues in a way that made them unique. If the speech was well received in Kansas, it would likely be successful in New York. Lincoln probably thought that the Eastern press would little note, nor would the world long remember, what he said in Kansas. His Kansas audiences became focus groups for the speech that launched Lincoln into the presidency.

Lincoln also had a personal reason for visiting. There was a strong connection between the prospects of the future president and Kansans. Slavery and Bleeding Kansas had captured the attention of the nation, they were the issues Lincoln had debated with Douglas, and the slavery issue had caused bloodshed and war in the Kansas Territory. America had created Kansas and Kansas was, in several ways, re-creating America. Finally, Kansas had six delegates in the upcoming Republican National Convention and those delegates were important to Lincoln. The *Elwood Free Press* had recently promoted a national ticket of William H. Seward for president and Abraham Lincoln for vice president. Lincoln knew that he had attracted attention in Kansas and decided it was time to visit its bloodstained soil.[12]

On November 29, Lincoln left Springfield, Illinois, and traveled west by train to the Mississippi River, crossed the river to Hannibal, and boarded the Hannibal & St. Joseph Railroad for the four-hour ride to St. Joseph, the end of the line on the pioneering railway completed that year, which pushed the farthest west of any line in the country.[13] On

Thursday afternoon, December 1, he arrived in St. Joseph, Missouri. The *St. Joseph Gazette* reported that "Old Abe will be lucky if he succeeds in doing for the Republicans of Kansas what he was unable to do for himself in Illinois." [14]

Lincoln was met at the depot by Mark Delahay and newspaper editor Daniel Webster "Web" Wilder, from Elwood, who was a leader of the Republican Party in the Kansas Territory and who had met Lincoln the summer before at Lincoln's law office in Springfield. To anyone seeing Lincoln for the first time, his appearance and mannerisms were startling. At 6 feet 4 inches, he dwarfed the Kansas men, and his coat hung like a gunny sack from his muscled shoulders. His arms, muscled from years of swinging an ax and outdoor labor, were longer than those of other men. His store-bought suits were typically too short in the sleeves and pant legs, leaving his trouser legs about an inch or two above his shoes. He had a peculiar, awkward gait, like he needed oiling. His legs were too long for his torso, and his hands and feet seemed too big. The ungainly giant the Kansans met weighed about 200 pounds. He was 50 years old and clean-shaven, which accentuated his chiseled cheekbones and kindly gray eyes looking out from under his bushy eyebrows. He wore a curiously mingled expression of sadness and humor. He shook hands as if he was pumping water from a well, as he said, "Howdy-do." [15]

Lincoln spoke with a rather high, frontier dialect in his everyday conversations. He said "wa-al" for "well," "keerful" for "careful," "cheer" for chair, "thar" for "there," "git" for "get," and "don't have any" was "ain't got any." The Kansans drove Lincoln in a horse-drawn carriage from the depot to a barbershop, where he got a shave and the locomotive cinders washed off his face, and then to the ferry to cross the Missouri River. [16]

The three men sat in the dirt on the river bank waiting for the ferry boat in the unseasonably warm afternoon. Wilder recalled, "As we sat there I remember being impressed with the wonderful length of Mr. Lincoln's legs. They were legs that could fold up; and the knees stood up like the hind joints of the Kansas grasshopper's legs. The buttons were off his shirt." Lincoln's stovepipe hat, which added eight inches to his height, caused him to appear to be over a foot higher than anyone else the Kansans had probably ever seen. The men crossed the Missouri River by ferry and arrived on Kansas soil at the river town of Elwood. [17]

Elwood had been established only three years earlier on the western bank of the Missouri River, but the town already boasted a population of more than 2,000 inhabitants. During these years, thousands of immigrants had disembarked at its wharfs from St. Joseph ferries and St. Louis steamboats. The settlers outfitted in Elwood before beginning their 2,000 mile, four-to-six-month trek by Conestoga wagons to Oregon and California.

Lincoln stayed at the Great Western Hotel, one of the largest in the Territory at three stories high. He had not scheduled a speech in Elwood, but its citizens begged him to address them. Along with horse racing and shooting contests, public speaking was a primary form of entertainment in 1859 frontier America. Although fatigued from the bruising train ride and "somewhat under the weather," he agreed. An Elwood man walked through the town late in the afternoon banging the hotel's dinner gong as he called out that Mr. Abraham Lincoln would give a speech that evening in the hotel's dining room.[18]

A large number of Elwood citizens assembled in the dining room to hear Lincoln. After some introductory comments, he addressed the history of slavery in America:

> "You may examine the debates . . . that framed the Constitution . . . and you will not find a single man saying that slavery is a good thing. They all believed it was an evil. They made the Northwest Territory, the only territory then belonging to the government, forever free. They prohibited the African slave trade. Having thus prevented its extension and cut off the supply, our fathers of the Republic believed slavery must soon disappear. . . ."[19]

Lincoln's speech approached the extension of slavery issue from a fresh perspective: by citing the lessons and precedents of the American past. As noted earlier, the phrase "our fathers" carried a special resonance for Bible-reading Americans of 1859. Lincoln demonstrated that the secular fathers of America, when they brought forth our new nation, opposed slavery and expected it to end. The speech "was received with great enthusiasm."[20]

The next morning, fierce, cold winds caused the temperature to plummet. Lincoln left Elwood for Troy in an open buggy, driven by Daniel

Wilder's 30-year-old brother, the dapper, mustached newspaperman Able Carter ("A.C.") Wilder, who was the secretary of the Kansas Republican State Central Committee. Wilder later served in the Frontier Guard.

Lincoln's next stop was in Troy, a raw frontier town and the county seat of Doniphan County, where he was met by the German-American leader John Hatterscheidt, who at three inches over six feet, was almost as tall as Lincoln. Troy consisted of a shabby wooden courthouse, a tavern, and a few shanties. The prairie wind shook the buildings and cut the faces of the travelers. Forty or fewer people assembled in the little, bare-walled courthouse to hear Lincoln's speech. A member of the audience reported:

> "The long, angular, ungainly orator rose up behind a rough table.
> . . . In a conversational tone, he argued the question of slavery in
> the territories, in the language of an average . . . farmer. . . . I was
> . . . drawn by the clearness and conciseness of his argument. Link
> after link it was forged and welded, like a blacksmith's chain. He
> made few assertions, but merely asked questions: 'Is this not true?
> If you admit that fact, is it not this induction correct?' Give him
> his premises, and his conclusions were inevitable as death.[21]

Lincoln used the plain language of the prairie to connect with his listeners and persuade.

From Troy, John Hatterscheidt and A.C. Wilder drove Lincoln approximately 18 miles southeast in a carriage to Doniphan, another Missouri River town, named after Mexican War hero Alexander William Doniphan. The weather had continued to be cold. Hatterscheidt gave Lincoln a lantern, which he placed under his buffalo robe to provide a little heat. Lincoln made his third Kansas speech in Doniphan's hotel. Little has been discovered of the text of the speech, but the crowd was probably small and the speech short.

The next morning Lincoln was driven in a carriage to Atchison, arriving at the Massasoit House Hotel late in the afternoon. Many of Atchison's citizens, including Mayor Samuel C. Pomeroy, swarmed the hotel lobby to shake hands with Lincoln as he warmed himself by the wood-burning box stove. The short, stout Pomeroy, who had moved to Lawrence in 1854, was a Massachusetts man and an agent for the New

England Emigrant Aid Society. In October 1856 he had been arrested along with other Free State men for anti-slavery activities before being released by Governor Geary under intense public pressure. Pomeroy then moved to Atchison, where, with the financial backing of Massachusetts abolitionist and wealthy entrepreneur Thaddeus Hyatt, he purchased a leading pro-slavery newspaper, the *Squatter Sovereignty*, and changed it to anti-slavery. Robert McBratney also met Lincoln in Atchison. McBratney was a lawyer and newspaperman from Ohio who had moved to Atchison in 1857 to partner with Pomeroy to purchase the *Squatter Sovereignty*. Pomeroy, McBratney, and Hyatt later served in the Frontier Guard.[22]

At eight o'clock that evening, Lincoln gave a speech to a large crowd in the Methodist Church, which offered the most seating in the town for public addresses. Mayor Pomeroy introduced Lincoln to the crowd. As Lincoln walked up the aisle and took his place at the pulpit, a member of the audience described him as "awkward and forbidding, but it required few words for him to dispel the unfavorable impression." In the audience was a leading pro-slavery leader in Kansas, former Missouri Attorney General Benjamin F. Stringfellow, who had declared that Kansas could never be a Free State because "no white man could break prairie." Lincoln joked that if that were true, he himself must be black, for he had broken prairie many times. When Lincoln told the audience that he intended to conclude his speech after about an hour and a half, the crowd insisted that he continue. He ended up speaking nearly two and a half hours.[23]

The next morning, after breakfast, the delegation from Leavenworth found Lincoln in the hotel barroom by a red-hot box stove, telling vulgar jokes and stories to a crowd of stage drivers, bartenders, bull whackers, and other rough characters, who responded "with boisterous . . . laughter." Lincoln's jokes and stories were as rough as their teller. They were full of bawdy, raw, outhouse humor. As a flatboat man and frontiersman, Lincoln often heard and reveled in barnyard anecdotes that became a staple of his storytelling. He often told stories considered appropriate for male ears only, such as the story recounted from Ethan Allen's visit to England, when his English hosts teased him by hanging a picture of George Washington in a privy. When his hosts asked him what he thought of the location of the picture, far from being offended, Allen replied, "There is nothing that will make an Englishman shit so quickly as the sight of General Washington." Charles C. Brown told William Herndon, "Lincoln met me and said, 'Brown, why is a woman like a barrel?'" Brown could not answer. "Well," said Lincoln, "you have to raise the hoops before you put the head in."[24]

As his visit to Atchison's hotel barroom illustrates, Lincoln was a pleasure to be with; he had a quick and lively wit and a bottomless supply of stories and hilarious jokes. Men love to laugh and be entertained, perhaps more so in rough frontier towns, which offered little formal entertainment. Lincoln was likable, and the enjoyment he gave kindled comradeship and gratitude, which was not forgotten when Lincoln faced a crisis. Other biographers have noted and marveled at Lincoln's remarkable friendships—some of them hardly more than bystanders—that kept turning up in his life. Abe "liked to be with men when he liked to be with anyone. . . . He was one of those manly men, whose mind made him seek masculine minds." From this homely and awkward figure, gloomy by nature, it was also a matter of amazement to find such abundant warmth and wit.[25]

Irish immigrant James Normile, who worked in the hotel and was man-grown at 15, was one of those gathered at the stove whom Lincoln entertained and captivated. Fifteen may seem young, but on the frontier, there was no time for boyhood. One was a child, and then one was a man. By the age of 12, most boys were farming, guarding the stock, hunting in the woods with a rifle to put food on the table, working on flatboats, or swinging a pickax in the mines, with little time for anything else. At 15, a boy on the frontier knew the smell of powder smoke, the kick of a rifle butt against his shoulder, and the thud of an ax on a log. Normile would soon serve as one of the youngest members of the Frontier Guard. Lincoln kept the Leavenworth delegation waiting for nearly a half-hour before leaving with them for that town, which was 20 miles south over rough, frozen wagon roads.[26]

Lincoln's visit to Leavenworth was one of the biggest events that had ever occurred in the river town. Politics was a high card on the frontier. A political speech brought out the whole territory. A crowd with a band and many buggies met Lincoln just outside of Leavenworth, and there was a parade organized by the German-American Turners into town past crowds of cheering people.[27]

Leavenworth was founded in May 1854, shortly after the signing of the Kansas-Nebraska Act, by pro-slavery men from Weston, Missouri. Located three miles south of the U.S. Army's Fort Leavenworth, it was a rough place with crooked streets and an almost impenetrable growth of underbrush. By 1859, it was a dusty, brawling, frontier river town and the largest city between St. Louis and San Francisco, boasting a population of approximately 10,000 citizens. The city's growth was spurred by the freighting firm of Russell, Majors, and Waddell, which had a contract to haul supplies to the Western United States Army posts, including Fort Leavenworth. The firm employed over 6,000 teamsters and owned over 45,000 oxen.

Leavenworth's levee was paved with cobblestones, giving the city the first steamboat landing west of St. Louis. Although Leavenworth had been founded by pro-slavery Missourians, it was now the home of a significant number of German-American and Free State men. The German-Americans in Leavenworth gave Abe a rousing welcome. John Vaughn delivered the welcoming speech. The German-Americans then fired "Old Kickapoo," the cannon they had captured, which gave a welcome in thundering tones.[28]

Lincoln spoke that night at Job Stockton's "Stockton's Hall" to perhaps the largest crowd ever to gather in Leavenworth. With his hands clasped before him, Lincoln began to speak. He slowed his delivery to help his listeners in an era without loudspeakers:

> Ladies and Gentlemen: You are, as yet, the people of a territory; but you probably soon will be the people of a state of the Union. . . . You have to bear a part in all that pertains to the administration of the national government. That government from the beginning has had, now has and must continue to have a policy in relation to domestic slavery. It . . . must take one of two directions. It must deal with the institution as being wrong, or as not being wrong.

Lincoln first provided a historical overview of the Founding Fathers' actions barring the foreign slave trade and prohibiting slavery in the federal territories, demonstrating that the government's early policy was based on the idea of slavery being wrong and tolerating it only as far as required. He then addressed the Kansas-Nebraska Act, which he argued was based on opposite ideas—that is, the idea that slavery is not wrong. He explained:

> You . . . furnish the example of the first application of this new policy. At the end of about five years, after . . . fire, and bloodshed . . . you have, at last, secured a free-state constitution. . . . You have at last, at the end of all this difficulty, attained what we, in the old Northwest Territory, attained without any difficulty at all. Compare . . . this new policy with that of the old, and say whether, . . . the way adopted by Washington and his peers—was not the better.

Lincoln began his equally extraordinary second section of his speech by purporting to address his remarks beyond his listening audience. He did so by employing the rhetorical device of *prosopopoeia*, an argument directed against an absent person or, in this case, an absent section of the country: the South. Lincoln pummeled his imaginary Southern listeners with a series of charges and dares, much to the delight of his audience: [29]

> [My opponents] . . . greatly fear the success of the Republicans would destroy the Union. Why? Do the Republicans declare against the Union? Nothing like it. Your own statement of it is, that if the Republicans elect a president you won't stand it. You will break up the Union. That will be your act, not ours. To justify it, you show that our policy gives you just cause for such desperate action. Can you do that? When you attempt it, you will find that our policy is exactly the policy of the men who made the Union. Nothing more and nothing less. Do you really think you are justified to break up the government rather than have it administered by Washington and other good and great men who made it, and first administered it? If you do, you are very unreasonable; and more reasonable men cannot and will not submit to you. . . . Old John Brown has just been executed for treason against the state. We cannot object, even though he agreed with us in thinking slav-

ery wrong. That cannot excuse violence, bloodshed and treason. It could avail him nothing that he might think himself right. So, if constitutionally we elect a [Republican] president, and therefore you undertake to destroy the Union, it will be our duty to deal with you as old John Brown has been dealt with.

Lincoln concluded his brilliant performance with an appeal to all that they vote in the upcoming election to preserve freedom. He was cheered loud and long by the largest political crowd ever to gather in the Kansas Territory. Henry Villard called Lincoln's speech "the greatest address ever heard here."[30]

It is likely that almost every Free State and Republican man within hundreds of miles was in attendance. Certainly, one of the founders of Leavenworth, 59-year-old George H. ("Uncle George") Keller was there. Keller was a Kentuckian, like Lincoln, who enlisted in the Army for the War of 1812 but who was refused because of his young age. Keller was a farmer and cattleman before he helped to found Leavenworth and open the Leavenworth Hotel. In 1856, pro-slavery men had taken Keller prisoner and confined him in a blockhouse in Weston, Missouri. He escaped and fled to Nebraska before returning to Leavenworth. Twenty-nine-year-old attorney Henry Fields, employed as clerk of the court of Leavenworth, was also likely in attendance. Lawyer Martin Conway, the Kansas territorial delegate to the Republican National Committee, was also likely there and met Lincoln. Conway's tie-breaking vote three weeks later sent the Republican presidential convention to Chicago, much to Lincoln's benefit. Charles Francis de Vivaldi, an Italian revolutionary who fled the failed 1848 Italian revolution and then founded and edited an anti-slavery newspaper in Manhattan, KT, was also likely there. All of these men later served in the Frontier Guard.

Lincoln's speech evidences his mastery of grammar, logic, and rhetoric. Grammar is the anatomy of discourse. Logic is the science of reason. Rhetoric is the art of persuasion. Grammar gives command of language; logic command of thought; and rhetoric command of men. Rhetoric takes the flow of language and heightens it a bit by repeating and paralleling elements, by bringing out the beauty of natural rhythms, so as to emphasize the idea by calling our attention to the wonders of the language carrying it. It is the manipulation of words for persuasive ends. The fact that 50 men from the Kansas Territory traveled 1,000 miles of primitive roads 16 months later to protect Lincoln is a powerful testament to Lincoln's skills and charisma.[31]

After the speech, Lincoln visited with Daniel Anthony, A.C. Wilder, and Marc Parrott, who were staying across the street from Lincoln's hotel. Parrott was the KT representative in the U.S. Congress. Their room contained beds, chairs, and an old box stove, which could eat wood enough to keep one man busy carrying fuel up the stairs and two or three men poor paying for it. The men stayed long enough for all of the wood in the room to be devoured by the gluttonous stove. It was a cold night and none of the men wanted to leave long enough to go for wood. Parrott had sent the men great sacks full of patent office reports from Washington to distribute. When the fire died down, two or three bulky books went into the stove. As the books were heaved into the stove, one of the men asked, "Mr. Lincoln, when you become president will you sanction the burning of government reports by cold men in the Kansas Territory?" "Not only will I not sanction it, but I will cause legal action to be brought against the offenders," Lincoln jested. He sat in the room for hours, "his feet against the stove, his chair tipped back . . . swapping tales." Anthony, Wilder, and Parrott would soon serve in the Frontier Guard.[32]

On Sunday, December 4, Lincoln took a break from politics in favor of spending the day relaxing and having dinner at the Delahay home on Kiowa Street with the Delahay family and a few guests. Lincoln quickly made friends with the five Delahay children. After supper, when nobody but the Delahay family was present, he pulled off his tight-fitting shoes as they sat around the fire in the back parlor, poking fun at the size of his gargantuan feet. He told the children story after story, much to their delight. Lincoln's habit, at the close of one of his favorite stories about frontiersmen chased by Indians, was to end by saying, "They got away." Then he rose up to his full height and said, "Now I must get away."

Lincoln stayed with the Delahay family for three days, and his visit was a great occasion for them. Mrs. Delahay honored their guest by using her best china at every meal. The children, dressed in their Sunday best, were allowed to dine with their company every night. Mrs. Delahay kept a Minton Jug on her parlor mantel. Lincoln, obviously having no idea as to the value of the china pitcher, took it outside to fetch some fresh water. Mrs. Delahay heard the pump handle rattle and creak and then begin a rhythmical speaking. She saw Lincoln clank the pitcher against the iron mouth of the pump, chipping the lip. Lincoln, unaware of the accident, came back into the house and offered the fresh water to Mrs. Delahay who, being the perfect hostess, did not change her pleasant demeanor (although she apparently never used the pitcher again).[33]

It is clear from letters between Mark Delahay and Lincoln prior to Lincoln's December 1859 visit that Lincoln was very familiar with Lane, at least by newspaper accounts, before Lincoln visited Leavenworth. Lincoln had no doubt been reading Lane's speeches, which had been published in Illinois, and came to admire Lane's courage and ability to move men with his words. Lincoln apparently met Lane at the Delahay home during his visit. Mrs. Delahay identified "Gen. J. H. Lane" as one of her dinner guests who dined with Lincoln. Daniel Wilder, another dinner guest, expressed surprise at how quickly Lane and Lincoln became close friends.[34]

At two o'clock on Monday afternoon, Lincoln gave his final Kansas speech at Stockton's Hall to an immense audience, which generally followed that of his earlier Leavenworth speech. In all, Lincoln had spoken six times on Kansas soil and in the Missouri River towns, and with each speech the size and enthusiasm of the crowd grew. Square-jawed Leavenworth newspaper editor John Vaughn, who would soon serve in the Frontier Guard, summed up Lincoln's visit: "He has sown seed that [will] be productive of great good. We part with him regretfully. . . . And we wish for him a long life and the honor benefiting such a gallant Captain in the Army of Freedom. His words have drawn him closer to our hearts. He is our friend—the friend of Kansas.[35]

The next day, Tuesday, was set for the election for governor, and Lincoln stayed to witness the roughneck spectacle of democracy in action on America's frontier. Lincoln believed that elections "were like 'big boils'—they caused a great deal of pain before they came to a head, but after the trouble was over, the body was in better health than before." Republican candidate Charles Robinson beat the Democratic candidate Samuel Medary by a vote of 7,848 to 5,401. On Wednesday, December 7, Lincoln left Leavenworth for Springfield. He apparently traveled back to St. Joseph by horse and buggy, as the river was frozen, preventing steamboat travel.[36]

Lincoln returned to Illinois with fond memories of Kansas. He told his friends back in Illinois that he was "delighted with his visit and with the cordial reception he met with from the people of Kansas." To a supporter, Lincoln daydreamed that if he needed to suddenly remake his life in an entirely new location, he might head West and try Leavenworth, showing the depth of affection he had for the men he met there. The same men would soon prove that they felt the same way about Old Abe.[37]

Shortly after Lincoln's departure from Kansas, the Kansas Republican Party, meeting in Lawrence, selected John Hatterscheidt as a delegate to the Republican National Convention in Chicago. Hatterscheidt's selection was in recognition of the contribution he and other German-Americans made to help turn the tide to make Kansas a free state.[38] Could they work a similar miracle for Abe Lincoln's nomination and election as president?

8

The Road to the
White House

Lincoln's rise from a washed-up congressman and frontier lawyer to president "was a masterpiece of apparent levitation." The work that went into it—the letter writing, the cultivation of influential newspaper editors, the occasional cunning ploy, was for the most part kept hidden. Publicly, Lincoln denied that he was contemplating the presidency when he visited the Kansas Territory in early December 1859. But he knew about the approaching Republican National Committee meeting in New York City a few weeks later, at which the 25 delegates (one from each of 24 states and the Kansas Territory) would decide where to hold the Republican presidential convention.[1]

At the December 21, 1859, Republican National Committee meeting at the Astor House in New York, supporters of former New York Governor William H. Seward, U.S. Senator Salmon P. Chase, and former U.S. Representative Edward Bates argued that the convention should be held in their respective candidate's home states of New York, Ohio, or Missouri. Norman Judd, Lincoln's friend and advocate, represented Illinois at the meeting and argued for Chicago "as a good neutral ground." The vote was apparently tied 12/12 between Chicago and St. Louis until the Kansas Territorial delegate, Martin F. Conway (who had met Lincoln less than three weeks before in Leavenworth), voted for Chicago, sending the convention to Illinois by the narrow margin of a single vote.[2]

If the members of the committee had been aware that Lincoln was a serious contender, Judd's argument for Chicago as the site of the convention because it was a neutral location would have been rejected. Had the convention been held in the favored St. Louis, Edward Bates, the presidential contender from Missouri, would hold the advantage for the nomination. Now, the advantage was Lincoln's.[3]

Lincoln's goal of making himself better known outside the West had received a boost when he received an invitation in October 1859 to speak in New York City. His lecture was eventually scheduled for February 27, 1860. Nearly 1,500 men came to hear this "Western man" speak in the large hall of Cooper Union. William Cullen Bryant, the poet and Republican editor of the *New York Evening Post*, introduced the evening's speaker: "The great West, my friends, is a potent auxiliary in the battle we are fighting, for freedom against slavery." He added, "These children of the West, my friends, form a living bulwark against the advance of slavery, and from them is recruited the vanguard of the armies of liberty. One of them will appear before you this evening in person." And with that, he presented frontier politician and lawyer Abe Lincoln.[4]

Lincoln then essentially repeated his Leavenworth anti-slavery lecture. His appearance, accent, and pronunciation were so awkward to Eastern eyes and ears that one critic reported that he said to himself, "Old fellow, you won't do; it's all very well for the wild West, but this will never go down in New York." But as Lincoln warmed to his subject, "his face lighted as with an inward fire; the whole man was transfigured. I forgot his clothes, his personal appearance, and his individual peculiarities. Presently, forgetting myself, I was on my feet with the rest, yelling like a wild Indian, cheering this wonderful man." Also seated in the crowd was New York City's most powerful newspaper editor, Horace Greeley, of the *New York Tribune*.[5]

Lincoln played on his Western roots during the speech by poking fun at the Democrats for failing, as they vowed, to sweep certain state elections "like fire sweeps over the prairie in high wind." Lincoln capped his speech by a ringing warning to would-be secessionists in the South. When he came to his dramatic ending: "Let us have faith that right makes might and in that faith let us, to that end, dare to do our duty, as we understand it," the hall erupted in thunderous applause. The audience waved handkerchiefs, threw their hats into the air, and cheered for ten minutes. It was a thrilling speech to his listeners and, later, readers, and transformed Lincoln from an obscure frontier lawyer into a viable national contender for his party's presidential nomination.

The speech allowed Lincoln to prove his appeal beyond the confines of the Western frontier that produced him. It demonstrated to the East that he was a far more serious, learned, dignified figure than the prairie-bred storyteller who mesmerized and entertained rowdy crowds on the debate trail in 1858. Lincoln "awoke the next morning to find himself famous." Northeastern German-Americans, upon whom the Republican Party was depending for its election hopes, were eager to read the speech. In fact, the first foreign language translation of the speech was in German, and appeared in the German language *New-Yorker Demokrat.*[6]

Long before Abe Lincoln traveled to Kansas and met John Hatterscheidt, he recognized the importance of the German-American vote. In fact, the quiet alliance between Lincoln and German-Americans became one of the important factors in Lincoln's nomination and election in 1860. Just as the German-Americans helped turn the tide in the Kansas Territory, they were also a key element in Lincoln's improbable election as the 16th President of the United States.

By 1860, Lincoln had been championing German-American rights for many years. In the 1850s, the American Party, more commonly referred to as the Know-Nothing Party, became a power in Northeastern legislatures, with a political agenda that included imposing limits on the voting rights of immigrants. The movement was a response to a massive influx of foreigners, particularly Germans and Irish. Between 1845 and 1855, close to three million immigrants, representing over 14 percent of the total population, emigrated to the United States, creating resentment as jobs became scarce in certain places.

Members of the Know-Nothings, the name of which implies that members were not to divulge the group's secrets, were required to be native-born citizens, Protestants, and opponents of the Catholic Church. Abe Lincoln had expressed his opposition to the Know-Nothings as early as 1855: "I am not a Know-Nothing. That is certain. How could I be?

How can anyone who abhors the oppression of Negroes be in favor of degrading white people?"[7]

Much of the German immigration was in the key states (for purposes of the presidential election) of Illinois, Indiana, Ohio, and Wisconsin. John C. Fremont, an opponent of slavery, had lost in these states in the 1856 presidential election. Looking ahead to 1860, Lincoln and other Republican leaders knew that it was critical for Republicans to have the German-American vote in these key swing states if they were to win.

Recognition of German voting power came at a time when many German-Americans began to realize that the Republican Party could represent their interests. The Republican Party, originally created in response to opposition to the Kansas-Nebraska Act, was opposed to the extension of slavery in the West and supported free labor in the territories. Immigrants were also eager to claim land in the West. But Pro-Slavers opposed opening the vast Western lands for settlement in the Homestead Act, fearing it would lead to more free states. President Buchanan vetoed the Homestead Act and handed the Republicans a strong cause to fight for in the 1860 presidential campaign. In addition to the abolitionists, the other group strongly opposed to the Kansas-Nebraska Act was German-American immigrants. For them, the issue was not only slavery; another provision of the Act restricted voting privileges and the right to hold office in the new territories to citizens, who had to swear to support the Constitution (which allowed slavery).[8]

In May 1859 Lincoln had, at great cost and at a time of financial difficulty, secretly purchased a printing press for $500 for a German language newspaper. Lincoln's secret contract was with a German-American publisher, Theodore Canisius. The agreement provided that "Canisius will publish the newspaper for the Republican Party until the presidential election of 1860," when the press would then become his property. The address of Canisius's printshop was the "East side of Fifth Street, between Jefferson Street and the Public Square." Lincoln's Springfield, Illinois office was only a few feet away at 6th Street and Adams, bordering the town square. With an obliging printing press at his disposal, Lincoln was in an ideal position to reach out and win over German-American voters. Lincoln's purchase of the printing press to create an alliance with the

German-American voters is strong evidence of Lincoln's belief that these voters were critical.[9]

On May 9, 1859, an anti-immigrant law went into effect in Massachusetts. The Massachusetts state legislators amended the Massachusetts constitution to prevent naturalized citizens (including recent German-American immigrants) from voting until two years after obtaining citizenship. The law prevented the participation of many German-Americans in the 1860 presidential election. Only days after Lincoln's purchase of the press, Canisius published a letter from Lincoln in which Lincoln responded to the Massachusetts legislation and vigorously defended the voting rights of German-Americans. Lincoln's letter generated a storm of editorials and articles in German papers nationwide, and generated much favorable publicity for Lincoln with the crucial German-American vote. In fact, German-American editors were some of the first to publicly declare for Lincoln as a viable presidential candidate. On April 5, 1860, a prominent journalist and Turner wrote a front-page editorial in favor of Lincoln in Indiana's leading German language newspaper. It took less than a week for the national paper of the Turners to follow.[10]

During the spring of 1860, the charismatic and now famous Jim Lane went on speaking tours for Lincoln in the most hotly-contested districts in the critical swing states of Illinois and Indiana (Lane's former home, where he had many contacts and was quite popular and influential), supporting Lincoln's bid for the presidency. Lincoln's friends believed if they could convince the Indiana delegates to support Lincoln at the May Republican Convention other states' delegates may follow.[11]

In May, as Illinois Republicans prepared for their state nominating convention, the state campaign manager, Judge Richard J. Oglesby, was talking with one of Lincoln's country cousins, a pioneer farmer named John Hanks. Hanks mentioned that 30 years earlier, he and Cousin Abe had split fence rails together when they were clearing land. Oglesby drove to the location in his buggy with Hanks, and they managed to find what Hanks said was the very fence. The two men grabbed a couple of rails and loaded them into the buggy.

On May 9, delegates gathered in the convention hall. Just before the formal ballot, Oglesby arose and announced that a certain person wanted "to make a contribution to the Convention." This was Hanks's cue. He and another man came marching up the center aisle carrying the two old rails, which were freshly festooned with red, white, and blue streamers and large banners reading: "Abraham Lincoln, The Rail Candidate for President in 1860." The effect was electric. The convention echoed with delegates' cheers as excited Republicans threw hats and canes into the air. Lincoln was brought to the speaker's platform and made to tell the story of how, in his early 20s, he had split rails, built a log cabin, and cultivated a small farm down on the Sangamon River. He was unanimously nominated the next day.[12]

It is hard to imagine today how some lengths of old lumber could electrify a large crowd of politicians. But the split-rail fence was a powerful symbol in the nineteenth century and a brilliant emblem for Lincoln's campaign. It was a distinctively American symbol of the West. It was often the first structure a pioneer would build after clearing the land. Building split-rail fences was hard work. The fences represented independence and private ownership, and yet also a sense of community, since neighbors often pitched in to build them. They "epitomized America's working class and its rural way of life." They were homely yet strong, a product of the frontier, like Lincoln himself.[13]

Symbols of the pioneer West "spoke to the Republicans' commitment to block the westward spread of slavery." Split rails also powerfully evoked the party's "free labor" ideology: a belief in the "dignity of the independent workingman," in contrast to "the slave-owning aristocrat whose livelihood depended on slaves." When compared to men who despised physical labor and depended upon work done by others, these old pieces of wood became eloquent anti-slavery symbols.[14]

Even more potent was the image of Lincoln himself as a rail-splitter. Campaign posters portrayed Lincoln as a mighty he-man, sleeves rolled up and muscles bulging as he wielded an enormous mallet. For the past two decades America had been governed mostly by the genteel alumni of the finest colleges in the East. The White House's current occupant, James Buchanan—"Granny Buck" to his detractors—was openly mocked as effeminate. It was hoped that Lincoln "would be a different kind of president."[15]

When Republicans from across the country gathered four days later for the national convention in Chicago, rails found their way into that convention hall too. John Hatterscheidt, as a Kansas delegate to the convention, worked behind the scenes to orchestrate German-American opposition to Bates and support for Lincoln. He worked with Gustav Koerner, who met with the Indiana delegation, which was leaning toward Bates, and told them German Republicans would not vote for Bates. Koerner told the delegates that if Bates was nominated, "the Germans will bolt!" Bates later laid the blame for his defeat at the convention upon the German-Americans: "A few Germans—Koerner of Illinois scared the timid men of Indiana into submission." Indiana's abandonment of Bates began to turn the tide for Lincoln. Horace Greeley wrote: "The unanimity of the Indiana delegation for Lincoln was the cause of Lincoln's nomination." In Springfield, news of Lincoln's nomination caused "the hearty Western populace [to] burst forth in the wildest manifestations of joy . . . Lincoln banners, decked in every style of rude splendor, fluttered in the high West wind."[16]

From the moment it began, the 1860 presidential race emerged as one of the most surprising and dramatic moments in American politics. In the weeks after his startling nomination, Lincoln benefited from a split in the Democratic Party. As Stephen Douglas began closing in on the nomination, Southern Democrats conditioned their support for Douglas on his support for new constitutional protections for slavery. In response, Northern Democrats insisted that they would not abandon their popular sovereignty platform. For the first and only time in American history, a major political party rent itself in two, with Northern Democrats nominating Douglas and Southern Democrats supporting John C. Breckenridge of Kentucky, the young, dashing vice president and defender of slavery. Adding to the confusion, a coalition of Know-Nothings and ex-Whigs ran John Bell, a former Tennessee senator. To win the election, the Republicans needed to capture any combination of two states among Pennsylvania, Illinois, and Indiana—a goal made easier by the divided opposition.

As summer gave way to fall, the race reached a fever pitch. Ironically, the most famous and feared person in America was also, throughout the summer and fall of 1860, one of its least visible. Lincoln, the consummate political animal, was constrained by tradition to sit out the most electrifying campaign of his life. Following the precedent set by almost every presidential nominee since Washington, he did not go on a speaking tour, which would have appeared unseemly.

The logic behind this display of disinterestedness flowed from fears of the country's founders of tyrannical leaders who aggressively sought and protected power. And so Lincoln sat in his office in Springfield, Illinois, and attended to his law practice, leaving it to others to deliver speeches, pen broadsides, and work enormous crowds that gathered at Republican campaign rallies, while he communicated and coordinated behind the scenes with his friends and those speaking on his behalf.[17]

One of those with whom Lincoln communicated and visited often was William Marsh, an Englishman who had first moved to the Kansas Territory in 1854 before moving to Springfield in 1858. Marsh had published political articles in the *Springfield Journal*, which brought him to Lincoln's attention. Lincoln became a frequent guest of the Marsh household, and Mrs. Marsh began teaching music to Mr. Lincoln's children. Marsh assisted in Lincoln's campaign by forming an English, Irish, and Scottish club, whose members' votes would help Lincoln defeat Stephen Douglas. Marsh later served in the Frontier Guard.[18]

In the election run-up, the party sent its best campaigners to the southern border districts of the crucial battleground states of Indiana and Ohio, where the Republican Party was most vulnerable. In September 1860, Jim Lane spoke in Indianapolis, Dearborn, and Lawrenceburg, in southeastern Indiana. John Hatterscheidt spoke in southern Indiana and in Indianapolis. In early November, just days before the election, he spoke in German to a crowd of thousands of German-Americans, praising Lincoln and explaining why German-American voters must cast their votes for Lincoln in order to protect their rights and interests.[19]

Lincoln won the presidential election with a plurality of only 39 percent of all votes cast, but by carrying Indiana and Illinois, he had a commanding majority of 180 votes in the Electoral College. In 10 Southern states Lincoln did not receive a single vote. For more than two generations, slave owners had controlled national politics. Now their winning streak was over. Lincoln would become the first anti-slavery president since John Quincy Adams.

Following Lincoln's election, Mark Delahay wrote Lincoln that Hatterscheidt contributed "important services upon the stump in southern
Indiana." The chairman of the Republican Central Committee of Indiana confirmed that Hatterscheidt "labored for weeks with great success
among our German friends." How had Lincoln managed to defeat Stephen Douglas, who had so decisively defeated him for the Senate just two
years before? Reporting from Springfield, Henry Villard, correspondent
for the *New York Herald*, made a remarkable assertion about Lincoln's
election: "In Ohio, Illinois, Indiana, Iowa, and Wisconsin, Republicans
now openly acknowledge that their victory was, if not wholly, at least to a
great extent, due to the . . . German ranks." Villard believed that Lincoln
owed his election to German-Americans.[20]

But over one-half of the country did not want Lincoln elected. The
month before the election, U.S. Army Major David Hunter wrote Lincoln from Leavenworth to tell candidate Lincoln that on a recent visit
to the East, a Southern woman who had been spending the summer
among her friends and relatives in Virginia told Hunter that "a number
of young men in Virginia had [vowed] to cause your assassination, should
you be elected." That same month, Captain George W. Hazard warned
Lincoln that the army in Washington was in the hands of secessionists,
mostly Virginians. Hazard identified General William S. Harney, General Joseph E. Johnston, Colonel John B. McGruder, and Major Pierre
Beauregard as among these men, all of whom would soon be wearing
Confederate uniforms.[21]

After his election, Lincoln began receiving baskets full of hate mail,
mostly from Southern locations, threatening him with assassination.
Before leaving Springfield for Washington, Lincoln carried an armful
of such letters to a cabinetmaker's shop below his third-floor office and
asked if he could throw them in the stove. The shopkeeper asked Lincoln
if he could keep the letters instead, and the president-elect agreed. One
representative of the so-called "hot stove" letters read: "Sir you will be
shot on 4 March 1861 [the date of Lincoln's inauguration]." Lincoln also
received warnings from concerned citizens who claimed to have knowledge of assassination plots.[22]

On December 22, 1860, *New York Tribune* editor Horace Greeley
wrote Lincoln, warning him, "Your life is not safe, and it is your simple

duty to be very careful of exposing it." In Lawrence, Kansas Territory, Jim Lane was also hearing reports that pro-slavery men were boasting that Lincoln would never live to be inaugurated. On January 2, 1861, Lane sent a letter to Lincoln's home in Springfield offering to provide Lincoln with "1,000 true Kansans armed and organized to protect your inauguration." Lincoln declined the offer, believing such efforts unnecessary.[23]

Following Lincoln's election, the senators from South Carolina were the first to withdraw from Congress. On January 21, 1861, senators from Mississippi, Alabama, and Florida followed. Later that same day, with the pro-slavery senators no longer present to block it, the Senate passed the bill making Kansas a state. Kansas had been a test case for the pro-slavery men. Their defeat in Kansas had been perhaps the most significant they had suffered in the 234-year-old American history of the hideous institution. It shocked and terrified them. Many saw it as the beginning of the end of slavery. They realized that because they had failed to make Kansas a slave state, which bordered on the slave state of Missouri, they would have little chance to make slave states of other, more remote western states.

Slave owners argued that the same Constitution that Lincoln held dear was also the source of their right to own slaves. Thus, the very thing that bound the Union together—the Constitution—also bound up within that Union the slavery of African-Americans. The constitutional crisis had reached a climax as the nation now added Kansas as a new free state, and would eventually add even more free states in the West. If only new free states joined the Union, the number of states advocating freedom might reach the three-quarters requirement necessary for constitutional amendment abolishing slavery. Secession and war were therefore inevitable, at least from the point of view of many slave owners, and many decided to begin looking for a pretext to secede from the Union. They found a convenient one in the election of Abe Lincoln.

On February 11, 1861, the "Lincoln Special"—Abraham Lincoln's private train—began its slow journey from Springfield, Illinois, to Washington, carrying the president-elect to his inauguration. The trip was a challenge, even if Lincoln had not been the subject of assassination plots. There were no nonstop trains. There was no single railroad that ran the entire way. Over a dozen regional lines, each independently owned and operated, would need to shuttle the president-elect from one city to the next, changing locomotives and cars at each location.

A private detective, Alan Pinkerton, uncovered startling evidence of a conspiracy to assassinate Lincoln on February 23, during his next-to-last stop at Baltimore. Baltimore was, other than Washington itself, the only heavily secessionist city of the major stops along Lincoln's train route that held slaves. And it wanted to keep them. If Maryland seceded, Baltimore would suddenly occupy an enviable place in the new Confederacy—a vital link of railroads to Washington and points north, south, and west, a vital port to the world, and a vital seat of commerce. Almost every resident of the city would potentially benefit.[24]

Maryland men despised Lincoln. In several Maryland counties, Lincoln received but a single vote; in two counties he received none at all. The men in one Maryland County so despised Lincoln that they demanded that all who voted for Lincoln—six men—leave the county.[25]

Long a site of mob violence, Baltimore, the birthplace of John Wilkes Booth, was a hotbed of violent secessionists. The largest city of a border slave state, Baltimore was home to paramilitary groups dedicated to killing Lincoln. For decades prior to 1861, gangs of thugs had terrorized Baltimore, earning it the nickname "Mob City." During this period, Baltimore's murder rate climbed dramatically, thanks to gangs known as "Plug Uglies" and "Black Snakes." These gangs controlled territories through which Lincoln's train must travel while passing through Baltimore. At least one suspected gang member was a Baltimore constable. These gangs formed a convenient, ready-made army of assassins.[26]

Potentially predictive of the welcome Baltimore might extend Lincoln was the reception the city had given president-elect Buchanan four years earlier. Buchanan, who had not been the city's choice, received abusive treatment as he passed through Baltimore on his way to Washington for his inaugural in March 1857. While traveling from the railroad depot to the City Hotel, gangs of men stoned his carriage and pelted his guard with bricks. As a result of the assault, Buchanan lost his appetite, declined dinner, and quickly and quietly left the city. But the Baltimore thugs followed him into Washington, firing revolvers outside his hotel. If the Baltimore thugs had heaped such abuse on the Democrat Buchanan, a defender of slave owners' rights, how much worse would it be for the Republican Lincoln?

Pinkerton's evidence established that the leaders of the Baltimore assassination plot against Lincoln included the chief of police, the mayor, and future colonels and generals in the Confederate Army. Baltimore's chief of police, Marshall Kane, was a violent secessionist who tended to employ any means necessary to justify his ends. Kane was a future Confederate officer and possible Confederate spy. A loyal officer warned Lincoln that Kane "would glory in being hanged for having stabbed a 'black republican president.'" Despite the obvious risks to Lincoln's safety traveling through Baltimore, neither Kane nor Baltimore's mayor, George William Brown, had any plan to protect Lincoln. Brown was an avid pro-slavery secessionist who had not even invited Lincoln to visit the city.

Nor had Maryland's slave-owning governor, Thomas Holliday Hicks, extended an invitation to Lincoln to travel to Baltimore. There is evidence, written in his own hand, that Governor Hicks wanted Lincoln dead. On November 9, 1860, unhappy with the election of an anti-slavery president three days earlier, an election that he admitted to have "done all properly in my power to prevent," Hicks wrote to his friend Maryland Congressman Edwin H. Webster bemoaning Lincoln's victory. Governor Hicks's letter was written in the context of his attempt to supply arms to a company of Maryland militia. Hicks raises the question in the letter: "Will they [the company to whom arms were to be supplied] be good men to send out to kill Lincoln and his men?"[27]

Other than Major David Hunter and Lincoln's friend, the 6 foot 4 inch, burly Ward Hill Lamon, who acted as Lincoln's unofficial bodyguard, and a couple of Lincoln's military acquaintances, Lincoln was without protection. In February 1861 there was not yet a United States Secret Service. No Federal Bureau of Investigation. No Central Intelligence Agency. No well-trained special federal agents who could be dispatched to dangerous locations to gather intelligence relating to a threatened presidential assassination or overthrow of the government. Clandestine operations, to the extent they were practiced, fell upon the shoulders of private detectives.

Lincoln traveled on a train pulled by a wood-burning steam locomotive. The engine had a tall, bulbous smokestack that poured forth pungent clouds of pine smoke. In addition to the smoke, the wood-burning engine often generated live sparks, some of which descended on the passengers. Wood-burning stoves heated the cars, and candles or whale-oil lamps lit the space at night. Locomotives threw sparks and ash high into the air and were not permitted to pass through the heart of most cities because of the fire hazard they created. A Baltimore city ordinance prohibited rail travel through the downtown area. Therefore, railcars had to be decoupled and drawn by horses through the streets between the Calvert Street and Camden Street stations. The transfer took 30 minutes if all went well—plenty of time for an attack or an assassination.

Pinkerton's informants told him that 20 assassins, armed with revolvers and knives, planned to surround Lincoln's train in Baltimore on Calvert Street on February 23 at 2 P.M. while it was being horse-drawn between the stations. The conspirators planned to rush into the rear of the car and murder Lincoln by bullet or blade, escape out of the forward door, and run through the crowd to a rum shop near the docks, where a waiting schooner would sail out of the bay, taking the assassins to safety in Mobile, Alabama. While Pinkerton was undercover in Baltimore, he also overheard Baltimore Police Marshal George P. Kane tell a cluster of secessionists that he would not be "giving a police escort." Although he could not be sure Kane was referring to a police escort for Lincoln, Pinkerton knew of no other upcoming event in Baltimore that might need a police escort except for Lincoln's arrival.[28]

Pinkerton convinced Lincoln to leave Harrisburg, Pennsylvania, on a special train so that he arrived secretly in Baltimore in the middle of the night. Much to Lincoln's later embarrassment when the press found out, Pinkerton also convinced Lincoln to wear a disguise when traveling through Baltimore. Lincoln's only companion was Ward Lamon, who was armed with two revolvers, a bowie knife, a blackjack, and a pair of brass knuckles. The transfer by horse of Lincoln's railcar was accomplished without incident, and an exhausted but relieved Lincoln arrived safely in the middle of the night on February 23 at the Baltimore & Ohio railroad depot at the foot of Capitol Hill in Washington. He startled a dozing clerk when he checked into Willard's Hotel.[29]

Mrs. Lincoln and her young sons, meanwhile, followed later that same day on the train upon which Abe Lincoln was to have traveled.

They were rudely welcomed to Baltimore with loud cheers—for Jefferson Davis. As their car was drawn slowly through the streets by a team of horses, mobs of men and boys surrounded it, rocking it violently back and forth and forcing the windows open as they screamed threats and obscenities at the terrified family. The would-be assassins were surprised and furious that Lincoln was not on the train. No police escort was initially on hand, but one finally arrived and the police rescued the Lincolns in the nick of time.[30]

Meanwhile, the Peace Conference, a meeting of more than 100 of the leading politicians of the day, was taking place at Willard's Hotel in Washington, in a desperate final effort by the individual states to resolve the secession crisis without bloodshed. With the seven states of the Cotton South already committed to secession, all hope for preserving the Union rested on the eight slaveholding states representing the Upper and Border South, with the states of Virginia and Kentucky playing key roles. Governor Robinson appointed future Frontier Guard members Martin Conway and Henry Adams to attend the conference on behalf of Kansas.[31]

By 10 A.M. on February 23, 1861, Willard's Hotel was buzzing with excitement. Rumors of Lincoln's early, unannounced arrival were being whispered. The unexpected report that Lincoln had arrived in Washington fell like a sledgehammer on the Southern delegates to the Peace Conference. Lucius E. Chittenden, the delegate from Vermont, observed firsthand the stunned reaction of certain Southern delegates to the news of Lincoln's safe arrival. Chittenden happened to be seated between James A. Seddon of Virginia, later the Confederate Secretary of War, and Waldo P. Johnson, afterwards a Confederate general, from Missouri. Chittenden recalled that Mr. Seddon's slave approached Seddon during the meeting and handed him a scrap of paper. Chittenden reported: "Mr. Seddon glanced at it, and passed it before me to Mr. Johnson, so near to my face that . . . I could not avoid reading it. The words written upon it were 'Lincoln is in this hotel!' The Missourian [Waldo P. Johnson] was startled as by a shock of electricity. He must have forgotten himself completely, for he instantly exclaimed, 'How the devil did he get through Baltimore?' With a look of utter contempt for the indiscretion of the impulsive trans-Mississippian, the Virginian [Seddon] growled, 'What would prevent his passing through Baltimore?' There was no reply, but the occurrence left the impression on one mind that the preparations to receive Mr. Lincoln in Baltimore were known to some who were not [Baltimore residents]. . . . No event of the Conference . . . produced so much excitement."[32]

Following Lincoln's arrival, rumors of assassination plots were heard daily in Washington. It was openly predicted that the secessionists would kill Lincoln before he could be inaugurated. If Lincoln died before the inauguration, who would become president in March? His vice president? The runner-up in the November 1860 election, the pro-slavery Democratic vice president, John C. Breckenridge of Kentucky? The Constitution was unclear on the point, but one thing was certain—pro-slavery Supreme Court Chief Justice Roger Taney would decide.

An openly pro-slavery militia company drilled nightly in Washington's streets, to the delight of the pro-slavery mayor, who would eventually be jailed for sedition. Lincoln was to accept the oath of office and give his inaugural address upon a wooden platform that was being erected on the steps of the partially completed Capitol building. The night before, General Scott had received information that the rebels intended to place explosive charges under the platform on which Lincoln would stand to take the oath of office. Scott immediately placed men under the steps, and at daybreak, a trusted guard of district troops formed in a semicircle at the foot of the great stairway and prevented all entrance. He also ordered that riflemen be placed in each window of the two wings of the Capitol, which overlooked the wooden platform.[33]

At around noon on March 4, 1861, President Buchanan left the White House for the last time as President to gather up his successor at Willard's Hotel. Buchanan arrived moments later, bareheaded and all alone, in a simple, open carriage, at the hotel's 14th Street entrance. He got out and entered the building. Lincoln and Buchanan emerged from Willard's about an hour later and entered the carriage. The carriage, now protected in part by a company of German-Americans, known as the Turner Rifles, began the mile-long ride down Pennsylvania Avenue to the Capitol.[34]

On April 4, Jim Lane was elected as the first Republican U.S. senator from the newly-minted state of Kansas. Lane hurried to Washington, knowing that the attempted assassination of the President was imminent and a general assault upon the city probable. Many Northerners, however, were not ready to actually kill their Southern countrymen. They preferred to think of the South in the terms that Lincoln used: as estranged brethren who needed to be brought back into the national fold.

For many pro-slavery men, however, the hatred of all blacks and abolitionists had been absorbed during childhood and drilled into them during their adult lives, leaving no room for reason. For such a man, the loss of an arm would come easier than the loss of prejudice. Many slave owners openly gloated at the prospect of slaughtering Northerners. "We will glut our carrion crows with their beastly carcasses and leave their bleaching bones to enrich our soil," wrote a Virginian in the *Richmond Dispatch*. "Virginians, welcome the invaders with bloody hands to hospitable graves," wrote another. These threats would soon become reality.[35]

9

The Jayhawks

By Thursday, April 18, as Lane was gathering his Kansas Jayhawks at Lincoln's request, rumors were flying. It was said that 5,000 armed Confederates were marching from Richmond to attack the city. Washington residents could see a rebel flag flying above Alexandria, Virginia. At night, they saw the menacing red eyes of Confederate campfires across the Potomac. The campfires were rumored to be the staging ground for thousands of troops. The cascade of rumors threw the city into a panic, and at Willard's Hotel, "one would have thought an invading army were at the very gates."[1]

Lane was one of the most famous military leaders of the day. Local newspapers reported that his experience as a commander in Mexico and Kansas "commended him as an accomplished officer, brave and skillful," and "Gen'l Lane's" popularity resulted in hundreds of men rallying to his call to protect the White House. Lane and his men had been severely outnumbered by pro-slavery armies in the Kansas Territory, but they had survived and prevailed due to their fighting skills, cunning, and bravery. Could they do it again, when the stakes were even higher?[2]

Washington residents began hoarding food. Most bought their food daily at public markets. Much of their meat, poultry, milk, eggs, and other perishables came from the surrounding countryside. Confederate troops could easily block farm wagons from crossing the bridges to Washington, stop fishing boat boats from sailing up the Potomac to deliver their catch, and starve the city. In this atmosphere of fear, residents also began arming themselves. Shops selling guns and ammunition ran out of stock, and there was a brisk trade in secondhand weapons. Even President Lincoln began practicing his marksmanship with a rifle, taking shots at a woodpile on the south lawn of the White House, using targets made out of congressional stationery.[3]

That morning, U.S. Army Colonel Robert E. Lee received an urgent request to come to the house of Francis Preston Blair, who was the father of an old friend. A graduate of West Point, the 54-year-old Mexican War veteran was among the most experienced and respected soldiers in the army. His father was a Revolutionary War hero, and his wife the great-granddaughter of Martha Washington. Lee lived in one of northern Virginia's grandest mansions, located on a hilltop with a commanding view of the woods and the Potomac River. He owned over 200 slaves, some of whom he hired out to other plantation owners to supplement his income.

Lee knew that Virginia's Secession Convention was secretly meeting in Richmond to debate the calls for secession. He rode his carriage away from his Virginia estate at Arlington down a long hill to the Potomac and over the bridge toward the white buildings of Washington. Beneath him, the river rushed by, on whose banks poison ivy and oak grew in sinister wreaths. He reached Blair's home on Pennsylvania Avenue across from the White House, climbed out of the carriage, and saw an old man standing on the porch—it was Francis Blair.

Blair brought Lee into a study, a large and impressive room with shelves lined with hundreds of books. Blair told Lee that President Lincoln had authorized Blair to offer Lee the command of the U.S. Army, the highest-ranking military position within the President's power to proffer, to command an army that was being formed to put down the rebellion and preserve the Union. Lee had not expected the offer. His mind raced as he sat for a long moment before replying. "Sir, would you please convey my deepest gratitude to the President, but I must decline your offer. I am opposed to secession, but my greatest loyalty is to Virginia. I would rather resign from the Army and return to my fields at Arlington than to lead an invasion." Blair thanked Lee and wished him well.[4]

Lee then rode around the corner to U.S. Army headquarters, located in the Winder Building, to discuss his dilemma with General Scott, who described Lee as the "very best soldier I have ever seen in the field." Scott sat in his office in a huge leather chair and stood with a painful effort. Lee saw the stiff movement, the slow struggle. Scott held out a huge, worn hand, smiled with a warmth Lee remembered well from their days in the Mexican War, and the two men sat facing each other across Scott's shiny oak desk. The lines in Scott's face were deeper, his gray hair now thinner, and his tired eyes redder, the eyes of a man whose time was past. General Scott made the offer official; Lee's arrival in Richmond several days later indicated his answer.[5]

Soon after, two Union delegates from western Virginia, who had fled Richmond the night before fearing for their safety, told President Lincoln that Virginia had seceded in secret in order to quietly confiscate the public property within her borders before the decision was known. The "Mother of Presidents," Virginia had been the home of many of the Founding Fathers, including George Washington and Thomas Jefferson. Virginia's secession lent legitimacy to the Confederate cause, and Lincoln feared other slave states, such as Maryland, Arkansas, North Carolina, and Tennessee, would follow. Virginia was also the most populous state in the South, and Richmond's Tredegar Iron Works was one of the few Southern foundries capable of manufacturing heavy armaments. Virginia's secession was a crushing blow to the Union.

General Scott was no longer optimistic that the city could ward off a Confederate attack. He complained to Lincoln that he was "placed between many fires." He worried that the Confederates would place artillery on Arlington Heights, the site of Lee's mansion, and that shells from there "could easily reach the White House." He feared the Confederates would have an easier time capturing the city than did the British 47 years earlier, given the weakness of Washington's defenses. Not only must he defend Washington, but he had to also defend Fort Monroe, a critical military installation in Hampton, Virginia, and Gosport Navy Yard at Norfolk, Virginia (now Norfolk Naval Shipyard). With its strategic location, immense dry dock, and great supply of cannons and guns, the naval installation was indispensable to both sides.[6]

That afternoon, having received a steady stream of reports that Baltimore secessionists planned to attack Union troops traveling through Baltimore, Secretary Cameron telegraphed Maryland Governor Hicks that "the President had been informed that threats are made and measures taken by an unlawful combination of misguided citizens of Maryland to prevent by force the transit of U.S. troops across Maryland on their way, pursuant to order, to the defense of this capital." Cameron reminded Hicks that he must take immediate effective measures against an attack on Northern troops. Otherwise, the "most deplorable consequences" for Maryland would result. A growing mob of Baltimore citizens had already traveled to Washington and were lurking outside the National Hotel at the northeast corner of Pennsylvania and 6th Street, where they taunted and threatened passersby. The National Hotel was the primary competitor to Willard's and was favored by Southerners and secessionists. John Wilkes Booth customarily stayed at the National when in Washington.[7]

President Lincoln, cautiously confident in Jim Lane's loyalty, skills, and judgment, quickly accepted Lane's offer of soldiers, principally from Kansas. That evening, Lane and about 60 other men marched with a fierce pride down Pennsylvania Avenue from Willard's to the White House. The majority of the Kansans were battlefield veterans from the Western group of men who had emigrated to the Kansas Territory from the then-frontier states of Ohio, Indiana, Illinois, Iowa, and Wisconsin. They thrived on the rough, masculine good nature and the shouts and yells of the border towns of the frontier West. They marched side by side, bristling with rifles and huge Walker and Navy Colt revolvers, and "presented a formidable appearance." From Leavenworth came 22 men, from Lawrence another 14, and yet another 16 came from Atchison, Topeka, Big Springs, Grasshopper Falls, Osawatomie, Doniphan, Manhattan, Junction City, Burlingame, and other small Kansas towns. Newspapers reported that Lane's men had "seen hard service on the frontiers" and were "most experienced shots, and are impatient to avenge the wrongs they had suffered in Kansas." Years on the frontier had melted away any softness they might have had and left behind a hard core of rawhide resilience. It took a strong man to survive in the Kansas Territory—and they had survived.[8]

Most of them felt a fierce loyalty toward Lincoln, who had been a champion of their Free State cause for years and who had endured personal hardship to travel in the dead of winter to the Kansas Territory 16 months earlier when these men had called upon him. They would now answer Lincoln's call and fight to protect the life of their President. Among them were

Joseph Cody, the grizzled uncle of William, soon to be known as "Buffalo Bill"; James Holmes, "the Hornet," who had fought with John Brown at the Battle of Osawatomie; George Smith, who carried a pro-slavery bullet in his chest from the Battle of Fort Titus; Dan Clayton, who marched with a limp, caused by a pro-slavery bullet in his ankle; Patrick Townsend, who had been attacked by pro-slavery men in Lawrence; Henry Adams, who had backed down pro-slavery men in Atchison; Thomas Ewing, who had stood up to armed Missourians' efforts to commit election fraud; Mexican War and Third United States Cavalry veteran John Taylor Burris; William Ross, who had risked his life when he refused to surrender an African-American man to armed pro-slavery men in Lawrence; Jared Phillips, whose pinned sleeve covered the stump of his arm taken by pro-slavery bullets; Ed Daniels, who had led an armed group of Free State men from Iowa into the Kansas Territory; and nearly 20 other former Kansas Free State fighters, including Dan Anthony, Marc Parrott, Tom Bancroft, Sidney Clark, Sam Greer, Dave Gordon, Merritt Insley, John Jenkins, George Keller, Robert McBratney, Turner Sampson, Philip Schuyler, Tom Shanklin, Chester Thomas, Leicester Walker, George Warren, and Anthony Wilder. Many of these men carried a gut-level dislike, even hatred, for pro-slavery men, and the fight with the Confederates would be personal.

There was also a strong contingent of German-American fighters, led by John Hatterscheidt. The Germans included U.S. Navy veteran Lorenzo Holtslander, Prussian army veteran Frederick Gottfried Hesse, 35-year-old Charles Forster from Berlin, tough 26-year-old Guido Joseph Ilges from Prussia, 48-year-old Frederick William Bogen from Darmstadt, and 28-year-old John A. Gareis from Bavaria. The men elected Jim Lane as captain of the company, Mark Delahay as First Lieutenant, Job Stockton as Second Lieutenant, David Gordon as First Sergeant, Mexican War veteran John Burris as Second Sergeant, John Hatterscheidt as First Corporal, and John Jenkins as Second Corporal.[9]

Many of the Kansas men were rugged frontiersmen and seasoned veterans of border fighting. Most were battle-scarred Westerners—plainsmen, hunters, horsemen, and gun hands. Many were crack shots and trail-tough fighters who had survived six years of hardship on some of the roughest and most dangerous frontier in the world by their toughness and fighting ability. They were men who knew the sound of gunfire and who would not run when the enemy shot at them. Newspapers quickly began reporting that the Kansas "Jayhawkers" were a rugged and dangerous lot, and some of the capital's deadliest sharpshooters.[10]

For some of these men, fighting was their primary stock in trade. Willard's was the finest hotel many of them had ever seen. These were men of campfires, saddles, and Colt revolvers; the only carpet with which many were familiar was Kansas prairie grass, the only chandelier the stars. They were loyal men who stood by their friends. If you made trouble with one of them, you bought trouble with all. They had fought together in the past, side by side, shoulder to shoulder. If they were to fight together again, they would stand by one another until they were dead or put out of action. Lane knew from the Kansas struggles that one man, backed with fighters such as these, could make a difference—even when most thought the situation hopeless.

Lane, perhaps more than any other man in the city, knew the extreme danger Lincoln faced and the likelihood of an assassination attempt. The Pro-Slavers in the Kansas Territory had made numerous attempts on Lane's life during the five years leading up to the Civil War. Would they attack a man in his home, in the presence of his wife and children? Lane and the Kansans knew from bitter experience that pro-slavery men would not hesitate to do so. Generations of pioneer ancestors did not allow these men to take an attack upon one's home lightly. One had a home; one defended it. This was something they understood perfectly well, particularly men like Jared Phillips, whose home had been attacked by pro-slavery men two years earlier, and his brother murdered. Now, he and the others were in Lincoln's home, to defend Lincoln from attack.

Cassius Clay of Kentucky, who formed another small band of pro-Union men who were garrisoned at Willard's Hotel, insisted that his men and Lane's men should be uniformed. Lane, who had learned his military lessons in the field rather than in schools, refused. He knew from the guerrilla warfare he had waged in the Kansas Territory that the last thing a smaller force wanted to do was to give the enemy an accurate count and an easy identification of who and where they were. That was a sure way to die. He must protect Lincoln with wit and wiles rather than strength. His tactics had worked in the KT, and he would now use them again. Lane explained this to Clay; the Frontier Guard went without uniforms.[11]

Lincoln's secretary led the men to the East Room of the White House. The East Room is approximately 80 x 37 feet and is the largest of the 31 rooms in the house. The room was heated by two large fireplaces. In contrast to the opulence of the East Room, the rest of the White House was "a dirty, rickety concern." Unattended for years, the White House had come to look like "an old and unsuccessful hotel." Paint was peeling from the columns of the portico, and the glass of the front windows was streaked with dust. The public rooms had worn, tobacco-stained rugs, torn curtains, broken chairs, and the walls were badly in need of painting. Its wallpaper was greasy in places where visitors had brushed against it with sweaty hands.[12]

On the first floor were the family and state dining rooms; the East Room, where past occupants had staged large receptions; and several parlors—the Blue, Red, and Green rooms—where the President and Mrs. Lincoln entertained visitors. Upstairs, on the west side of the building, were the family quarters, including an oval-shaped library that the Lincolns used as a family room, and separate bedrooms for the President and Mrs. Lincoln, their sons Tad and Willie, and Robert, who was away at Harvard.[13]

Lincoln came down from his second floor office to greet the men. Major David Hunter then presented Lane with a gleaming new saber. Lane, waving the huge sword, sternly ordered his men to conduct a rudimentary drill for Lincoln, similar to the drills they had performed in Lawrence while readying themselves to defend the town from attack. Defending Washington would not be much different than defending Lawrence—in both, men's lives hung in the balance. Lane was a military man, accustomed to command and the handling of fighting men, and it showed.[14]

Lincoln's first impression of the men, as the firelight flickered on their weathered faces, was good. They were tough, competent men. Some had suffered appallingly in the Kansas Territory and were not in a benevolent mood toward pro-slavery men. Some were even bent on revenge. It was obvious that Lane knew most if not all of the men and that they greatly respected him. They had been by Lane's side in battle in Kansas, and they carried their wounds and scars as badges of honor. Lane assured Lincoln they were fierce fighters. Having fought together before, they would now stand with each other until they were dead or a prisoner.[15]

Lincoln knew many of the men from his visit to the Kansas Territory, including John Hatterscheidt, Marcus Parrott, Dan Anthony, Joseph Cody, A.C. Wilder, John Vaughn, William Ross, Robert McBratney, Samuel Pomeroy, George Keller, Henry Fields, Martin Conway, and James Normile. Some were kin, who stuck to the family tradition of helping one another. Clark Hanks was Lincoln's second cousin. Mark Delahay was married to Hanks's sister, and Lincoln had stayed with Delahay during his visit to Leavenworth. Young Norton Vedder was Clark Hanks's nephew. James A. Jenkins was born in Harden County, Kentucky, Lincoln's birthplace. The Jenkins cabin was six miles from the Lincoln cabin. James was a fierce feuder and fighter. James's brother, Wycliffe, was a boyhood friend of young Abe. During the Black Hawk war, Wycliffe was in the same company of the Illinois militia. Lincoln had tried cases with Jeff Dugger in Illinois. He had ridden in carriages across the Kansas frontier with John Hatterscheidt, Dan Anthony, and A.C. Carter, and had dined with Jim Lane in Leavenworth.[16]

The men from Kansas knew each other; most were friends who respected each other. They had worked together, risked their lives and property for six years, and had smelled powder smoke together, and nothing binds men like sweat and gunsmoke. The sense of comradeship known in the Kansas Territory battles had been near ecstasy for some, like James "the Hornet" Holmes. They were ready to give up their life for Lincoln and each other.

Although they were small in number, they were veterans of the sort of trouble that lay before them. The Mexican War and fields of Bleeding Kansas were brutal training grounds for Lane and his men. They knew little of parades, only that war was a matter of killing and survival. They were not amateurs going to war: they were seasoned soldiers, perhaps some of the most experienced fighting men in the country—an elite company of light infantry.

Lane glanced at his men, sober over their coffee, their rough-hewn faces thrown into relief by the firelight. He felt a kinship with them. Some of them were of the sort he might never have encountered had he not come to the Kansas Territory, and they were, in some cases, men whom he would not have chosen for friends, but when the Confederates attacked, they would stand by until death, if need be. If he had to face serious trouble, he could not face it with a better company of men. As a result of six years of war in Kansas, he came to have a thorough knowledge of their characters. He knew whom he could trust. He knew their troubles, trials, tribulations: Delahay, who drank too much; Holmes, who was touchy and could be hard to get along with; and Clayton, Smith, and Phillips, who bore scars and mutilated limbs caused by pro-slavery bullets, a constant, painful reminder of the breed of the men they now faced, again.

Even among the non-Kansas men, there were familiar faces and common acquaintances. The emergency the men faced changed even strangers among them into a group of men who had joined hands in a common cause. They had something in common now, and there was a comradeship between them—they were outmanned and knew the need for readiness to fend off an expected fierce attack by the Confederates. Lane and his men fully expected that they would be attacked and that some, perhaps all, might die.

There was also a contingency of New England men, most of whom had settled in Lawrence, KT. Recently elected U.S. Senator Samuel Pomeroy may have been the leader of this group, although neither Pomeroy nor any other of the other New England contingent was elected by the men to be an officer in the Guard. Others in the New England group included Dan Anthony, A.C. Wilder, Martin Conway, William Hutchison, Robert McBratney, Philip Schuyler, and Sam Tappan.

The Kansans slept that night with their heads to the walls, touching elbows on the carpet of the East Room, under gaslight from three enormous chandeliers, their rifles stacked down the center of the room. Many of the rifles had been fitted with saber bayonets: broadly curving steel blades that could, in an instant, turn a gun into a spear. Two long rows of Kansas Jayhawks slept on their bedrolls on each side of the rifles on the carpet while guards made their rounds around the room and protected the entrances to the White House and its grounds.

Lane positioned sentries at all entrances, including the basement. He had learned working with these men in Kansas that victories are won in the mind before they are won upon the ground. Lane knew that he must create doubt in the rebels' minds, make them hesitate to attack. He ordered that sharpshooters be posted on the flat roofs of the White House and the nearby five-story Winder Building, the location of army headquarters. The roofs provided excellent views of the approaches and good fields of fire. Lane wanted the Confederates to know if they attacked the White House that experienced, cold eyes would be looking down rifle barrels at them.[17]

Lane wanted no pillows for his men, knowing that a man can't hear well with a pillow around his ears. He wanted his men to sleep light and safe, and wake up easy. He knew from his experience in Kansas that those who sleep too soundly may never awaken. Lane slept outside Lincoln's bedroom door with a rifle, revolver, and the naked blade of his sword.[18]

Lane ordered 30-year-old David H. Bailey to guard the north door of the East Room. Late that night, there was a rap on the door. Bailey opened it and found Abe Lincoln and Jim Lane waiting to come in. Silence reigned; the lights were turned down and shadows of gloom seem to flit over the historic room. The soldiers were asleep, breathing heavily; the polished steel of bayonets glittered under the somber light. The tramp of sentinels in the halls and on the flagstones outside emphasized the ominous tone of the great drama of the day.

Not a word was spoken for some minutes. The President was wrapped in his own thoughts and there passed across his face a sad, weary look, an expression of deep but troubled thought, as if he were trying to solve the great problem before him. He stood in the midst of the military camp in his own home, but while there was dread portent in the surroundings, his face seemed to reflect a sense of security in the presence of these loyal men, upon whom he was relying to protect his life and the lives of his family. The spell was broken by General Lane, who whispered something to the President, and the two men withdrew.[19]

Around midnight, Jean Davenport Lander, a famous stage actress and socialite, knocked on the White House door, saying she urgently needed to speak to the President on matters concerning his personal safety. Lincoln had already gone to bed, however, and so Lincoln's young assistant secretary, John Hay, met with her in the White House doorkeeper's room. She told Hay that she had spoken to two Virginians who had come into town in a great hurry to buy new saddles. One of the men had bragged to her that he and a half dozen others, including a violent slaveholder from Richmond named Ficklin, "would do a thing within 48 hours that would ring throughout the world." Based upon other details he gave her, she concluded that the men intended to assassinate or capture the President. Hay woke Lincoln to tell him the grim news. B. F. Ficklin of Richmond was later arrested for conspiring to assassinate the President.[20]

John Hay observed the arrival of Lane's Frontier Guard. Recognizing the desperate and historic nature of the event, Hay began his Civil War diary that night. The fame of Lane and his Jayhawks had preceded them. Hay noted in his diary that these men were the Jayhawks, and Lane was their leader: "The White House is turned into barracks. Jim Lane marshaled his Kansas Warriors today . . . into the East Room. . . . It is a splendid company . . . of Western Jayhawkers." It was fitting that Lane, who set the image of the Jayhawk into motion during Bleeding Kansas, should be recognized as its foremost representative at the beginning of the national conflict that the Kansas crisis foreshadowed. Hay concluded: "Kansas had supreme possession of the White House. Two long rows of Kansans . . . Generals and Jayhawkers were dozing upon each side, and the sentinels made regular beats around them." Clifford Arick reported in his official proceedings of the Frontier Guard that those who were not on patrol "slept by their guns."[21]

As Lincoln's young secretary, John Hay, got ready for bed he wrote the last sentence of the day's diary entry, describing the "tempest of great excitement" that all felt on "the brink of an expected invasion." Frontier Guard John Burris was making his rounds as Sergeant of the Guard during the night when he heard a rhythmic rumbling, which he feared was Confederate troops crossing over the planks of the Long Bridge into the city. He hurried to the roof of the Winder Building, just west of the White House and closer to the river, where Tom Ewing was on guard. Ewing heard the same noise resounding from the bridge, even louder, and he told Burris that he too feared that it was caused by crossing Confederate infantry. As the sun rose, however, the relieved men discovered the noise had been made by the wheels of wagons hauling barrels of flour across the wooden planks into the beleaguered city. How much longer would their luck hold?[22]

10

The "Men Who Stood Off an Entire Army"

On Friday morning, April 19, Washington residents awoke and were momentarily relieved that no attack had come during the night. In the early-morning darkness, a plot to burn Willard's Hotel to the ground was narrowly foiled. Filling most of a city block on 14th Street, between F Street and Pennsylvania, Willard's had 150 guest rooms, lecture and meeting halls, and a massive bar and dining room where hundreds of patrons feasted daily on fish, oysters, venison, and champagne. Nathaniel Hawthorne said that it was "much more justly called the center of Washington and the Union than either the Capitol, the White House, or the State Department." Fifteen bundles of flammable material were discovered hidden in various parts of the hotel, with slow matches attached.[1]

The front page of the *New York Herald* shouted, "Virginia Seceded—Washington . . . to be the Battle Field." Southern newspapers were predicting an imminent attack on the capital: "There is one wild shout of resolve to capture Washington City," wrote the editor of the *Richman Examiner*. "The filthy cage of unclean birds must and will be purified by fire. . . . Many indeed will be the carcasses . . . that will blacken the air upon the gallows." They called Lincoln "Old Ape," a low "flat boatman," and a "tyrant." General Scott was a "vile traitor" and a "fuss-and-feathered tyrant." Northerners were "Hessians" (German-Americans) and

"Jayhawkers." Southern newspapers reported Confederate troops were in Alexandria "drilling and the Confederate flag is flying," and "the Capital must soon fall into the hands of our troops."[2]

Rumors and signs of a possible attack were everywhere. The Confederates could be seen in the Virginia hills overlooking the city with spyglasses watching the White House. At the Capitol, volunteers were fortifying the entrance with iron and barrels of cement meant for the half-finished dome. Lane gave passionate speeches in Washington in support of the Union, seeking to encourage more men to join his Frontier Guard. As he did in Kansas, Lane was one of the first men in Washington who declared war on the Pro-Slavers, now Confederates. He denounced secession "as treason and secessionists as traitors!" The traitors in Washington would have "received the rope and the limb" in Kansas! Five years ago, "Jeff Davis had me indicted for treason" because Lane had tried to get Kansas into the Union "a little irregularly, and now what should I do with Jeff Davis, who wants to go out irregularly [secede]?" The crowd cheered and roared in laughter. Lane thundered he "was for war" against those who had taken up arms against the government.[3]

Lane called upon all of his military training and experience battling the pro-slavery men in the Kansas Territory. He anticipated from his successful defense of Lawrence that the Confederates would hesitate to attack a fortified position, defended by experienced, veteran fighters. He had learned that victory is sometimes easier won with words than a gun—and the results were better. He spread false rumors that the Frontier Guard had swelled to 500 fighting men. He ordered his men to be conspicuous in their patrols around the White House, and he took every opportunity to make the enemy think the Guard's numbers were far greater than they were. Having heard Burris's and Ewing's report about the nighttime noise on the bridge, Lane ordered some of his men to noisily march back and forth on the wooden Long Bridge after dark, making as much noise as possible. He hoped that the Confederates swarming in the woods across the river would believe that they were facing a small army, and would delay attacking. Lane's tactic worked—his men "made enough [noise] for a whole army."[4]

In an effort to force the Confederates away from Washington and as a show of force and confidence in his men, Lane also spread rumors that his men intended to march across the Long Bridge and attack. Lane did not want to give the Confederate army a chance to get set and in position for an attack. He wanted to attack, or at least make them think he would attack, to keep them off balance. Union spies reported to Lane that the Confederates on the other side of the Potomac were "more alarmed at Lane and his force of sharpshooters than by John Brown's raid on Harpers Ferry." The Confederates with military experience knew there were only two kinds of fighting men—good ones and dead ones. You either learned or you died. Lane and his men had learned and survived, and the Confederates hesitated to attack.[5]

The news as to possible reinforcements, however, was gloomy. At Baltimore (only 38 miles away), a mob attacked the men of the Sixth Massachusetts Volunteers Regiment as they hurried through the city, using the same route Lincoln had taken seven weeks earlier. The Baltimore rebels overwhelmed the volunteer soldiers, knocking them down as they wrenched muskets from sweaty hands. The soldiers fired a volley in the hope of dispersing the mob, but the rebels responded violently and nearly 20 soldiers and citizens were shot dead, killed by bricks and paving stones, or seriously wounded.

At about 2 P.M. President Lincoln received an urgent telegram from Baltimore Mayor George Wilson Brown, an outspoken pro-slavery secessionist, and Maryland's Governor Thomas H. Hicks, a slave-owner who wanted to keep his slaves at all costs. They reported on the attack and warned: "Send no troops here. We will endeavor to prevent bloodshed." News of the attack in Baltimore quickly spread across the country, first in telegrams, then in newspapers' extra editions. The date of the attack resonated profoundly in the North. April 19, 1861, was the anniversary of the battle of Lexington, which touched off the American Revolution. Before the Sixth Massachusetts men left Boston, they had already deemed themselves the "Minutemen of 61," because they were the first regiment to respond to Lincoln's request for troops. Two of the men in the regiment who were killed were grandsons of original Minutemen who had fought in the Revolutionary War.[6]

Pro-slavery newspapers viewed the Baltimore bloodshed in a different light. The Baltimore mob was compared to the heroes of the Revolutionary War, throwing off not the tyranny of England but the "execrable yoke of Lincoln." The mob attack and killings were praised and held up as a heroic example of revolutionary resistance. The attack was seen as a sign that Maryland was tilting to the Confederacy, which would ensure the capture of Washington and the "expulsion of Lincoln and his bodyguard of Kansas cutthroats from the White House."[7]

As news of the Baltimore riot swept Washington, fear caused many residents to panic, setting off another rush to leave the city. The news upset Mary Lincoln, who was afraid an attempt would be made to assassinate her husband. Young Hay had to do some "dexterous lying" to calm her down. By nightfall, malignant rumors swept Washington that the Baltimore mob was now on its way to the city. Lincoln's secretary, John Nicolay, reported that "a vigilant watch is out at all the possible directions of approach."[8]

That night, a small number of troops from the Sixth Massachusetts Regiment, bloodstained, bandaged, and on crutches, finally arrived by train at the capital. As they filed out of the train cars and into the dark, dingy depot carrying their wounded, men and women who were too old to flee the capital threw their arms around the soldiers' necks and kissed them, great tears streaming down their cheeks, blessing them and calling them their deliverers. The men lined up to march to the U.S. Senate chamber and the open rotunda beneath the incomplete dome of the Capitol, which was assigned to them as their quarters. They had eaten nothing since morning and were very hungry, but they had to wait until the next morning before food could be found.

About 9:30 P.M., President Lincoln appeared in the chamber, escorted by men from the Frontier Guard. He shook hands with each soldier, paying particular attention to the wounded, and had kind words for all. The President made a few remarks, congratulating the men on being the first troops to arrive for the defense of the capital. The wife of Frontier Guard Ed Daniels then stepped up upon an ammunition box and sang the Star-Spangled Banner. The grim-faced soldiers enthusiastically joined in the chorus, some with tears running down their faces. Lane vowed: "The blood of these [Sixth Massachusetts] men is not shed in vain." After the Frontier Guard men returned to the White House, Clifford Arick solemnly noted: "The anniversary of the Battle of Lexington and the day of the Battle of Baltimore."[9]

That night, many Washingtonians again expected an attack on the city. After the bloody riot against the Sixth Massachusetts Volunteers in

Baltimore, residents realized that Washington faced danger on all fronts: from Maryland to the north and east, and Virginia to the west and south. About midnight, John Hay recorded in his diary that Lane's Westerners "were quietly asleep on the floor of the East Room and a young guard loafed around the furnace fires in the basement." The young man moved Hay: "Good-looking and energetic young fellow, too good to be food for gunpowder." John Nicolay wrote that he feared an attack was imminent: "We have rumors that 1,500 men are gathered and under arms at Alexandria seven miles below here, supposed to have hostile intentions against the City, and an additional report that a vessel was late this evening seen landing men on the Maryland side of the river." He concluded that "all these things indicate that if we are to be attacked . . . [i]t will happen tonight."[10]

SATURDAY, APRIL 20

By Saturday morning, Washington was nearly a ghost town. The city was isolated. Maryland rebels had torn up the railroad tracks leading north, burned railroad bridges, and destroyed telegraph lines. There were rumors that the rebels were attacking the Gosport Navy Yard. At 8 A.M., General Scott's carriage pulled up to the front steps of the White House. Scott's gout made it painful for him to walk up the stairs to Lincoln's second-floor office, so Lincoln came down to save Scott the effort. Each day brought new conflicts and decisions as Lincoln struggled to right the beleaguered Union. As Lincoln walked down the grand staircase, he found a three-man Baltimore delegation bearing a letter from Baltimore's Mayor Brown and Governor Hicks informing him that it was "not possible" for more Union soldiers to pass through Baltimore, unless the President was willing to bear "responsibility for the bloodshed" that would follow.[11]

At nearly the same time, news reached the White House that the critical bridges on the rail lines to the north and west of Baltimore had been burned and destroyed. General Scott had warned Lincoln two days before that if rail transportation and communication were broken at Baltimore, in "ten days, Washington would be in a state of starvation and be likely to fall into the hands of the secessionists." Maryland rebels also cut the telegraph lines that ran along the railroad tracks and pulled telegraph poles from the ground so that the lines could not be easily repaired. There were also rumors that rebel militias planned to attack any Union troops that tried to pass through Maryland.[12]

The mood at the White House was one of desperation. The Lincoln administration had experienced a startling cascade of disasters to the Union cause: Virginia's secession on the 17th, Harpers Ferry lost on the 18th, Baltimore in arms and the North effectively blockaded on the 19th, the Gosport Navy Yard attacked on the 20th. On April 20, Colonel Robert E. Lee also submitted his formal resignation to the U. S. Army. Scott and Lincoln knew there would now be a tidal wave of defections by U.S. Army officers and troops following Lee's example. The feeling of isolation and despair was now acute. For the third consecutive night, Hay recorded in his diary, there were "feverish rumors about the meditated assault upon this town."[13]

On the two prior nights, April 18 and 19, the fear of attack had been lessened by the arrival of a few troops from Massachusetts, however battered and ill-equipped. Tonight, everyone knew that no reinforcements had come, and with the rail lines to the North severed, it was now uncertain that any more troops would reach the city. It appeared that the Confederates might reach Washington before Union troops. H.D. Bird, the superintendent of Virginia's Southside Railroad, wrote to Confederate Secretary of War Leroy Walker: "Lincoln is in a trap. . . . One dash and Lincoln is taken." Arick recorded the mood of his fellow defenders: "A universal gloom and anxiety sits upon every countenance." "When will reinforcements come?" Arick wondered. "Will it be too late?"[14]

Lane escalated his propaganda campaign. He went to the War Department and, for the benefit of Confederate spies and sympathizers, demanded that he be allowed to take his "600 fighting Devils across into Virginia and clean out the rebels for murdering Union men over there." Almost simultaneously, Arick recorded that Union spies were reporting that the Confederates now believed the Frontier Guard were "400 or 500 strong." The Confederates believed Lane's threat that his "desperados had been reconnoitering and intend [to attack the Confederate] forces at Alexandria." This caused the rebels in Alexandria to focus on defensive measures, buying Washington a little more time.[15]

When Lane heard that rebels were refusing to allow federal troops to pass through Baltimore, he growled that the city would be open to federal troops in two days or "Baltimore will be laid in ashes." Lane wrote a note to Lincoln seeking authority to bring a Union force from the north through Baltimore to protect Washington. He closed by assuring Lincoln that he was "with you to the last." As a slave state, Maryland was a sister of the South. Baltimore was the South's largest port city, after New Orleans. Maryland men streamed daily to Harpers Ferry to join the rebels. Yet Lincoln knew that Maryland had not yet removed its star from the spangled banner. Thus, Lincoln must be judicious—and patient. He denied Lane's request.[16]

Due to Lane's reputation and recruiting efforts, the ranks of the Frontier Guard swelled to over 116 men, including Ed McCook, who had arrived on the last train into the city. Only one year earlier, McCook was living in a cabin in Central City, located in the far west of the Kansas Territory, with other adventurers. The 27-year old, with a thick black mustache and long sideburns, was a charismatic and natural leader. In the fall, the tough men of Arapahoe County elected McCook to the Kansas Territorial legislature. After riding 800 miles to Lecompton, and fighting Kiowa warriors along the way, he discovered that his district was not included when Congress voted Kansas into the Union as a free state. Instead, Arapahoe County had been included in the newly designated Colorado Territory.

After learning of the recent threats caused by the secession of Virginia and other Southern states, McCook decided to travel to the capital to aid in its defense and perhaps enlist in the army. He was on the last train to arrive in Washington from Baltimore before the rebels tore up the tracks. He had heard about Jim Lane's company and hurried to the White House to join his uncle, Daniel McCook, in the Frontier Guard.

Daniel McCook, called "Judge" due to his election as a probate judge in the Ohio Valley, was a tall man with the commanding presence of a Scotch-Irish clan chieftain. He was handsome, with a square jaw and blue eyes, and had 12 children, including nine sons, eight of whom would soon fight for the Union during the Civil War. By April 1861, 62 years of winters and failed investments had left Daniel's face deeply lined, his hair a grizzled gray. McCook was good friends with U.S. Senator Stephen A. Douglas, who had landed McCook a job as a clerk in the U.S. House of Representatives. McCook was working as a lobbyist to promote the passage of a transcontinental railroad from Chicago to San Francisco for his good friend Senator Douglas.[17]

The recent arrivals also included Joseph J. Henry, one of the Henry family of gunsmiths. He may have carried with him the latest Henry 16-shot, .44-caliber lever-action repeating rifle. These rifles would soon become wildly popular with Union soldiers during the Civil War. To the amazed muzzle loader–armed rebel who had to face this deadly "sixteen-shooter," it was called that "damned Yankee rifle that was loaded on Sunday and fired all week." Oscar A. Hale from Vermont, the great-grandson of Revolutionary War hero Colonel Nathan Hale, was also in this group, as was John H. Houston, the cousin of the Texas Revolution war hero and Governor Samuel "Sam" Houston. Many of the second and third waves of men who joined the Guard were abolitionists, like Thaddeus Hyatt, who believed that Abe Lincoln was the best hope to bring about the end of slavery. George Rye was a tough saddle maker from Shenandoah County, Virginia, who had been charged with the felony of writing and publishing a letter encouraging slaves "to make insurrection." He had been burned in effigy by men in New Market, Virginia, for his abolitionist beliefs.[18]

That night, one-armed Frontier Guard Jared Phillips wrote his wife that Washington was a "beleaguered city. . . . Our communications are cut off. . . . We have about 120 men and are stationed in the East Room of the White house. . . . If we have a fight you will hear a good account of the Frontier Guard. I'm inclined to stay to see it out." He assured his wife that the men camped in the East Room of the White House were well armed, each with "two revolvers and a Sharps rifle with a bayonet." Phillips may have been exaggerating as to the number of Sharps rifles, however, in an effort to put his wife at ease as to his safety.[19]

SUNDAY, APRIL 21

On Sunday morning, Washington was ominously silent. As the remaining residents attended church services, the city was completely isolated from the North and had now lost mail service, so that residents could not send letters to families and friends or receive information. Arick reported that Washington had no means of knowing when expected reinforcements would arrive: "No reliable word can be had as to the whereabouts of the New York Seventh and other forces known to be moving hither." As a result, "unabated anxiety prevails." Worse, the lines from Alexandria to the south were still operational, "notifying the rebels of our exposed condition."[20]

When Lincoln recalled the events of April 1861 one year later, he described the city's isolation: "Mails in every direction were stopped," while telegraph lines were "cut off by the insurgents" and "all the roads and avenues to the city were obstructed." At the same time, the "military and naval forces . . . called out by the government for the defense of Washington . . . were prevented from reaching the city by organized and combined treasonable resistance. The capital was put into the condition of a siege." Despite his entreaties, his wife Mary refused to leave his side. She sat up all night fully dressed, waiting to be captured.[21]

The danger and apprehension of attack was now visibly starting to affect Lincoln's demeanor, revealing what his aides saw as genuine apprehension. "The events of Friday, Saturday, and Sunday," April 19–21, said Nicolay and Hay, "exhibited a degree of real peril such as had not menaced the capital since the British invasion in 1814." Lincoln was growing shorter in temper, particularly about the failure of Northern troops to arrive. "Now go away!" he shouted at a visitor who clung to him, repeating his request for a job over and over. "Go away!" Lincoln exclaimed, "I cannot attend to all these details. I could as easily bail out the Potomac with a teaspoon!" On the evening of April 21, Illinois Representative Philip B. Fourke found Lincoln and his cabinet "hourly expecting an attack from the Virginia side, but determined to hold their ground to the last."[22]

Fortunately, Lane continued to be successful in his disinformation campaign. Arick recorded that it was being reported by Confederates in Virginia that "Lane has 1,000 men" and intended to invade Alexandria the next day. Again, the Confederates delayed attacking the White House, choosing to fortify defensive positions. Lane ordered those of his men who knew the surrounding terrain to ride to Baltimore, Annapolis, and Alexandria in disguises to gain intelligence and learn the plans of the Confederates, and report back to him. One of Lane's spies may have been William Hoban, who would also soon serve as a spy for the Union army.[23]

What was it like being with the men in the East Room? Many of the men's manners were rough-hewn, as might be expected of frontiersmen. They were used to the rough horseplay of the frontier, and their language was often likely foul, as they were thrown together in an all-male society. The language likely made the boys turning into men feel tough and like members of the group. They probably told crude jokes to relieve the tension. They cooked their dinners in the fireplaces. They argued and perhaps even fought with each other. The result of these shared experiences was a closeness unknown to outsiders.[24]

MONDAY, APRIL 22

Dawn broke, but the city was strangely quiet. Henry Villard noted as he walked on Pennsylvania Avenue that "an extraordinary change had taken place at the capital" since he left Washington five days earlier. "I could almost count the people in sight on my fingers. The whole city had a deserted look." It seemed "as though the government of the great nation had been suddenly removed to an island in mid-ocean in a state of entire isolation." Frederick Douglass, writing from Pennsylvania, said we "opened our papers, new and damp from the press, trembling, lest the first line should tell us that our National Capital has fallen." General Scott reported to Lincoln that a force of 1,500–2,000 Confederate troops was preparing to attack Fort Washington, and that another 2,000 troops were on Baltimore & Ohio Railroad cars from Harpers Ferry "to join in a general attack on this Capital."[25]

Many Washington residents began to fear starvation. Food became scarce, and the price of flour skyrocketed beyond the reach of all but the wealthiest. The impatient question heard again and again in the Executive Mansion was, "Why don't the troops come?" Others asked, "Will it be too late?" Arick reported that there was a rumor that the New York Seventh regiment had been "attacked, cut up and driven back."[26]

When yet another group from Baltimore called to demand that no troops be allowed to pass through the city and that the Confederacy be recognized, the President lost his customary patience and scolded them: "You, gentlemen, express great horror of bloodshed, and yet would not lay a straw in the way of those who are organizing in Virginia and elsewhere to capture this city . . . I must have the troops. . . . And they [must] come through Maryland. They can't crawl under the earth, and they can't fly over it. Those Carolinians are now crossing Virginia to come here to hang me."[27]

Once again, however, it may have been Lane's reputation, his skillful deployment of his men, making his force appear much larger, and his spreading of rumors exaggerating the strength of his force that saved Lincoln and the city. Arick recorded that Union spies reported the Confederates in Virginia were in "dread of James Lane and his John Brown horde." To Confederates, Brown was a crazed religious zealot who had been willing to die for his cause of freeing slaves—much like a martyr fighting a holy war. Calling Lane's men a "John Brown horde" reflected slave owners' fear that Lane's men were also martyrs who would fight to the death—and these men had already defeated, on several occasions, a much larger pro-slavery army in the Kansas Territory. Pro-Slavers were hesitant to fight them again.[28]

The Confederates also now believed that Lane had been planning his defense of the White House "for months" and had "been secretly assembling a force in Washington." It was rumored that Lane had so many men under his command that he was confident that he could "successfully repel an attacking army of 5,000" rebels with the fighters he had hidden around the city. Confederate spies desperately tried to solve the mystery of where Lane was hiding his men.[29]

The city was dark and deserted as the sun set. Theaters and stores had closed. A remaining jeweler marked his pieces down to "panic prices." The Frontier Guard marched conspicuously up and down in front of the White House, armed with rifles and Colt Navy revolvers. A glimmer of good news finally appeared on the horizon. It was reported the Eighth Massachusetts Volunteers and the Seventh New York Regiment had commandeered a ferry boat and had finally sailed into Annapolis Harbor. Their commanders, however, refused to allow them to sail up the Potomac River to Washington because they feared that enemy guns might shell them from the Virginia shore. They also worried that the ships captured by the Virginians from the Gosport Navy Yard might be lying in wait for them.[30]

General Scott asked Lane which soldier in the Frontier Guard was the best rider. Lane replied that Ed McCook was said to be the best. In fact, McCook did not like to be on foot doing guard duty because he felt more comfortable in the saddle. Scott ordered McCook and seven other men to ride to Annapolis carrying orders that the Union commanders there were to hurry their men to Washington immediately.[31]

TUESDAY, APRIL 23

The city was braced for an attack. General Winfield Scott came to dinner at the White House and spoke with Lincoln about the possibility of famine. None of the eight riders who Scott had ordered to ride to Annapolis had returned. The rumors of an impending attack by Virginians seemed more real than the hope of rescue from the North. A haggard-looking, worried Lincoln scanned the Potomac River with field glasses through the window of the Executive Office, looking for ships bringing troops and exclaimed, "Why don't they come! Why don't they come!"[32]

Unknown to Scott, one of the riders he had sent made it through to Annapolis. The other riders were killed, captured, or forced to turn back. The rider who arrived safely was Frontier Guard Ed McCook, who carried the urgent message that the capital was still in Union hands, and that Colonel Lefferts and his Seventh New York Regiment, and General Butler and his Eighth Massachusetts Regiment, were to speed their arrival of their troops to Washington as soon as possible.[33]

The news of the landing of the Union troops at Annapolis had spread throughout Washington, and many residents expected the troops to reach the city by Tuesday morning. This was urgent, as there were rumors General Beauregard had been seen on the outskirts of Washington the night before. Beauregard's arrival was quite possible, given that ample time had passed since the surrender of Fort Sumter for Beauregard to have reached Washington from Charleston—it was no more than three days by train from Richmond, and from there no more than another day to Alexandria. If Beauregard were near Washington, it would be very bad news for Lincoln, as Beauregard was one of the best siege warfare tacticians in America.

Another wave of panic washed across the city. The main roads out of Washington were once again clogged with people trying to flee in carriages, wagons, and on foot. As dangerous and desperate as the situation was, it was nothing new to Lane. Danger he had known for years. It was a way of life along the Kansas/Missouri border. It was a thing one accepted with the rising and setting of the sun, and one dealt with it as best as one could. Lane knew from experience fighting the Pro-Slavers in Kansas that he must not let the Confederates fight at a time and place of their own choosing; he must throw them off balance.

Lane's spies reported that the Confederates were gathering at the crossroads of Falls Church, Virginia, about seven miles from Alexandria, for a strike at the White House. He immediately ordered Frontier Guard Captain Job Stockton to take a detachment of men to ascertain the strength of the Confederates and, if possible, make a show of force and drive them away from the city. Stockton and his men were the first Union military force to invade a Confederate state, carrying aloft the national flag, the emblem of federal authority.[34]

Upon approaching Falls Church, Stockton saw a company of Confederate soldiers drilling in the town square. Instinctively, Stockton and his men charged. The Confederates scattered, not having time to take down their flag, which was flapping on top of a flagstaff. Stockton and his Kansas men took down the Confederate flag and brought it with them as they rode back to Washington—the first flag taken by Union forces in the Civil War. It was a striped flag, upon which was printed "State Sovereignty" on one side and "Virginia" on the other. Stockton's raid had the desired effect of causing the rebels massing in the Virginia hills to retrench, as they feared Stockton's raid may be a scouting party for a larger force.[35]

Lane hung the trophy outside the window of his room at Willard's Hotel, with a banner inscribed "Captured by the Frontier Guards upon the sacred soil of Virginia!" Within hours, thousands of people stood outside in the street staring up at the flag with excitement and amazement. Arick described the flag as "a terribly piratical-looking rag."[36]

Lincoln asked Lane to bring the flag to the White House. Lane handed it to President Lincoln about one o'clock in the afternoon during a cabinet session. General Scott was also in attendance. Lincoln raised the flag up and said: "What a miserable rag that is to fight for!" "Yes," replied

General Scott, "but it convinces me that Gen'l Lee has not yet reached Richmond. He'll have a better-looking flag."[37]

WEDNESDAY, APRIL 24

On Wednesday morning, the houses around Lafayette Square were shuttered and dark. The Capitol was barricaded with heaps of iron and marble ten feet high. The glimmers of hope many residents felt the previous day evaporated when they realized that Washington's situation was unchanged. Those Frontier Guard men who were woodsmen, and who could move quietly even among Indians, concealed themselves in the shrubbery surrounding the White House, expecting an attack at any moment.

Lane stationed soldiers in the basement, the hallways, and on the roof. "All were disappointed at the non-arrival of the New York Seventh," recorded Arick. "The worst apprehension prevails," he wrote, and the "anxiety of all is greater than any [day] which is passed." Anger began to mount against the Lincoln administration because of its failure to bring the Union troops by the most direct route—through Baltimore. Arick noted the growing skepticism that more troops would ever arrive in the capital: "Why do the reinforcements delay? No one it seems can tell. Yet it is asserted that they are in striking distance. Most . . . people doubt it."[38]

Lincoln met at the White House with members of the Sixth Massachusetts who had been wounded at Baltimore. His "impatience, gloom and depression were hourly increasing." Lincoln's expression was "perhaps the saddest ever shown upon the face of a man." He thanked the men for their patriotism and suffering and then confided his doubts openly: "I don't believe there is any north. The Seventh Regiment is a myth. . . . You are the only northern reality."[39]

There were now citywide food shortages, and the remaining groceries were scarce and expensive. The price of flour had more than doubled. Sabotage was discovered at the Washington Navy Yard: someone had filled recently manufactured shells with sand and sawdust instead of gunpowder, and a battery of cannon to protect the installation had been spiked. "We all know that if the cowards who are stimulating the rebellion had a leader and had the nerve," recorded Arick, "the city would fall a prey to its own traitors." Before falling asleep on the East room's floor, he wrote: "The destiny of the capital is really suspended by a hair."[40]

Fortunately, for Lincoln and the Union, Lane's propaganda efforts had paid off beyond Lane's wildest expectations. That day, Confederate Brigadier General Philip St. George Cocke, the commander of Confederate forces at Alexandria, Virginia, wrote Robert E. Lee that he hesitated to attack Washington because he believed there was "an army now numbering ten to twelve thousand men" in Washington.[41]

THURSDAY, APRIL 25

The day dawned with Washington on the lookout for any sign of the Seventh New York or Eighth Massachusetts regiments. At noon, loud cheers were heard on Capitol Hill from the Sixth Massachusetts men. From their elevated vantage point at the unfinished Capitol, they had spotted a train carrying soldiers of the Seventh New York waving from open windows of the passenger cars. They knew that the city was saved. The *New York World* proclaimed, "1,000 voices shouted with one acclaim: It's the Seventh Regiment! It's the Seventh! Hurrah for the gallant Seventh! Three cheers for the New Yorkers!" The sounds of jubilation soon reached the White House, which "gladdened the heart" of Lincoln. For the first time in ten days, Lincoln "seemed to be in a pleasant, hopeful mood."[42]

Arick wrote: "The 7th is here. Received with shouts and tears of joy as they move along the avenue. The way is open and others are to follow. All is safe now—everybody thinks so. Everybody says so. Everybody feels so." At 12:30 P.M., 1,000 men from the Seventh New York—unshaven and wearing filthy uniforms—left the B&O station and started marching down Pennsylvania Avenue toward the White House as the regiment's band played. They marched past the White House, with the stars and stripes flying in the bright sun. They snapped a marching salute to an exhausted and hollow-eyed President Lincoln, who was standing with Secretary Cameron under the White House portico. Mrs. Lincoln wept for joy.

The happy event transformed the exhausted President: Lincoln was now the "happiest-looking man in town as the regiment marched by him."[43]

In the Willard's Hotel lobby, General Lane stood on an empty keg and roared, "The point of danger is passed!" He told his men, "Boys, if the true history of this war shall ever be written you will be given the credit of saving the city, for sure as God lives they would have captured it but for you,—and boys—they would have captured it in spite of you and all hell if they had not been God-damned cowards!" With a defiant flourish he shouted, "Twenty-four hours ago they might have seized the capital. Now all Hell can't take it!" By wit and wiles, Lane had put a stronger enemy on the defensive and kept them there.[44]

FRIDAY, APRIL 26

On Friday afternoon, April 26, additional troops from Massachusetts and Rhode Island finally arrived. The arrival of the units cheered Lincoln, along with word that 8,000 additional troops had arrived in Annapolis and would march to Washington immediately. Washington was transformed overnight.

Arick recorded that "numerous arrivals from the north of brave and true men have given a Union spirit to Washington City unfelt by it for years." Residents again began to "regard ourselves more as citizens of a great nation." The Frontier Guard soldiers were later told by Union spies that the Confederates "would have attacked" but they "were afraid of those damned Kansans." The Confederates thought the Frontier Guard were "several thousand strong." Lane had out-generaled the pro-slavery soldiers, much as he had done six years earlier in the Kansas Territory.[45]

The Frontier Guard proved the theory that one soldier under cover was worth at least three in the open field. One author concluded that Lane and his Frontier Guard "saved the President's life, as all Southern men knew these men could and would shoot." Lane's ruse had saved Lincoln's life, and perhaps the capital. The service of the Frontier Guard was as important as that of the band of Spartans which, in a mountain pass, had stood off an army.[46]

Arick opined that the pro-Union Virginians who had fled from Virginia into the capital had now switched positions with the secessionist Virginians who thought Washington would soon be under Confederate control. "The poor Virginia exile today," wrote Arick of the pro-Union Virginians, "who with weeping eyes exclaimed, 'Alas! I have no country,' may take courage." As for the "traitors" in Virginia who wanted to seize the capital, they could only utter the sad refrain: "Mine was the land of Washington, and they have robbed me of it."[47]

SATURDAY, APRIL 27

By Saturday afternoon, enough federal troops had arrived that Lane wrote to Secretary of War Cameron: "I am satisfied the emergency has ceased that called our company into service. I should be pleased to . . . discharge the members ." Cameron later agreed: "I extend . . . my high appreciation of the very prompt and patriotic manner in which your company . . . defen[ded] the Capital." The Frontier Guard evacuated the East Room of the White House, but they had ruined the room's expensive carpet with their muddy boots, and gouged the entryway ceiling with their pikes and the bayonets extending from their muskets. As the men were leaving, Prentice M. Clark recalled that Lane handed Clark a rifle, saying, "You'd better take this along as a memento, it will probably be all the thanks that you'll ever get."[48]

The Frontier Guard formed in ranks in the East Room at the White House one last time to be mustered out during a ceremony in their honor. They stood at attention awaiting Lincoln's inspection. Walking down the ranks of the volunteers, Lane formally introduced each man to the President, who thanked them for their service. Lane then introduced Colonel John Vaughn of Leavenworth as the orator for the occasion. Vaughn addressed the President:

> Mr. President: Permit me to introduce to you the Frontier Guard, a company formed under the leadership of General James H. Lane, for the protection of the capital, at a time when great danger threatened. . . . A large portion of them have been in situations

of trial; when the dark cloud of peril overshadowed our Western border, under the command of their gallant leader they drove the invader from their soil. As far as they are concerned, "No compromise with rebels."[49]

Lincoln responded with a few remarks of his own. He thanked the men for their service to the nation, and then he placed their actions in the wider context of the national conflict, which he said he hoped would still end with a peaceful resolution. "I will not say that all hope has yet gone," he said. However, "if the alternative is finally presented and the Union is to be broken to fragments and the liberties of the people bartered away or fraternal blood be shed, you will probably make the choice . . . with which I will not be dissatisfied." Lincoln then happily presented each Frontier Guard soldier with a signed, elaborately printed "honorable discharge," even though they were never officially enrolled in the Union army.[50]

The mission of the Frontier Guard was over. A grateful President Lincoln accompanied the Guard to the south lawn of the White House to have their photograph taken. The men wore their Sunday best clothes, resplendent in frock coats and stovepipe hats—and held their rifles and muskets, affixed with towering bayonets. Lane's generalship, his disinformation campaign, and his fearsome reputation among the rebels had saved Lincoln's life. A greatly relieved Lincoln was enormously grateful for the bravery of Lane and his men in risking their lives to save the lives of Lincoln and his family members. "The departments of the Government contained so large a number of disloyal persons," said Lincoln later, "it would have been impossible to provide safely, through official agents only, for the performance of the duties." Referring to the Frontier Guard and others, he concluded: "I believe, that by these measures . . . the Government was saved from overthrow."[51]

Daniel McCook wrote that the capital was no longer at risk of being "occupied by the Southern Confederate troops," because the men of the Frontier Guard had been "a terror to evil doers." The rebels "took flight" and "we heard no more of hanging Lincoln." Historians later concluded that the presence of the Frontier Guard "no doubt prevented an attempt, then well understood to be organized for the purpose of capturing the President, and overturning the government by a *coup d'état* in Washington City." Frontier Guard member Tom Bancroft later said the Frontier Guard men "made such a display of strength by scattering out over a great territory and making a big show of their small numbers that the Southern troops who were just across the river feared to make an attempt to take the city, although it could easily have done against the handful who were doing their best by their wits to make up for their lack of numbers." Ward H. Lamon, Lincoln's former law partner and the newly appointed U.S. Marshall for Washington, said, "No more timely and effective service was at any time done during the war. There was never banded together a braver, more determined, set of men."[52]

Lincoln concluded, "I cannot speak so confidently about the fighting qualities of the Eastern men, . . . but this I know—if the Southerners think that man for man they are better than our . . . western men . . . they will discover themselves in a grievous mistake." He added, "Nothing is too good for 110 [*sic*] men who stood off an entire Army." He rewarded many members of the Guard with positions in the United States Army, knowing that they would be invaluable resources for, and add mettle to, the inexperienced Union troops. The service records of Lane and the soldiers of the Frontier Guard in the Civil War proved that Lincoln's confidence in them was well-placed.[53]

Lane received considerable publicity from his command of the Frontier Guard and became a national hero in the North. The Frontier Guard "marked the beginning of an intimate friendship with the President . . . which gave [Lane] prestige and influence that continued throughout the war." Lane had, against all odds, defeated the pro-slavery army in the Kansas Territory and the Confederates in Washington. Lincoln was now facing a similar but even more daunting task on a nationwide basis, and he would consult with Lane on Union strategy often during the war. By the end of April, Lane was handling all applications for appointments to political offices in Kansas for Lincoln. This gave Lane a near monopoly of federal patronage at the outset of his national political career.[54]

Lane continued to spend considerable time at the White House. On April 29, John Hay walked into Nicolay's room in the morning and found Lane sitting at a window taking turns looking through a spyglass at a Confederate flag flying over Alexandria. Lane said, "We have got to whip those scoundrels like hell. They did a good thing stoning our men at Baltimore and shooting away the flag at Sumter. It has set the great North a-howling for blood and they'll have it."[55]

Arick reported that "war-like rumors from the West" were being heard, including news that Missouri secessionists had seized federal armories near Kansas City and were preparing for a raid on Lawrence, Kansas. At the end of April, Lane ordered his Kansans in the Frontier Guard to return home to form the nucleus of two companies of troops to protect the country's critical Western frontier.[56]

11

"They Would as Soon Fight the Devil as to Fight Kansas Men"

At the outbreak of the Civil War, Lincoln believed it was vital that Missouri remain loyal to the Union. The American interior was a frontier of rivers: the Ohio, Mississippi, and Missouri were the highways into the heart of the country. And Missouri controlled traffic on these river networks, which were essential to access the northwest part of the continent, and Missouri's manpower and natural resources, including large deposits of iron, were critical to the war effort. Whoever controlled Missouri would hold the country by the heart.

There were currents pulling Missouri toward both the Union and the Confederacy. Although slavery was legal, most of Missouri's citizens were not slave owners. St. Louis had a large population of German-American immigrants who had no ties to the South. But many Missourians, particularly those who owned slaves, loathed Lincoln, the candidate of the less-than-a-decade-old Republican Party. In Kansas City, Lincoln had mustered only one of every 19 votes cast. Missouri would soon be a battleground coveted by both sides.[1]

Missouri's recently elected Governor Claiborne F. Jackson was a poker-playing, horse-trading, Little Dixie slave owner. Six years earlier, he had led nearly 1,000 Missourians, armed with rifles, pistols, bowie knives, and cannon, to Lawrence to fraudulently vote in the Kansas Territorial elections. Better to let the "Indian savages" keep Kansas forever, Jackson had said, since "they are better neighbors than the abolitionists, by a damn sight." Jackson now planned to assist the Confederacy in its bid for independence. In response to Lincoln's call for 75,000 men, Governor Jackson raged, "Your requisition is illegal, unconstitutional, revolutionary, inhuman . . . [and] not one man will the State of Missouri furnish to carry on such an unholy war." If Missouri left the Union, Kansas would be virtually isolated from the rest of the North and left at the mercy of its sister state.[2]

One of Lincoln's first significant military appointments after the fall of Fort Sumter addressed Kansas/Missouri border security. Lincoln was so impressed with Lane's military skill and success in guarding the White House that, shortly after the Frontier Guard was disbanded, Lincoln appointed Lane a brigadier general for the Kansas/Missouri border region. The appointment was unprecedented for a sitting U.S. senator and in violation of the Constitution.[3]

Lincoln clearly initiated the appointment. On June 20, 1861, he wrote Secretary of War Simon Cameron that he had been thinking about their conversation concerning Lane and the Kansas/Missouri border area. "I have been reflecting upon the subject, and have concluded that we need the services of such a man out there at once; that we better appoint him a brigadier general of volunteers today, and send him off with such authority to raise a force . . . as you think will get him into actual work quickest. Tell him when he starts to put it through, not to be writing or telegraphing here, but put it through."[4]

Lane's appointment authorized him to name the officers of Kansas state regiments, which was the primary gubernatorial prerogative as to the army. Lane's archrival, Kansas Governor Charles Robinson, was furious, and demanded Lane's appointment be reversed. Robinson argued that the appointment was unconstitutional, and he even sent a replacement senator to Washington to take Lane's Senate seat. Lincoln and his administration essentially ignored Robinson for several months.[5]

Lane ordered Frontier Guard Second Lieutenant Job Stockton to travel west to Leavenworth with some of the rifles and arms that had been provided to the Guard, in order to equip two companies of Kansas volunteers. When Stockton reached Chicago he had the guns and ammunition boxed up, marked "Fruit Trees," and consigned to a company in Denver, Colorado Territory. Stockton was able to successfully get the arms past the rebels along the Hannibal & St. Joseph Railroad, and at least 50 heavily armed bushwhackers at St. Joseph, Missouri, who were sitting on the steep banks of the Missouri River watching for arms bound for Fort Leavenworth.[6]

The First Kansas Infantry was raised under President Lincoln's call, in May 1861, for three-year volunteers to defend Kansas and fight the Confederates in Missouri and elsewhere. The men were recruited primarily from the counties of Leavenworth, Douglas (where Lawrence was the county seat), and Atchison. Stockton was commissioned to command Company G, First Infantry Kansas. The regiments joined the Union forces of Brigadier General Nathanial Lyon in his pursuit of the secessionist Missouri State Guard. Missouri had fought to make Kansas a slave state; Kansans would now fight to make Missouri a free state.

On August 10, 1861, Job Stockton gallantly commanded Company G at the first major Civil War battle in Missouri, the Battle of Wilson's Creek. The battle near Springfield, Missouri, was the first great battle of the Civil War west of the Mississippi. The Confederate army, about 13,000 strong, consisted primarily of militia. The rebels were led by former Missouri governor and Mexican War veteran Major General Sterling "Old Pap" Price. The 5,500 Union troops were led by the fiery, 43-year-old Union commander, General Nathanial Lyon, a West Point graduate and veteran of the Mexican War. Lyon's main column traveled over 260 miles, first by train from St. Louis to Rolla, which was approximately halfway to Springfield, and then by horse and foot to Wilson's Creek, at the end of a precarious supply line 200 miles from St. Louis.

In steaming, miserable conditions, the armies fought a slow fight up and around a hill on the banks of Wilson's Creek, which became known as "Bloody Hill." During the battle, the First Kansas established a reputation for bravery and discipline that was exceeded by none. The company formed in the face of the enemy, engaged a Confederate force four times their number, and held their ground under an uninterrupted and murderous fire of artillery and infantry. The First Kansas occupied the ground for two hours, repulsing or cutting to pieces one enemy regiment after another. During the six-hour battle, Major Samuel Sturgis told General Lyon: "These Kansas boys are doing the best fighting I ever witnessed."[7]

In the thick of the fighting, General Lyon was twice wounded and his horse shot out from under him before a bullet found his heart. The Union troops, almost out of ammunition, slowly pulled back, leaving the field to the enemy. The First Kansas went into battle with 664 men and officers, of whom 77 were killed and 255 wounded. Each side had suffered about 1,300 casualties, a considerably higher proportion of losses than at Bull Run. In fact, more men died per number of men engaged than in any subsequent battle. Shelby Foote described Wilson's Creek as "a reciprocal form of murder." Job Stockton's bravery and leadership was recognized and he was soon promoted to captain, commanding Stockton's Light Battery. Captain Stockton saw significant action in Missouri and Arkansas, and his exploits were recognized even in rebel newspapers.[8]

In the wake of recent Union defeats in the East and West, and a vacuum of military authority in Kansas, Lane stepped into a command position over three regiments: the Third, Fourth, and Fifth Kansas Volunteers, which made up the Kansas Brigade. Many Kansans feared an invasion from Missouri, and Lane's Brigade was Kansas's only protection. Much like he did when guarding Lincoln and the White House, he advocated that his troops advance into Missouri to keep the Confederates off-balance—and to prevent them from attacking Kansas.

Some of the Kansans in the brigade had suffered at the hands of the Missouri Pro-Slavers during the Bleeding Kansas days, and for these, their personal dislike no doubt caused them to harshly treat anyone they suspected of being a former Border Ruffian (now rebel). Several members of the Frontier Guard served in Lane's brigade, including Colonel John Burris and Captains David Gordon, Job Stockton, and Henry Adams. Lane led the brigade in fights against Confederate forces on September 3 and "drove back the enemy" after fighting them "for two hours twelve miles east of Fort Scott." He reported his losses at five killed and six wounded, adding that the "enemy has suffered considerably." On September 16, Lane sent 600 men and two howitzers against a rebel camp at Morristown, Missouri. They "routed the enemy," he wrote, "killing seven and capturing their entire camp equipage, tents, wagons, and some 100 horses." Lane's losses were two killed and six wounded.[9]

The pro-slavery Missouri newspapers editors demonized Lane and his soldiers, accusing them of theft of slaves and horses and mistreatment of women. On September 17, 1861, Lane drew up rules for his men, setting forth a strict standard for military conduct, which were read to the brigade. He wanted to prevent abuses that might spur otherwise-loyal Missourians into the Confederate ranks. Many of his men seem to have taken these orders to heart. A newspaper reporter described the behavior of Lane's soldiers while passing a secessionist farm in Missouri: "She was a secessionist and she had one son in the rebel army; but, as Lane told his men, his men were not at war with widows. This sort of discipline was observed all along the march. Not an apple or peach was touched without permission of the owner or the officer in charge." Slavery disappeared before the march of Lane's brigade. Slaves flocked to the brigade seeking freedom and protection, something which Lane was willing to give them, since they provided the labor force for their rebel owners. Because slave owners considered their slaves to be their most valuable property, they called Lane and his men thieves and "nigger stealers."[10]

The brigade was hailed as the savior of Kansas and the terror of Missouri. Lane and his brigade garnered national praise as heroic victors. The praise was not, however, universal within the Union ranks. There was always a difference in viewpoint between the soldier in the field and the man behind the desk. General Henry W. Halleck criticized the brigade for "the stealing of negroes, the robbing of farms and the burning of barns." General George B. McClellan denounced Lane for confiscating the "property of rebels." In short, the brigade was accused of engaging in what was later called "total war" during General William T. Sherman's 1864 march to the sea.[11]

Lincoln closely followed events in Missouri. On September 27, 1861, Lincoln telegraphed: "What news from up river?" The response was: "Lane has captured at Osceola large [quantity of] suppl[ies]." Osceola, Missouri, located at the head of navigation on the Osage River, was the great supply depot for the Confederates for all of southwestern Missouri and northwestern Arkansas. Steamboats were constantly traveling between St. Louis and Osceola, loading and unloading food, supplies, and raw materials at its wharves and storehouses. The Granby, Missouri, iron mines were operating at full blast about 25 miles southeast of Joplin. Twenty-five to 100 ore wagons rumbled daily to Osceola from Granby, their drivers shouting at the huge oxen leaning into the harnesses as they strained against great loads. The teamsters unloaded their ore on the wharves and made the return trip with their wagons loaded with salt, whiskey, boots, shoes, and merchandise. Osceola had two wholesale houses that did an immense business supplying southwestern Missouri and northwestern Arkansas.

After the Battle of Wilson's Creek, General Price had marched his men north to capture the Missouri River town of Lexington. Lane correctly determined that Price had counted on Osceola to resupply his army. Over 300 men from Osceola and the surrounding area had formed three companies in Price's army, and Price camped near the town several weeks later on his return march. Osceola was also the home of the aristocracy of the slaveholding oligarchy in the area, which had poured out men, supplies, and money for six years in their attempt to export slavery into Kansas.

Before marching into the area, Lane had sent out messages to the Missouri towns that if their citizens fired upon his men, he would burn the towns for harboring and supporting rebels. As Lane and his men approached Osceola from the southeast, about 30 rebels opened fire from the nearby woods. Lane's men returned fire and the rebels withdrew after killing at least one of Lane's men and wounding several others. Lane reported killing or wounding "15 or 20" of the rebels.[12]

A large secession flag was flying over the courthouse. Lane believed pro-slavery soldiers were holed up there, so he ordered his artillery to shell the building. Lane's officers decided the warehouses along the waterfront should be destroyed, including a large supply of whiskey, rather than be allowed to support rebels. They torched the buildings, which then spread to several nearby businesses and homes. Almost 200 slaves also escaped to freedom, which infuriated their owners. There were no reports at the time (or in the decades following) that Lane's men murdered prisoners or noncombatants, or otherwise mistreated Osceola's citizens.[13]

A few weeks after the Osceola attack, newspaper editor John Speer presented Lane as a liberator of slaves: "A few days ago we met two wagons full of slaves this side of Kansas City." They were wearing ragged, dusty clothes with no sleeves, pants ragged around their legs. Speer asked from where they came. "Are you running away?" "Oh no," responded an old woman, "Dey took us." "Who took you?" "Why, some of Lane's men! De blessed Kansas Jayhawks!" They asked how far it was to Lawrence, and rolled onward to freedom.[14]

West Point officers raised questions about Lane's command and the conduct of his soldiers. Major General David Hunter, commanding the Department of Kansas, criticized Lane's units because they failed to make timely reports, failed to conduct themselves with West Point spit and polish, and allegedly engaged in harsh tactics against the rebels in Missouri. Lane was also hampered in his military efforts by a lack of local support from Governor Robinson. In an effort to have Lane relieved from any military responsibilities for the border, Robinson wrote to federal authorities that there was "no danger of invasion," and that "I will guarantee Kansas from invasion from Missouri." Tragically, events soon proved Robinson wrong.[15]

In the Senate, Lane favored abolishing the Academy at West Point because so many of its graduates lacked common sense. "There is no board examination," he said, "to separate the stupid from those who have brains." At about the same time, Lane proposed an expedition led by him into Texas in command of 10,000 Kansas troops, including blacks, and 4,000 Indians. Lane thought the South needed to be hit hard on its vulnerable western flank, and he disliked the caution and the fuss of the West Point officers.[16]

Lincoln, frustrated with the inaction of General McClellan in the East, sympathized with Lane's bold proposal. Hunter told Lincoln, however, that he would have trouble defending Kansas with his existing resources, much less invading Texas. Hunter was also apparently angry and perhaps jealous about Lane's influence upon Lincoln. Lincoln admired Lane's audacity but did not want to disrupt the chain of command. He wrote at the end of December 1861 he was "sorry General Halleck is so unfavorably impressed with General Lane." He reminded Hunter, however, that he "who does *something* at the head of one regiment will eclipse him who does *nothing* at the head of a hundred."[17]

On February 10, 1862, Lincoln wrote a joint letter to Lane and Hunter that he wanted to use the services of both of them and "so far as possible, to personally oblige both." If Hunter could "consistently with the public service, and his own honor, oblige Gen. Lane, he will also oblige me." Hunter would not oblige. On February 16 Lane informed Lincoln: "All efforts to harmonize with Major General Hunter have failed. I am inclined to decline the brigadiership." Ten days later, Lane notified the legislature he intended to "return to my seat in the United States Senate."[18]

Lane and Lincoln were close friends during the war and shared a love of humor and practical jokes. One incident involved a Frontier Guard. Charles de Vivaldi had been a Catholic priest in Italy. He left the priesthood, married, and moved to the Kansas Territory in 1859. While in Kansas, he received a letter from the Pope appealing to him to renounce his wife and come back into the church. De Vivaldi refused, saying he would not give up his wife and son. A nervous and excitable man, de Vivaldi imagined every stranger to be a Jesuit sent to kill him. After serving in the Frontier Guard, de Vivaldi sought a political appointment. Lane decided to have some fun at de Vivaldi's expense. Lane told Lincoln and Secretary Seward how de Vivaldi feared the Jesuits, and Lane arranged for a meeting in Lincoln's office. Secretary Seward told de Vivaldi that Lincoln and he had considered de Vivaldi's request for an appointment and they had decided to send him to Rome. De Vivaldi dropped to his knees and pleaded, "Oh, Mr. Secretary, do not send me to Rome, they would kill me!" After Seward, Lincoln, and Lane were able to stop laughing, they told him they would send him to a consulate in Brazil.[19]

Another Lane trait admired by Lincoln was the senator's vision. Lane had an ability to form public opinion along lines he foresaw and championed. Prominent among the visions Lane pushed with Lincoln was attaching openly to the war the moral cause of freeing the slaves. The passage of a century and a half since the guns fell silent has linked the Civil War and the end of slavery as "tightly as lightning and thunder." But when the war began, only the abolitionists believed that the war must end slavery. Many felt, as the nation's founders, that the best course to hold the Union together was to avoid the issue.[20]

Lane, like Lincoln, first and foremost wanted to save the Union, let slavery stand or fall as it might. Lincoln also had constitutional scruples on freeing the slaves, but Lane, based on his experience fighting proslavery men during the Bleeding Kansas days, saw the firsthand practicalities of freeing the slaves as a means of weakening the enemy. He advised Lincoln to issue the Emancipation Proclamation almost at the beginning of the Civil War and advocated it in speeches in 1861, amid threats of assassination.

In July 1861 during a Senate debate on the Army Organization Bill, Lane told his colleagues in Congress: "The effect of marching an army on the soil of any slave state will be to instill into the slaves a determined purpose to free themselves. . . . There will be a colored army marching out of slave states while the army of freedom was marching in . . . . I do not propose to make myself a slave catcher for traitors and return them to their masters." Lane concluded: "They [the rebels] have brought upon us this conflict. If, in that conflict, the institution of slavery perishes, we will thank God that he has brought upon us this war."[21]

In an October speech in Leavenworth, Lane said:

We march to crush treason, and if slavery does not take care of itself, the fault is not ours. It can never be made our duty to defend it for the benefit of traitors.

In a November speech to his troops he said:

Let us be bold—inscribe "freedom to all" upon our banners, and appear just what we are—the opponents of slavery. In steadiness of purpose and courage, each soldier will be a Spartan hero. The spirit of the Crusader will be united with the iron will of the Roman, and an army of such soldiers is invincible.

By December, Lane argued that the successful prosecution of the war required that slaves be freed:

Withdraw [slavery], and this Rebellion falls of its own weight. The masters will not work, and they must eat. As the peasants of France rallied to the standards of Napoleon . . . , so will the slaves flock to ours.[22]

Lane illustrated his arguments with a story that made good sense to men schooled in the Western way of rough-and-tumble fights. In his speeches in Kansas and to his troops in the field, Lane often told the story of Joe Darrah:

> When I was a boy we fought prize fights on Saturday night with the other boys. One boy my age, Joe Darrah, had more muscle and skill than I. One Saturday, when we boys were swinging, poor Joe knocked his shin upon a rock, and I had him show his sore, and I marked well the spot that was wounded. That night, I kicked Joe in the shin the first opportunity, and he fled the field bellowing like a calf. I tell you, comrades and fellow citizens, that slavery is the sore shin of the Confederacy and you miss the opportunity of your lives if you fail to kick it whenever and wherever you can.[23]

Lane was a pioneer in urging the Army to field soldiers of color. He used America's military heroes as examples to make his points: "General Washington did not lie when he said his Negroes fought as well as white men. General Jackson did not lie when he paid that noble tribute to his black soldiers at New Orleans." In January 1862, to a crowd in Leavenworth, he told them how the Comanches had fought the Mexican troops in the Mexican-American War. Lane looked over his crowd and let the story sink in. He then brought his point home: "I don't say I would call the Comanches but I do say that it would not pain me to see the Negro handling a gun, and I believe the Negro may just as well become food for powder as my son." This was almost one year before black regiments were mustered into federal service.[24]

In August 1862, Lane wrote Secretary of War Stanton that he intended to form two regiments of black soldiers. Lane based his authority on two pieces of legislation enacted the month before: an amendment to the militia act that authorized the President to arm black men into "war service," and the second confiscation act, which deemed slaves captured from rebel masters as forever free. Lane's push for black soldiers was quite controversial. He did not follow public opinion on this issue—he led public opinion to a necessary political and military policy. On August 23 Secretary of War Stanton objected, saying the President had not given Lane the authority, and the black regiments "cannot be accepted into service." Lane proceeded to recruit and arm black soldiers in Kansas anyway. Lane later explained that Lincoln had orally promised Lane that the Kansas Black Regiment would be clothed and provided for until such time as they could be brought into battle. At the time, Lane was taking a big risk, but he may have seen black soldiers as a necessary resource to aid the Union cause.[25]

The formation of the infantry began in August. Regimental officers scoured Kansas counties looking for able-bodied men among the thousands of escaped slaves from Missouri. The unit had not yet been mustered into federal service, but its political and military backers made sure the recruits wore the blue uniforms of the U.S. military and carried the U.S. flag into combat. Lane gave these former slaves something more than uniforms and weapons. He gave them dignity and the opportunity to prove that they were men, not property. Another thing also separated them from white soldiers—the knowledge if they were captured by the Confederates, they faced almost certain death or a return to slavery.[26]

On October 29, 1862, the First Kansas Colored fought in Bates County, Missouri, near a low hill named Island Mound. This was the first time in American history that black soldiers fought the Confederates in the Civil War. For the First Kansas, this would be no battle over abstract principles—these men were fighting for their own freedom and that of their families. The two regiments numbered about 240 men, and were commanded by both black and white officers. Their orders were to attack a Confederate guerrilla force near the Toothman homestead, about nine miles on the other side of the Kansas/Missouri border.[27]

As the Kansans approached on Monday, October 27, their scouts identified a large party of mounted Confederate guerrillas. Though not every guerrilla owned a slave, all of them quaked with rage at the specter of black men carrying guns, since they fought to protect their economic livelihood based on slaves. Finding the enemy in a greater force than anticipated, the Kansans fortified the Toothman homestead and stacked fence rails to create breastworks and form a barricade. The soldiers called their quickly assembled defensive position "Fort Africa."

The Union officers learned from local residents that as many as 800 Confederates were gathering a few miles away for an attack. On Wednesday morning, Captain Henry C. Seaman sent two officers and 30 troops to look for food. Mounted rebels attacked them, yelling, "Come on you damned niggers," and forced them back to Fort Africa. The rebels then set fire to the prairie grass, hoping the wind would blow the fire toward the black troops to cover the Confederate attack or burn them out. Seaman set a back fire, which foiled the Confederates' plan. Seaman ordered a scouting patrol to get clear of the smoke and watch for enemy movement. About 400 mounted Confederates attacked the scouting party. The rebels attempted to run their horses over the black troops, who engaged them in hand-to-horse combat, with sabers swinging and pistols blasting. The main body of the First Kansas men then moved forward and fired on the mounted rebels, causing them to retreat.

When the gun smoke cleared, the Kansans found eight of their men dead and 11 wounded. Confederate losses are unknown, although some Kansans claimed between 30 and 40 killed. At Island Mound, in uniforms issued by a country that had not yet emancipated them, these former slaves displayed courage and tenacity under murderous fire from pro-slavery men. One of the rebel leaders later said the African-Americans "fought like tigers!"[28]

This small skirmish between black soldiers and bushwhackers in a remote location was covered extensively by *Harper's Weekly* and major national newspapers in New York, Philadelphia, and Chicago. With muskets on their shoulders and bullets in their pockets, former slaves had joined the political debate about their status and future, and helped guide their own destiny. They were the first former slaves and freed men to defeat Confederate forces in the Civil War. The battle at Island Mound was a real-world test that proved the hypothesis Lincoln set forth in his Gettysburg Address one year later: All men were created equal.[29]

Lane said the African-American soldiers "showed as much skill with their weapons as any troops who ever fought." Although he was not enlightened on racial issues, Lane countered the prejudice toward the soldier of color by the federal government: "When we put the uniforms of the United States on a person, he should be the peer of anyone who wears the same uniform, without reference to complexion." On these issues, Lane blazed a trail eventually taken by Lincoln and the military.[30]

The battlefield success of the First Kansas Colored, coupled with embarrassing Union losses elsewhere, emboldened Lincoln to muster black soldiers into the war and validated the need for black troops to fight to win "The Freedom War," as slaves and former slaves sometimes called the Civil War. On January 1, 1863, Lincoln signed the Emancipation Proclamation, which contained a controversial provision calling for the enlistment of black soldiers. Emancipating rebel slaves and using them as troops seems logical and inevitable to modern readers, but such an act was, at the time, a revolutionary and risky venture. Emancipation was not universally popular, even in the North, and no one could be sure how the officer corps, or the troops, and the Northern public at large would react to it. Lane's success in fielding soldiers of color provided assurance to Lincoln of the wisdom of the policy.

Lane became a vanguard of the Union's policy of "hard war." Lane argued:

> This war will never be successfully carried out so long as an army marches through slave states as a boat goes through a flock of ducks. They fly up on its approach and nestle down as soon as it has passed. The boat is safe and so are the ducks. When you march through a state you must destroy the property of the men in arms against the Government. This is war.

Lane's approach was carried into action by some of his Frontier Guard.[31]

After his service in the Frontier Guard, Tom Ewing returned to Kansas and was elected as the first chief justice of Kansas. In the summer of 1862, Lincoln called for another 300,000 Union soldiers, and he authorized Lane to recruit three new Kansas regiments. Tom Ewing resigned as chief justice to become Lane's colonel, with the authority to appoint the officers of his regiment. The appointment was yet another affront to Kansas Governor Robinson, who probably would not have appointed Ewing to regimental command. Lane had so much influence with Lincoln and Secretary of War Stanton that Lane told Ewing that if Governor Robinson would not commission Lane's officers, President Lincoln would. In a fit of pique, Governor Robinson asked Stanton how it was that Lane was "both Senator and Governor." [32]

During the fall and winter of 1862, the Confederate Army in northwest Arkansas had looked forward to wintering in the Fayetteville area in the midst of a region famed for its peach and apple brandies. In late

November, Union General Blunt sent 4,000 men, including Ewing's regiment, to strike at Confederate General Marmaduke's 8,000-man command. The armies met at Cane Hill, a cotton-milling region 20 miles southwest of Fayetteville. Ewing proved himself in the battle as a "hard-nosed leader, not content to push pins around a map at headquarters." The Kansas Brigade charged into a thick volley of Confederate fire. After firing, each man dropped his rifle butt onto the ground, grabbed a round from a cartridge box, tore at the paper with his teeth, rammed home a round, shouldered the gun, and fired at anything moving beyond the smoke and haze. The Confederate forces were primarily cavalry, and without infantry support, they could not hold against the determined Kansas assault, and retreated.[33]

Frontier Guard Second Sergeant John Burris's Tenth Kansas cavalry was one of the Kansas units that distinguished itself during the battle. In the battle of Cane Hill, the company suffered six dead and 67 wounded. The Kansas Brigade was successful in driving Confederate General Thomas C. Hindman's forces out of Missouri and south of the Arkansas River. Worse for Hindman, a 5-foot-tall Arkansan who made up in energy what he lacked in height, over 3,000 of his remaining conscripts having learned that the federal troops, consisting primarily of Kansans, were not easy to drive off, deserted over the next few weeks.

On December 7 Hindman's men again faced Ewing, Burris, and the Kansas regiments at the battle of Prairie Grove, Arkansas. The Confederates fled from the Kansas companies, leaving behind 5,000 muskets, 300,000 cartridges, and two artillery pieces. The battle accomplished what Union commanders wanted. Never again did a Southern army use northwest Arkansas as a staging area to invade western Missouri or Kansas. Union Captain Edmund Ross, the brother of Frontier Guard William Ross, reported that the rebel prisoners growled that they "would as soon fight the devil as to fight Kansas men."[34]

On March 13, 1863, Ewing was promoted by President Lincoln to Brigadier General for his courage and leadership at the bloody Battle of Prairie Grove. He was given command of the difficult District of the Border, which consisted of eastern Kansas and western Missouri, a hotbed of guerrilla activity. The Union army had gained control of the Missouri railroads, the Missouri River, and the northern counties in the state by the winter of 1861, but the western border with Kansas and that part of the state below the Missouri River became a devil's nightmare of guerrilla activity.[35]

Small bands of secessionist guerillas sprang up, fighting without official Confederate sanction or direction, referred to as "bushwhackers." Initially they consisted of small, mounted local bands. Soon, however, they grew in strength, skill, and effectiveness, until they began to attack federal troops, terrorize pro-Union civilians, and make raids into Kansas. Because they took no prisoners, to fight them meant two choices: fight or escape. To surrender meant death.

Missouri descended into a war of thousands of bloody incidents. The cycle of violence, with its escalating savagery by the guerrillas and ever-more-harsh reprisals by federal authorities, resulted in atrocities committed by all. Both sides prayed to the same benevolent God; both sides engaged in unholy brutality. Union General Fremont declared martial law and warned that civilians who aided the rebels would be shot. By 1862, rebel guerrillas swarmed across Missouri like the proverbial locusts of ancient Egypt. Abraham Lincoln understood the toll guerrilla warfare was inflicting. He lamented, "Each man feels an impulse to kill his neighbors, lest he first be killed by him. Revenge and retaliation follow. And all this among honest men. But this is not all. Every foul bird comes along, and every dirty reptile rises up."[36]

By March 1862, federal armies controlled St. Louis and its railroads and the towns along the railroad lines, in which they garrisoned troops who were often non-Missourians. The Confederacy would never establish a permanent base in Missouri. Tens of thousands of pro-slavery families remained hundreds of miles behind Union lines, living next door to Unionists, enraged by the Union occupation and its excesses on their doorsteps. And many families had young men of military age who had not gone south to join the regular Confederate Army.

As rebel guerrillas emerged from winter hibernation in the spring of 1863, the internal threat to Missouri became unprecedented. A Union soldier lamented that Missouri "was never so overrun with guerrillas. No one knows how to slow the flood." It was a warm and humid summer day when the sun rose over Lawrence on August 21, 1863, a day when Bleeding Kansas became bloodier. The Civil War had been raging over two years, but there was little evidence of the war in Lawrence, which was a sleepy but now prosperous hamlet that sheltered 2,000 souls. Brick buildings and white board homes lined its neat, well-ordered streets, and it boasted well-stocked stores, rich banks, fine homes with silver and jewelry, and white church steeples. It was said to be "the most beautiful city west of the Mississippi." All would change on that fateful day, when 26-year-old William Clark Quantrill and about 400 bearded, wild-haired guerrillas unleashed what was the largest mass murder of unarmed civilians in America until September 11, 2001.[37]

Lawrence was the home of the archenemy of Quantrill and the guerrillas, Jim Lane, and the heart of the Unionists and Jayhawks in Kansas. In persuading his fellow guerrillas to attack Lawrence, Quantrill claimed that Lane's Jayhawks had killed his older brother. (Despite Quantrill's claim, he did not have a brother.) Quantrill said, "We can get more revenge and more money there than anywhere else."[38]

Quantrill's mob rode into sleeping Lawrence at 5 A.M. and began killing, robbing, and burning. They slaughtered with guns, clubs, and bowie knives all men and boys old enough to carry a gun, often before the eyes of sobbing wives, mothers, and children, robbed banks, stole cash and valuables from the living and the dead, and burned homes and businesses. The nearly four hour orgy of death and destruction provided Quantrill enough time to order breakfast at the City Hotel and, when finished, shoot the proprietor in the head, enough time to turn Massachusetts Street into smoldering ruins, and enough time to kill 180 men and boys and create 85 widows and 250 fatherless children.[39]

The Lawrence massacre shocked the country and the world. Thousands of federal troops in the Kansas militia galloped after the guerrillas, but they fled back to the safety of Missouri's woods and ravines. Four days later, Brigadier General Ewing issued General Order No. 11, which commanded that Southern sympathizers living in the four eastern Missouri counties bordering on Kansas be expelled in an effort to stop guerrilla attacks into Kansas. The farmers' lands were the swamp from which the guerrillas emerged, and so Ewing decided to drain it.[40]

Ewing then took the war to the guerrilla bands operating in southeast Missouri. The new command was much like that in Kansas, small units of cavalry and a few forts in small towns defended by companies of infantry. Ewing's Kansas regiments proved extremely valuable to loyalist citizens, who knew the Kansas boys, unlike those in Missouri militia regiments, would not have relatives among the guerrillas and would pull no punches: "The Tenth Kansas Regiment tends to mollify the warlike propensities of our rebels, because they have a very distinct [idea as to in] what peculiar manner these Kansas boys are wont to settle accounts with bushwhackers."[41]

To the curious who met Tom Ewing and wondered if he was inclined to treat the rebels more kindly than his brother-in-law, General William T. Sherman, he quickly dispelled such notions. In June, Ewing's chief lieutenant reported: "Our men got in pursuit of the guerrillas . . . and three men who had been harboring them were taken, and, attempting to escape, were shot and killed." A later report describes the no-quarter fighting: "One [of the rebels] had the oath of allegiance in his pocket but the bullet missed the pocket and thus the oath failed to protect him."[42]

In October 1864 came Ewing's crowning wartime achievement. The war in 1863 had gone fairly well for the Union, with major victories at Gettysburg, Vicksburg, and Missionary Ridge. But in the spring and summer of 1864, when the Civil War was entering its fourth year, the situation of the Union army was grim. In the East, they had suffered terrible losses in the battles of the Wilderness (May 5 and 6), Spotsylvania (May 12), and Cold Harbor (June 3), while campaigns west of the Mississippi in Louisiana, Texas, and Arkansas had ended disastrously, allowing the Southern forces to assume the offense. Lincoln sought reelection in order to finish the war, but high Union casualties and his perceived mishandling of the war made Lincoln extremely unpopular. Senior Confederate officers fervently hoped the Confederacy could hang on and continue to bleed the Union army until the Democratic nominee, former Union General George McClellan, could be elected in November 1864. McClellan would then seek peace, leaving the war unfinished and slavery intact.

In May 1864, the Union had launched two invasions in an effort to turn the tide against the Confederacy. Grant's movement into Virginia pinned down Robert E. Lee around Richmond, but Grant suffered enormous casualties and the armies were deadlocked. Sherman's march into Georgia toward Atlanta was agonizingly slow. By August, every Confederate commander knew the primary purpose of the two main Confederate armies outside of Atlanta and Richmond were to keep Grant and Sherman from capturing those cities before November's election made George McClellan president. With McClellan already pledged to make peace, success on the battlefield was no longer required for the Confederates to survive; an illusion of success was good enough. If the Confederate army could break loose into the North and cause havoc, an embarrassed Lincoln would lose the 1864 election. The only option for such an invasion lay to the west of the Mississippi River, and the last rebel army in the Confederacy capable of attacking anything of significance was commanded by General Sterling Price.

On August 28, 1864, Price led a 15,000-man Confederate force from Arkansas, planning to attack St. Louis, burn the city's wharves and military supplies, and arm rebels with weapons from the massive St. Louis arsenal, which held with weapons for all U.S. Army troops west of the Mississippi. Price's chances of success were good, as there were only 6,500 scattered Union troops between Price's army and St. Louis. After St. Louis, Price intended to attack Kansas City, brush aside any Kansas militia, destroy Leavenworth, and turn south to burn Lawrence and Topeka. In addition to the military objectives, Price hoped that his invasion would lead to the overthrow of the loyal government of Missouri and the installation of a Confederate administration in Jefferson City.[43]

Ewing was the deputy commanding general for the Department of Missouri, under General William Rosencrans in St. Louis. Rosencrans ordered Ewing into southeast Missouri to report back on which route Price was taking toward St. Louis. On September 26, Ewing found himself at a small earthen fort called Fort Donaldson, which lay at the end of the railroad and telegraph lines 90 miles southwest of St. Louis near Pilot Knob, Missouri. Fort Donaldson was an octagon-shaped structure, 9 feet high and 10 feet thick, situated near a creek and on a slight rise surrounded by four small hills. Like a castle, the fort was also surrounded by a dry moat, with two rifle pits dug outside. Any Confederate army coming out of Arkansas had to march either through the Ozark Mountains or through the Arcadia Valley past the fort. Price chose the latter.

Ewing was the senior officer in command of 800 soldiers and 12 cannon in the fort who found themselves surrounded by Price's army. Price demanded that Ewing surrender, but Ewing had black civilians in the fort, and he expected the rebels might massacre them as they had months earlier slaughtered black soldiers at Fort Pillow, Tennessee, many of whom had surrendered and laid down their arms. As the author of Order No. 11, Ewing also had a price on his head. Ewing refused Price's demand that he surrender.

Ewing's band of heavily outnumbered soldiers fought off Price's repeated attacks from his force of 15,000 Confederates. Ewing's cannons and infantry, the latter firing from the rifle pits, caused terrible casualties among the rebels. Over 1,500 Confederates, representing the cream of Price's army, were shot down in a single afternoon. Ewing lost less than 200 men. The punishment Ewing inflicted on the Confederate divisions was so severe, it is said, that they never entirely recovered their morale during the rest of the campaign.[44]

At midnight, Ewing led a small force out of the fort under cover of darkness, through the Confederate lines, and escaped. Ewing's band then engaged in a successful fighting withdrawal to Rolla, Missouri. Ewing's men gave the Union army time to fortify its defenses around St. Louis, and Price's shattered force could not complete their intended attack on the city. Eastern newspaper writers hailed the Battle of Pilot Knob as the "Thermopylae of the West," and Ewing as a hero.

Price turned west, where outnumbered Kansas troops defeated his army on October 24 at the sprawling, three-day Battle of Westport, sometimes called the "Gettysburg of the West," which prevented Price from crossing the state line into Kansas. The approximately 29,000 soldiers involved in the battle made it the biggest Civil War battle west of the Mississippi River. Lane offered his services to Union General Curtis, who appointed Lane his aide-de-camp. Lane was on the front line, carbine in hand, swinging down from his saddle with the skirmishers to fire a volley or two before being driven back. Curtis reported, "Lane's experiences in former campaigns in Mexico and upon the Kansas border enabled him to be of much service in the field everywhere."[45]

Lane also continued to be useful to Lincoln in the East. In the Senate, Lane became a major player in advancing the transcontinental railroad and the various proposals for federal aid to the Pacific Railroad bill, a key Lincoln and Republican initiative. In 1864, the construction of the Kansas branch of the Union Pacific Railway was begun at Wyandotte,

Kansas. Before Kansans had realized what was going on, the road had already been graded and cleared, missing Lawrence and Topeka by three miles. Lane wrote a letter, signed by Lincoln and every Republican Senator, to the Union Pacific Railroad requesting that the railroad track be changed to run just north of the Kansas River across from Lawrence and Topeka. The railroad refused. When Lane met with them, they demanded $300,000 from Lawrence to change the location of the track. Lane loved Lawrence and had not forgotten the sufferings of her people at the hands of Quantrill's murderers just one year earlier. Lane told the railroad executives, "Your road shall go to Lawrence. You can't levy tribute on that burnt and murdered town." The railroad went to Lawrence.[46]

Lane also had his uses to Lincoln as an orator to the masses. Lincoln and other Republicans could threaten to unleash Lane and the mob he could arouse if calmer tempers did not prevail in negotiations, maintaining all the while their reputations as rational statesman. The "wild fanaticism" approach had its appeal in Washington and Kansas when the negotiations of the "counselors" seemed to lead nowhere. Lane was courted as a necessary, popular, and charismatic leader. He became one of the most popular men in Washington: Lane was "a great lion here and his room is filled with visitors; at this moment there is not a man in Washington more sought after."[47]

During the Civil War there was a pattern of consultation, mutual respect, and interest between the two men. Given Lane's reputation, particularly in the Southern press, as an irresponsible demagogue, this was a surprise and a concern to many. Charles Robinson was one of Lane's primary political opponents and personal enemies. Even odder, considering that he was a Republican governor, was that he was an enemy of Lincoln. Robinson wrote in June 1863: "The President is a poor weak man used by demagogues of the most worthless & corrupt character."[48]

Lincoln selected Lane to open his campaign for his reelection. Although it is hard to believe now, Lincoln was not a popular president during the first half of 1864. He operated in a perpetual crossfire from congressmen, governors, generals, office seekers, and ordinary citizens—all dissatisfied, and many sincerely convinced he was incompetent and leading the nation down the path of destruction. On March 30, 1864, Lane spoke in New York City at the Cooper Institute, where he praised Lincoln's accomplishments and defended Lincoln for not issuing the Emancipation Proclamation and arming black soldiers sooner. A few weeks later, the Kansas State Republican Convention met at Topeka and elected Lane and former Frontier Guards A. C. Wilder and Merritt H. Insley as delegates to the upcoming Republican National Convention in Baltimore. Lane was also elected as a delegate to the Grand Council of the Union League, which assembled in the same city the day before the convention.[49]

During the June 1864 Republican presidential convention in Baltimore, appalling charges were made against Lincoln, and it appeared he might not be renominated. Lane then arose near the front, in the middle aisle of the hall, turned around, and made an emotional appeal:

> I am speaking individually to each man here. Do you, sir, know in this broad land, and can you name to me, one man whom you could or would trust, before God, that he would have done better in this matter than Abraham Lincoln has done, and to whom you would be now more willing to trust the unforeseen emergency or peril which is to come? That unforeseen peril, that perplexing emergency, that step in the dark, is right before us, and we are here to decide by whom it should be made for the Nation. If we nominate any other man than Abraham Lincoln we nominate ruin!

Lincoln was renominated.[50]

Vice President Hamlin, like Lincoln, also sought to be renominated. Lincoln, however, told Lane that he favored Governor Andrew Johnson of Tennessee, a strong war Democrat, and he sent Lane to engineer the delicate deal. When the delegates were about to renominate Hamlin, Lane said, "No, Mr. Lincoln feels that we must recognize the South in kindness. The nominee will be Andy Johnson."[51]

Nearly 20 other Kansans in the Frontier Guard also bravely fought for the Union and distinguished themselves during the war. The war records of but a few will be mentioned here. As a captain in the 18th U.S. Infantry, George Washington Smith commanded eight companies and was brevetted for "gallant and meritorious conduct" at the Battle of Chickamauga, Georgia, and he was promoted to lieutenant colonel for "conspicuous gallantry" at the Battle of Jonesboro, Georgia. He fought in 19 general battles, over 30 skirmishes, and was under fire 63 times. He lost two adjutants, two orderlies, and two horses under fire at Chickamauga alone.[52]

Sam Hartman first enlisted and fought with the First Kansas Brigade. He then enlisted in Company E, 79th Pennsylvania, and was commissioned a second lieutenant. His gallantry caused him to be promoted to first lieutenant and later, captain. Captain Hartman served on the staff of General Russo, who commanded the division under which the 79th Pennsylvania, "Lancaster's Own," fought with such great bravery and terrible loss at Perryville.[53]

Back East, other former members of the Frontier Guard also became famous Union Army generals and soldiers.

12

The Fighting McCooks

By July 1861, the Northern three-month enlistments were almost up, and Congress and the Northern press were pressuring Lincoln to act. About 35,000 Union citizen-soldiers were gathered in the Washington area. Their commander was General Irvin McDowell, a tall, stately, and somewhat pompous-looking man. McDowell was a former officer on Winfield Scott's staff, with no battle experience. For the most part, the 90-day recruits in McDowell's command were greener than meadow grass and would need several months of training before they would be ready for battle.

After Virginia's secession, the Confederate government had accepted Virginia's invitation to move its capital from Montgomery, Alabama, to Richmond, Virginia. The Confederate Congress scheduled its next session to meet in Richmond on July 20. Horace Greeley's *New York Tribune* blazed forth with a standing headline: "Forward to Richmond! The Rebel Congress Must Not Be Allowed to Meet There on 20 July." Other newspapers picked up on the cry of "On to Richmond." Northern public opinion demanded an invasion onto Virginia soil to crush the Confederate army.[1]

Abraham Lincoln ordered General McDowell to come up with a plan to strike the Confederate army encamped at Manassas, a rail junction in northern Virginia linking the main rail lines to the Shenandoah Valley and the deep South. Manassas was about 35 miles south of Washington, and if the Confederate army could be defeated there, the way would be clear to Richmond. McDowell drew up plans for a flanking attack on the 20,000 Confederate soldiers defending Manassas Junction. If McDowell's troops could push through the Confederate lines, there would be little to stop them from marching straight into Richmond. The Confederate troops were under the command of the dapper General Pierre G.T. Beauregard, the victor at Fort Sumter. So far the war had been a series of minor fights and skirmishes, most of which had been won by the Union in western Virginia.

McDowell's plan was good—for experienced troops led by veteran officers. At a White House strategy conference on June 29, McDowell pleaded with Lincoln for a postponement of the attack until he could train the new three-year enlisted men. Lincoln told McDowell, "You are green, it is true, but they are green, also; you are all green alike." The President ordered McDowell to begin his offensive.[2]

Happy to be on the march, a vivid assortment of Northern volunteers marched with a swaggering gait, eager for a fight. Most of them were members of state militias, and their uniforms were as diverse and colorful as the Northern states from which they came. Massachusetts men wore blue. Regiments from New Hampshire wore gray, and Vermont mountaineers marched in green. New Yorkers were the most flamboyant. Their Fire Zouaves wore exotic and colorful uniforms similar to those worn by French troops in North Africa—red hats with yellow tassels, short blue coats, yellow cummerbunds, and baggy red breeches. Much of the Union Army resembled a theater troupe going to a frolic instead of a fight.

Behind them, in the dusty distance racing to catch up, careened a carriage driven by the commanding figure of Frontier Guard Daniel McCook, armed with a Colt revolving rifle. Four members of Congress accompanied him, planning to fight as civilian volunteers beside their constituents. Judge McCook planned to fight beside his eighth son, Charlie, who was a private in Company I, Second Ohio, Second Brigade, First Division. Charlie's division had the honor of leading the army south. Catching up to the division about three miles from Manassas, McCook and his congressional comrades got their first taste of battle at Blackburn's Road over Bull Run Creek.[3]

Judge McCook could hear the sounds of battle, the deep rumble of artillery fire, and the high chatter of muskets. He saw flags floating through white smoke, and a black cannon spouted red fire from round lips at the limits of his vision. He ducked his head as a shot whickered over him. There was wreckage everywhere, smoking earth, naked stumps of trees. He saw a dead horse lying in a black mound in the steaming heat, a splintered wagon, a severed foot. The sky was overcast with blowing white smoke, the smell of hot guns, blasted earth, and splintered trees. Then he smelled the odor of dead meat on the wind.

Slinging his rifle over his shoulder, he ran onto the field in his hat and coat to carry wounded men from the bloody field, while he dodged bullets cutting leaves. His clothes were soon wet and soaked with blood. The hillside was alive with death. At least 19 Union soldiers in Charlie's division were dead, 38 wounded, and 26 missing. The temperature was 95 degrees. The soldiers were exhausted after fighting in their sweat-stained wool uniforms under the blazing sun, and sought shade and rest.

The next day, General McDowell ordered the Second and Third divisions, led by Brigadier Generals David Hunter and Samuel P. Heintzelman, to cross the Bull Run Creek and attack the Confederates. Judge McCook, on a hillside above the action, alternated between taking shots at enemy cavalry with his rifle and conversing with other congressional observers and reporters. By noon it appeared to McCook and others on the hillside that the battle was won. The Confederates had retreated into the woods and disappeared. Washington civilians who had come out to watch the battle began celebratory luncheon parties.

About one in the afternoon, McDowell ordered the Union infantry to attack the Confederates. Unfortunately, the rebels had been reinforced, and there was mass confusion about uniforms. Some Confederate officers still wore their old blue regular U.S. Army uniforms, and many soldiers on both sides wore gray. In the confusion and smoke, friends shot friends and foes went unscathed. Instead of a quick Union victory, the battle raged on savagely.

About four in the afternoon, fresh Confederate troops began running onto the battlefield. They were the last of 12,000 reinforcements who had arrived by train from the Shenandoah Valley to increase the Confederate army to 32,000. The Union soldiers had no reinforcements and began to retreat, sometimes being fired upon by their own men.[4]

Judge McCook, running back to a field hospital to warn his son Charlie of the Confederate attack, discovered a Confederate infantry attack on the Union left flank. He climbed a fence to direct artillery fire on the rebels. Meanwhile, a Confederate cavalryman charged Charlie McCook, who attempted to keep the rebel's horse at bay with his bayonet. "Surrender!" yelled the Confederate. "No!" shouted Charlie, "Never to a rebel!" Circling behind him, the horseman shot Charlie in the back. "Now, damn you, will you surrender?" "Never," cried the boy. The cavalryman then went after Charlie with his sword.[5]

Judge McCook started to raise his rifle at the Confederate, but a Union soldier blew the rebel out of his saddle. The devastated father picked up his bloody son and carried him to the field hospital, where the surgeon told him the wound was not fatal and the boy could be moved for further medical attention. McCook drove Charlie to the little town of Fairfax Courthouse, where the taverns, inns, and homes were serving as hospitals. An army surgeon who removed the bullet in Charlie's lower torso discovered the wound was fatal. Daniel McCook lay on the bed beside his son, who died in his grieving father's arms about 2:30 that morning.

After the battle, both sides seemed infected with a gloom, a sense this was now very real, the abstract political rhetoric replaced by the clear, sickening knowledge many men were going to die. That evening, in the Willard's Hotel lobby, Judge McCook told the crowd the story about his son who refused to surrender. Charlie's cousin, Frontier Guard Private Ed McCook, held up the fatal bullet and swore the entire McCook clan—fathers, uncles, brothers, and cousins—would fight the Confederates in Charlie's honor. From that day forward they were called "The Fighting McCooks." The next day, Judge McCook wrote, "I leave tomorrow for the banks of the upper Potomac with my rifle in search of game. I'm determined to pay the boys across the river for Bull Run."[6]

Several other members of the Frontier Guard also bravely fought during the Battle of Bull Run. Frontier Guard and Kansan Leicester Walker, whom Abraham Lincoln appointed as a second lieutenant of the Second United States Cavalry (later changed to the Fifth Regular Cavalry), distinguished himself during the battle. Walker went on to fight at the Second Battle of Bull Run, Fair Oaks, Malvern Hill, and Antietam, among others.[7]

Frontier Guard First Sergeant David Gordon fought in the battle as a second lieutenant in the Second U.S. Calvary. Gordon was captured by the Confederates and sent to Libby Prison in Richmond, and then to prisons in South and North Carolina before he was released in August 1862 as part of a prisoner exchange. He rejoined his regiment just before the Battle of Fredericksburg. Gordon was later promoted to captain in the Second U.S. Calvary and received a brevet to Major, U.S. Army, for gallant and meritorious service at the Battle of Gettysburg. In 1864 Gordon served with the regiment during the Wilderness Campaign and Sheridan's two raids. He commanded the regiment through the Battle of Deep Bottom on July 27-28, 1864, and during the majority of the Shenandoah Campaign from August to October 1864, before retiring as a brigadier general.[8]

In October 1861, Frontier Guard Judge Daniel McCook fought at Bolivar Heights, Maryland, with the 28th Pennsylvania, earning mention in the official report of Colonel John Geary, who noted "Daniel McCook . . . gun in hand, volunteered and rendered much service during the engagement." In November, McCook enrolled as a captain in the Ohio Militia, after having fought several battles in civilian garb and, more than once, narrowly escaping death.[9]

On August 6, 1862, Judge McCook's third son, Robert, now a brigadier general, was ambushed and murdered by rebel guerrilla Frank Gurley and his men in Tennessee. The next spring Judge McCook was promoted to major and commissioned as a paymaster with the Army of the Ohio. Shortly after, on July 21, 1863, McCook charged a Confederate skirmish line along the banks of the Ohio River near Buffington Island while pursuing his son Robert's murderer, Frank Gurley, who was thought to be with Confederate Brigadier General John Hunt Morgan's "Raiders." McCook was shot from his horse still clutching his rifle.

That evening McCook died, one month after his 65th birthday and two years to the night after he had nursed his dying son Charlie. The Cincinnati *Daily Commercial* newspaper pronounced: "The whole state and country will be shocked by the . . . death of Major Daniel McCook, the well-known father of so many distinguished soldiers. . . . Let all homage be rendered to the memory of a model patriot!"[10]

Judge McCook's nephew, Frontier Guard Ed McCook, soon became one of the Union's most distinguished generals. In recognition of McCook's courage and equestrian skill in riding through rebel lines to order Union soldiers to come to Washington, General Scott offered McCook a second lieutenant's commission in the elite First U.S. Cavalry. Two days later, on May 10, 1861, Ed wrote to his Connecticut cousin about his commission and the sacrifice he made by leaving behind "all that I possess in the world" in the mountains, "that lawless country where only the strong arm protects your rights." He knew his absence would mean "utter ruin" for all that he worked for in the Kansas Territory (now Colorado), but he would rather do his duty than possess "all the wealth that lies buried in those lonely mountains."[11]

McCook was ordered to report to Carlisle Barracks, Pennsylvania, where he awaited the arrival of the First U.S. Cavalry on its way east from Fort Leavenworth. During encampment outside of Washington in Virginia, Ed wrote to his cousin he was confined to bed as a result of "an injury received from a vicious horse." The "vicious horse" was, in truth, a case of syphilis that landed him in the hospital for several weeks. By the time Ed was able to sit upon a horse, the Battle of Bull Run had been fought. By November, Ed was on his way to distinction as major of the Second Indiana Cavalry, Fourth Division, Army of the Ohio.[12]

Cavalrymen were the elite of the army. They were paid more than infantrymen, and were finely mounted on chestnut and gray horses. McCook was soon bronzed by the sun and wind, his shoulders square under his blue cavalry overcoat, short blue jacket with yellow braid, polished boots, gleaming brass spurs, and wide leather belt that held his six-shot revolver and glistening, clanking saber. He rode 30 miles per day when on the march, and slept under the stars with his head on his saddle and horse tethered to his wrist.

In the spring of 1862, General George P. Buell's Army of the Ohio marched south to join Grant's Army of the Tennessee. McCook, now colonel of his regiment, arrived with his men the night of April 6 at the Battle of Shiloh, just as Grant's forces were almost driven into the Tennessee River. The Union reinforcements turned the tide of battle the next morning, and the Confederates were forced to retreat from the bloodiest battle in U.S. history up to that time.

In September McCook was given command of the 1,100 men of the First Brigade of the Cavalry Division in Buell's Army of the Ohio. After fighting at the Battle of Perryville, Kentucky, on October 8, he was with General William S. Rosencrans at Murfreesboro in the spring of 1863. McCook soon commanded the Second Brigade, First Division, Cavalry Corps, in Rosencrans's Army of the Cumberland. After Rosencrans was defeated at the Battle of Chickamauga, in North Georgia, on September 19, 1863, he retreated to Chattanooga, Tennessee.

A Union wagon train started south to resupply the Army of the Cumberland. On October 3, a 10-mile long Union supply train, with 800 mule-team wagons, wound its way through Tennessee bound for Chattanooga. Confederate General Joseph Wheeler, with nearly 6,000 troops, discovered the great prize near Anderson's Crossroads. After an eight-hour attack, Wheeler's army marched off with half the mules and wagons—the rest he ordered to be killed and burned.

McCook, scouting the valley with two regiments, saw the black smoke pointing a finger to the sky and dashed to the train, but reached the charred remains too late. Galloping past burning wagons and dead mules, McCook caught up with the Confederate army about dusk. His men charged the rebels and engaged them in running battles. McCook's men fought like demons and recovered most of the wagons and about 500 mules, killing over 120 rebel troops and taking over 60 prisoners, including nine officers.[13]

McCook and Brigadier General George Crook, commanding the Second Division, pursued Confederate General Wheeler and fought him in several battles. Finally, Wheeler, with many of his troops dead or wounded, retreated south of the Tennessee River. McCook, commended by Rosencrans, looked forward to receiving his general's star as a result of the action. Unfortunately for McCook, two weeks later, Rosencrans was removed from command, leaving McCook as the only colonel in the army exercising a major general's command.

After three more months of hard wintertime fighting, in February 1864, McCook applied for a 20-day leave of absence to ride to Washington to meet with President Lincoln. He was startled to see how much two years of war had aged the great man since McCook had served as a Frontier Guard. Anxiety and sleepless nights had taken their toll. Lincoln's shoulders sagged, his long neck emerged gauntly from his turned-down collar, and his cavernous, ancient eyes were sunken deep in his haggard face. But Lincoln had not forgotten McCook, who, during the first week of the war when Lincoln's life hung by a thread and most had fled, had the courage to remain and protect the President. On April 23, 1864, Lincoln nominated McCook for brigadier general; four days later he was confirmed by the Senate.[14]

One week later, Brigadier General Edward McCook commanded the First Cavalry Division, Army of the Cumberland, as Sherman began his campaign for Atlanta. After failing in battles on July 20 and 22 to penetrate the city with infantry and artillery, Sherman switched to his cavalry. One of the South's finest fighters, Lieutenant General John Bell Hood, was firmly entrenched in the city. On July 27, Sherman ordered McCook and his 3,500 cavalry and General Stoneman, with 5,000 cavalry, on a sweeping raid around the city to wreck the Macon & Western Railroad, Hood's main supply line. Sherman's order stated: "I send by the right a force of about 3,500 cavalry, under General McCook, and around by the left about 5,000 cavalry, under General Stoneman, with orders to reach the railroad about Griffin." McCook and Stoneman were to join forces the evening of July 28 near Lovejoy Station.

McCook's troopers, armed with new Spencer seven-shot repeating carbines, revolvers, and sabers, trotted out of camp at 4 A.M. in a torrential downpour. Reaching the town of Palmetto about 6 A.M., they tore up two and one-half miles of railroad tracks, downed telegraph lines, destroyed freight cars, and torched 100,000 bales of cotton, 300 sacks of flour, and large quantities of bacon and tobacco. They then attacked and destroyed a five-mile-long Confederate supply train, capturing 72 rebel officers and 350 privates who had been asleep inside.[15]

After trading their tired mounts for fresh horses, they rode toward Fayetteville. Reaching the town before dawn, prisoners in tow, they captured another 130 Confederates, mostly officers, sleeping in homes near the town square. After destroying some of the town's supplies, McCook galloped out at 5 A.M. headed for Lovejoy Station, 30 miles south of Atlanta. He reached his rendezvous at 7, 12 hours late. Stoneman was not there. Neither was there evidence that he arrived early and left. McCook found out later that Stoneman had deviated from the planned rendezvous in an effort to rescue the 33,000 Union prisoners at the infamous prisoner of war camp at Andersonville. While waiting for Stoneman, McCook carried out his orders by burning the railroad depot, ripping up two and one-half miles of railroad track, tearing down five miles of telegraph poles and wires, and burning several railroad cars containing cotton, tobacco, and bacon. By this time he had destroyed 1,160 wagons and 2,000 mules badly needed by Confederate General Hood.[16]

At about 2 p.m., McCook, resting his men, was warned by his scouts that a large cavalry force was approaching from the east. It was Confederate General Wheeler. Having wasted precious hours waiting for Stoneman, McCook was forced to abandon his effort to encircle Atlanta and instead ride back the way he had come. Worse, nearly 1,000 Confederate soldiers, forced to stop on trains due to wrecked rails, jumped out to defend the smoking town of Palmetto and attacked McCook as he tried to pass. McCook's men were exhausted and they were burdened with several hundred prisoners, who slowed them down.

General Wheeler caught up to McCook's rear guard and turned his full wrath upon McCook's forces. Surrounded and outnumbered, McCook met with his commanders to consider the Confederate demand for surrender. McCook's commanders asked to be allowed to cut their way out with their brigades. McCook agreed. "Save yourselves and your commands," he ordered.[17]

While McCook and 1,200 men held off the enemy, Colonels John Claxton and William Torrey fought their way out and their brigades scattered. McCook then led his 1,200 cavalrymen in a surprise charge through the Confederate lines. Having broken through, McCook and his men rode through woods and swamps until they reached the Chattahoochee River, where they captured some boats and made their way to Marietta. Sherman, who had feared McCook was dead or captured, sent a relieved dispatch on August 3: "General McCook is safe. He is in with 1,200 of his command."[18]

The days of August 1864 were some of the darkest of the Civil War for the Union. What was supposed to be a quick war had stretched into years. Patience, along with patriotism, wore down. The numbers of deaths in battle were appalling. General Ulysses S. Grant had lost 55,000 men during his campaign in Virginia, but Richmond remained in Confederate hands and Southern defiance was undiminished. Public horror at the lengthening casualty lists fueled opposition to the war. Draft resistance became epidemic, while desertions skyrocketed. Editors in Northern newspapers demanded, "Stop the War." The Confederates were hopeful that Northerners, sick of the slaughter, would defeat Lincoln at the polls and sue for peace. If the Confederacy could hold onto Atlanta and Richmond, independence might follow.

Even Republican stalwarts were desperate and considered the President's reelection "an impossibility." Lincoln expected to lose. At the end of August, he asked members of his cabinet to sign a sealed document whose contents he did not disclose. The contents were later revealed as:

> This morning, as for some days past, it seems exceedingly likely that this Administration will not be reelected. Then it will be my duty to so cooperate with the President-elect, as to save the Union between the election and the inauguration; as he will have secured his election on such ground that he cannot possibly save it afterward.[19]

On August 10, however, Sherman used his infantry to encircle Atlanta and finally cut Hood's supply line. Hood was forced to evacuate Atlanta and Sherman marched in. After arduous months of maneuvering across northern Georgia, on September 3 Sherman telegraphed the War Department: "Atlanta is ours, and fairly won." Sherman's military victory helped ensure Lincoln's political victory two months later at the polls. Lincoln, running on the Union Party ticket, a combination of Republicans and War Democrats, won 55 percent of the popular vote and carried every loyal state except Kentucky, Delaware, and New Jersey.[20]

The week after Lincoln's victory, Sherman started on his 256-mile march across Georgia to the sea. Designed to break the South's will to continue fighting, Sherman's march destroyed over $100 million in property in a 50-mile-wide swath through Georgia, leaving a wasteland of blackened chimneys. Thirty-two days later, Sherman arrived in Savannah.

Sherman then began fighting his way up the eastern seaboard to join Grant at Petersburg. Lee's men were exhausted. But Confederate President Jefferson Davis refused to admit defeat. So Secretary of War Stanton ordered a massive cavalry raid through the Deep South to destroy the factories that made the weapons that allowed the South to continue fighting. On March 22, 1865, Brigadier General McCook led over 4,000 lean and hard cavalrymen out of Chickasaw Bluff, Mississippi, on the largest Union cavalry raid of the Civil War.

McCook's First Division was one of three divisions commanded by Brigadier Generals Ed McCook, Eli Long, and Emery Upton in the Army of the Mississippi, commanded by Major General James Harrison Wilson. Wilson and McCook did not get along. Wilson, a West Pointer who went strictly by the book, disliked McCook's tendency to toss the text aside as he improvised on the march. Most of McCook's troopers were experienced, savvy fighters, having spent four years in the saddle. They carried Spencer repeating carbines and 100 rounds of ammunition, and were well supplied with rations and food for their horses.[21]

McCook's troopers wrecked ironworks, rolling mills, and blast furnaces in northern Alabama before riding for the shipbuilding city of Selma. Confederate General Nathan Bedford Forrest, with 11,000 men in widely scattered forces, vowed to fight to the bitter end. Discovering the Union cavalry's presence, Forrest tried to unite his scattered forces to protect the city. Forrest had fought 50 battles during the war, inflicting over 16,000 Union casualties. He was a fearsome foe. One of McCook's brigades, however, riding on the spur of speed, covered 15 miles in two hours and captured and destroyed a bridge over the Cahaba River, preventing two of Forrest's divisions from reaching him. With only part of his force, Forrest was badly outnumbered and beaten at Montevallo. Fighting again at Ebenezer's Church, he was wounded by a saber and fell back into Selma. Wilson stormed the city on April 2 and captured it, destroying the armament industry and capturing 2,700 prisoners. Forrest escaped.[22]

McCook, having missed the Selma fighting due to destroying the bridge over the Cahaba, was given the honor of marching on Montgomery, Alabama, the "Birthplace of the Confederacy." At sunrise on April 12, as McCook's troops appeared on the outskirts of the city, the town mayor and a delegation of citizens rode out to surrender. McCook accepted the surrender and ordered the Stars and Stripes be raised over the Alabama Statehouse. When Wilson arrived, the entire army made a victorious march into the city. McCook and Wilson, their bright brass buttons and brilliant epaulets shining, rode at the head of the column, with sabers drawn. Behind them troopers trotted four abreast. The parade lasted nearly all day. It was the fourth anniversary of the attack on Fort Sumter. Southerners glared silently from their windows.[23]

On April 9, Lee surrendered to Grant at Appomattox Courthouse. Shortly thereafter, on Good Friday, Lincoln was shot by John Wilkes Booth at Ford's Theater while watching a performance. Frontier Guard and Union Army soldier Thomas Bancroft stood at the head of the stairs in Ford's Theatre, holding excited audience members back while President Lincoln was being carried downstairs. Bancroft saw blood dripping from the back of Lincoln's head onto the theater floor and steps as the President passed by. Lincoln died the next day.[24]

The day after Lincoln's death, Frontier Guard Prentice Clark was in the National Hotel when he overheard a conversation between two men about the assassination, one of whom was a servant of Mary Surratt, and the other turned out to be Lincoln conspirator Lewis Thornton Powell (a.k.a. Lewis Payne). Clark followed one of the men to the Kirkwood Hotel but lost him in the crowd. Clark provided the information to the police, leading them to stake out Mary Surratt's boarding house and capture Surratt and Payne. Other members of the Frontier Guard, including Sidney Clarke, traveled with Abraham Lincoln's funeral train to Springfield, Illinois, where they acted as pallbearers.[25]

Three weeks after Lincoln's assassination, some of McCook's troops helped capture the fleeing president of the Confederacy, Jefferson Davis. That same day, McCook, with the remainder of his men, accepted the rebel surrender of Florida in Tallahassee. Florida was the last Confederate state east of the Mississippi to surrender. Ordering the Stars and Stripes raised over the Florida Statehouse, McCook directed his artillery to fire one salvo for each of the 35 states in the now indivisible Union. Lincoln would have approved.[26]

Numerous other members of the Frontier Guard also fought bravely and with distinction during the war. Oscar Hale was a lieutenant colonel of Company D, Sixth Regiment Vermont Volunteers, and he fought at all of the regiment's battles from Yorktown to the Virginia Valley before being wounded at the Battle of Charles Town. Joseph Henry was captain of Company H in the Ninth New Jersey Volunteers. He was killed at Roanoke Island, North Carolina, when a Confederate cannonball crushed his chest.[27]

Ed Daniels was a colonel in the First Wisconsin Cavalry Regiment and fought at L'Anguille Ferry, Arkansas, and Pilot Knob and Cape Girardeau, Missouri. During the first half of 1863, he was part of General McCook's expedition to the rear of Atlanta. James H. Northcott was a private in the same company and received nine wounds in battle, leading to his discharge. Edward Spicer enlisted in the Union Army, 10th Heavy Artillery, New York, and served bravely in many bloody battles until he mustered out on August 24, 1865.[28]

The German-Americans in the Frontier Guard also fought bravely and had distinguished war records. German-Americans were the largest ethnic contingent to fight for the Union. About 216,000 native Germans served in the Union Army. New York supplied the largest number with 36,000, Missouri with 30,000, and Ohio with 20,000. Scores of individual regiments consisted entirely of German-Americans. New York and Ohio each provided ten divisions dominated by German-born men. The men from Deutschland were soon referred to as "Dutchmen" by other soldiers. The German-Americans demonstrated discipline and efficiency under fire. General Lee was reported to have said, "Take the Dutch out of the Union Army and we'll whip the Yankees easily."[29]

Frederick Bogen enlisted in the New York 41st Infantry Regiment as a commissioned officer and helped defend Washington until April 1862, before moving into Virginia and fighting in several battles. In June 1862, at the Battle of Keys Cross, Bogen was shot in the leg. In May 1863 at Chancellorsville, Bogen received another gunshot wound. Bogen recovered and rejoined his regiment in time for the July 3 Battle of Gettysburg.[30]

Lincoln appointed Guido Ilges captain in the 14th U.S. Infantry Regiment. Ilges was cited by brevets to major and lieutenant colonel for gallant service in action at the Battles of the Wilderness and Spotsylvania, Virginia. John Gareis was a sergeant in the 1st Regiment Maryland cavalry in Captain Wetschky's Company B. He had been promoted to first lieutenant by the Battle at Brandy Station, where he was wounded and captured. William G. Hoban worked as a spy for the Union. He interviewed General Beauregard at Manassas Junction and sent a report on rebel troop strength and intentions three weeks before the first Battle at Bull Run. He was involved in the arrest of Confederate spies Cyrus F. Sergeant and Octavius Hill, and he helped capture Confederate guerrilla John H. Boyle.[31]

Lincoln said, "Nothing is too good for 110 [*sic*] men who stood off an entire army."[32] He backed up his words with plum political appointments for about 30 members of the Frontier Guard who did not serve in the Union Army. These appointments are listed in Appendix II. After the war, members of the Frontier Guard played important, and surprising, roles in post-bellum America.

13

Aftermath

After Lincoln's death, Lane championed Lincoln's, now President Andrew Johnson's, policy of reconciliation with the South. Unfortunately, the radical Republican Congress did not embrace Lincoln's "with malice towards none" approach. Lane's statesmanship was excoriated by the radical Republicans, who believed that they were entitled to the spoils of war. Kansas Republicans, having suffered for ten years at the hands of pro-slavery Missourians, pilloried Lane for abandoning radical Republican principles.[1]

Lane went into the Civil War from one world and had come out of it into another. He may have never recovered from Lincoln's assassination. When newspaper editor John Speer visited the senator at his farm in late June 1866, he joked that he heard Lane was ill but thought that Lane was worth a dozen dead men yet. Lane responded by paraphrasing scripture: "The pitcher is broken at the fountain. My life is ended." On July 1 he shot himself and lingered ten days before he died. Lane was a man who had lost a powerful friend and whose tumultuous world had come to an end. At his funeral the preacher said that Lane had been for Kansans "dear to our hearts as he certainly was to his friend Lincoln."[2]

Others, including former Kansas Governor Charles Robinson and, later, his widow were not so kind to Lane. Robinson was irrational about Lane, describing Lane and John Brown as being single-handedly responsible for the violence in Kansas (apparently assuming that the pro-slavery men would have willingly allowed fair elections so that their slaves and source of wealth could be taken from them). Robinson described Lane as aggressive and almost feral, "pawing the earth, beating the air and bellowing . . . like a bull of Basham." Robinson thought Lane was "destitute of principles or convictions of any kind," and that Lane corrupted all who touched him and corrupted Lincoln. "To know that this man [Lane], who was constantly plotting against the peace of his own state," Robinson wrote, "was sustained in Washington by the president was most disheartening and discouraging, and when the full history of his course relating to Kansas affairs shall be written, it will cause a stain upon his [Lincoln's] otherwise honorable name that will not out." In June 1863 Robinson reached a startling, even treasonous, conclusion: "If Genl. Lee would take the President prisoner . . . I think we would be the gainers, even though Washington was lost at the same time." Robinson's hatred of Lincoln tends to discredit his charges against Lane.[3]

The New Englanders who immigrated to the Kansas Territory had viewed slavery as a sin, while the Western men viewed it as unfair competition. The New Englanders were unable to oust slavery from Kansas with moral arguments and passive resistance, and resented the vulgar Westerners' use of violence to accomplish what the New Englanders could not do with words. The New Englanders preferred to make their man, Charles Robinson, the hero of Bleeding Kansas.

After an 1879 meeting of territorial pioneers, those who had been in the New England Emigrant Aid Company began their campaign to revise history. "It was believed necessary to destroy the characters of both Lane and Brown that the work they did in Kansas in aid of freedom might be discredited and condemned." They characterized Lane as wild and fanatical, of questionable morals and motivations, and argued that his suicide was evidence of his depravity, even insanity. The Pro-Slavers had associated Lane with the more radical abolitionist John Brown, an association that Lane did not dispute and may have encouraged when fighting pro-slavery armies in the KT and defending Lincoln in the White House, but on the issue of slavery Lane did not turn radical until late in the territorial period, and perhaps not until the Civil War. But his political enemies decided what better way to diminish Lane than to associate him with the fanatical John Brown, who had the Pottawatomie

Massacre associated with his name? Thus, late in the twentieth century, Lane and Brown were shaped into a pair of wild-eyed, antislavery killers.[4]

Robinson on the other hand, was portrayed as the calm, educated statesman, untainted by the Westerner's low morals, as his steady hand guided Kansas to freedom. But it was not Charles Robinson who rallied the North to the cause of making Kansas a free state in the summer of 1856, it was Jim Lane. It was not Robinson's name that struck terror through the ranks of the Pro-Slavers, it was Lane's. Lane became a powerful senator, Robinson a failed one-term governor. Lane warned and protected Kansas against the Price invasion of 1864. Robinson called Lane's warning a political ploy and then did nothing during the battles that resulted from the invasion. Robinson even blamed Quantrill's attack on Lawrence on Lane, and he argued that his own home was spared by Quantrill's men because Quantrill had said Robinson had done "all he could to preserve peace on the border." One has to wonder what survivors of the Lawrence massacre thought about such a statement from Robinson.[5]

But the New Englanders succeeded. In 1883 Charles Robinson wrote about Lane's killing of Gaius Jenkins in a biased account that misstated the facts. He alleged that Lane was a murderer who had shot Jenkins in cold blood while he was drawing water from the well, that Lane was acquitted in a rigged court by "partisans," and that he used his influence as a senator to win his land claim case. Of course, Lane was no longer around to correct the record. Because of these efforts, the publication in 1892 of Robinson's biased *The Kansas Conflict*, "and the later Libby Custer–like campaign of his widow, Sara, with her wealth and influence, on behalf of her husband's reputation, followers of Kansas history began considering Robinson as the hero of Bleeding Kansas, and Lane a lesser man, both in deed and character."[6]

Other less-biased contemporaries thought much of Lane. A strictly religious and moral New Englander, Isaac Goodnow, wrote: "It has been with the greatest interest that I have carefully watched the labors and the influence of this wonderful man. . . . He is the man for the hour and fills a place in our history that no other man can." Sidney Clarke, who served under Lane in the Frontier Guard and was later a United States representative from Kansas, wrote of Lane: "When other men hesitated, he went forward with faith and courage." He was, thought Clarke, a "comprehensive statesman, and his breadth of vision was as wide as the world in which he lived. . . . There was but little hypocrisy in his nature." Historian John Speer's 1896 *Life of Gen. James H. Lane: "Liberator of Kansas"* portrayed Lane as a misunderstood figure who died early and was pilloried by his enemies in later years. In Speer's view, the demonization of Lane began with the move of the federal government and Democratic Party against a Kansas resisting ratification of the Lecompton constitution, and it escalated due to Robinson's ambition and the demonization of Lane by Pro-Slavers and political rivals.[7]

Wendell Stephenson's scholarly account in 1930 portrayed Lane as a consistent loyalist for Kansas, and Stephenson believed in Lane's influence with Lincoln. Stephenson thought there was "an element of truth" in Robinson's statement that Lincoln "believes nothing from Kansas unless it is first indorsed [*sic*] by General Lane." Other historians concluded that there was a "strong attachment between these two men."[8] The rough-hewn Lane, with his "uncouth manners," was probably more like Lincoln than the educated, "austere" Dr. Robinson.[9]

More recently, historian Lloyd Lewis has argued that Lane has been treated unfairly by history. "Where a man stands in history," Lewis said, "depends upon who keeps the record; more than that, it depends upon who lives to keep the record." There were, he said, "for the sake of objectivity . . . still too many midland biographers and historians and professors blandly adopting the historical viewpoints of New England—a natural thing, perhaps, for men whose dream is to be called someday to a full professorship at Harvard." To such men, "Lane was particularly unattractive, and they failed to grasp his peculiar genius." Lewis characterized Lane as a practical man who loved Kansas and freedom, and who had much in common with his close friend, Abe Lincoln. Recent biographies of Lincoln have acknowledged that Lincoln had a good deal of the Lane-type manipulative politician in him.[10]

Lewis also focused upon an important general truth about the source of the relationship between Lane and Lincoln—Lane's usefulness to Lincoln in many ways. At the center of that was Lane's attractiveness as a person and an orator to the masses, if not to the Eastern insiders. Whether on the stump or simply sitting across the table, Lane was a memorable personality—a presence so powerful that some said they avoided him for fear of being "charmed out of their principles." Lane's presence, attraction, and personal magnetism are difficult to communicate across time. No politician, especially the embattled Lincoln, could afford to ignore that kind of charisma.[11]

Recently, Kansas historian Craig Miner speculated that there was something else between Lane and Lincoln—"a personal affinity based not only on common experience but upon a deeper understanding the two men shared."[12] Lane in the flesh was a human being of warmth and sensibility. He was married, had four children, and had experienced the death of his child, like Lincoln. The stories are legion of Lane's compassion, his kindness, his loyalty, and his disregard for financial success. "No night was too dark," John Ingalls wrote, "no storm too wild, no heat or cold too excessive, no distance too great, to delay his meteoric pilgrimages, with dilapidated garb and equipage, across the trackless prairies from convention to convention."[13]

Minor noted that an amateur psychologist might conclude that Lane's frenetic energy and frequent "low" spells might have been symptoms of what would now be called bipolar disorder. One observer described Lane as "grand, gloomy and peculiar" and felt "there always appeared to be something weighing on his mind—something which seemed to be causing trouble." The last statement corresponds to many made about Lincoln. Lincoln's law partner, William Herndon, once wrote of Lincoln that "melancholy dripped from him as he walked." A friend noted, "No element of Mr. Lincoln's character was so marked, obvious and ingrained as his mysterious and profound melancholy." Sometimes, a stranger might have thought from his behavior that Lincoln had gone insane.[14]

Gary Wills notes that such a "Hamlet"-like melancholy was—at least so long as it did not move into actual insanity—an attractive feature for Lincoln in his times, as it may have been for Lane. Historian Leverett Spring thought Lane and Lincoln both had a "noble discontent with the world," but that Lincoln, unlike Lane, had "the refuge of books and their rationalizing calm." Perhaps these two men, both homely, both tall, both carelessly dressed, and both magnetic partly due to their mysterious emotional volatility, "found an understanding, if not an attraction, in each other?"[15]

The battle over Lane's legacy continues today. Proponents of the "Lost Cause"—those who argue the Civil War was primarily fought over states' rights, not slavery—continue to demonize Lane, much like their posthumous attacks on General Ulysses S. Grant that tore his reputation to tatters. Certain of these advocates also argue that William Quantrill was a noble patriot who massacred civilians in Lawrence only in response to Lane's alleged atrocities in Osceola. They attempt to portray Quantrill as a family-loving patriot and protector of women, consistent with the myth that pro-slavery men were honorable toward their wives and women in general (at least white women). They compare this alleged standard of conduct to that of Northern men, who they generally accuse of licentious and disrespectful behavior toward women. They claim "scores of women [were] deflowered and dishonored" by Lane, and that he took "stolen silk dresses from Osceola to his many mistresses in Lawrence." I found no facts to support these claims, nor do their advocates provide factual support. It is true that Lane, like Lincoln, had marital difficulties, and that his wife filed for divorce on grounds of desertion when he was traveling about the country raising support for the Free State cause. They reconciled, however, and by all outward appearances were content at the time of his death. For all of the outrageous accusations made against Lane by his enemies, one historian concluded: "You cannot brush him aside. Always a figure of titanic accomplishments comes striding back through the fog."[16]

Other members of the Frontier Guard fared better than Lane after the war. On June 21, 1865, Major General Ed McCook married a beautiful 19-year-old heiress, Mary Thompson, from Peoria, Illinois, whose parents had left her a fortune from iron manufacturing and distilling. The next year, President Johnson appointed McCook to a four-year term as minister to Hawaii. President Johnson then appointed McCook to a four-year term as governor of the Territory of Colorado. Ed was thrilled to return to his beloved Rocky Mountains. Unfortunately, his wife died at the age of 27 after a long bout with tuberculosis. McCook remarried in Denver in 1884, and his financial interests made him one of the wealthiest men in Colorado.[17]

Tom Ewing was heavily involved in defending President Andrew Johnson against impeachment efforts and successfully lobbied the key vote against impeachment, U.S. Senator Edward G. Ross of Kansas, who served under Ewing in the 11th Kansas Regiment. In 1870 Ewing returned to his native Lancaster, Ohio, where he practiced law for the next decade and managed investments in railroad and telegraph companies. In 1879 he was defeated in a close election for governor of Ohio.[18]

In 1868 Major Leicester Walker went west with his troops to fight Indians. He was stationed at Fort Lyon, Kansas, where he served as the fort commander. In the spring of 1869, Major Walker marched his 400 men to Fort McPherson, Nebraska, and fought in several Indian battles along the Republican River. On July 1, he fought in the battle of Summit Springs, Colorado, where Chief Tall Bull was killed, along with many braves. In January 1871 Walker resigned from the army and began raising cattle on a ranch in Nebraska.[19]

In June 1873 George Smith, as second lieutenant, joined Company H in the Ninth Cavalry, which was famous for its regiments of "Buffalo Soldiers." He served in the New Mexico Territory, where he fought the Apaches. On August 19, 1881, Smith was shot twice in a battle with Apache Indians near Fort Bayard, New Mexico Territory. The battle raged from ten in the morning until two in the afternoon. His men begged him to dismount, but Smith replied, "Not while breath is still in me." Smith continued to command until he finally fell from his saddle. His African-American troops bravely fought on, and then carried his body from the battlefield.[20]

After the war, David Gordon served for 25 years on the frontier, first at Fort Leavenworth, Kansas, then Fort Lyon, Colorado, then Fort Russell, Wyoming Territory. His duties included protecting settlers, fighting Plains Indians, and performing escort duty for travelers on the eastern slope of the Rockies. It was said, "There is scarcely a stream of water on the east slope of the Rockies that he has not camped on while fighting . . . and performing his duties." He was a brigadier general on May 23, 1896, when he retired. The last living member of the Frontier Guard, he died on January 30, 1930.[21]

Clifford Arick became president of Ames Manufacturing Company, which manufactured cannons, guns, swords, bayonets, and cavalry supplies for the government. The company also cast bronze statuary and made the huge bronze doors of the Capitol in Washington. John Hatterscheidt served as U.S. Consul to Moscow until 1866, when he was replaced by Frontier Guard Philip Schuyler's nephew. John Burris returned to Olathe, Kansas, a small town 20 miles southwest of downtown Kansas City, Missouri, and resumed his law practice. In 1865 he was elected a member of the Kansas House of Representatives, of which he was soon elected as speaker. In 1866 he was elected the county attorney of Johnson County, and in 1869 he was appointed as the first judge of the Tenth Judicial District in Olathe, the seat of Johnson County.[22]

In 1866 President Andrew Johnson appointed Frontier Guard Martin Conway as consul to Marseille, France. In 1868 Addison Danford was elected attorney general of Kansas. In 1869 Orsamas Irish was appointed U.S. consul at Dresden, Germany. He was later appointed as the assistant chief of the Bureau of Engraving and Printing, and eventually he became chief of the Bureau. In 1870 Frontier Guard Phineas Hitchcock was elected as U.S. senator from Nebraska. In 1874 President Grant appointed John Jenkins secretary of Colorado. Jenkins became acting governor when Frontier Guard Ed McCook's appointment as governor was pending and before it was made final. From 1882 to 1887, Frontier Guard Zenus F. Moody served as governor of Oregon.[23]

Many members of the Frontier Guard were pioneers, explorers of unknown territories and ideas. It is perhaps not surprising, then, that many were also highly successful and creative inventors, authors, poets, and artists. Thaddeus Hyatt patented a panel made of iron and small glass discs, designed to allow natural light into the cellars under city sidewalks. He made a fortune and built factories in New York and London. In 1877 he published a book on reinforced concrete, and he later published a book on aerial navigation and the possibility of manned flight.[24]

In 1875 Frederick G. Hesse was appointed chair of industrial mechanics in the University of California. Hesse's hydraulic engineering work contributed to the early development of hydroelectric power plants in California. James Eddy built and operated "Angels Flight," an inclined cable railway in Los Angeles. William D. Nichols patented and sold the highly successful and cutting-edge "Nichols Centennial Windmill." Delano T. Smith worked to promote the idea of a railroad under Broadway in New York City, and he received a charter for the first subway in New York.[25]

John Wesley Jones was a pioneer painter who became famous for his Great Pantoscope of California, the Rocky Mountains, Salt Lake City, Nebraska, and Kansas. Addison A. Wheelock became a leading lecturer on spiritualism and editor of *American Spiritualist*. William Marsh published a highly acclaimed book, *Songs and Poems*. Joseph C. Howells was an inventor who received many patents on items such as fire-hose nozzles, secret pockets for clothing, and glass vessels. He was also an acquaintance of Walt Whitman and a member of a "Free Love Movement." Frederick Abner Brown was the agent and manager for Jane Combs, a famous stage actress. The couple married in August 1864 and traveled the world touring and performing for the next four decades. On March 8, 1893, Brown and Combs stayed at the Eldridge House in Lawrence, Kansas, where she was starring in *Bleak House* at the Lawrence Opera House.[26]

Many Kansans in the Frontier Guard remained close friends throughout their lives, and held periodic meetings and reunions after they left the White House. In March 1864, Dan Wilder married the eldest daughter of Frontier Guard member John B. Irvin. In 1912, Frontier Guard David Gordon married Belle Vedder Fleming, the sister of Frontier Guard Norton Vedder. Her mother, Indiana Hanks, was a second cousin of Abraham Lincoln's mother. Frontier Guard Cunningham Hazlett was appointed administrator of the estate of Horatio Ames, of Ames Manufacturing Company, Clifford Arick's company.

Frontier Guard Robert L. Ream played a significant role in Abraham Lincoln's legacy. Ream was poor, but his 16-year-old daughter, Vinnie, was a genius at sculpting. Ream asked Lincoln if he could introduce his daughter to him. Lincoln agreed and immediately took a liking to her. Lincoln at first objected to her request to make his bust, saying that there was no reason why anyone would want to make the likeness of so "homely a man." He finally relented because she was poor, with naught but her ambition, and he agreed to sit for what turned out to be a half hour each day for five months in 1864 so that she could complete the bust, which Lincoln apparently greatly admired.[27]

Vinnie later said: "During much of it [the time she spent with Lincoln] he stood by his window and looked sorrowfully upon the world outside. I never saw him other than sad. . . . I always felt that this was because my half-hour with him was one of relaxation when he fell into the mood that to him was natural. I am sure that the man I saw was the real Lincoln, and that a monumental melancholy always weighed upon his heart. Many times have I seen Lincoln weep. I was such a small bit of a girl and was very boyish in form and appearance that the President often said that I made him think of Willie [Lincoln's 11-year-old son, who died on February 20, 1862, likely of typhoid fever]. These thoughts were the occasion of the great tears that I saw so often course down his cheeks."[28]

After Lincoln's assassination, Congress decided to commission a marble statue of Lincoln for the rotunda in the Capitol. It asked the great artists of the world to submit models for the statue. There were scores of competitors, and among them Vinnie Ream, now 18 years of age, submitted the clay model that she had so studiously made of Lincoln in his presence. Of all the submissions, she had caught the spirit of the man, and her model appealed to those who knew Lincoln best as being the thing that would perpetuate him as he really was, and hand down to posterity the actual Lincoln.

Ream did not know that she had received the commission until one day General Sherman called upon her at her studio and asked her to accompany him to the Capitol building. When they entered one of the galleries of the Senate chamber, a dignified body rose *en masse* and waived a multitude of handkerchiefs and applauded loudly. Ms. Ream turned to General Sherman and congratulated him upon the demonstration that was being given in his honor, but the general told her that it was she who was being honored for her selection to create the statue of Lincoln.

Ream was given a room for her studio next to the one occupied by Lincoln's friend, Judge David Davis of the Supreme Court, who became her constant adviser and critic in her sacred task. She approached the work with reverence and trembling hands, and had taken the proportions of the figure from the bloodstained garments that President Lincoln had worn on his last night. She worked six years on the statue. During the time she spent in the Capitol modeling the figure, she had constant visitors, including almost all of the senators and representatives, who were deeply interested in the work.

Many former soldiers also came, some on crutches, and told how father and son, brother and brother, had met upon the battlefield, only to die in each other's arms. She heard stories of time spent in Confederate prisons, and of friends who died at Shiloh, Antietam, and in the wilderness. Her studio was lighted by a huge fireplace, one of the last ones in the Capitol. It took up one entire side of the room, and was kept blazing with great logs six feet in length. The old soldiers liked to linger there. It was their campfire, and as the glow from the blazing hearth lighted up the clay image, the name Lincoln was ever on their lips.[29]

The finished sculpture was an exact likeness of Abraham Lincoln, with a face sadder than was ever worn by man. In January 1870 the statute by Ms. Ream was unveiled in the Capitol at Washington to universal acclaim and praise. To this day, many people visiting the statue weep upon seeing Lincoln's countenance, so masterfully was it captured by this young daughter of a Frontier Guard.

Epilogue

The question of slavery's future was fought over in the Kansas Territory and the victory locally won that finally demanded the Emancipation Proclamation, and culminated in the surrender at Appomattox and the death of the hideous institution. The bloody Kansas victory was won by men from Indiana, Ohio, Illinois, New York, Pennsylvania, Massachusetts, Iowa, and Wisconsin, who risked their lives battling superior numbers of pro-slavery soldiers from South Carolina, Missouri, Alabama, Georgia, and Mississippi. Pro-slavery men had ruled the nation from its inception and seemed to be strengthening from year to year, until some of its leaders boasted in the halls of Congress that they would live to call the roll of their slaves in the shadow of Bunker Hill. No one, not even Abe Lincoln, had predicted the results or foreseen the outcome in the KT— one of the most remarkable victories in the history of human freedom.

The Kansas Territory fighting was about property rights versus human rights, about hard men and violent conflict. When Jim Lane took hold of the Free State cause, its defenders were being defeated by a fierce and merciless opponent, backed by the federal government. In the fall of 1855, when 1,200 armed men had surrounded Lawrence and were on the verge of attacking and wiping out the Free State stronghold, Lane quickly organized the outnumbered Free Staters and led them to lightning victories that struck terror in the pro-slavery men in Missouri and across the South, to the very shores of Charleston's harbor. He had the courage to speak out against the Pro-Slavers and the U.S. administration, including President Pierce, who supported the pro-slavery men, when doing so put his life in danger and subjected him to numerous assassination attempts. Assembling and leading an anti-slavery Free State legislature was treasonable insurrection, according to President Pierce and the pro-slavery Kansas Territorial governor, who ordered Lane indicted for treason. President Pierce called Lane a revolutionary—and he was—but like Sam Adams and Patrick Henry.

Lane was brave, bold, and courageous. He loved Kansas and freedom and in turn was loved by the Western men in the territory, who willingly put their lives in his hands. He charmed no more by physical beauty than did Lincoln. But he had a magnetic personality and presence, and all agreed, whether shouting in cowhide or whining in broadcloth, that Lane was a marvel as a speaker. Like Lincoln, contemporaries thought Lane's effectiveness as a speaker came from psychological insight and sympathy with common folk as a result of unerring intuition. Lane's zeal for the anti-slavery cause was all the greater because he had once been a sinner who supported Stephen Douglas's popular sovereignty view and the Kansas-Nebraska Act. None who heard him speak against the evils of slavery doubted his sincerity. The institution was, he said, "an emanation from hell."[1]

Lane's opponents charged that he was wild and reckless, but he demonstrated no recklessness during the Mexican War, or during the six years of war in Kansas, or during his defense of Abe Lincoln in the White House. Reckless men did not live long in the KT. It was a land that required courage, but intelligent courage. Lane may have purposely groomed an image as wild and reckless, because he believed it might buy his outnumbered forces time by keeping the enemy off-balance and wondering about his next move, causing them to hesitate to attack.

It is hard to imagine how the Free State men would have prevailed in Kansas without Lane. Who else would have bridged the gap between the anti-slavery Westerners and the New England abolitionists? Certainly not Charles Robinson. Who could have rallied the North to the Free State cause in the summer of 1856? Who could have taken control of and led the Free State forces? Without Lane, events in the Kansas Territory and during the first ten days of the Civil War probably would have turned out differently, and probably not for the best for Kansas or for the nation.[2]

The Jayhawks who served under Lane in the Frontier Guard earned their spurs fighting in the Kansas Territory. They were crack shots, skilled with revolvers and bowie knives. Hardship and conflict had been their daily companions for six years, keeping their bodies conditioned and their minds prepared. The frontier was a school that taught and required character and self-reliance. Nearly 50 Jayhawks had served their apprenticeship as soldiers under Lane during the bloody fighting in the KT. The KT provided practical experience in survival when facing a deadly enemy—experience that paid off in the Civil War. If Bleeding Kansas had not happened, these experienced and feared soldiers would not have existed, and Abe Lincoln may not have survived the first week of the Civil War.

Some Eastern historians have minimized the significance and violence of Bleeding Kansas, sniffing that it paled in comparison to the mass slaughter that occurred during the Civil War. Although the battles in the Kansas Territory were generally small, were the bullets less deadly? The blades less sharp?

The Frontier Guard was one of the most cohesive and experienced fighting units in the country. Many had gone to Kansas and served their apprenticeship as military men with General Lane during the bloody fighting in that border state. They valued experience over titles and credentials; they were fighters, and the Confederates wanted no part of them. The men tended to be loyal—they stuck together, and a fight with one of them was a fight with all. When the life of a man they considered a friend was threatened, they needed no more reason than that to come to his aid. They were Lincoln's band of brothers, and they were willing to die to defend their President. These self-reliant soldiers stood alone, together, to defend Abe Lincoln.

Eastern historians have ignored or trivialized the role of the Frontier Guard, describing them as "hotel guests." Far from it. They were some of the bravest, toughest, most experienced fighters in the country—as their later service during the Civil and Indian wars demonstrated. They marched up Pennsylvania Avenue one evening in the spring of 1861, a handful of men with a handful of weapons, not sure if they would live to see the sun rise over the half-finished Capitol dome. The ten days following the fall of Fort Sumter were a hinge of American history, a decisive moment at which the outcome of the Civil War hung by a thread—Lincoln could have been captured or killed, the Union lost, and slavery preserved. Theirs was a mission for heroes, and their presence saved lives. If there was any "luck" involved in the Confederate failure to attack the White House, that luck was the residue of Lane's design.[3]

Lane commanded some of the most distinguished men in the young country, including state supreme court judges, governors, and members of both houses of Congress. Nearly 100 of them distinguished themselves in military or civil service during the Civil War. Scores of them stood firm under withering fire. They had learned in Bleeding Kansas to fight dismounted, behind cover, rather than gloriously charging the enemy in the open, sabers shining. They favored Sharps rifles, repeating carbines, and Colt revolvers. Western toughness added mettle to the Union army— many of its volunteer "shopkeeper" soldiers had never fired a weapon at another man. There were no better fighters, in either Army, than men like Generals Ed McCook, Tom Ewing, and Jim Lane. The German-Americans who served in the Frontier Guard also distinguished themselves in the Union Army, along with over 216,000 of their countrymen.

The number of lawyers (about 20 of the Kansas men and almost 50 total) who served in the Frontier Guard was surprising. But describing these men as lawyers is like describing Doc Holliday as a dentist. Many of them were as skilled with a gun as with a pen. These were tough frontier lawyers who scraped out a living on the very edge of civilization. They were a new breed of fighting man—the educated soldier. In many ways, they reflected many of the soldiers who soon fought for the Union. They were men who did not depend on slaves for their livelihood. Rather, they believed that they could be successful based on the fruits of their own labor and enterprise. They were independent, quintessential Republicans of their day, much like Lincoln himself.

Many of the men came from fighting stock. At least one of them had fought in the War of 1812; at least six had fought in the Mexican War; and many of their grandfathers and fathers had fought in the American Revolution. John Burris's grandfather fought at the battle of Yorktown. His maternal grandfather was a sergeant major under General "Mad" Anthony Wayne and fought in the Indian campaigns in Ohio. George Febiger's grandfather had been a colonel in the Revolutionary War and was one of Washington's most trusted officers. Oscar Hale's grandfather was Colonel Nathan Hale of the Revolutionary War. Clark Hank's father was a soldier in the war of 1812, and his grandfather fought in the American Revolution. Zenus Moody's and Chester Thomas's grandfathers served as soldiers in the Revolutionary War. Daniel McCook had eight sons, seven of whom fought for the Union, and the oldest, Dr. Latimer McCook, tended to wounded Union soldiers on 38 battlefields. McCook and three of his sons, Robert, Daniel Jr., and Charles, died of wounds received in action during the Civil War.[4]

The diversity of the men who served in the Guard is startling. One might expect to find soldiers, abolitionists, political opportunists, and personal friends and relations of Lincoln's, but poets, writers, artists, photographers, and inventors? Lincoln was somehow able to reach and inspire them all. Lincoln's law partner, William Herndon, later recognized the remarkable friendships that kept turning up in Lincoln's life: "The bonds he [made] were destined to stand the severest of tests. His case never became so desperate but [that] a friend came out of the darkness to relieve him."[5]

Easterners typically underestimated Lincoln and Lane. Considering them crude frontiersmen, university-trained lawyers were surprised to find themselves outsmarted. Considering them unlettered, college graduates were surprised to hear them quote the Bible and Shakespeare. Considering them uncouth for telling raunchy stories, "proper" Easterners were awed by the power and poetry of their speeches. Both were different from most men, with magnetic personalities and the ability to read the moods of others and motivate them to action. They were both entertaining public speakers with emotional intelligence, eccentric geniuses in their own ways, who suffered from depression.

Lane went to Bleeding Kansas in 1855 and rode the storm to the United States Senate. Lincoln bestrode the Kansas issue in 1858 and rode the tempest to the presidency. The two interacted in significant public ways. Lane praised Lincoln on the stump in Illinois and Indiana in 1860 and at the conventions in the presidential campaigns of 1860 and 1864. Lincoln threw unprecedented patronage Lane's way after Lane's Frontier Guard saved Lincoln's life, and he supported Lane's ambition for military glory, both in the face of fierce opposition from Lane's enemies, particularly Governor Charles Robinson. Lane was Lincoln's political viceroy in Kansas and sometimes, perhaps, in the whole region west of the Missouri River. Lane early advised Lincoln to recruit and arm black soldiers, issue the Emancipation Proclamation, and institute a "total war" policy—advice that foreshadowed federal policy.

Lincoln was assassinated and became a secular saint; Lane took his own life less than a year later, and his character was assassinated by Robinson and Lane's pro-slavery enemies. Lane was deeply anguished over Lincoln's assassination. His despair was amplified when Republicans rejected Lincoln's desire that the South be forgiven rather than punished and excoriated Lane for attempting to carry out Lincoln's wishes. But it is the work a man does that matters. In a matter of less than ten years, Jim Lane was responsible for Kansas becoming a Free State and saving Abraham Lincoln's life and, with it, the Union, leading to the ultimate destruction of slavery. Either of these accomplishments should make Jim Lane a household name.

Lincoln commented once on the unfairness of written history. The "living histories," he said were the best examples of history, "but those histories are gone. They can be read no more forever. They were a fortress of strength; but, like invading foemen could never do, the silent artillery of time has done; the leveling of its walls." Lane and the Frontier Guard were casualties of time. But the lives of those who were Lincoln's companions give us a clearer and more dimensional picture of the President himself. For many, Lincoln is a marble monument, devoid of flesh and blood. But for Lane and the soldiers of the Frontier Guard, Abe was a man—they shook his huge hand, gazed into his gray eyes, felt his breath, and shared laughs over earthy stories and bawdy jokes. Those who knew and walked with Lincoln have passed away, and the last man who ever heard his voice or grasped his hand has left the earth. But by studying those close to Lincoln, we can gain insights into the great man.[6]

Abraham Lincoln may have been one of the few men who really knew and understood Lane. Lincoln and Lane were brought together not by political association and expediency, but by the ropes of a strong friendship. Asking why Lane appealed to Lincoln makes one wonder whether more should not be made of the remaining stump of the man who was once the King of Kansas and the Lion of Washington. Lane was one who "studied men and knew every avenue to the human heart . . . a man strong in his friendships and not less implacable in his hatreds," who backed words with action and risked his life for Lincoln and others. That was doubtless what Lincoln saw and admired in him.[7]

The men of the Frontier Guard were descendants of the same stock as the Kentucky riflemen who fought with Andy Jackson in the Battle of New Orleans and the Texans who fought at the Alamo. They plowed the furrows, built their shelters against the wind, and survived their own personal Alamos. They were there when the country was young and wild; they knew the smell of gunsmoke and buffalo chip fires. And they were underdogs who held off the Confederate army. Lincoln never forgot Jim Lane and his howling heroes from the KT. Perhaps we should remember them too.

The 116 Timeline

February 12, 1809	Lincoln's birth in Hardin (now LaRue) County, Kentucky.
June 22, 1814	Lane's birth in Lawrenceburg, Indiana.
1833	Lincoln admitted to Illinois bar.
1840	Lane admitted to Indiana bar.
November 29, 1841	Lane marries Mary Baldridge.
November 4, 1842	Lincoln marries Mary Todd.
1846–1848	Lane serves as a Colonel in the Mexican War.
December 6, 1847– March 4, 1849	Lincoln serves in U.S. House of Representatives.
February 22, 1847	Battle of Buena Vista (near Monterrey), Mexico.
1850–1852	Lane serves as Lt. Governor of Indiana.
December 1852– March 1854	Lane serves in U.S. House of Representatives.
May 30, 1854	Kansas-Nebraska Bill signed by President Franklin Pierce.
June 10, 1854	Isaac Cody moves his family to Salt Creek, Kansas Territory.
September 18, 1854	Isaac Cody stabbed in back, Salt Creek, Kansas Territory.
October 3, 1854	Lincoln and Douglas speak at Springfield, Ill. Hall of Representatives.
March 30, 1855	1st Kansas Territorial election—1,000 Missourians under Claiborne Jackson armed with guns, knives, and two cannons arrive in Lawrence to vote.
April 22, 1855	Lane arrives in Lawrence, Kansas Territory.

April 30, 1855	Free State man (McCrea) shoots pro-slavery man (Clark).
June 8, 1855	Free State Convention in Lawrence.
June 27, 1855	Lane is Chairman of Lawrence Democratic Convention.
July 1855	Kansas Territorial Legislature meets in Pawnee.
August 14–15, 1855	First Convention in Lawrence of Free State men—Lane takes active part; speech invoking the "caution of Washington."
September 5, 1855	Big Springs Convention—Free State party formed—resolutions reported by Lane.
September 19–20, 1855	Free State Convention at Topeka—Lane elected chairman of committee to form a Free-State Constitution.
October 1855	Delahay's newspaper office destroyed in Leavenworth, Kansas Territory.
October 6, 1855	John Brown arrives at Osawatomie, Kansas Territory.
October 9, 1855	Election of delegates to Topeka Constitutional Election.
October 23– November 11, 1855	Topeka Constitution Convention—Lane elected president on October 24 and gives speech.
November 15, 1855	Free State script issued, signed by "J.H. Lane, Chairman, Executive Committee, Kansas."
November 21, 1855	Coleman (pro-slavery) kills Dow; Sheriff Jones arrests Free State man, Branson, with whom Dow lived.
November 26, 1855	Free State men rescue Jacob Branson.
December 1855	Lane supervises construction of rifle pits and leads defense of Lawrence.
December 7, 1855	Kansas Territory Governor Shannon travels to Lawrence; consults with Lane; Barber murdered.
December 8, 1855	Gov. Shannon, Robinson, and Lane ride to pro-slavery camp at Franklin, Kansas Territory.
December 15, 1855	Barber's funeral/Lane speech calling Dow and Barber first martyrs of freedom in Kansas.

March 4, 1856	Lane elected chairman of Executive Committee of Topeka legislature.
April 1856	Lane goes to Washington to present Kansas Memorial.
April 19, 1856	Sheriff Jones shot.
May 5, 1856	Kansas Territory Judge LeCompte indicts Free State leaders, including Lane, Robinson, and Parrott.
May 10, 1856	Charles Robinson arrested by pro-slavery officials.
May 19–20, 1856	Senator Sumner's "Crime against Kansas" Speech.
May 21, 1856	Pro-slavery militia sack and burn Lawrence.
May 22, 1856	Senator Sumner is beaten nearly to death.
May 24, 1856	John Brown's men kill five pro-slavery men along Pottawatomie Creek.
May 26, 1856	Battle of Black Jack, Kansas Territory.
May 29, 1856	Lincoln's "Lost Speech" at Bloomington, Illinois.
May 31, 1856	Lane gives speech in Chicago courthouse square "fresh from the smoking ruins of Lawrence."
May 31, 1856	Lincoln writes letter from Springfield, Illinois, to Joshua Speed: "that Kansas will form a slave Constitution and, with it will ask to be admitted into the Union, I take to be an already settled question."
Summer 1856	Pro-slavery men blockade travel on the Missouri River by Free State men and seize Free State arms and supplies.
June 5, 1856	John Brown releases his prisoners captured at Black Jack to Col. Edwin V. Sumner and Lt. J.E.B. Stuart.
June 6, 1856	Brown's Station is burned to the ground.
July 4, 1856	Col. Edwin V. "Bull" Sumner disperses Free State Legislature.

August 7, 1856	Lane leads 400 settlers into Kansas down Lane Trail from Iowa through Nebraska City to Topeka.
August 12, 1856	Lane's men attack Fort Franklin.
August 15, 1856	Lane's men attack Fort Sanders.
August 16, 1856	Lane's men attack Fort Titus.
August 30, 1856	Battle of Osawatomie, Kansas Territory.
September 1, 1856	Pro-slavery men attack Phillips brothers in Leavenworth; William Phillips is murdered by pro-slavery men; Jared Phillips loses his arm.
September 14, 1856	2,700 Southerners threatening Lawrence.
September 16, 1856	Blanton's letter regarding scalping by pro-slavery men, fog of smoke from burning houses.
October 10, 1856	Federal soldiers stop Daniels' expedition of 200 men and confiscate their weapons.
February 1857	Joseph Cody moves his family to Grasshopper Falls, Kansas Territory.
March 6, 1857	U.S. Supreme Court decides *Dred Scott* case, ruling that Mr. Scott, a slave who had spent part of his life in a non-slave territory, could not sue for his freedom because African-Americans were not citizens of the United States.
March 10, 1857	Isaac Cody dies of pneumonia; stab wounds suffered earlier listed as contributing factors.
July 18, 1857	Topeka Convention passes General Order No. 1 authorizing Jim Lane to organize militia companies in order to protect ballot boxes on election day.
August 26, 1857	Free State Convention at Grasshopper Falls (today Valley Falls), Kansas Territory; Lane appointed to Executive Committee.
September 7, 1857	Lecompton Constitutional Convention drafts Lecompton Constitution, which sustained slavery in the state and protected the rights of slave owners.

September 15–16, 1857	Free State Convention at Topeka; Lane serves as president.
November 14, 1857	Lane's Leavenworth speech, "Kansas is a slave state now."
December 3, 1857	Lawrence Convention; Lane chairman of Resolutions Committee.
December 7, 1857	Kansas Territorial Legislature makes James Lane a major general in the Territorial Militia.
December 17, 1857	Lane enrolls about 150 men as first members of Kansas Jayhawks at Sugar Mound (now Mound City), Kansas.
January 1, 1858	Lane to speak in Atchison/Free State men ride to Atchison, Kansas.
January 4, 1858	Kansas Territory elections in which Lecompton Constitution rejected by voters; Ewing monitors Kickapoo voting.
January 5, 1858	Free State men capture Kickapoo cannon.
March 25, 1858	Lane is president of Leavenworth Constitutional Convention.
May 1858	Lane enters into law partnership with James Christian in Lawrence, Kansas.
May 19, 1858	Massacre on Marais des Cygnes; five Free State men murdered.
June 3, 1858	Lane shoots Gaius Jenkins.
June 6, 1858	Lincoln's "House Divided" speech in Springfield, Illinois.
July 1858	Lane's preliminary hearing regarding Gaius Jenkins' death, charges dismissed on grounds of self-defense.
August 1858	Kansas Election—Lecompton Constitution defeated.
August 21, 1858	Lincoln begins first of seven debates with Stephen Douglas at Ottawa, Illinois.
November 1858	Lincoln loses Illinois U.S. Senate election to Stephen A. Douglas.

March 9, 1859	Leavenworth and Pike Peak's Express (predecessor to Pony Express) makes its first run.
May 18, 1859	Kansas Republican Convention at Osawatomie, Kansas Territory.
July 29, 1859	Wyandotte Constitution.
October 15, 1859	Lincoln invited to speak in New York City.
October 16, 1859	John Brown's raid on Harpers Ferry.
November, 1859	Lincoln's letter agreeing to speak in Kansas Territory.
December 1, 1859	Lincoln arrives in Elwood, Kansas Territory.
December 2, 1859	John Brown hung.
December 4, 1859	Lincoln meets Lane in Leavenworth.
December 7, 1859	Lincoln leaves Kansas Territory.
December 21, 1859	Republican National Committee meeting to decide on location for Republican Presidential Convention.
February 27, 1860	Lincoln's Cooper Union speech in New York City.
May 13, 1860	Republican Presidential Convention in Chicago.
November 1860	Lincoln elected president.
January 2, 1861	Lane's letter to Lincoln offering 1,000 Kansans to protect Lincoln.
January 29, 1861	Kansas admitted to Union.
February 11, 1861	Lincoln leaves Springfield, Illinois, on "Lincoln Express."
February 23, 1861	President-elect Lincoln arrives at the Baltimore & Ohio Depot.
March 4, 1861	President Lincoln's inauguration.
April 4, 1861	Lane elected as one of Kansas' first U.S. senators.
April 8, 1861	Stockton's letter to Lincoln offering 1,000 Kansas troops.
April 12, 1861	Rebels attack Ft. Sumter.
April 13, 1861	Union troops at Ft. Sumter surrender; Lane arrives in Washington, speaks to crowd outside Willard's Hotel.

April 15, 1861	Lincoln calls for 75,000 federal troops.
April 17, 1861	Virginia secedes.
April 18, 1861	Francis P. Blair offers the command of the Army to Colonel Robert E. Lee.
April 18, 1861	Rebels attack federal armory at Harpers Ferry, Virginia.
April 18, 1861	Lincoln meets with Lane at the White House.
April 18, 1861	Frontier Guard formed at Willard's Hotel.
April 18, 1861	Frontier Guard marches to White House and camps in East Room.
April 19, 1861	6th Massachusetts Regiment is attacked in Boston.
April 20, 1861	Rebels attack Gosport Navy Yard.
April 20, 1861	Rebels seize Liberty, Missouri, arsenal.
April 21–22, 1861	Frontier Guard captures rebel flag at Falls Church, Virginia.
April 23, 1861	Hay hears Lane at dinner: Baltimore will be open Thursday or "Baltimore will be laid in ashes."
April 25, 1861	Seventh New York regiment arrives in Washington.
April 25, 1861	Sixth Massachusetts regiment arrives at Washington's rail depot after fighting a mob in the streets of Baltimore.
April 27, 1861	Lincoln's speech to Frontier Guard; Lane writes to Cameron that the need for the Frontier Guard has passed.
April 29, 1861	Lane in Nicolay's room looking at rebel flag in Alexandria and says the rebels have set North "howling for blood."
May 13, 1861	Frontier Guard disbanded.
May 24, 1861	Ellsworth dies trying to take rebel flag from Marshal House, Alexandria, Virginia.
May 24, 1861	Union troops seize Arlington Heights and Alexandria.
June 18, 1861	Lane confers with Lincoln.

June 20, 1861	Lincoln wrote to Cameron: 'We'd better appoint him [Lane] a brigadier general of volunteers today."
July 16, 1861	Union forces begin 25-mile march from Washington to Bull Run.
July 21, 1861	Confederate Army defeats Union Army at Bull Run, Virginia.
July 22, 1861	Defeated Union Army flees back to Washington.
August 3, 1861	Rebel spy, Mrs. Greenhow, arrested.
August 15, 1861	Lane confers with Lincoln.
August 24, 1861	Washington's Mayor Berret arrested for disloyalty.
September 1, 1861	Lane's general order barring taking of loyal citizens' goods.
September 17, 1861	Lane issues General Order 4, "No Jay-hawking shall be allowed."
September 22, 1861	Lane's brigade (Montgomery) burns Osceola (1860 census shows 40 dwellings and 265 white inhabitants).
September 27, 1861	Lincoln's telegraph: "What news from up river?"
October 8, 1861	Lane's speech at Stockton's Hall, Leavenworth— slavery could not survive march of federal army; lay waste the property of traitors; war could not be won "if army marches through slave states like a boat goes through a flock of ducks."
November 1, 1861	General Winfield Scott retires as Army general-in-chief, replaced by General McClellan.
December 18, 1861	Lane appointed brigadier general of volunteers.
Winter of 1861–1862	Union Army camps near Washington, prepares for battle, and builds a circle of forts around the city.
January 17–23, 1862	Lane confers with Lincoln.
February 20, 1862	Lincoln's son Willie dies.
March 21, 1862	Lane's appointment as general cancelled.
April 16, 1862	Act of Congress ends slavery in the District of Columbia.

August 4, 1862	Lane opens recruiting office in Leavenworth for 1st and 2nd Colored Infantry.
August 23, 1862	Stanton writes Lane that black troops could not be accepted into service.
August 24, 1862	*Leavenworth Daily Times* article calls for guerillas to be exterminated.
August 28–30, 1862	Second Battle of Bull Run.
September 5, 1862	General Lee's army turns away from Washington and invades Maryland, seizing Frederick.
September 6, 1862	Under General McClellan, the Army of the Potomac marches north through Washington and Rockville, Maryland, in pursuit of Lee's Army.
September 6, 1862	Lane meets with Lincoln.
September 17, 1862	General McClellan wins battle against Lee at Antietam Creek near Sharpsburg, Maryland.
September 22, 1862	President Lincoln issues the preliminary Emancipation Proclamation.
October 29, 1862	1st Kansas Colored Infantry fights rebels at Island Mound, Missouri.
November 5, 1862	Lincoln removes General McClellan from command. General Burnside takes his place.
December 13, 1862	Army of the Potomac under General Burnside defeated at Battle of Fredericksburg, Virginia.
January 1, 1863	Emancipation Proclamation takes effect.
January 25, 1863	General Hooker replaces General Burnside as commander of the Army of the Potomac.
May 4, 1863	General Lee's army again defeats the Army of the Potomac with great losses at Chancellorsville, Virginia.
June 3, 1863	Lee's army begins invasion of the North.
July 3, 1863	Army of the Potomac under General Meade defeats Lee's army at Gettysburg.
August 21, 1863	Quantrill's massacre of civilians at Lawrence, Kansas.

August 22, 1863	Hay tells Lincoln that Quantrill will murder Lane if he catches him.
September 15, 1863	President Lincoln suspends writ of habeas corpus throughout the Union.
November 19, 1853	Gettysburg Address.
March 12, 1864	Lt. General Grant named general-in-chief of Union Army.
March 30, 1864	Lane's speech at Cooper Institute to open Lincoln's reelection campaign.
April 13, 1864	Lane tells Hay that Lincoln must guard against assassination.
April 24–5, 1864	Lane at White House.
May 5–8, 1864	Great battle occurs between the armies of Lee and Grant in the Virginia Wilderness.
May 8–19, 1864	Armies collide again in another large battle near Spotsylvania Court House.
June 3, 1864	Lee's and Grant's armies fight at Cold Harbor; Grant fails to break through, suffers large losses.
June 6, 1864	Lane consults at length with Lincoln; Lane's speech for Lincoln at the Republican National Convention.
June 7, 1864	Republican Convention nominates Lincoln for a second term.
September 2, 1864	Atlanta falls to General Sherman's army.
September 27, 1864	Battle of Pilot Knob, Missouri.
October 24, 1864	Battle of Westport, Missouri.
November 8, 1864	Lincoln reelected President.
November 15, 1864	General Sherman's army leaves Atlanta—starts march through Georgia.
December 21, 1864	General Sherman captures Savannah, Georgia.
December 22, 1864	Lane meets with Lincoln.
January 31, 1865	The Thirteenth Amendment abolishing slavery passes Congress.
February 3, 1865	Peace Conference between Lincoln and Confederate Commissioners held on *River Queen* in Hampton Roads, Virginia.

March 4, 1865	President Lincoln's second inauguration.
April 2, 1865	General Grant breaks through Confederate line at Petersburg.
April 3, 1865	Richmond falls; President Davis flees.
April 9, 1865	General Lee surrenders his army at Appomattox Court House.
April 14, 1865	President Lincoln shot at Ford's Theater.
April 15, 1865	President Lincoln dies in early morning at the Petersen House across the street from Ford's Theater. Vice President Andrew Johnson sworn in as president.
April 19, 1865	Funeral of President Lincoln held in East Room of White House.
July 1, 1866	Lane shoots himself.
July 11, 1866	Lane's death.

Bibliography

BOOKS

Adams, James O., ed., *The History of Salisbury, New Hampshire*. Manchester, N.H.: William E Moore, 1890.

Andreas, A.T. *History of the State of Kansas*. Chicago: Western Historical Company, 1883.

Andreas, A.T. *History of the State of Nebraska*. Chicago: Western Historical Company, 1882.

Ayres, Carol D. *Lincoln and Kansas: Partnership for Freedom*. Lawrence, Kan.: Sunflower University Press, 2001.

Bailes, Kendall E. *Rider on the Wind: Jim Lane and Kansas*. Shawnee Mission, Kan.: Wagon Wheel Press, 1962.

Ballou, Adin. *An Elaborate History and Genealogy of the Ballous in America*. Providence, R.I.: E. L. Frederick & Son, 1888.

Bancroft, Hubert Howe. *History of Nevada, Colorado and Wyoming: 1540-1888*. San Francisco: History Co., 1890.

Banasik, Michael E., ed. *Reluctant Cannoneer: The Diary of Robert T. McMahon of the 25th Independent Ohio Light Artillery*. Iowa City, Iowa: Press of the Camp Pope, 2000.

Baron, Frank. *Abraham Lincoln and the German Immigrants: Turners and Forty-Eighters*, sup. vol. 4. Topeka, Kan.: Society for German-American Studies, 2012.

Barry, Louise. *Beginning of the West: Annals of the Kansas Gateway to the American West*. Topeka, Kan.: Kansas Historical Society, 1972.

Basler, Roy. *The Collected Works of Abraham Lincoln*, 8 vols. New Brunswick, N.J.: Rutgers University Press, 1953.

Beebe, Levi. *A Sketch of the Samuel Phillips Family.* Pittsfield, Mass.: Sun Printing Co., 1892.

Benedict, Bryce. *Jayhawkers: The Civil War Brigade of James Henry Lane.* Norman: University of Oklahoma Press, 2009.

Black, Robert C. *The Railroads of the Confederacy.* Chapel Hill: University of North Carolina Press, 1952.

Blackmar, Frank W., ed. *Kansas: A Cyclopedia of State History, Embracing Events, Institutions, Industries, Counties, Cities, Towns, Prominent Persons, Etc.,* Vol. I. Chicago: Standard Publishing Co., 1912.

———. *The Life of Charles Robinson.* Topeka, Kan.: Crane & Co., 1902.

Borit, G. S., ed. *Why the Confederacy Lost the Civil War.* New York: Oxford University Press, 1992.

Brownlee, Richard S. *Gray Ghosts of the Confederacy: Guerrilla Warfare in the West,* 1861-1865. Baton Rouge, La.: Louisiana State University Press, 1958.

Burke, Diana M. *On Slavery's Border: Missouri's Small Slave-Holding Households,* 1815-1865. Athens, Ga.: University of Georgia Press, 2010.

Burke, W.S. *Official Military History of Kansas Regiments during War for the Suppression of the Great Rebellion.* Leavenworth, Kan., 1870.

Burlingame, Michael. *Abraham Lincoln: A Life.* Baltimore: Johns Hopkins University Press, 2008.

———. Michael Burlingame and John R. T. Ettlinger, eds. *Inside Lincoln's White House: The Complete Civil War Diary of John Hay.* Carbondale, Ill.: Southern Illinois Press, 1999.

———. Michael Burlingame, ed. *Lincoln's Journalist: John Hay's Anonymous Writings for the Press, 1860-65* (Carbondale, Ill.: Southern Illinois University Press, 1998.

———. Michael Burlingame, John R. Turner Ettlinger, eds. *Inside Lincoln's White House: The Complete Civil War Diary of John Hay.* Carbondale, Ill.: Southern Illinois University Press, 1997.

———. *The Inner World of Abraham Lincoln,* Urbana, Ill.: University of Illinois Press, 1994.

Carter, Robert A. *Buffalo Bill Cody: The Man Behind the Legend.* New York: John Wiley & Sons, 2000.

Castel, Albert E. *Civil War Kansas: Reaping the Whirlwind*. Lawrence, Kan.: University of Kansas Press, 1997.

―――. *William Clarke Quantrill: His Life and Times*. New York: Frederick Fell, 1962.

―――. *A Frontier State at War: Kansas, 1861-1865*. Ithaca, N.Y.: Cornell University Press, 1958.

――― and Thomas Goodrich. *Bloody Bill Anderson: The Short, Savage Life of a Civil War Guerrilla*. Mechanicsburg, Pa.: Stackpole Books, 1998.

Collins, Robert. *Jim Lane: Scandal, Statesman, Kansan*. Gretna, Louisiana: Pelican Publishing, 2007.

Connolly, Thomas L. *Marble Man: Robert E. Lee and His Image in American Society*. Baton Rouge, La.: Louisiana State University Press, 1978.

Connelly, William E. *James Henry Lane, the Grim Chieftain of Kansas*. Topeka, Kan.: Crane & Co., 1899.

Cordley, Richard. *History of Lawrence*. Lawrence, Kan.: Lawrence Journal Press, 1895.

Crittenden, Lucius E. *Recollections of Abraham Lincoln and His Administration*. New York: Harper's Brothers, 1891.

―――. *Invisible Siege: The Journal of Lucius E. Crittenden*, April 15, 1861–July 14, 1861. San Diego: Americana Exchange Press, 1969.

Cutler, William G. *History of the State of Kansas*. Chicago: A.T. Andreas, 1883.

Davis, William C. *Brother against Brother: The War Begins*. Alexandria, Va.: Time Life Books, 1983.

Donald, David Herbert. *Lincoln*. New York: Simon & Schuster, 1995.

―――. *Why the North Won the Civil War*. New York: Simon & Schuster, 1960, 1996.

Drake, Madison J. *History of the Ninth New Jersey Volunteers*. Elizabeth, N.J.: Journal Printing House, 1889.

Duncan, Patricia A. *Tallgrass Prairie: The Inland Sea*. Kansas City, Mo.: The Lowell Press, 1978.

Edwards, John N. *Noted Guerrillas, or the Warfare of the Border*. St. Louis: H. W. Brand & Co., 1879.

————. *Shelby and His Men, the War in the West.* Cincinnati, Ohio: Miami Printing and Publishing Co., 1867.

Edwards, William C. *The Lincoln Assassination—The Rewards Files.* Google E-Book, 2012.

Ellis, Mark R. *Law and Order in Buffalo Bills Country: Legal Culture and Community on the Great Plains, 1867-1910.* Lincoln: University of Nebraska Press, 2007.

Etcheson, Nicole. *Bleeding Kansas: Contested Liberty in the Civil War Era.* Lawrence, Kan.: University Press of Kansas, 2004.

Etulain, Richard W. *Lincoln Looks West: From the Mississippi to the Pacific.* Carbondale, Ill.: Southern Illinois University Press, 2010.

Fellman, Michael. *Inside War: The Guerrilla Conflict in Missouri During the American Civil War.* New York: Oxford University Press, 1989.

————. *Citizen Sherman: A Life of William Tecumseh Sherman.* New York: Random House, 1995.

Fehrenbacher, Donald E. *Collected Works of Abraham Lincoln.* Stanford, Cal.: Stanford University Press, 1996.

————. *Abraham Lincoln, Speeches and Writings.* Library of America, 1989.

Ferguson, Ernest B. *Freedom Rising: Washington in the Civil War.* New York: Vintage Books, 2004.

Fish, Reeder M. *The Grim Chieftain of Kansas.* Clarion Book Print, 1885.

Flood, Charles Bracelen. *Grant and Sherman.* New York: Farrar, Straus & Giroux, 2005.

Foote, Shelby. *The Civil War: A Narrative.* 3 vols. New York: Random House, 1974.

Foster, Gaines M. *Ghosts of the Confederacy: Defeat, The Lost Cause, and The Emergence of the New South, 1865 to 1913.* New York: Oxford University Press, 1987.

Furnas, J. C. *The Americans: A Social History of the United States, 1587-1914.* New York: G. P. Putnam's Sons, 1969.

Gallagher, Gary W. & John T. Nolan eds. *The Myth of the Lost Cause and Civil War History.* Bloomington, Ind.: Indiana University Press, 2000.

Galloway, John D. *The First Transcontinental Railroad.* New York: Dorset, 1889.

Gates, Theodore B. *The War of the Rebellion.* New York: P.F. McBreen, 1884.

Gilmore, Donald L. *Civil War on the Missouri-Kansas Border.* Gretna: Pelican Publishing Co., 2006.

Glaab, Charles N. *Kansas City and the Railroads.* Lawrence, Kan.: University of Kansas Press, 1993.

Goodheart, Adam. *1861: The Civil War Awakening.* New York: Vintage Books, 2011.

Goodrich, Debra. *The Civil War in Kansas: Ten Years of Turmoil.* Charleston, S.C.: The History Press, 2012.

Goodrich, Thomas. *Black Flag: Guerrilla Warfare on the Western Border, 1861-1865.* Bloomington, Ind.: Indiana University Press, 1995.

———. *War to the Knife: Bleeding Kansas, 1854-1861.* Mechanicsburg, Pa.: Stackpole Books, 1998.

———. *Bloody Dawn: The Story of the Lawrence Massacre.* Kent, Ohio: Kent State University Press, 1991.

Goodwin, Doris K. *Team of Rivals.* New York: Simon & Schuster, 2005.

Grant, U. S. *Personal Memoirs.* New York: Penguin Putnam, 1999: C.L. Webster, 1885.

Gwynne, S. C. *Empire of the Summer Moon: Quanah Parker and the Rise and Fall of the Comanches, The Most Powerful Indian Tribe in American History.* New York: Scribner, 2010.

Hall, Henry. *America's Successful Men of Affairs: The City of New York.* New York: New York Tribune, 1895.

Hay, John. *Inside Lincoln's White House.* Carbondale: Southern Ill. Univ. Press, 1997.

Hinton, Richard Josiah. *John Brown and His Men.* Harpers Ferry: Funk & Wagner Co.,, 1894.

Hoeflich, Michael H. *Justice on the Prairie: 150 Years of the Federal District Court of Kansas.* Kansas City, Mo.: Rockhill Books, 2011.

Hoffer, William James. *The Caning of Charles Sumner: Honor, Idealism and the Origins of the Civil War.* Baltimore: Johns Hopkins University Press, 2010.

Holzer, Harold. *Lincoln at Cooper Union: The Speech That Made Abraham Lincoln President.* New York: Simon & Schuster, 2004.

————. *Abraham Lincoln as I Knew Him: Gossip, Tributes and Revelations from His Best Friends and Worst Enemies.* Chapel Hill, N.C.: Algonquin, 1999.

Horan, James D. *The Authentic Wild West: The Lawmen.* New York: Crown Publishers, Inc., 1980.

Horton, James Oliver & Lois E. eds. *Slavery and Public History: The Tough Stuff of American Memory* (Chapel Hill: University of North Carolina Press, 2006).

Hunter, Lewis C. *Steamboats on the Western Rivers: An Economic and Technological History.* New York: Dover Publications, Inc., 1949.

Hurt, R. Douglas. *Agriculture and Slavery in Missouri's Little Dixie.* Columbia, Mo.: University of Missouri Press, 1992.

Jenkins, Warren Y. *The Jenkins, Boone, and Lincoln Family Records.* No publisher listed, 1925.

Johnson, Mark Wells. *That Brave Body of Men: The U.S. Regular Infantry and the Civil War in the West.* Cambridge, Mass.: Da Capo Press, 2003.

Kagen, Neil, ed. *Eyewitness to the Civil War.* Washington, D.C.: National Geographic Society, 2007.

Kansas City Historical Company. *History of Johnson County, Missouri.* Kansas City, Mo.: Kansas City Historical Co., 1887.

Kaplan, Fred. *Lincoln: The Biography of a Writer.* New York: Harper Collins Publishing, 2008.

Keckley, Elizabeth. *Behind the Scenes: or, Thirty Years a Slave, and Four Years in the White House.* G. W. Carlton & Co.: 1868.

Klein, Maury. *Union Pacific: The Birth of a Railroad.* New York: Doubleday & Co. Inc., 1987.

Klein, Michael J. *The Baltimore Plot: The First Assassination Conspiracy, 1860-1861.* Yardley, Pa.: Westholme Publishing, 2008.

Lee, Richard McGowan. *Mr. Lincoln's City: An Illustrated Guide to the Civil War Sites of Washington.* EPM Publications, 1981.

Leopold, Patrick. *Gray's Doniphan County History: A Record of the Happenings of Half a Hundred Years.* Roycroft Press, 1905.

Leslie, Edward E. *The Devil Knows How to Ride: The True Story of William Clarke Quantrill and His Confederate Raiders.* New York: Random House, 1996.

Lockwood, John and Charles. *Siege of Washington: The Untold Story of the Twelve Days That Shook the Union.* New York: Oxford University Press, 2011.

Luthin, Reinhard H. *The First Lincoln Campaign.* Gloucester, Mass.: P. Smith, 1964.

Madison, James. *Notes of Debates in the Federal Convention of 1787.* New York: W.W. Norton, 1966.

Malin, John C. *John Brown and the Legend of Fifty-Six.* Philadelphia: American Philadelphia Society, 1942.

Mansfield, Edward D. *The Life and Services of Lieut. General Scott.* New York: N.C. Miller, 1862.

Masters, Edgar Lee. *Lincoln, the Man.* New York: Dodd, Mead, 1931.

McCandless, Perry. *A History of Missouri.* Columbia, Mo.: University of Missouri Press, 1972.

McClure, Alexander Kelly. *Abraham Lincoln and Men of War-Times: Some Personal Recollections of War and Politics during the Lincoln Administration.* New York: Times Publishing Co., 1892.

McCullough, David. *Truman.* New York: Simon & Schuster, 1992.

McDonald, Will H. *An Illustrated History of Lincoln County, Nebraska and Her People.* American Historical Society, 1920.

McPherson, James M. *The War That Forged a Nation: Why the Civil War Still Matters.* New York: Oxford University Press, 2015.

———. *Abraham Lincoln and the Second American Revolution.* New York: Oxford University Press, 1991.

———. *Battle Cry of Freedom: The Civil War Era.* New York: Oxford University Press, 1988.

———. *Ordeal by Fire.* New York: Alfred A. Knopf, 1982.

Miers, Earl Schenck. *Lincoln, Day by Day.* Lincoln Sesquicentennial Commission, 1960.

Miner, Craig. *Seeding Civil War: Kansas in the National News 1854-58.* Lawrence, Kan.: University Press of Kansas, 2008.

———. *Kansas: The History of the Sunflower State, 1854-2000.* Lawrence, Kan.: University Press of Kansas, 2002.

Mettendorf, Ernest. *Between Triumph and Disaster: The History of the 46th New York Infantry, 1861 to 1865.* Eden, New York: self-published, 2012.

Monaghan, Jay. *The Civil War on the Western Border, 1854-1865*. Boston: Little, Brown, 1955.

Morgans, James Patrick. *John Todd and the Underground Railroad: Biography of an Iowa Abolitionist*. McFarland, 2006.

Moulton, Gary E., ed., *The Definitive Journals of Lewis & Clark*. Lincoln, Neb.: University of Nebraska Press, 1986.

Mountcastle, Clay. *Punitive War: Confederate Guerrillas and Union Reprisals*. Lawrence, Kan.: University Press of Kansas, 2009.

Muehlberger, James P. *The Lost Cause: The Trials of Frank and Jesse James*. Yardley, Pa.: Westholme Publishing, LLC, 2015.

Nash, Gerald D. *Creating the West: Historical Interpretations of 1890-1990*. Albuquerque: University of New Mexico Press, 1991.

National Historical Company. *History of Clay and Platte Counties, Missouri*. St. Louis: National Historical Co., 1885.

Neely, Jeremy: *The Border Between Them: Violence and Reconciliation on the Kansas-Missouri Line*. Columbia, Mo.: University of Missouri Press, 2007.

Nichols, Bruce. *Guerrilla Warfare in Civil War Missouri, 1862*. Jefferson, Mo.: McFarland & Co., Inc., 2004.

Nicolay, Helen. *Lincoln's Secretary: A Biography of John G. Nicolay*. New York: Longmans, Green, 1949.

Nicolay, John. *The Outbreak of the Rebellion*. New York: Scribner's, 1882.

Nicolay, John G. & John Hay, *Abraham Lincoln: A History*. New York: Century Co., 1890.

Nolan, Frederick. *The Lincoln County War: A Documentary History*. Sunstone Press, 2009.

Oates, Stephen D. *To Purge This Land with Blood: A Biography of John Brown*. Amherst, Mass.: University of Massachusetts Press, 1970.

———. *The Whirlwind of War: Voices of the Storm, 1861-1865*. New York: Harper Collins, 1998.

Palmquist, Peter E. *Pioneer Photographers of the Far West: A Biographical Dictionary, 1840-1865*. Stanford University Press, 2002.

Paxton, W.M. *Annals of Platte County, Missouri*. Kansas City, Mo.: Ramfre Press, 1965, *reprint*.

Phillips, Williams. *The Conquest of Kansas, by Missouri and Her Allies*. Boston: Phillips, Sampson & Co., 1856.

Pierce, Frank H. III., *The Washington Saengerbund, A History of German Song and German Culture in the Nation's Capital.* Washington: The Washington Saengerbund, 1981.

Piston, William Garrett. *Wilson's Creek.* Charlotte: North Carolina University Press, 2000.

Podair, Jerald E. *Dictionary of Virginia Biography*, Vol. 3, edited by Sara B. Bearss et al. Richmond, Va.: Library of Virginia, 2006.

Potter, David M. *The Impending Crisis: America Before the Civil War, 1848-1861.* New York: Harper Perennial, 2011.

Prentice, Noble L. *History of Kansas.* Topeka, Kan.: 1899.

Puelo, Stephen. *The Caning: The Assault That Drove America to Civil War.* Yardley, Penn.: Westholme Publishing, 2012.

Quiett, Glenn Chesney. *They Built the West: An Epic of Rails and Cities*, New York: D. Appleton-Century Co., 1934.

Reynolds, David S. *John Brown, Abolitionist: The Man Who Killed Slavery, Sparked the Civil War, and Seeded Civil Rights.* New York: Vintage Books, 2005.

Robinson, Charles. *The Kansas Conflict.* New York: Harper & Brothers, 1892.

Rosa, Joseph G. *Wild Bill Hickok: Sharpshooter and U.S. Marshal of the Wild West.* New York: The Rosen Publishing Group, 2004.

Rossbach, Jeffrey. *Ambivalent Conspirators: John Brown, the Secret Six, and a Theory of Slave Violence.* Philadelphia: University of Pennsylvania Press, 1982.

Russell, William Howard. *My Diary North and South.* Boston: H.P. Burnham, 1863.

Saul, Norman E. *Concord and Conflict: The U.S. and Russia, 1867-1914.* University of Kansas Press, 1966.

Scott, William Force. *The Story of a Cavalry Regiment: The Career of the Fourth Iowa Veteran Volunteers; From Kansas to Georgia, 1861-1865.* New York: G. P. Putnam's Sons, 1893.

Sherman, William T. *Memoirs of General William T. Sherman.* New York: D. Appleton & Co., 1875.

Shumway, Grant Lee. *History of Western Nebraska and Its People.* Western Publishing & Engraving Co., 1918.

Slotkin, Richard. *Gunfighter Nation: The Myth of the Gunfighter in 20th Century America*. New York: Harper Perennial, 1993.

Smith, Ronald, D. *Thomas Ewing Jr.: Frontier Lawyer and Civil War General*. Columbia, Mo.: University of Missouri Press, 2008.

Speer, John. *Life of General James H. Lane: The Liberator of Kansas*. Garden City, Kan.: Speer 1896.

Spencer, Thomas M. *Power on Parade, 1877-1995*. Columbia, Mo.: University of Missouri Press, 2000.

Spring, Leverett W. *Kansas*. Boston: Houghton Mifflin, 1890.

Spurgeon, Ian Michael. *Soldiers in the Army of Freedom: The First Kansas Colored, the Civil War's First African-American Combat Unit*. Norman, Okla.: University of Oklahoma Press, 2014.

———. *Man of Douglas, Man of Lincoln: The Political Odyssey of James H. Lane*. Columbia, Mo.: University of Missouri Press, 2008.

Stauffer, John. *Giants: The Parallel Lives of Frederick Douglass and Abraham Lincoln*. New York: Grand Central Publishing, 2008.

Steiner, Mark E. *An Honest Calling: The Law Practice of Abraham Lincoln*. DeKalb, Ill.: Northern Illinois University Press, 2006.

Stephenson, Wendell H. *Publications of the Kansas State Historical Society Embracing the Political Career of General James H. Lane*, Vol. III. Topeka, Kan.: Kansas State Printing, 1930.

Sutherland, Daniel E. *A Savage Conflict: The Decisive Role of Guerrillas in the Civil War*. Charlotte, N.C.: University of North Carolina Press, 2009.

Sword, Wiley. *The Historic Henry Rifle: Oliver Winchester's Famous Civil War Repeater*. Lincoln, R.I.: Andrew Mowbray, 2002.

Tarbell, Ida. *Life of Lincoln*. New York: Doubleday & McClure, 1903.

Tate, Thomas K. *Under the Iron Eyelids: A Biography of James Henry Burton, Armorer to the Nations*. Google E-Book.

Thompson, Heber S. *The First Defenders*. n.p.; First Defenders Association, 1910.

Tripp, C.A. *The Intimate World of Abraham Lincoln*. New York: Free Press, 2005.

Twain, Mark. *Life on the Mississippi*. New York: Penguin, 1984. (Orig. pub. 1883.)

The United States Biographical Dictionary, Kansas Volume. Chicago: S. Lewis & Co., 1879.

Villard, Henry. *Memoirs of Henry Villard, Journalist and Financier, 1835-1900*. Boston: Houghton Mifflin, 1904.

Villard, Oswald Garrison. *John Brown 1800-1859: A Biography Fifty Years After*. Boston: Riverside Press, 1910.

Von Drehl, David. *Rise To Greatness: Abraham Lincoln and America's Most Perilous Year*. New York: Henry Holt, 2012.

Waugh, John C. *Reelecting Lincoln: The Battle for the 1864 Presidency*. New York: Crown Publishers, Inc., 1992.

————. *Lincoln and McClellan: The Troubled Relationship between a President and His General*. New York: Hargrave McMillan, 2010.

White, Richard. *It's Your Misfortune and None of My Own*. University of Oklahoma Press, 1993.

Winick, Jay. *April 1865: The Month That Saved America*. New York: HarperCollins Publishers, 2001.

The War of the Rebellion: A Compilation of the Official Records of the Union and Confederate Armies. 127 Vols., Washington, D.C.: Government Printing Office, 1880-1901.

Weber, Thomas. *The Northern Railroads in the Civil War, 1861-1865*. New York: King's Crown Press (Columbia University), 1952.

Whalen, Charles and Barbara. *The Fighting McCooks*, Bethesda, Md.: Westmoreland Press, 2006.

Wilder, Daniel R. *The Annals of Kansas*. Topeka, Kan.: Kansas Publishing House, 1886.

Williams, Walter, ed. *A History of Northwest Missouri*. Chicago: Lewis Publishing Co., 1915.

Wills, Garry. *Lincoln at Gettysburg: The Words That Remade America*. New York: Simon & Schuster, 1992.

Wilson, Douglas L. *Lincoln's Sword: The Presidency and the Power of Words*. New York: Alfred A. Knopf, 2006.

————. *Herndon's Informants: Letters, Interviews, and Statements about Abraham Lincoln*. Chicago: University of Illinois Press, 1998.

Woodson, W.H. *History of Clay County, Missouri*. Topeka, Kan.: Historical Publishing Co., 1920.

Wunder, John R. *The Nebraska-Kansas Act of 1854*. Lincoln, Neb.: University of Nebraska Press, 2008.

——. *Law and the Great Plains: Essays on the Legal History of the Heartland*. Westport, Conn.: Greenwood Press, 1996.

NEWSPAPERS

Atchison Daily Globe
Baltimore Sun
Chariton (Iowa) Herald
Charleston Mercury
Cincinnati Inquirer
Daily News Democrat
Emporia Gazette
Emporia Weekly News
Evening Star (Washington, D.C.)
Jonesville Daily Gazette
Kansas City Evening Star
Kansas City Journal of Commerce
Kansas City Star
Kansas City Times
Kansas Crusader of Freedom
Kansas Free State
Lawrence Daily Journal
Lawrence Republican
Leavenworth Times
Liberty Tribune
Milwaukee Morning Sentinel
Missouri Republican
Missouri Valley Register
Missouri World
National Tribune
Nevada State Journal
New York Herald
New York Times

New York World
Providence Evening Press
Topeka Daily Capital
Quincy Daily Whig
Richmond Conservator
Richmond Missourian
The Ripley Bee
Red Wing Sentinel
Sioux City Journal
Springfield Republican
St. Joseph Daily News
St. Joseph Gazette
St. Joseph Herald & Tribune
St. Joseph Morning Herald
St. Louis Dispatch
St. Louis Globe (later *St. Louis Globe-Democrat*)
St. Louis Republican
The Daily Argus
The National Republican (Washington)
The Topeka Capital-Journal
Wall Street Journal
Willmer Tribune (Minnesota)
Winfield Courier

ARTICLES

Arnold, Isaac H., "The Baltimore Plot to Assassinate Abraham Lincoln," *Harper's New Monthly Magazine*, Vol. 37, No. 217 (New York: Harper and Brothers, 1868): 123–28.

Ball, Durwood, "Scapegoat? Col. Edwin B. Sumner and the Topeka Dispersal," *Kansas History: A Journal of the Central Plains*, Vol. 33 (Autumn 2010): 165–83.

Baron, Frank, "James H. Lane and the Origins of the Kansas Jayhawk," *Kansas History: A Journal of the Central Plains*, Vol. 34, No. 2 (Summer 2011): 115–27 .

————. "German Republicans and Radicals in the Struggle for a Slave-Free Kansas: Charles F. Kob and August Bondi," *Yearbook for German-American Studies* 40 (2005): 3–26.

Bassler, Roy, P., ed., "James Quay Howard's Notes on Lincoln," *Abraham Lincoln Quarterly*, Vol. IV, No. 8 (December 1947).

Bird, Roy, "Jim Lane's Misnamed Frontier Guard Had a Lofty Charge to Protect the President of the United States," *America's Civil War*, Vol. 12, Issue 1 (March 1999): 8–11.

Brinckerhoff, Fred H., "The Kansas Tour of Lincoln the Candidate," *Kansas History: A Journal of the Central Plains*, Vol. 31 (Winter 2008-2009): 275–93.

Caldwell, Martha B., "When Horace Greeley Visited Kansas in 1859," *Kansas Historical Quarterly*, Vol. 9, No. 2 (May 1940): 115–40.

Castel, Albert, "Jim Lane of Kansas," *Civil War Times Illustrated*, Vol. 12 Issue 10 (February 1974): 22–20.

————, "Kansas Jayhawking Raids into Western Missouri in 1861," *Missouri Historical Review* 54, No. 1 (October 1959): 1–11.

————, "Order No. 11 and the Civil War on the Border," *Missouri Historical Review* 57, No. 4 (October 1962): 357–68.

Delahay, Mary E., "Judge Mark W. Delahay," Kansas Historical Collection, X (1907).

Drake, Ross, "The Law That Ripped America in Two," *Smithsonian* 9 (Winter 2009).

Etulain, Richard W., "Abraham Lincoln Looks West," *Wild West Magazine* (April 2009).

Finkelman, Paul, "The End of War and Slavery Yields a New Racial Order," *American Bar Journal* (April 2011).

Goertner, Thomas Grenville, "Reflections of the Frontier Soldier on the Sand Creek Affair as Revealed in the Diary of Samuel F. Tappan," Master's Thesis (1959).

Gower, Calvin W., "Gold Fever in Kansas Territory: Migration to the Pike's Peak Gold Fields, 1858-1860," *Kansas Historical Quarterly*, Vol. 39, No. 1 (Spring 1973): 58–74.

Grinspan, Jon, "Young Men for War: The Wide Awakes and Lincoln's 1860 Presidential Campaign," *The Journal of American History* (Sept. 2009).

Holzer, Harold, "Lincoln's Tough Guy," *Civil War Times* (June 2014): 72–77.

———, "An Inescapable Conflict," *American Bar Journal* (April 2011): 45.

Howes, Cecil, "Pistol-Packing Pencil Pushers," *Kansas Historical Quarterly*, vol. 13 no. 2, (May 1944): 116–38.

Hutton, Paul Andrew, "Living the Legend: Super Scout Buffalo Bill Cody," *Wild West Magazine* (February 2009): 26–35.

Isley, W.H., "The Sharps Rifle Episode in Kansas History," *American Historical Review*, Vol. 12, No. 3 (April 1907).

Kremer, Gary R., "The Abraham Lincoln Legacy in Missouri," *Missouri Historical Review*, Vol. 103, No. 2 (January 2009): 108–19.

Langsdorf, Edgar, "Price's Raid and the Battle of Mine Creek," *Kansas History: A Journal of the Central Plains*, Vol. 37, No. 2 (Summer 2014).

Langsdorf, Erich, "Jim Lane and the Frontier Guard," *Kansas Historical Quarterly* Vol. 9, No. 1 (1941): 13–25.

———, "Thaddeus Hyatt in Washington Jail," *Kansas Historical Quarterly*, Vol. 9, No. 3 (August 1940): 225–39.

———, "S.C. Pomeroy and the New England Emigrant Aid Company, 1854-1858," *Kansas Historical Quarterly*, Vol. 7, No. 4 (November 1938): 227–45.

Lanham, Paul, "Terror in the Dark—The Confederate Guerrilla Boyle," Prince Georges County Historical Society, January 1975, Vol. III, no. 1.

Lauk, Jon, "The Silent Artillery of Time: Understanding Social Change in the Rural Midwest," *Great Plains Quarterly* 19 (Fall 1999).

Lewis, Lloyd, "The Man the Historians Forgot," *Kansas Historical Quarterly*, Vol. 8, No. 1 (February 1939): 85–103.

"Lincoln in Kansas," *Kansas Historical Collections*, Vol. 7 (1902): 536–52.

Miner, Craig, "Lane and Lincoln: A Mysterious Connection," 186 *Kansas History: A Journal of the Central Plains,* Vol. 24 No. 3 (Autumn 2001): 186–89.

Montgomery, Rick, "The Rise & Fall of a Cowtown," *The Kansas City Star Magazine* (Dec. 9, 2012).

Muehlberger, James P., "Lincoln's Mercy: A Confederate Spy and a Missouri Lawyer," *Journal of the Missouri Bar Association*, Vol. 68, No. 6 (November-December 2012): 340–43.

———, "The Kansas Lawyer Who Saved Lincoln's Life," *Journal of the Kansas Bar Association*, Vol. 80, No. 2 (February 2011): 34–43.

———, "Reflections on Lincoln's Kansas Campaign, *Journal of the Kansas Bar Association,* Vol. 78, No. 10 (November/December 2009): 24–36.

Napier, Rita G., "Origin Stories and Bleeding Kansas," *Kansas History: a Journal of the Central Plains*, Vol. 34, No. 1 (Spring 2011): 28–39.

Rosa, Joseph G., "Colt's 'Old Navy' Model Revolvers Found a Ready Market in the West," *Wild West Magazine* (December 2009): 66–67.

Shepherd, Allen L., "Gentile in Zion: Algernon Sidney Paddock and the Utah Commission, 1882-1886," *Nebraska History* 57 (Fall 1976).

Six, Fred N., ed., "Eyewitness Reports of Quantrill's Raid," *Kansas History: A Journal of the Central Plains* 28 (Summer 2005): 94–103.

Solomon, Margaret, "A Bloomer Girl Conquers Pike's Peak," *American History Illustrated* (January 1984): 40–47.

Sorensen, Theodore C., "A Man of His Words," *Smithsonian* (Winter 2009).

Spring, Leverett, "The Career of a Kansas Politician," *American Historical Review* (1898).

Stone, Charles P., "Washington on the Eve of War," *Century Illustrated* (July 1883).

Stashower, Daniel, "Lincoln Must Die," *Smithsonian* (February 2013): 74–89.

Strasdenraus, P.J., "Immigrants or Invaders," *Kansas Historical Quarterly*, Vol. 24, No. 4 (Winter 1958): 394–98.

Sutherland. Daniel, E., "The Missouri Guerilla Hunt," *Wild West* (September 2009).

Taylor, David G., *Business and Political Career of Thomas Ewing Jr.: A Study of Frustrated Ambition*, Ph.D. Thesis, University of Kansas (1970).

Tegeder, Vincent G., "Lincoln and the Territorial Patronage: The Ascendancy of the Radicals in the West," *The Missouri Valley Historical Review*, Vol. 35, No. 1 (June 1948): 77–90.

Turk, Eleanor L., "The Germans of Atchison, 1854-1859: Development of an Ethnic Community," *Kansas History: A Journal of the Central Plains*, Vol. 2, No. 3 (Autumn 1979): 44–71.

Villard, Henry, "Recollections of Lincoln," *Atlantic Monthly*, February 1904.

Weiss, Earl J., "Western Lawmen: Image and Reality," *Journal of the West* (January/Winter 1985): 23–32.

Whitney, Henry Clay, "Lincoln's Last Speech, Now First Published from the Unique Report," *McClure's Magazine* (September 1896).

Appendix I:

Author's Transcript of the Frontier Guard Roll & Other Proceedings

Library of Congress
0013 578 998 7
Records, 1861–1908

FRONTIER GUARD ROLL & OTHER PROCEEDINGS

The capture of "Fort Sumter" by traitors, having stimulated "treason" at Washington City, every Union loving sojourner (?) threat, at once felt the live-wish (?) solicitude for its safety. The anticipated arrival of troops under the President's Proclamation of April 15, 1861, at an early day; was the hope of all. Gen. James H. Lane of Kansas, having reached the Federal Capitol April 13th was not an idle or disinterested observer of passing events. The rebels were not unknown to him. He had met them on other fields in other days; and now clearly saw them in the distance. Attended by a few of his old "Companions in Arms" he formed on the

17th, a nucleus, around which was to be rallied once more, the opponents of Atchison, Stringfellow, Titus, Bufford & Company, in vindication, not of freedom in Kansas; but of Constitutional Government in America. Co-operated with by a few of Gen. Lane's admirers from many portions of the Union, such was the substance of their private speculations at No. 12 Willard's Hotel, Washington City, April 17, 1861.

APRIL 17, 1861

Gen. Lane had an interview with the President of the United States in the morning . . .

APRIL 18, 1961

. . . making known his purpose to be at the service of the Government, at the Command of the President, when the "critical moment" arrived.

At the invitation of the President of the United States, about noon Gen. Lane and his band were assigned the delicate and responsible duty of defending the "White House," and were invited without delay to enter on that duty, in military order.

In response to the invitation of the President, a meeting was held at Gen. Lane's home No. 12 Willard Hotel about 2 o'clock P.M. at which the following names were enrolled for military service, in discharge of the assigned duty, to be known and designated by order of Gen. Lane, as the "Frontier Guard."

ROLL OF FRONTIER GUARD

No.	Names	Age	Height	Col. of Hair	Residence	Remarks
1	James H. Lane	47	5.11	Dark Brown	Lawrence, KS	Honorable lv to disband
2	Mark M. Delahay	42	5.11	Very Dark	Leavenworth City, KS	Honorably Discharged
3	Job B. Stockton	27	5.9	Dark	Leavenworth City, KS	"
4	D.S. Gordon	28	5.8	"	Leavenworth City, KS	"
5	J. T. Burris	32	5.9	Light	Leavenworth City, KS	"
6	J.P. Hatterscheidt	32	6.3	"	Leavenworth City, KS	"
7	J.W. Jenkins	25	5.9	Dark Brown	Lawrence, KS	"
8	H.J. Adams	45	5.11	"	Lawrence, KS	"
9	R. McBratney	21	5.7	⸺	Atchison, KS	"
10	D.A. Clayton	32	5.10		Leavenworth City, KS	"
11	M.H. Insley				Leavenworth City, KS	"
12	Sidney Clark				Lawrence, KS	"
13	J.W. Eddy	29	5.8½	Light	Batavia, IL	"
14	G.F. Warren	38	5.5½	"	Lawrence, KS	"
15	J.N. Northcott	52	6	"	Centralia, KS	"

continued on next page

No.	Names	Age	Height	Col. of Hair	Residence	Remarks
16	T. Sampson	46	5.7	"	Lawrence, KS	"
17	W.W. Ross	31	5.11	Brown	Topeka, KS	"
18	Samuel C. Pomeroy	45	5.11	Dark	Atchison, KS	"
19	Chester Thomas				Auburn, KS	"
20	D.H. Bailey	30	5.9½	Dark	Leavenworth City, KS	"
21	Jeff L. Dugger				Leavenworth City, KS	"
22	Thos. Shankland	50	6	Light	New York City	"
23	P. H. Townsend	36	5.11	Dark	Big Spring, KS	"
24	Samuel Gilson	38	5.7	Brown	Weston, MO	"
25	J. W. Jenkins	47	5.4	"	Petersburgh, IL	"
26	S.W. Greer		5.10	"	Leavenworth, KS	"
27	G. Ilges	24	6.1	"	IN	"
28	C. Hazlett	27	5.10	Light	Morristown, OH	"
29	Thomas Ewing, Jr.	31	6.1	Black	Leavenworth City, KS	"
30	W. Parker Wright	37	5.4	Sandy	Nevada, NY	"
31	T. H. Sypherd	30	5.7	Dark	Kansas City, MO	"
32	D.W. Kelsey	40	5.7	"	Onopolis, NE	"
33	J.A. Cody	41	5.9	"	Grasshopper Falls, KS	"
34	J.R. Meredith	40	6	"	Omaha City, NE	"

No.	Names	Age	Height	Col. of Hair	Residence	Remarks
35	Anthony J.Bleecker				New York City	"
36	S.D. Leibe	50	5.11	Dark	Pottsville, PA	"
37	Geo. Bassett	30	5.8½	Brown	Washington City/Lawrence	"
38	Franklin Webster	36	5.8 ½	"	Chicago, IL	"
39	Geo. L. Febiger	37	6.2	Dark	Wilmington, DE	"
40	Leicister Walker Jr.	26	6	Light	Maysville, KS	"
41	George Rye	51	5.10	Light	Woodstock, Shenandoah, Va	"
42	N.J. Vedder	15	4.7		Washington City	
43	W.G. Hoben	35	6.	Black	New York	"
44	Robt. L. Ream	51	5.10	Gray	Washington City	"
45	Wm. B. Waugh	43	5.10	Dark	Leavenworth City, KS	"
46	P.L. Hartman	27	5.6	"	Lancaster, PA	"
47	Danford					
48	Jared Phillips	32	5.10	Black	Leavenworth City, KS	"
49	E. Daniels	39	5.7	"	Rippon, WI	"
50	Wheelock	28	5.6	"	SanFrancisco, CA	"
51	Chas. F. DeVivaldi	36	5.9	"	Manhattan, KS	"
52	G.H. Keller	60	5.11	Gray	Leavenworth City, KS	"

continued on next page

No.	Names	Age	Height	Col. of Hair	Residence	Remarks
53	H.C. Fields	29	5.8	Black	Leavenworth City, KS	"
54	O.H. Irish	30	5.9	Dark	Nebraska City, NE	"
55	J. Wesley Jones	35	5.10	Brown	Melrose, MA	"
56	G.B. Way	50	6.2	Dark	Urbana, OH	"
57	Charles Forster	31	5.9	Light	Evansville, IN	"
58	G.W. Fisher	63	6	Gray	Urbana, OH	"
59	Fredrick A. Brown	18	5.9	Light	Buffalo, NY	"
60	W. S. Merrill				Rochester, NJ	"
61	W.H. Russell	57	6.1	Gray	Kansas City, MO	"
62	Nathaniel I. Wilcox	56	5.9	Light	Fredrick Schuyler Co., IL	"
63	C. W. Pollard	33	5.4	Brown	Marietta, OH	"
64	H. W. DePuy	39	6	Gray	Omaha City, NE	"
65	Clifford Arick	34	6	Brown	Steubansville, OH	"
66	J.H. Holmes	28	5.6	Black	NM	"
67	O. H. Benjamin	31	5.8	"	Lexington, MO	"
68	P.W. Hitchcock	28	5.10	Light	Omaha City, NE	"
69	W. A. Bucher	62	5.8	Gray	New York City	"
70	S. Sisson	60	6	"	Louisville, KY	"
71	J.E. Mindenhall	24	5.8		Richmond, IN	"

No.	Names	Age	Height	Col. of Hair	Residence	Remarks
72	Jas. Bryan	65	5.11	Gray	Cambridge, MD	"
73	H.S. Paddock	28	5.9	Dark	Omaha City, NJ	"
74	B. A. Barnes	33	5.11	Brown	Wilkesbarre, PA	"
75	Daniel McCook	62	6.2	Gray	Grandtower, IL	"
76	Edward M. McCook	27	5.10	Dark	Central City, CO	"
77	Joseph Chas Howells	38	5.7	Light	Madison, WI	"
78	Victor Smith	38	5.9	"	Cincinnati, OH	"
79	G. W. Smith	24	5.10	Brown	Lawrence, KS	"
80	Charles Champion	35	5.5	"	Negro Hill, CA	"
81	J.H. Clinton	22	6.2	Brown	Jennings Co, IN	"
82	L. Holtslander	40	5.10	Light	Oberlin, OH	"
83	J.J. Henry	25	5.10	Black	Scranton, PA	"
84	E.G. Chambers	41	5.9	Dark	Bucyrus, OH	"
85	James Normile	17	5.9	"	Doniphan, KS	"
86	H.H. Brown	53	5.10	Gray	Buckeys Town, IN	"
87	H. M. Gibbons	25	5.6	Black	Portland, OR	"
88	W.D. Nichols	34	5.10	Light	Davenport, IA	"
89	E. Spicer	27	5.10	Brown	Lawrence, KS	"

continued on next page

No.	Names	Age	Height	Col. of Hair	Residence	Remarks
90	O.A. Hall	23	5.7	Dark	Worcester, MA	"
91	J.R. Carpenter	42	5.10	Light	Washington, DC	"
92	F.G. Hesse	33	5.7	Dark	Washington, DC	"
93	Constant Freeman Smith	26	5.7½	Light	Washington, DC	"
94	John Ayer	35	5.9	Dark	Hannibal, MO	"
95	Ira Freeman Jr.	30	6	"	Baltimore, MD	"
96	Fredrick Bogen	46	5.10	Brown	New York City	"
97	Thaddeus Hyatt	45	5.7½	"	Washington City	"
98	D.T. Smith	30	5.7	Light	Minneapolis MN	"
99	E.G. McLaren	25	5.10	Black	Lewiston Fulton Co. IL	"
100	James M. Lasco					
101	W. Perkinson	55	5.10	Gray	Baltimore, MD	"
102	Geo. W. Lee	31	5.6	Brown	Steilacoum (?), Pierce Co. NJ	"
103	Joseph Heiman	30	5.8	Light	Philadelphia, PA	"
104	P.M. Clark	33	6.2	Light	Springfield, ME	"
105	T.W. Jennings	28	5.10	Dark	Washington, DC	"
106	Jas. T. Sample	39	5.8½	Dark/Curly_	Stickleyville (?), PA	"
107	Geo. R. McIntyre	26	5	Dark Brown	Warren, ME	"
108	Thomas D. Bancroft	23	6.3	Light	E. Avon NY	"

No.	Names	Age	Height	Col. of Hair	Residence	Remarks
109	A.J. Dean	45	5.11½	Sandy	Allegheny City, PA	"
110	Elisha Wallace	69	5.9	"	Syracuse, NY	"
111	Wm. Zearing	31	5.6	Dark	Princeton, IL	"
112	Mark N. Garton	27	5.7	Light	Washington, DC	"
113	Cooper K. Watson	51	6	Gray	Tippers, OH	"
114	Rosewell Hart					
115	Elias Wampole	55	5.9	Gray	Philadelphia, PA	"
116	John C. Vaughan	65	5.10	Sandy/Curly	Leavenworth, KS	"

An election for officers was gone into and resulted as follows:

James H. Lane	Captain
Mark M. Delahay	1st Lieutenant
Job B. Stockton	2nd Lieutenant
David S. Gordon	1st Sergeant
J.T. Burris	2nd Sergeant
John P. Hattersheidt	1st Corporal
J.M. Jenkins	2nd Corporal

Thus organized, the "Frontier Guard" marched under orders to the President's house where they arrived April 18, 1861 8 o'clock P.M. The Company was immediately formed in the East Room. Gen. Lane received from the Secretary of War in the presence of the President his sword and at once proceeded to arm his Company, which was done.

The Company stacked their arms up the centre of the East Room about 12 A.M. A guard being formed, the remainder of the men slept by their guns.

APRIL 19, 1861

The anniversary of the "Battle of Lexington" and the day of the "Battle of Baltimore."

The Massachusetts Regiment with their wounded arrived in Washington amidst intense excitement and anxiety, about 5 o'clock P.M.

The "Frontier Guard" returned to duty at 8 o'clock P.M. The city agitated by incredible rumors and all apprehending the worst. Gen. Lane said to his men, "The blood of these men is not shed in vain."

APRIL 20, 1861

A universal gloom and anxiety sits upon every countenance, 700 Massachusetts men, about as many Pennsylvanians and the City rife with treason and the streets full of traitors. For the present the President should go round Baltimore—But when will re-enforcements come and will it be too late? Such are the inquiries on every mind, and now the "Frontier

Guard" is represented 400 or 500 strong. Commanded by the notorious Jim Lane and comprised of his desperate Kansas followers. It is said that the Braves across the Potomac are more alarmed at this than Wise was by John Brown. It is reported also that these desperados have been over reconnoitering and intend visiting the forces at Alexandria Monday noon.

APRIL 21, 1861

Unabated anxiety prevails and no reliable word can be had as to the whereabouts of the N.Y. 7th and other forces known to be moving hither—numerous arrivals from Virginia. Exiled *fugitives*, they report as rumors in Virginia that Jim Lane has 1,000 men and that the country stands in terrible awe. Apprehending an attack, Lieutenant Stockton directed to encourage the most incredible rumors and to proclaim an immediate purpose to invade. In the meantime let every man stand to his post, be patient and watchful.

APRIL 22, 1861

No reliable news from the forces supposed to be moving hither. Rumors of the 7th being attacked. Cut up and driven back—numerous arrivals from Virginia. The people over the way in dread of Jim Lane and his John Brown horde as they say. It being now declared that apprehending this result for months, Lane has been secretly accumulating a force here—the strength of which none will know until it is attacked. It is asserted that Lane feels perfectly able with his force, to successfully repel an attacking army of 5,000 men. This is believed across the Potomac. Where Lane's men all stay is the mystery on this side.

APRIL 23, 1861

The Rail Road having passed into the hands of the government, a better feeling prevails to-day—a rapid movement from toward Baltimore being thereby prevented. It is confidently asserted also that the 7th is nearby and will be in to-night. An advance guard of Lane's men under Lieut.

Stockton returned from Virginia, having captured a "Secession flag"—a terribly piratical looking rag.

APRIL 24, 1861

All are disappointed at the non-arrival of the N.Y. 7th and the worst apprehension prevails. With the Guard, this has been a sad day and the anxiety of all is greater than any which has passed. Why do the re-enforcements delay & no one it seems can tell. Yet it is asserted that they are in striking distance. The most of people doubt it. We all know that if the cowards who are stimulating this rebellion had a leader and had the nerve, this city would fall a prey to its own traitors. So the destiny of the Capitol is really suspended by a hair. Wellington never wished for Blucher more than we do for Lefferts.

APRIL 25, 1861

The 7th is here. Received with shouts and tears of joy as they move along the avenue. The way is open and soon others are to follow. All is safe now—everybody thinks so. Everybody says so. Everybody feels so. The Frontier Guard have a jubilee at their quarters, and Gen. Lane regales them with a speech. He says "The point of danger is past. Secession may howl but the Union is safe. Twenty-four hours ago they might have seized the Capitol—now all H-L [Hell] can't take it."

APRIL 26, 1861

Numerous arrivals from the south of brave and true men have given a Union spirit to Washington City unfelt by it for years. At length we begin to regard ourselves once more as the citizens of a great nation. The poor Virginian exile to-day. Who with sweeping eyes exclaimed "Alas! Alas! I have no Country" may take courage and was to the traitors who to-day oppress him! The same Virginian said "Mine was the land of Washington, and they have robbed me of it."

Alexandria, so near Mt. Vernon, boasts of her united treason against the government of Washington.

The Guard have not failed to have "a chief among em taking notes." They missed the figure when they undertook to out brag us. We caught them in the act. To this day they can't count.

APRIL 27, 1861

Last night the Guard were on duty at the Navy Yard and stood guard on the bridge all night. "nobody hurt."

The continued arrivals of large numbers of troops, rendering an attack on the city improbable, and a successful one impossible, in connection with the war-like rumors from the West induced Gen. Lane to seek authority to disband his company at this point and discharge them from the service, intending to transfer as many of them with their arms as desired to go to Kansas.

With this view he addressed the following note to the Secretary of War:

Headquarters Frontier Guard
Washington City April 27, 1861
To Hon Simon Cameron
Secretary of War

Sir:

In consequences of the arrival of large numbers of troops in this city, I am satisfied the emergency has ceased, that called our Company into Service. If you concur in this opinion, I should be pleased to receive authority from you to disband said Company and to honorably discharge the members thereof from the Service.

Very truly
J. H. Lane
Capt Comdg

To this note Gen Lane rec'd the following reply:

War Department April 27 1861
Gen. James H. Lane

Sir:

In reply to your letter of this day's date, stating that, in conse-
quence of the arrival of large numbers of troops in this city, the
emergency has ceased which called the Company commanded
by you into service, and that you would be pleased, therefore, to
have authority to disband your Company and have an honorable
discharge from service for it. Concurring fully with you, I read-
ily grant you the authority asked for, and, in doing so, I beg to
extend to you, and through you to the men under your command,
the assurance of my high appreciation of the very prompt and
patriotic manner in which your Company was organized for the
defence of the Capitol and the very efficient services rendered by
it during the time of its existence.

Very Respectfully
Countersigned Simon Cameron

"Cheerfully Approved Secy of War".
A. Lincoln

APRIL 27, 1861

Our rect. of the foregoing correspondence the "Guard" resolved itself
into a business meeting by calling Col. Mark W. Delahay to the Chair.
Col. D. having made a few remarks thanked the Company for the honor
conferred and took his seat.

On motion Clifford Arick was elected Secretary of this meeting.

On motion the President of this meeting was authorized to appoint
a committee of five who shall procure certificates of discharge for the
members and officers of this Company.

On motion two others were directed to be added to said Committee.

Clifford Arick, C.F. DeVivaldi, George L. Febiger, Joseph Charles Howells, Edward Daniels, T.W. Jones and Daniel McCook were appointed said Committee.

On motion a unanimous vote of thanks was given for Gen. Lane, Col. Delahay, Capt. Stockton and the other officers of the Guard for their cheerful and gentlemanly bearing toward its members.

On motion a unanimous vote of thanks was given to Chap. Hunter U.S.A. for his kindness and generous attention to the Guard since its organization.

On motion a unanimous vote of thanks was tendered the President of the United States and his Cabinet. Also Lieut. Gen. Scott for the generous confidence refused in the "Frontier Guard." We might have hoped for an opportunity wherein to test its worthiness in the last extremity. We rejoice it was not presented.

On motion of Col. Vaughan the following resolutions were unanimously adopted:

On motion said Committee were directed to wait on the President and report to this meeting.

Gen. Schuyler addressed the Meeting.

Gen. Lane addressed the Meeting.

Col. Vaughan, Chairman of the Committee, to wait on the President, reported and 3 o'clock was set apart as the hour at which the Company should call at the White House.

The "Frontier Guard" visited the President at this hour appointed.

Gen. Lane introduced the Company and personally Col. Vaughan who for the occasion had been named our Judge Advocate.

Col. Vaughan addressed the President at some length and in conclusion declared that he was authorized "on behalf of the brave men with whom he stood associated to say that much as we would deprecate the shedding of fraternal blood, our motto is, and will ever be, "No Compromise with Rebels."

The President replied substantially in conclusion—"I have desired as sincerely as any man. I sometimes think more sincerely than any other man that these difficulties might be settled without the shedding of fraternal blood. I will not say all hope of this is gone. But if the alternative is finally presented, whether the Union is to be broken to fragments and the liberties of the people bartered away or fraternal blood be shed. <u>You</u> will probably make the choice or alternative with which I will not be dissatisfied."

The Company immediately retired and repaired to No. 12 Willard Hotel.

The Committee on Certificate of Discharge reported the form and style of the same adopted to wit.

A Vignette. "White House" east view. Encircled in German text by the words "United States of America" to be followed by the letter of Gen. Lane to the Secretary of War heretofore appearing in the minutes. This to be followed by the Secretary's reply as before set forth. In each case the signatures to present "facsimiles" the whole to conclude as follows:

By authority vested in me as Captain of the Frontier Guard, I, James H. Lane, do hereby certify that, a member of said Company, served his country in defence of the National Capitol at a time of great peril, when threatened by hordes of traitors: said service commencing on the 18th day of April 1861 and ending on the date hereof. I also by virtue of said authority do hereby honorably discharge the said from the service of the United States. Given under my hand at the East Room of the Executive Mansion at Washington City this day of, 1861.

To be signed—"J. H. Lane Capt."
Attested.
M.W. Delahay   1st Lieut.
J.B. Stockton   2nd Lieut.
Either or both

Thereupon the meeting adjourned to meet at No. 12 Willard on Monday next.

Pursuant to adjournment no business transacted. Adjourned to May 3, 1861.

Pursuant to adjournment, Secretary ordered to issue discharges to members standing fair on the Rolls or application. Whereupon this

Meeting adjourned to meet again in the public call of the President and Secretary, upon this our motion at the request of ten of the members.

MAY 3, 1861

This is to certify that the foregoing are the substantial memoranda of facts and incidents connected with the organization, service and discharge of the Frontier Guard.

Clifford Arick　　　　Mark W. Delahay
Secretary　　　　　　President

Appendix II:

Frontier Guard Timelines

(Research by Debby Lowery and Judy Sweets)

Henry Joseph Adams (1816–1870)

1816, Feb. 10, Henry Joseph Adams was born in Rodman, Jefferson County, New York. He was the son of Joseph and Azula [Henry] Adams. [*Findagrave*, www.findagrave.com (Shelli Bailey, submitter)]

1841, Sept. 16, Married Abigail "Abby" R. Gibson, Cincinnati, Ohio. [Ibid.]

1845, Aug. 22, Daughter Anna Gibson Adams born at Walnut Hills near Cincinnati, Ohio. [Ibid.]

1855, March, Moved to Lawrence, Kansas Territory [*Findagrave*, op. cit.]

1856, Senator in Free-State Legislature. [*Legends of Kansas* (www.legends ofkansas.com/people-a.html#HenryJ.Adams)]

1857, Elected first Free-State Mayor of Leavenworth, Kansas Territory. [*Daily National Intelligencer*, Apr. 22, 1857, p.3]

1861, April, In Frontier Guard. [*History of Kansas*, Noble L. Prentis, 1899, Topeka, Kans., pp.96–97]

1861, Sept. 5, Additional paymaster, Volunteers.

1862, Married Mary A. Ward, at Leavenworth, Kans. [*Findagrave*, op. cit.]

1864, Aug. 22, Dismissed as paymaster. [*Findagrave*, op. cit.]

1870, June 2, Died at Waterville, Kans., and buried in Oak Hill Cemetery at Atchison, Kans. [*Findagrave*, op. cit.]

Daniel Read Anthony (1824–1904)

1824, Aug. 22, Daniel R. Anthony, born Adams, Mass., was a son of Daniel and Lucy Anthony, and a brother of Susan B. Anthony. [*Legends of Kansas*, "Historic People of Kansas," www.legendsofkansas.com (a web property of Legends of America) and *American Civil War Research database*]

1854, June, Member of the first party sent to Lawrence, Kansas Territory, by the New England Emigrant Aid Society. [*Legends of Kansas*, op. cit.]

1857, Anthony settled in Leavenworth, Kansas Territory, where he would remain for the rest of his life. [Ibid.] An abolitionist, Anthony assisted African-American William Matthews with Underground Railroad activities in Leavenworth, Kansas Territory. [Ibid.].

1861, January, Established the *Leavenworth Conservative*. [Ibid.]

1861, Apr. 15th, Anthony arrived at Willard's Hotel, Washington, D.C. [*Evening Star*, April 15, 1861, p.4].

1861, April, Member of Frontier Guard. ["Soldiers of Kansas: The Frontier Guard at the White House, Washington, D.C., 1861," *Transactions of the Kansas State Historical Society*, Vol. 10, pp.419–21]

1861, June 13, Shooting between Anthony and R.C. Satterlee. Satterlee was killed. [Ibid.]

1861, Sept. 29, Anthony was commissioned as a lieutenant colonel in Seventh Kansas Cavalry and served until he resigned on Sept. 3, 1862. [*Legends of Kansas*, American Civil War Research Database].

1861, Oct. 29, Promoted to lieutenant olonel. [American Civil War Research Database, op. cit.]

1862, Sept. 3, Anthony resigned from the 7th Cavalry. [Ibid.]

1863, Elected mayor of Leavenworth. [*Legends*, op. cit.]

1864, Jan. 21, Anthony married Miss Annie F. Osborn of Edgartown, Mass. [Ibid.]

1864, March, He purchased the [Leavenworth] *Bulletin.* [Ibid.]

1871, The *Leavenworth Times* came into his possession. [Ibid.]

1872, Anthony was elected mayor of Leavenworth again. [Ibid.]

1874, He was appointed postmaster in Leavenworth by President Grant. [Ibid.]

1904, Nov. 12, Daniel R. Anthony died in Leavenworth and is buried in Mount Muncie Cemetery, Lansing, Leavenworth County, Kans. [www.findagrave.com]

Clifford Arick (1826–1875)

1827, December, Clifford Arick was born in Ohio. [*U.S. Federal Census,* Roll M432_661, 125B]

1852, July 1, He married Josephine C. Templeton in Belmont County, Ohio. [*Ohio Marriages 1803–1900,* database online, www.ancestry.com]

1861, Apr. 5, He was appointed Junior Assistant Examiner at the Patent Office in Washington, D.C. [*Scientific American,* Vol. 4, Munn & Co. (1861), p.250]

1861, April, Member of the Frontier Guard.

1862, Arick made an application for a patent of the "Eureka" ordnance projectile. [D. Van Nostrand, *Van Nostrand's Magazine,* Vol. 1 (1869), p.1059]

1875, Jan. 20, Arick became president of Ames Manufacturing Co. [Thomas K. Tate, *Under the Iron Eyelids: A Biography of James Henry Burton, Armorer to the Nations* (Google eBook), p.329]

1875, Sept. 23, Clifford Arick died of apoplexy in Poughkeepsie, New York, where he had gone to place his daughter at Vassar College. [*National Republican* (Washington, D.C.), Sept. 25, 1875]

1875, Sept. 28, He was buried at Oak Hill Cemetery in Washington, D.C. [www.findagrave.com.]

John Ayer (1825–1863)

1825, Dec. 22, John Ayer was born. [U.S. Civil War Soldier Records and Profiles, 1861–1865]

1850 or 1852, June 27, John Ayer married Lydia Ann Bowen in Bangor, Penobscot County, Maine. [Maine, *Marriages, 1771–1907* Index and www.familysearch.org]

1859, Sept. 19, John Ayer was the general freight agent for Hannibal & St. Joseph Railroad based in Hannibal, Mo. [*Bangor Daily Whig and Courier*, Sept. 19, 1859]

1860, John Ayer listed as a general freight agent of the Hannibal & St. Joseph Railroad. [*Missouri State Gazetteer and Business Directory*, Southerland & McEvoy (1860), p.104]

J. T. K. Hayward was an early promoter of the Hannibal & St. Joseph Railroad and a former mayor of Bangor, Maine. He moved to Hannibal to supervise the construction of the railroad and, in 1862, raised a militia composed almost entirely of railroad employees.

1860, Aug. 21, In the 1860 census, John Ayer was living in Ward 2, Hannibal, Marion County, Mo. He was age 35, a railroad agent, born in Maine. Living with wife Lydia N. Ayer, age 28, born in Maine, and son William Ayer, age 5, born in Maine. [U.S. Federal Census, Roll M653_632, p.787]

1860, December, "John Ayer, Railroad" was included in Hannibal's *Daily Evening News* on a list of men who voted Republican but was "still considered respectable and law abiding who would not be guilty of doing anything unbecoming gentlemen and law-abiding citizens." ["List of Republican Voters in Marion County," *Hannibal Daily Courier*, 1889 article, Rootsweb]

1861, April, Frontier Guard at the White House, Washington, D.C.

1862, Aug. 14, John Ayer enlisted as a commissioned officer in Company H, 16th Infantry, Maine Volunteers. [U.S. Civil War Soldier Records and Profiles, 1861–1865 (database online)]

1862, December, Captain John Ayers was wounded in the knee at the Battle of Fredericksburg and captured by the Rebel Army.

1863, February, Captain John Ayers died in Libby Prison in Richmond, Va., of wounds. [*U.S. Registers of Deaths of Volunteers, 1861–1865.* (database online)]

1863, May 19, John was buried at Mount Hope Cemetery in Bangor, Maine. [www.findagrave.com]

Henry G. Babcock (1825–1884)

1825, May 14, Born in Otsego County, N.Y. [*U.S. Passport Applications, 1795–1925*], Henry was the son of Gurdon Babcock and Almira Starkweather. [Stephen Babcock, *The Babcock Genealogy* (np, 1903), p.270]

1851, He was in the junior class at Union College, with residence listed as Schenectady, N.Y. [*U.S. School Catalogs, 1765–1935*]

1852, Senior class at Union College with residence in Germany [Ibid.]

1860, Henry G. Babcock, 35, lawyer, born New York, living with Gurdon and Almira Babcock and family in Wisconsin. [1860 Federal Census, Columbus, Wis.]

1861, April, Frontier Guard.

1861, June, He was appointed to a clerkship at the Patent Office. [*Evening Star,* June 10, 1861, p.2]

1861, Oct. 29, Married Mary Van Buskirk in Washington, D.C. [*DC Marriages, 1811–1950*]

No date, Henry G. Babcock v. Mary E. Babcock, divorce. [Wis. Historical Society, Wis. Circuit Court (Dane County): Divorce Case Files, 1839–1928, Reel 6, Item ID 288]

1884, Feb. 5, Died in Asheville, N.C. [Stephen Babcock, *The Babcock Genealogy* (np, 1903), p.270]

David H. Bailey [Hon.] (1830–1897)

1830, Sept. 27, David H. Bailey born, Wilmington, Clinton County, Ohio, son of Micajah Bailey. ["Ancestral File," database, *David H. Bailey Family Tree*] (http://familysearch.org/pal:/MM9.2.1/MWXS)

1861 April, Served in Frontier Guard, Washington, D.C.

1861, May 8, He married Clarissa Harlan, Clinton County, Ohio. [*David H. Bailey Family Tree*, op. cit.]

1862, Mar. 10, Son Barclay Harlan Bailey, born Leavenworth, Leavenworth County, Kans. [Ibid.]

1863, Aug. 18, Daughter Susanna Bailey, born Leavenworth, Kans. [Ibid.]

1867, Daughter Maria Antoinette Bailey born Clinton County, Ohio [Ibid.]

1870, Bailey left for his post as Consul in Hong Kong, China. [*Cincinnati Enquirer*, 23 Sept. 1870, p.4]

1873, **Oct. 19** Son Harlan Bailey born, Hong Kong, China. [Ibid.]

1876, Micajah Bailey [father of David H. Bailey] died from prescription mistake by druggist.

1877, **Dec. 14**, Hon. David H. Bailey of Ohio nominated Consul to Shanghai. ["Appointments,"*Daily Register*, Rockford, Ill.), Dec. 15, 1877, p.2]

1883, Harlan Bailey was born. [Bailey Family Tree, op. cit.]

1897, **Jan. 22**, Died Cincinnati, Ohio; buried Sugar Grove Cemetery, Wilmington, Ohio [*Bailey Family Tree*, www.familysearch.org]

Isaac Denny Balch (1835–1889)

1835, **Apr. 18**, Balch was born in Newburyport, Mass., the son of John Balch and Laura Amelia Denny Balch. [Galusha Burchard Balch, *Genealogy of the Balch Family in America* (E. Putnam, 1897), p.313]

1856, Graduated from Bowdoin College. [Nehemiah Cleaveland, *History of Bowdoin College* (J. R. Osgood & Co., 1882), p.704]

1857, He taught at Limington Academy. [Ibid.]

1858, Taught in Kennebunkport. [Ibid.]

1859, Taught in Plaquemine, La. [Ibid.]

1860, Lived with John and Laura Balch and siblings in Newburyport. [1860 Federal Census, Newburyport Ward 5, Essex, Mass.]

1860, Studied law in Newburyport, Mass. [Cleaveland, p.704]

1861, **April**, Frontier Guard. [# 58 on list of 164]

1861, **Apr. 29**, Enlisted in Company A of the 3rd District of Columbia Infantry Battalion for defense of the City of Washington for a term of three months. [American Civil War Research Database]

1861, **June 10**, 3rd D.C. Infantry expedition to Rockville, Md. [Ibid.]

1861, **July 7**, Expedition to Great Falls, Md. [Ibid.]

1862, Admitted to the bar in Cincinnati, Ohio. [Cleaveland, p.704]

1863–1864, Practiced law in Jersey City, N.J. [Ibid.]

1864–1867, Mercantile business in N.Y.C. [Ibid.]

1870, **Jan. 7**, Listed as a clerk at the Custom House [1870 Federal Census, N.Y. Ward 16, Dist. 7]

1880, June 7, Listed as lawyer and Deputy Collector at the Customs House [1880 Federal Census]

1889, Feb. 16, Died in East Orange, Essex, N.J. [N.J., *Deaths and Burials Index*, 1798–1971]

Thomas D. Bancroft (1837–1917)

1837, Thomas D. Bancroft born in Ohio, son of David and Louisa (Thomas) Bancroft of New York. [*Wyandotte County and Kansas City, Kans. Hist. and Biographical*, The Goodspeed Publishing Co., Chicago (1890), p.500]

1839, Bancroft family returned to New York. [Ibid.]

ca. 1853, [age 16] He left home. [Ibid.]

ca. 1855, [age 18] Came to Kansas Territory. [Ibid.]

1856, At 18, T.D. Bancroft served as Captain of a company under John Brown during the Border War in Kansas. ["Dr. Bancroft to Talk of Lincoln," *Quincy Daily Whig*, Quincy, Ill., Aug. 8, 1908, p.8; "[Bancroft] joined the Free-State troops, then under the leadership of Gen. James Lane and John Brown"] [op. cit., Wyandotte County, 1890]

1856/57, Bancroft returned to his father's home. [Ibid., p.500]

ca. 1857, Attended Genessee Wesleyan Seminary and College in Lima, Livingston County, N.Y. [Ibid., p.501]

ca. 1860, "Served as Capt. of a wide-awake company during Lincoln's campaign." [Ibid., p.501]

1861, Jan. 28 "Went to Washington, D.C. and was present at the Capitol building and heard many of the farewell speeches made in the Senate and House of Reps by seceding members." [Ibid., p.501]

1861, Married Susie Archer of Washington, D.C. [Ibid., p.502]

1861, Mar. 4, "Mr. Bancroft was present at the first inaugural of Abraham Lincoln, afterward making his personal acquaintance." [Ibid., p.501]

ca. 1861–1862 Son William T. Bancroft was born. [Ibid., p.502].

1861, April, Bancroft was among the first to join the [Frontier Guard], "made up of men who had formerly fought in the Kansas Border Ruffian War. . ." [Ibid., p.501]

"During the Civil War, Bancroft fought in the volunteer service in twenty or more battles and skirmishes." [Ibid., p.501].

1862, First wife died. [Ibid.]

1863, Involved in arrest of Mr. Annis and his brother, who tried to invest or buy contraband goods in Baltimore through T.D. Bancroft, who claimed to be a detective. [www.fold3.com]

1864, Mar. 9, Appointed as Sutler for the Regiment, 1st Conn. Cav. [Ibid.]

1864, May 5–7, Fought in Wilderness Battle with Gen. Sheridan. [*Wyandotte County Biography*: op. cit., p.501]

1864, Dec. 14, Dismissed as Sutler 1st Conn. Cav. for neglect of duty since April 1864. [*Fold3*]

1865, Apr. 4, Assassination of Lincoln; Dr. Bancroft was at the Ford Theater, Washington, D.C.

He stood at the head of the stairs while President Lincoln was being carried downstairs and across the street to the building where Lincoln died. [*Buffalo Morning Express*, Buffalo, N.Y., 1905] Bancroft picked up program stained with Lincoln's blood from theater floor.

1879, Went west, settled in Kansas City, Kansas, with wholesale grocer's firm. [Wyandotte County Bio., op. cit., p.501]

1880, Married Miss Elida Smith, a native of New Jersey [Ibid., p.502].

1888, Began organization of a Sunday school for children in Kansas City at the Opera House. [Wyandotte County Bio., op. cit.] Kans.

1893, May 23, Free public baths and swimming pool, conceived by Rev. Dr. T. D. Bancroft, opened in Kansas City, Kansas. [*Kansas City Star*, May 24, 1893, p.1, col. 4]

1895, T.D. Bancroft and wife, Elida, enumerated in Kansas State Census in Wyandotte County, Kans. He is listed as a philanthropist. [Source: 1895 Kansas State Census, household #653 and family #672, p.99]

1896, January, The Tabernacle in Kansas City, Kansas, erected by T.D. Bancroft for benefit of the poor, burned down. After the fire, Bancroft moved to Cripple Creek [Colo]. [*Kansas City Star*, Jan. 29, 1896]

1900, June 19, Bancroft, with wife, Eliza S., at 1616 Washington Ave., 9th Precinct, Denver, Arapahoe County, Colo. [U.S. Federal Census 1900, Arapahoe County, Colo.]

1905, Bancroft at Salida, Colo., establishing a home for consumptives. [*Buffalo Morning Express*, 1905]

1906, October, Bancroft of Denver, Colorado, touring the East to raise money for houses for consumptives. His career "included service with John Brown and a permanent acquaintance of Abraham Lincoln." [untitled article, *Olympia Daily Recorder*, Olympia, Wash., Oct. 1, 1906, p.2]

1910, Wrote pamphlet: "The Assassination of Abraham Lincoln was the Greatest Tragedy the World has Ever Known . . ." [McLellan Lincoln Collection, Brown University]

1912, June, T. D. Bancroft of Portland, Ore., visiting in Grand Rapids, Mich., gave a lecture about the assassination of President Lincoln. ["Old Frontier Guard Saw Lincoln Shot . . . ," *Grand Rapids Press*, Grand Rapids, Mich., June 21, 1912, p.24]

1917, Nov. 23, "T. D. Bancroft of El Monte, California, a lecturer on the life of President Lincoln, found [dead] in room in a lodging house here." [Providence, R.I.] "Death due to gas poisoning. Leaves son W. T. Bancroft of Kansas City, Missouri, and daughter Mrs. Estelle Temple of Baltimore." [*Boston Herald and Journal*, Boston, Mass., Nov. 24, 1917, p.2, col. 7]

1917 Buried, Pocasset Cemetery, Cranston, Providence County, R.I. [www.findagrave.com]

John Kemp Bartlett (1832–1899)

1832, Bartlett born was born in New York City, the son of John Bartlett and Sarah Paschell, Quakers from Easton in Talbot County, Md. [Clayton Hall, *Baltimore: Biography* (Baltimore: Lewis Historical Publishing Co., 1912), p.600.

1858, Oct. 12, He married Virginia Cowgill (a Quaker). They moved to Kansas. [Ibid.]

1858–1863, He was editor of the *Leavenworth Times*. [William G. Cutler, *History of the State of Kansas*]

1861, Apr. 18, Member of the Frontier Guard.

1863, October, He sold his interest in the *Leavenworth Times* and moved to Philadelphia. There he entered into the oil production business in Pennsylvania. [Clayton Hall, p.600]

1874, Moved to Talbot County, Md., and continued in the oil industry. [Ibid.]

1876, Moved to Baltimore. [Ibid.]

1899, July 15, He died in Baltimore and was buried in Friends Cemetery, Baltimore, Maryland.

George Agur Bassett (1832–1885)

1832, George A. Bassett was born in N.J., son of Agur and Olive Bassett of Connecticut. His father was a saddler.

1841, The Bassett family moved to Washington, D.C. [*National Republican*, Sept. 12, 1876]

1856, Nov. 6, George Bassett married Clarinda M. Williams.

1860, Aug. 4, Clarinda Bassett was listed in the census in the household of her father, James Williams in Washington, D.C. The family lived close to Edwin M. Stanton. [*U.S. Census,* Roll M653_103, 375]

1860, Dec. 21, Bassett was Vice President of the Republican Ass'n. [*National Republican*]

1861, Mar. 4, George A. Bassett was included on the list of people invited to Lincoln's Inaugural Ball to be held Mar. 6. [*National Republican*, March 4, 1861]

1861, Apr. 13, He accepted the commission of Captain of the First Regiment of the Infantry of the District of Columbia. [*Letters Rec'd by the Office of the Adjutant General, 1861–1870,* www.fold3.com]

1864, Oct. 27, Wife Clarinda died at 27. [*Interment in the Historic Congressional Cemetery*]

1865–1866, Ad in several papers for a real estate brokerage and attorneys for claims against the government naming Geo. A. Bassett, Esq., clerk of Committee of Ways and Means in the House of Representatives, as an associate. [*Daily National Republican,* Jan. 20, 1866]

1871–1873, Bassett listed in Washington, D.C. City Directory as clerk, Ways and Means Committee.

1873, February, Investigation of the Ways and Means Committee. Charges of corruption were brought against Judge C. T. Sherman and George A. Bassett, clerk. [*Evening Star*, Feb. 17, 1873]

1876, September, He was a clerk for the Postal Commission. [*Index to the Misc. Documents of the House of Representatives for the Second Session of the 45th Congress* (Google eBook), p.74]

1880–1885, Listed in the Washington, D.C. City Directory as clerk in the Treasury Office.

1885, Feb. 9, George Agur Bassett died of pneumonia and was buried. [Website: *Congressional Cemetery, Association for the Preservation of the Historic Congressional Cemetery*]

John Hogan Benton (1829–1914)

1829, June 10, John Hogan Benton was born in Brownstown, Indiana. [*Wash. Times,* Sept. 12, 1914, p.10]

1848–50, He received his education at Asbury University in Greencastle, Ind. [John Hoban Benton, *David Benton, Jr. and Sarah Bingham, Their Ancestors and Descendants and Other Ancestral Lines* (Boston: David Clapp & Son, 1906), p.55]

1849–1860? Employed in Indiana as bookkeeper, merchant, civil engineer, and assistant secretary of the state senate. [*Washington Times*, op. cit.]

1851, Married Mary Ray in Indiana. (She died in 1889.) [Ibid.]

1857, Summer–Fall, Traveled to Kansas with his friend John F. C. Tanner. [Benton, p.55]

1860, Aug. 4, John H. Benton appointed secretary of the Republican Central Committee of Jackson County, Ind. ["Republican Meeting at Brownstown," *Seymour Times* (Ind.), Aug. 9, 1860, p.2]

1861, March, Moved to Washington, D.C., where he took a clerkship at the Census Office. [Benton, p.55]

1861, Apr. 19, He was "at the B&O Station in the evening of April 19, 1861, when the 6th Mass. Inf. arrived, fresh from the assault of the Baltimore mob, and marched with it to its quarters in the Senate wing of the capital; and that same evening, we [I] enlisted in General 'Jim' Lane's Frontier Guard, and with it bivouacked that night in the East Room of the White House. The company was drawn up in line at midnight, and was reviewed by President Lincoln." [Benton, p.56]

His honorable discharge from the Frontier Guard was printed in his book. [Benton, p.58]

1862, August, He was "a voluntary nurse, stretcher-bearer, and field hospital assistant on the battlefield of Second Bull Run leaving the city on Saturday evening while the battle was still in progress and the roar of the conflict distinctly heard—reaching the field under a flag of truce on Monday morning—leaving it with the last ambulance train on Friday afternoon and arriving home at midnight." [Benton, p.56]

1863, April, Transferred to the Pension Office. [Benton, p.56]

1864, July, Became a member of the Pension Office Guards, "but with the disappearance of the enemy, the company was disbanded." [Benton, p.56]

1875–1876, Chief of the invalid branch of the pension office. ["John H. Benton Hale and Hearty," *Washington Herald,* June 11, 1911, p.14]

1882, Member of the board of review for the Pension Office until retirement. [Ibid.]

1890, October, Married Maria Louisa Webster (she died in 1910). [*Washington Times,* ibid.]

1896, Jan. 8, A group of survivors of the Frontier Guard was organized, with John H. Benton chosen as President. ["Frontier Guards Organize," *Evening Star,* Washington, D.C., Jan. 9, 1896]

1903, Retired from Pension Office.

1914, Sept. 11, Died in Washington, D.C. [*DC, Select Deaths and Burials,* 1840–1964]

Anthony James Bleecker (1799–1884)

1799, Oct. 22, Anthony James Bleecker was born in New York City, the son of James and Sarah (Bache) Bleecker. He was educated at Dr. Eiginbrodt's Academy in Jamaica, Long Island. [Henry Hall, *America's Successful Men of Affairs: The City of New York* (*New York Tribune,* 1895) pp.89–91]

1823, He joined the successful New York real estate brokerage and auction business established by his grandfather. ["An Old New-Yorker Gone" (*New York Times,* Jan. 18, 1884), p.8]

1837, Appointed U.S. Marshal of the Southern District of New York by Martin Van Buren [Ibid.].

1855, He was instrumental in founding the Republican Party in New York City [Ibid.].

1856, Ran as the first Republican candidate for mayor on Freemont's ticket [Ibid.].

1861, Mar. 30, He wrote Lincoln asking for an appointment as Naval Officer or as Surveyor of the Port of New York. [Abraham Lincoln Papers at the Library of Congress, *American Memory* (memory.loc.gov)]

1861, April, Member of the Frontier Guard. "Besides the Western Jayhawkers it [the Frontier Guard] comprises some of the best material of the East. Senator Pomeroy and old Anthony Bleecker stood shoulder to shoulder in the ranks." [John Hay, *Complete Civil War Diary of John Hay* (SUI Press, 1999), p.1]

He was "an inimitable raconteur, whose stories convulsed Abraham Lincoln with laughter . . ." [Henry Mills Alden, *Harper's Monthly Magazine,* Vol. 77 (Harper & Brothers, 1888), p.936]

1862, Appointed by Lincoln as Assessor of Internal Revenue for the Eighth District of New York, a position which he held for six years. ["An Old New-Yorker Gone," ibid.]

1863, He was appointed Chairman of the Commission to extend Central Park [Ibid.].

1871, Appointed to a commission to appraise every square inch of property to which the City held any claim when "Boss" Tweed wished to issue additional municipal bonds [Ibid.].

1884, Jan. 17, Bleecker died of a stroke and was buried in Trinity Churchyard Cemetery [Ibid.].

Frederick William Bogen (1813–1885)

1813, Jan. 7, Frederick William Bogen was born in Hesse, Darmstadt, Germany. [*Petitions for Naturalization Filed in New York City 1792–1989* (www.ancestry.com) database online]

1850, Frederick W. Bogen, 37, clergyman, lived in Suffolk, Maine, with wife Sarah. [1850 Federal Census]

1851, *The German in America,* by F. W. Bogen, was published. It was an introduction of American life to German immigrants and was printed in German on one page and English on the other. [Google eBook]

1851, Aug. 21, His Naturalization Petition was filed in the Massachusetts District Court. [*New York, Naturalization Petitions, 1794–1906* (www.ancestry.com) database online]

1861, April, He was a member of the Frontier Guard.

1861, Nov. 1, He enlisted in the New York 41st Infantry Regiment at Hunter's Chapel, Va., as a commissioned officer with the rank of Chaplain. [*U.S. Civil War Soldiers Records and Profiles, 1861–1865* (www.ancestry.com) database online]

1863, May, He was wounded at Chancellorsville. [Letter to Edwin M. Stanton, March 22, 1865 (www.fold3.com/image/#284431251)]

1863, June 22, Recovered to join his regiment at Goose Creek in Loudoun County, Va. [Ibid.].

1863, July, He was at the Battle of Gettysburg [Ibid.].

1863, August, His regiment then went to Folly Island, off the coast from Charleston [Ibid.].

1863, Dec. 6, Mustered out because of bad health. [*New York Civil War Muster Roll Abstracts 1861–1900;* Letter to E. M. Stanton]

1864, January–April, Traveled to Germany. [Letter to E. M. Stanton]

1864, May, Worked temporarily for the Treasury Department in Washington, D.C. [Ibid.]

1864, September, He took part in the presidential election campaign, speaking to the German-born citizens of Indiana [Ibid.].

1865, Mar. 22, Sent a letter to Edwin M. Stanton requesting transportation to Ship Island, Miss., to join the 74th Colored Infantry in the capacity of Chaplain [Ibid.].

1869 through 1885, Listed as a clerk at the Pension Office in the City Directory. [*City Directories for Washington, D.C.,* www.fold3.com]

1885, Mar. 18, He was admitted to the veteran's hospital in Togus, Kennebec, Maine, with a disability from a gunshot wound of left ankle joint. [*U.S. National Homes for Disabled Soldiers 1866–1938*, (Ancestry.com) database online]

1885, May 4, Bogen died at the hospital and was buried in Togus Nat'l Cemetery in Togus, Maine [Ibid.].

Alexander H. Brown (1804–1873)

1804, Sept. 17, Alexander H. Brown was born. [www.findagrave.com] He was the son of Matthew Brown. [*Jacob Engelbrecht Death Register of Frederick County, Maryland, 1820–1890* (Monrovia, Md.: Paw Prints, Inc., 1996), p.28]

His father had been a newspaper editor in Baltimore but moved to Frederick County around 1807 to farm and raise sheep on his estate, Fleecy Dale. [Rachel A. Minick, *History of Printing in Maryland, 1791–1800* (Archives of Maryland Online), p.45]

1831, June 4, Alexander H. Brown was a committee member at the district meeting of the National Republican Party held at Buckeystown, Md. [William J. Grove, *History of Carrollton Manor, Frederick County, Maryland* (Lime Kiln, Md., 1922), p.51]

1832, Apr. 24, He was appointed postmaster at Point of Rocks, Frederick County, Md. [*Appointments of U.S. Postmasters, 1832–1971*]

1832, Advertised as a forwarding agent and commission merchant at the depot at Point of Rocks. [*Frederick Town Herald,* June 30, 1832, p.4]

1861, April, He was a member of the Frontier Guard.

1873, Aug. 15, He died in Frederick County, Md. [*Jacob Engelbrecht Death Register,* p.28]

1876, Nov. 8, His remains were removed from Maryland and buried at Oak Hill Cemetery in Washington, D.C. [www.findagrave.com]

Frederick Abner Brown (1842–)

1842, Oct. 8, Frederick Abner Brown was born in Lockport, Erie County, New York, the son of William Otis Brown and Olivia E. Clarke. [Adin Ballou, *An Elaborate History and Genealogy of the Ballous in America* (Providence, R.I.: E. L. Freeman & Son, 1888), p.467]

1846, His family moved to Buffalo, where his father was a leading merchant on the Central Wharf, shipping grain from the West to

European markets. He had 16 ships on the Great Lakes and a large interest in the grain elevators in Buffalo. [Ballou, p.467]

1861, April, Frederick was a member of the Frontier Guard.

1864, Aug. 14, Frederick Brown married Jane Coombs. [Ballou, p.467] She was a popular tragedienne with a career that lasted six decades. He later worked as her agent and as the manager for her Jane Coombs Theater Company.

1865–1870, He worked as a commission merchant in Buffalo, New York, with an office on the Central Wharf. [*City Directories of Buffalo, New York,* www.fold3.com]

1880, Frederick Brown and wife Jane lived in New York. [*1880 U.S. Federal Census, New York, N.Y.*]

1889, Oct. 19, "F.A. Brown, agent of the Jane Coombs Co., is at the St. George." ["Social and Personal," *Evening Sentinel* (Santa Cruz, Cal.), p.3]

1893, Mar. 8, F. A. Brown and Jane Coombs stayed at the Eldridge Hotel in Lawrence, Kansas. She was starring in *Bleak House* at the opera house. [*Lawrence Daily Journal,* March 9, 1893, p.4]

1910, Apr. 16, Frederick Brown, age 59, Appraiser, lived in the Bronx in New York with wife Jane C. Brown, age 58. [*1910 U.S. Federal Census, Bronx Assembly District, New York, N.Y.,* p.3B]

John B. Brown (1807–1867)

1807, July 16, John B. Brown was born in Richfield, Otsego County, New York. ["Obituary," *New York Daily Tribune,* Dec. 24, 1867]

1849, He moved to Alexandria County, Va., where he became the leader of the Republican Party in Virginia.

1856, He was an elector for Fremont. ["Obituary"]

1860, He was a delegate to the Republican National Convention at Chicago, which nominated Lincoln for President. On his way home, he was arrested on the charge of circulating incendiary documents, which included the *New York Tribune,* the *Washington Star,* and the *Baltimore Sun.* He was thrown in jail and made to pay $2,000 bond. ["Obituary"; "Arrest for Circulating Incendiary Documents," *New York Times,* June 12, 1860, p.4]

1861, $1,000 was offered for him by Rebel authorities. ["Obituary"]

1861, April, He was a member of the Frontier Guard.

1861, Received an appointment in Washington that he held for five years. ["Obituary"]

1867, Dec. 9, He died in Washington, D.C. ["Obituary"]

James Bryan (1796–1869)

1796, May 4, James Bryan was born in Maryland. [www.findagrave.com] He was the son of Charles Bryan and Margaret. [Edward C. Papenfuse et. al., *Biographical Dictionary of the Maryland Legislature, 1635–1789,* Archives of Maryland (msa.maryland.gov) Vol. 426, p.521]

1819, Jan. 5, He first married Emily Woodward Lecompte. [www.findagrave.com]

1820s, He was the Secretary of the Auxiliary Colonization Society in Dorchester County, Md. [Am. Colonization Soc'y, *Annual Report* (Washington: Davis & Force, 1823), p.173]

1836, Aug. 3, James Bryan married, second, Mary Ann Pattison. [www .findagrave.com]

1849, June 4, He freed a family slave, whom he had recently bought from his brother, Joseph H. Bryan, in consideration of the attachment formed to her by his deceased sister, Rebecca. [*Dorchester County Court Chattel Records, 1852–1860,* Archives of Maryland (msa. maryland.gov) Vol. 776, p.189]

1850, July 22, James Bryan, 54, was a merchant in Dorchester County, Maryland, and lived with his wife Mary A. Bryan and children. [1850 U.S. Federal Census, Dist. 1, Dorchester, Md.]

1860, Apr. 20, When the Republican State Convention assembled in Baltimore, it was broken up by mob violence. They moved to a private house to meet and selected James Bryan as one of the delegates to attend the Convention in Chicago. [John Thomas Scharf, *History of Baltimore City from the Earliest Period to the Present Day* (Baltimore: L. H. Everts, 1881), pp.126–27]

1860, July 11, James Bryan, 64, lived on Taylor's Island in Dorchester County, Md., at the residence of his son, James L. Bryan, a physician. [1860 U.S. Federal Census, Dist. 4, Dorchester, Md.]

1869, Jan. 19, Died and was buried in Christ Episcopal Church Cemetery, Cambridge, Md.

John Taylor Burris [Col.] (1828–1916)

1828, Dec. 22, Born Butler County, Ohio [*A Standard History of Kansas and Kansans*, William E. Connelley, Topeka. Chicago: Lewis Publishing Co., 1918 [transcribed by students from USD 508, Baxter Springs Middle School, Baxter Springs, Kans., November, 1997]. http://skyways.lib.ks.us/genweb/archives/1918ks/biob/burrisjt.html

    Spent youth in Kentucky and taught school there [Ibid.].

1847, Went to Iowa [with the Mounted Rifles]; served in Mexican War from that state [Ibid.].

1849, Oct. 4, Married Martha Ann McGannon [William G. Cutler's *History of the State of Kansas, first published 1883 by A.T. Andreas*] [*Part 5, Johnson County*], http://www.kancoll.org/books/cutler/johnson/johnson-co-p5.html

1852 Burris opened a hotel at Fredonia, Iowa [Ibid.].

1853 Was admitted to bar [Ibid.].

1855 Elected judge of County Court [Ibid.].

1858 Settled in Olathe, Johnson County, Kansas Territory [Ibid.].

1859 Elected member of Wyandotte Constitution Convention [Ibid.].

1861 Served as sergeant in Lane's Frontier Guard, Washington, D.C. [Ibid.] Appointed District Attorney of Kansas. [Ibid.].

1861, August, Became Lt. Col. 4th Kansas Infantry [later became 10th] [Ibid.].

1865, Mar. 13, Promoted to Colonel (Brevet, Vol.) [*American Civil War Research Database*™, Copyright 1997–2013 Historical Data Systems, Inc.]

1865, Aug. 20, Mustered out of 10th Kansas [Ibid.].

1865, Burris resumed the practice of law in Johnson County, Kansas. [Cutler, op. cit.]

1865, Elected to Kansas House of Representatives, served as speaker [Ibid.].

1868, Appointed judge of the 10th Judicial District [served 1869–1870] [Ibid.].

1868, Burris was President of the Republican State Convention. [*Kansasipedia*, Kansas State Historical Society, Topeka, Kans., https://www.kshs.org/kansapedia/john-taylor-burris/17058

1869, Elected to lower house of legislature. [Connelley, op. cit.] Organizer of Fort Scott and Gulf Railroad [Ibid.].

1890–1901, Served as judge of the 10th District [Ibid.].

1910, Living in Olathe, Johnson County, Kans. [U.S. Federal Census]

1916, Dec. 4, Died in Los Angeles, Cal. [*Kansas City Star*, Dec. 6, 1915, Vol. 78, No. 291, p.4]

John R. Carpenter (1819–1862)

1819, John R. Carpenter was born in New York. He was the son of William Carpenter and Alice Dexter. [DAR Records, Mrs. Marion Carpenter Hall Blackburn, Application # 30047]

1839, Dec. 23, He married Miriam H. Mosier Tanner, a widow, in Perth, Montgomery County, N.Y. [Widow's Pension, *Case Files of Approved Pension Applications of Widows and Other Dependents of Civil War Veterans,* NARA Catalog ID #300020]

1850, John R. Carpenter, 31, was a millwright living in Fairfax County, Virginia, with his wife, Miriam, and children Samuel, Louisa, Jane, Phoebe, and John. [*1850 U.S. Federal Census, Fairfax County, Va.*]

1860, He worked as a mechanic in Wash., D.C., and lived with his wife and children. [*1860 U.S. Census*]

1861, April, Member of the Frontier Guard.

1861, July 23, He enlisted in Companies F and S of the 1st District of Columbia Infantry with the rank of Chaplain. The regiment had duty in defense of Washington. [National Park Service (www.nps.gov)]

1861, Oct. 21, As Chaplain of the District of Columbia Volunteers, he was one of the committee who met at Trinity Church. [*Evening Star,* Oct. 21, 1863 ("Chronicling America"), p.3]

1862, January, His regiment guarded the railroad near Bladensburg, Maryland, until May, then had duty for the defense of Harpers Ferry until June. [National Park Service]

1862, June, The 1st District of Columbia Infantry was in Shenandoah
   Valley, along with the 60th New York Regiment Volunteers until
   August. [National Park Service]
1862, August, "Mr. Carpenter was taken sick with typhoid fever in
   August, went home, and died. He was a good man, always at his
   post, and much beloved by his regiment. I think he was connected
   with the Methodist Episcopal Church." [Richard Eddy, Chaplain,
   History of the Sixtieth Regiment New York State Volunteers (Philadelphia, PA: published by author, 1864), p.121]
1862, Aug. 22, John R. Carpenter died. [Widow's Pension]
1862, Aug. 26, He was buried in Glenwood Cemetery in Washington,
   D.C. ["Funeral of Rev. J. R. Carpenter," *Evening Star,* Aug. 27,
   1862 ("Chronicling America"), p.3]

Edward George Chambers (1819–1898)

1819, June 4, Edward G. Chambers was born in Dublin, Ireland. His
   parents died when he was young. [William Henry Perrin, et al.,
   *History of Crawford County and Ohio: containing a history of the
   earliest settlement to the present time; a history of Crawford County;
   bibliographic sketches of some of the early settlers and prominent men,
   etc.* (Chicago: Baskin & Batty, 1881), p.888]
1833, Aug. 20, He came to America at age 14, on a ship from Liverpool.
   [Ancestry.com, *New York, Passenger Lists, 1820–1957*]
1833, He first worked with a crew on the Delaware & Raritan Canal. He
   was then hired as a crew manager for the Boston & Providence
   Railroad. [Perrin, *History,* p.888]
1835, He moved to Crawford County, Ohio, where he learned carpentry.
   [Perrin, *History,* p.888]
1839, Married Elizabeth Henderson. [Perrin, *History,* p.888]
1842, He started preparatory school at Oberlin College. [Ancestry.com,
   Catalog of Officers and Students in Oberlin College Institute]
1845–1848, He graduated from Oberlin College with an A.B. degree.
   [Ancestry.com, *U.S. School Catalogs, 1765–1935*]
1848, He taught school in Bucyrus, Ohio, for six months, then moved
   to Groveport, Ohio, and taught there for three years. [Perrin, *History,* p.888]

1856–1858, He worked as paymaster for the Pittsburg, Fort Wayne & Chicago Railroad. [Perrin, *History,* p.888]

1860, Chambers, age 40, farmer, lived in Crawford County, Ohio, with his wife, Elizabeth, and children. [*1860 U.S. Federal Census, Whetstone Township, Crawford County, Ohio*]

1861, Mar. 6, He went to Washington, D.C. with Ohio Senator Benjamin Wade and secured a position as a clerk on the Committee of Territories, of which Wade was chairman. [Perrin, *History,* p.888]

1862, He was appointed secretary of the Joint Committee on the Conduct of War. Benjamin Wade was chairman of that committee. [Perrin, *History,* p.888]

1866, Superintended the construction of the harbor at Frankfort, Ohio and lived there for two years. [Perrin, *History,* p.888]

1867, When a town plan was drawn up for Frankfort City, he was involved in building the town. [*The Traverse Region,* p.302]

1870, June, Lived in Crawford County, Ohiohio. [*1870 U.S. Census, Whetstone, Crawford County, Ohio*]

1881, He was secretary of the Crawford County Agricultural Society. [Perrin, *History,* p.888]

1890, Listed on 1890 Veteran's Schedule as Edward G. Chambers, Private in Frontier Guard for Defense of Washington, 13 Apr 1861–27 Apr 1861, 14 days. [1890 Veteran's Schedule, Crystal Lake, Mich., p.3]

1898, Feb. 28, Chambers died in Bucyrus, Ohio. [Ancestry.com, *U.S. School Catalogs*]

Charles Champion (1826–1879)

1826, Charles Champion was born in Philadelphia, Pennsylvania [NARA, *Passport Apps 1795–1905,* No. 566612]

1850, Aug. 7, He lived in Spring Garden, Pa. with his parents, Thomas and Rachael Champion, and his three brothers, Thomas, Jr., Newton, and John. His father was a mechanical engineer with several patents. The sons were trained in mechanics and metalworking. [*1850 U.S. Federal Census, Spring Garden, Ward 6, Philadelphia County, Pa.*]

1850, He went by ship to San Francisco. [U.S. Passenger and Immigration Index (www.ancestry.com)]

1852, **December,** Lived in Sacramento County, California. [Cal.State Census, 1852]

1860, He was living with his family in Washington, D.C. [*1860 U.S. Federal Census*]

1860, **July,** He and his brother Thomas, Jr. received a patent for an improvement in gas regulators. [*Annual Report of the Commissioner of Patents,* (U.S. Gov't Printing Office, 1861), p.543]

1861, **April,** He was a member of the Frontier Guard.

1863, **May 1,** Married Catherine E. Hyde. [*District of Columbia Marriages, 1811–1950*]

1867–1872, He was vice president and president of what was variously called the Republican Club and the Republican Central Committee. [*Evening Star,* "Chronicling America"]

1869, He was on the Board of Aldermen for the Sixth Ward of Washington. [Poore, Benjamin, *Congressional Directory for the First Session of the Forty-First Congress of the USA* (1869), p.101]

1873–1879, He worked as a clerk in Washington, D.C. [*Washington, D.C. City Directory*]

1879, **Aug. 20,** Died at age 54. [*Washington Post* (Ancestry.com Historic Newspapers)]

1879, **Aug. 22,** He was buried in the Congressional Cemetery in Washington, D.C. [Internment Index]

Thomas Champion (1833–1912)

1833, Thomas Champion was born in Pennsylvania. He was the son of Thomas and Rachel Champion and the younger brother of Charles Champion, also of the Frontier Guard.

1850, The Champions lived in Philadelphia. [*1850 U.S. Census, Spring Garden Ward 6, Phila., Pa*]

1852–1863, The family lived in Washington, D.C., where Thomas Sr. was employed at the naval yard building engines and boilers for steamers. ["From Thomas Champion," *The Papers of Andrew Johnson: 1864–1865* (Univ. of Tenn. Press, 1986), p.476]

1861, **April,** He was a member of the Frontier Guard.

1863, July, Thomas Champion, age 31, Boilermaker, single, no previous military service, residence Washington, D.C. [*U.S., Civil War Draft Registrations Records, 1863–1865*]

1863? He and his family moved back to Philadelphia, where they "repaired plates for ironclad vessels." ["From Thomas Champion"]

1870, He was listed on the census as a blacksmith, living in Philadelphia with his widowed mother and a younger brother. [*1870 U.S. Federal Census, Phila. Ward 20, Dist. 66, Philadelphia, Pa.*]

1912, Nov. 6, He died and was buried in Fair Hill Burial Ground in Philadelphia.

Prentiss M. Clark (1827–1914)

1827, Oct. 26, Prentiss M. Clark was born. [*Maine, Births and Christenings, 1739–1900* (Index, Family Search)] He was the son of Samuel C. Clark and Sallie Dow. [*U.S. Sons of the American Revolution Membership Applications, 1889–1970,* Membership # 3263]

1850, Lived as a schoolteacher in Springfield, Maine. [*1850 U.S. Federal Census, Springfield, Penobscot, Maine*]

1860, Employed as a book and map seller and lived with his wife, Augusta, and their two daughters, Lillian and Emily. [*1860 U.S. Federal Census, Springfield, Penobscot, Maine*]

1861, April, Member of the Frontier Guard.

1861, September, Clerk at the Indian Office of the Department of the Interior in Washington, D.C. [*Register of Officers and Agents, Civil, Military, and Naval on the Thirtieth of September, 1861* (Washington: U.S. Gov't Printing Office, 1862), p.82]

1865, Apr. 16, He was involved in the capture of Lewis Thornton Powell (aka Lewis Payne) at Mary Surratt's house the day after Lincoln's assassination. [William C. Edwards, *The Lincoln Assassination– The Rewards Files* (Google eBook, 2012), pp.143–48]. In July 1865 his sister Roxinda married George F. Robinson, who was credited with saving the life of Secretary of State Seward when he was attacked by Lewis Thornton Powell. [George Foster Robinson Family Tree (Ancestry.com)]

1866, July, The Committee on Claims awarded Clark $500 for his help in the capture of the would-be assassin. [Clara E. Laughlin, *Death of Lincoln* (New York: Doubleday, Page & Co., 1909), 312–15]

1870, Moved to Minneapolis with his wife and daughters. [*1870 U.S. Census, Mineapolis, Minn.*]

1871, While living in Minnesota, he was appointed to a clerkship at the Patent Office in Washington. [*Register of Officers and Agents, Civil, Military, and Naval, on the Thirtieth of September, 1871* (Washington: Gov't Printing Office, 1872)]

1880, Moved to San Antonio, Texas. [*1880 U.S. Federal Census, San Antonio, Bexar, Texas*]

1884, Mar. 11, Married second, Adelaide Sabine, in Washington D.C. [*District of Columbia, Select Marriages, 1830–1921* (Ancestry. com) database online)]

1900, He and Frances Adelaide Sabine Clark lived in Newport, Minn. [*1900 U.S. Census, Newport, Minn.*]

1905, Lived in St. Paul, Minnesota. [*Minnesota, Territorial and State Censuses, 1849–1905*]

1907, "An account in a newspaper stating that Gen. Gordon was the last survivor came to the attention of P. M. Clark of Los Angeles, Calif., who wrote Gen. Gordon that he had supposed he (Clark) was the last one living. Mr. Clark related several incidents that proved to qualify him as one of the survivors of that old guard." ["Gen. Gordon, Ninety, Was Guard for Lincoln," *Washington Star,* May 30, 1922]

1910, Lived in Long Beach, California. [*1910 U.S. Census, Long Beach Ward 4, Los Angeles, Cal.*]

1914, Sept. 17, died in Los Angeles. [*California, Death Index, 1905–1939* (Ancestry.com) database]

Sidney J. Clarke (1831–1909)

1831, Oct. 16, Sidney Clarke was born in Southbridge, Massachusetts. [His grandfather was in the Revolutionary War and his father was in the War of 1812.] [*Parsons Daily Sun,* June 22, 1909, p.4]

ca. 1849, He engaged in mercantile pursuits at Worcester, Mass., wrote for a number of publications, and "soon earned the reputation of being a clear, concise and forcible writer." [Ibid.]

1854, Became editor and proprietor of the Southbridge Press [in Massachusetts] for five years. [Ibid.]

1856, A "Free-soiler" who became identified with the Republican Party. [Ibid.]

1858, Came west and located at Lawrence, Kansas Territory. [Ibid.]

1860, Married 1st wife, Henrietta Ross Clarke (1835–1873). [www.find agrave.com]

1860, Son, Sidney Ross Clarke, was born. [ibid]

1861, April, Member of Frontier Guard. [*Topeka Daily Capital*, March 22, 1909, p.3]

1862, Appointed Assistant Adjutant General of Volunteers in the Union Army by President Lincoln. Studied law in the office of General Lane and was his private secretary. [*Parsons Daily Sun,* op. cit.]

1862, Became a member of the Kansas Legislature. [Ibid.]

1862, Son, George Lincoln Clarke, was born. [www.findagrave.com]

1863, Chairman of the Republican State Committee. [*Parsons Daily Sun,* op. cit.]

1863, "Became the Assistant Provost Marshal General for Kansas, Nebraska, Colorado, and Dakota." (Headquartered in Leavenworth, Kans.) [Sidney Clarke biography, *Kansas Memory,* http://www.kansasmemory.org/item/213865]

1863, Aug. 21, Sidney Clarke and family lived on Tennessee Street, Lawrence, Kansas, and survived the Quantrill Raid. ["*Eyewitness Reports of Quantrill's Raid.* Letters of Sophia Bissell and Sidney Clarke," edited by [Justice] Fred N. Six, Kansas History: A Journal of the Central Plains 28 (Summer 2005), pp.94–103, http://www.kshs.org/publicat/history/2005summer_six.pdf]

1864, Elected to U.S. House of Representatives. [Ibid.]

1865, He was at Ford Theater the night Lincoln was assassinated. [Sidney Clarke (biography).]

1865, Served as pallbearer at President Lincoln's funeral (accompanied body of President Lincoln from Washington, D.C. to burial place in Springfield, Illinois). [*Topeka Daily Capital,* March 22, 1909, p.3]

1866, Reelected to Congress. [*Parsons Daily Sun,* op. cit.]

1870, Rebublican candidate for U.S. Senate but was defeated. [Ibid.]

1878, In the Kansas Legislature, elected Speaker of the House. [Ibid.]

1879, Dec. 10, Married Miss Dora Goulding. [*Lawrence Daily Journal,* Dec. 12, 1879, p.4, col. 1]

1889, Moved from Lawrence to Oklahoma; became an advocate for Oklahoma statehood. [www.findagrave.com and Clarke biography, http://www.kansasmemory.org/item/213865]

1891, Attended funeral of Chester Thomas, former Frontier Guard member. ["Sid Clark attends the Funeral of Chester Hays," *Topeka Daily Capital,* April 3, 1891, p.8]

1896, Jan. 10, Met with some surviving members of the Frontier Guard in Washington, D.C. to form a committee. ["Survivors of the Lane Guard," *Kansas City Gazette,* Jan. 16, 1896, p.6]

1909, June 18, Clarke died in Oklahoma. [www.findagrave.com]

1909, Buried Fairlawn Cemetery, Oklahoma City, Oklahoma County, Okla. [www.findagrave.com]

Daniel A. Clayton, Jr. (1828–)

ca. 1828, June, Daniel A. Clayton born in Maine. [U.S. Federal Censuses, 1860 and 1900]

1856, July, D.A. Clayton, Jr. gave receipt for supplies received to G.W. Hutchinson and William Hutchinson. [Kansas Memory, Kans. HS, Item 90099, James Blunt Collection #281, Box 1, Folder 4, DaRT 90099, item #1, p.2]

1856, D. A. Clayton [wounded] in the ankle—[from list of those] severely wounded "on the Free-State side at the battles of Franklin and Titus' Camp" [*History of the State of Kansas,* William G. Cutler, 1883] and "List of Wounded on the Free State side" [*Philadelphia Inquirer,* Sept. 5, 1856, p.2].

1860, July 24, D.A. Clayton, age 33, born Maine, carpenter living in Leavenworth, Kansas Territory, living with wife [?] Melvina, age 28, born Ky. and son, Arthur, age 1, born Mass. [1860 U.S. Cen-

sus, 4th Ward Leavenworth City, Leavenworth County, Kansas
Territory, Dwelling #1545, Family #1387, 156]

1861, In Frontier Guard, Washington, D.C.

1863, Daniel A. Clayton, Clerk, Treasury Department, born Maine,
"from whence apprenticed," Kansas, compensation [$]1,200.
[Source: Register of Officers and Agents, Civil Military, Army or
Navy in service of the United States, 13 Sept. 1863, U.S. Dept. of
Interior, Washington, Gov't Printing Office, 1864]

1868, H.C. Fields and D. A. Clayton were elected "by acclamation as
delegates to the Republican County Convention to be held in
Leavenworth." [*Leavenworth Times*, Sept. 26, 1868, p.4]

1870, June 18, Daniel A. Clayton, farmer living in Delaware Township,
Leavenworth County, Kansas [married July 1869], Lilly, wife[?],
Arthur, age 11 at home, born Kans., Minnie, age 9, born D.C.

1880, Living in St. Louis, Missouri, D.A. Clayton, 50, born Maine,
Lizzie J., age 45, born W.Va., Frank R., age 7, born Kans., Zelpah,
M. [female], age 4, born Mo. [1880 U.S. Federal Census]

1897, Feb. 25, D.A. Clayton of 2739 Bacon Street was appointed and
qualified a temporary clerk in the special tax department of the
B.P.I. [*St. Louis Republic*, Feb. 26, 1897, Vol. 89, No. 242, p.12].

1900, June, Daniel Clayton, Clerk Street Department, born June 1828,
Maine [both parents born Maine], age 71, married 45 years; Eliza-
beth Clayton, wife, born Dec 1833, born Va. [both parents born
Va.]. She was mother of 7 children, 5 still living; Frank R. Clay-
ton, born June 1873, Kans., age 26, single, deputy sheriff; Zilpah
Clayton, born June 1877, age 22, single, born Mo. [1900 U.S.
Census, St. Louis, Ward 21, House #2739 Bacon Street, Dwelling
142, Family 191, p.220, Sheet 10]

J. Henry Clinton (1839–1862)

1839, Feb. 12, J. Henry Clinton was born in Indiana, the son of David
E. Clinton and Jane Butler from Scott County, Kentucky. [Public
Member Tree, Ancestry.com]

1861, April, A member of the Frontier Guard, he enlisted in the 12th
Indiana Volunteer Infantry, Company A, for three years. [www
.findagrave.com]

1862, Aug. 17, The 12th Indiana Volunteer Infantry mustered in at Indianapolis. [The Civil War Index (www.civilwarindex.com)]

1862, Aug. 30, Clinton died in Battle of Richmond, Ky., age 23. [Public Member Tree, Ancestry.com.]

1862, He was buried in Vernon Cemetery in Jennings County, Indiana. [www.findagrave.com]

Joseph A. Cody (ca. 1813–1911)

1813/1814, Jan. 12, Birth of Joseph A. Cody, Canada [www.family search.org], Toronto, Peel County, Canada [Mundia.com], son of Philip J. Cody and Lydia Martin. Uncle of William F. Cody.

1853, 21 June, Marriage to Elvira Coble [Cable], Cuyahoga County, Ohio. [*The Daily Cleveland Herald* (Cleveland, Ohio), Wednesday, June 22, 1853, Issue 149, col. D; *Ohio marriages*, www.family search.org]

1857, June, Joseph A. Cody and one other in household, settled in Kansas Territory. [1859 Kansas Census [Voter], Grasshopper Falls, Jefferson County, Kansas Territory, 14]

1858, May, J.A. Cody, editor and proprietor of the newspaper, *Grasshopper,* in Jefferson County, Kansas Territory—subsequently *The Crescent* for several months. [*Kansas Quarterly*, 1941]

1860 Joseph A. Cody, 46, lawyer [?], living in Grasshopper Falls Twp., Jefferson County, Kansas Territory, with others. Mrs. Joseph A. Cody not listed in household at this time. [1860 U.S. Federal Census, Grasshopper Falls, Jefferson Co., Kansas Territory, p.9]

1861, April, Served as a Private in the Frontier Guard, Washington, D.C.

1861, May 14, 1861–Apr. 14, 1862, Joseph A. Cody appointed Indian agent at the Upper Platte Agency in Nebraska Territory [now Wyoming] May 14th, 1861. [Edward E. Ayer Manuscript Collection (Newberry Library), Chicago, Ill. Printed form, signed by President Abraham Lincoln]

1862, Mar. 24, Joseph A. Cody ordered removed as Indian agent of Upper Platte Agency by order of Abraham Lincoln. [*Executive Proceedings of the Senate of the United States of America from Dec. 2, 1861 to July 17, 1862 inclusive*, Vol. XII, Washington, D.C. 1887, p.182]

1865, J. A. Cody, 52, farmer, living in Grasshopper Falls Township with wife, E. C. Cody, age 32, J. Cody, age 2, daughter. [1865 Kansas State Census, Grasshopper Falls, Jefferson County, Kans.]

1870, Jos. A. Cody, 56, living in Grasshopper Falls Township, Jefferson County, Kansas, with wife, Elvira, 37, and daughter, Josephine, 7, and 3 others. [1870 U.S. Census, Jefferson County, Kans., p.42]

1875, J.A. Cody, 62 [?], Gentleman [?], b. Canada, came from Ohio to Kansas; E.C. Cody, wife, age 43, and Josie, daughter, age 12 were living in Valley Falls Township*, Jefferson County, Kansas, with two others. [Kansas Census, Valley Falls, Jefferson County, Kans., p.44] *Grasshopper Falls later became Valley Falls.]

1878, Oct. 23, Joseph A. Cody died, buried Lakeview Cemetery, Cleveland, Cuyahoga County, Ohio.

Martin F. Conway (1829–1882)

1829, Nov. 19 Martin Franklin Conway, born in Charleston, S.C. [Obituary, *New York Times*, Feb. 18, 1882, p.2]

1843, Left school at age 14 and learned the printer's trade in Baltimore, Md. [Ibid.]

1851, Studied law. [Ibid.]

1851, Conway married Emily Dykes. [Ibid.]

1852, He was admitted to the bar. [Ibid.]

1854, Moved to the Kansas Territory, initially working as correspondent for the *Baltimore Sun*. Then resumed practice of law. [Ibid.]

1860, Elected as representative to the U.S. Congress under the Wyandotte Constitution. [Ibid.]

1861, January, Conway spent the day the Emancipation Proclamation went into effect with Ralph Waldo Emerson, William Lloyd Garrison, Wendell Phillips, and Julia Ward Howe. [Ibid.]

1861, January, Elected 1st U.S. congressman from Kansas [Republican]. Served until March 3, 1863. [Ibid.]

1861, January, He put forth a resolution in Congress to recognize the Confederacy and then wage war on the South as a war between nations. [Ibid.]

1861, W.F. Conway, listed in John T. Burris's account as being in the Frontier Guard, Washington, D.C.

1866–1869, Appointed by President Andrew Johnson and served as consul to Marseilles, France. [Ibid.]

1873, October, Martin Conway was arrested for firing shots at Samuel C. Pomeroy, former U.S. senator from Kansas. ["Ex-Senator Pomeroy Shot," *The New York Times*, Oct. 12, 1873, p.1].

Ca. 1873, After the shooting of Pomeroy, Conway became a patient at St. Elizabeth, Wash., D.C. [Ibid.]

1882, Feb. 15, Martin F. Conway died age 52, buried in Rock Creek Cemetery, Washington, D.C. [Ibid.]

Addison Danford (1829–1901)

1829, July 4, Addison Danford born in Laconia, Belknap County, New Hampshire [Source: *Transactions of the Kansas State Historical Society 1907–1908,* Vol. X, State Printing Office, Topeka, 1908, p.210]; son of Ebenezer Danford. [*Portrait and Biographical record of the state of Colorado,* Chapman Publishing Co., Chicago, Ill. (1899), p.448]

Ca. 1835, He moved with family to Kane County, Ill. [ibid., 448]

Ca, 1845, Addison Danford began study of medicine. [ibid., 448]

Ca. 1849, He graduated in the medical department of La Porte [Ind.] University. [ibid., 448]

1850, He graduated from Keokuk Medical College, Keokuk, Iowa, with an M.D. degree. [ibid., 448]

1850, Addison Danford, age 21, b. NY, physician listed in Geneva, Kane County, Ill. census with other family members. [Source: 1850 U.S. Federal Census, Kane County, Ill.]

ca. 1850–1852, Practiced medicine. [Chapman, op. Cit., p.448]

1854–56 Danford decided to engage in Mercantile Business. [ibid., 448]

1856, Moved to Mound City, Linn County, Kans. [ibid., 448]

1857, Danford became the first lawyer in Mound City (Linn County), Kans. [Part 6, [Chapter Linn County, Kans.], William G. Cutler's *History of the State of Kansas* (was first published in 1883 by A. T. Andreas, Chicago, Ill.)]

1857 and 1858, Addison Danford was a member of the House of Representatives, Kansas Territory. [*Martin*, op. cit.]

1861, April, In Frontier Guard, Washington, D.C.

1863, September, Moved to Fort Scott, Kans., and engaged in practice of law. [op. cit., p.448]

1865, Danford was state senator from Fort Scott, Kans. [Cutler, op. cit.]

1868, He was elected Attorney General of State of Kansas. [Ibid.]

1869, Jan. 11–1871, Jan. 9, Danford served as Kansas Attorney General. [www.kshs.org (Kans.HS)]

1875, He moved from Fort Scott, Kans., to Colorado Springs, Colo. [Chapman, op. cit., p.447]

1885, A. Danford, lawyer, age 56, born New Hampshire and Lucy, his wife, age 44, born Vermont living in Leadville, Lake Colorado, Colo. [Colorado State Census, 1885. Family Search, www.family search.org]

1901, Sept. 29, Addison Danford died, Colorado Springs, Colo. ["Former Resident Dies in the West," *St. Charles (Ill.) Chronicle*, Oct. 25, 1901 [Danford Family, www.genforum.com]

Edward Dwight Daniels (1828–1916)

1828, Jan. 19, Edward Dwight Daniels was born in Cambridge, Mass., the son of Nathaniel Daniels and Nancy Hays Daniels. [J. E. Podair and the Dictionary of Virginia Biography, "Edward Dwight Daniels (1828–1916)," www.encyclopediaVirginia.org]

1843–1846, He attended Oberlin College. [Ibid]

1848, Moved to Ripon, Wisconsin, to live in a cooperative agriculture community. [Ibid]

1853, He was appointed Wisconsin's first state geologist. [Ibid.]

1856, Daniels led the State Kansas Aid Society of Wisconsin and led expeditions to Kansas. [Ibid.]

1857, He was one of the state commissioners of geology in Wisconsin. [Ibid.]

1859, Mar. 1, Married Ione Gove. [Ibid.]

1861, April, He was a member of the Frontier Guard.

1861, Summer, Daniels was authorized by the War Department to raise the 1st Wisconsin Cavalry. He subsequently raised two more companies. [First Wisconsin Cavalry (www.secondwi.com/wisconsin-regiments/frstWiscavalry.htm)]

1862, Mar. 19, His regiment arrived at Benton Barracks in St. Louis, where Daniels was placed in command of the post and assigned to the District of Southeast Missouri. [Ibid.]

1862, May, He led several raids into Illinois and Arkansas. [Ibid.]

1863, Feb. 3, He resigned because of poor health. [Podair (encyclopediavirginia.org)]

1868, Feb. 26, Daniels bought Gunston Hall, a plantation in Fairfax County, Va., with a plan to start a cooperative community of farmers and artisans. [Ibid.]

1871–1874, He purchased and ran the Richmond *Evening State Journal*. [Ibid.]

1871, Ran an unsuccessful campaign for State Senate in Virginia. [Ibid.]

1872, Ran for U.S. House of Representatives and lost. [Ibid.]

1881, Testified at trial of Charles Julius Guiteau for the assassination of President Garfield. [Ibid.]

1882, He founded the Society to Promote Industrial Education. [Ibid.]

1885–1886, Edited *Our Country*, a labor newspaper in New York City. [Ibid.]

1886, His wife, Ione, left him to live with her adult children in Nebraska and Iowa. She died in 1899. [Ibid]

1891, June 18, Daniels sold Gunston Hall, keeping a small plot of land for himself. [Ibid.]

1901, He married second wife, Julia E. Rennie. [Ibid.]

1916, Apr. 19, Died in Fairfax County, Va., and buried in Arlington National Cemetery.

Henry Walter DePuy (1820–1876)

1820, September, Henry Walter DePuy was born in Pompey Hills, Onondaga County, N.Y. His father was Jacob Rutsen DePuy and his mother was Polly Hibbard Clement. [*Reunion of the Sons and Daughters of the Old Town of Pompey* (Pompey, N.Y., 1875) (HATHI Digital Trust Library), p.395]

1836, He published the *Fayetteville Times* in Onondaga County, N.Y. at age 16. [Ibid.]

1837, Studied law, but didn't like the profession and returned to journalism. [Ibid.]

1840, Edited the *Cortland Democrat* in Courtland County, N.Y. [Ibid.]

1842, Henry W. DePuy married Theodosia E. Thomas. [*Sons of the American Revolution Applications, 1889–1970* (Ancestry.com) database online]

1848–1850, He established the *Rockford Free Press,* a Free-Soil paper. [Charles R. Church, *History of Rockford and Winnebago County, Ill.* (Rockford, Ill.: W. P. Lamb, 1900) p.219, Google Books]

1851, He published *Kossouth and His Generals with a Brief History of Hungary.* [Charles Dudley Warner, *A Library of the World's Best Literature—Ancient and Modern*, Vol. XLII, p.140]

1853, He published *Ethan Allen and the Green Mountain Heroes of '76, With a Sketch of the Early History of Vermont.* [Ibid.]

1853–1854, Private Secretary to New York Governor Horatio Seymour. [Unknown Author, *Reunion of the Sons and Daughters of Pompey,* p.396]

1855, Nov. 2, Henry DePuy married again, Elvira Merrick Gilchrist. [*New York Evening Post,* U.S., Newspaper Extractions from the Northeast, 1704–1930 (Ancestry.com) database online]

1856, He served as U.S. Consul in Baden, Germany. [U.S. Dep't of State, *Foreign Service List* (U.S. Gov't Printing Office, 1857), p.iv]

1856, He published *Louis Napoleon and the Bonaparte Family.* [Charles Dudley Warner, *A Library of the World's Best Literature,* p.140]

1858, Depuy was elected to the Nebraska Territorial House of Representatives. [Nebraska Historical Society, *Transactions and Reports of the Nebraska State Historical Society* (Lincoln, Neb., 1887), p.262]

1859, DePuy was elected Speaker of the House. [Nebraska State Historical Society, p.288]

1861, Mar. 30, Was appointed by Lincoln as agent to the Pawnee Indians. [*Evening Star,* April 30, 1861]

1863, Dec. 31, Lincoln nominated DePuy for agent of the Indians of the Upper Missouri. [U.S. Congress, *Journal of the Executive Proceedings of the USA* (D. Green, 1887), p.367]

1870–1872, Henry W. DePuy lived in Brooklyn, N.Y. [*U.S. City Directories* (Ancestry.com) database]

1876, Feb. 2, Died in New York City. ["Obituary," *New York Times,* Feb. 6, 1876]

Charles Francis de Vivaldi, [Count] (1824–1902)

a/k/a Carlos Francisco Alberto Julio Lorenzo de Vivaldi

1824, July 12, Charles Francis de Vivaldi [*The Mercury*, Manhattan, Kans. Oct. 2, 2005] born Sardinia. [1860 U.S. Federal Census, Riley County, Kansas Territory]

1848, "Revolutionary agitator" in Italy. [Source: "A Vivaldi Timeline," *Hesch History Blog*, http://heschistory.blogspot.com/2012/08/a-devivaldi-timeline.html, compiled by Larry Royston and Marlys Hesch Sebasky from book *Vivaldi en la Patagonia*, by Juan José, Kopp (2012)]

1849, Exile to France. [Ibid.]

1851, July 9, Francois de Vivaldi, one of five clergymen who arrived in St. Paul, Minn. from France with Father Cretin [*North American*, Philadelphia, Pa., Aug. 4, 1851]

1851–? Served at Long Prairie, Minn. at Winnebago Indian Mission.

1857, Moved to Green Bay, Wis. and meets widow, Mary Lowe Meade. [Royston and Sebasky, op. cit.]

1858, July 23, Marriage to Mrs. Mary Frances [Lowe] Meade, in Brown County, Wis. [Wisconsin Marriages 1836–1930, www.family search.org]; wife was "a Chippewa Woman" [Mr. S.D. McDonald letter, "An Early Kansas Character," *Kansas City Gazette*, Kansas City, Kans., June 2, 1892, p.4, col. 3]

1859, Lived in Wyandotte, Kansas Territory.

1859, April 18, Daughter, Corinna Alberta Vivaldi, born Wyandotte, Kansas Territory [Royston and Sebasky, op. cit.]

1859, May 18, Charles de Vivaldi was on the Platform Committee at the 1st Republican Convention in KT, held at Osawatomie. [*History of Kansas*, William G. Cutler, ed. (Chicago, A.T. Andreas, 1883, p.172)]

1859, Editor and founder of the *Western Kansas Express* antislavery newspaper, Manhattan, Kansas Territory.

1860, De Vivaldi chosen mayor of Manhattan, Kansas Territory. [*Emporia Weekly News*, June 16, 1860]

Ca. 1861, De Vivaldi went to Washington to obtain a foreign appointment. [S. D. McDonald letter]

1861, In Frontier Guard, Washington, D.C.

1861, Dec. 21, President Lincoln appoints de Vivaldi Consul to Santos
   [Brazil]. [*Journal of the Senate, Including the Journal of the Executive Proceedings of the Senate*, Vol. 37, Issue 2, p.27]

1867, de Vivaldi's Consulate ends, he moves to Rio de Janeiro, Brazil.
   [Royster and Sebasky, op. cit.]

1882, May, Vivaldi leaves marriage. [Ibid.]

1882, January–1883, March, Year of repentance, Casa San Carlos [Ibid.]

1884, March, Resumes priesthood, Chubut, Patagonia, mission. [Ibid.]

1888, August, Appointed honorary Canon, Cathedral of Buenos Aires,
   Argentina. [Ibid.]

1902, Jan. 22, de Vivaldi died in Paris (age 78). [Ibid.]

Jefferson Lewis Dugger (1826–1863)

1826, Sept. 1, Jefferson Lewis Dugger was born in Madison County,
   Ill., the son of Jarrett Dugger (1792–1850) and Mary McAdams
   Dugger (1793–1871). [www.findagrave.com]

1850, He was a merchant living in Carlinville, Ill. [*1850 Federal Census,
   Carlinville, Macoupin, Ill.*]

1852–1855, He edited the *Macoupin Statesman,* a Whig newspaper in
   Carlinville. [Frank William Scott and Edmund Jane James, *Newspapers and Periodicals of Illinois, 1814–1879* p.41.]

1854, Married Mary E. Gill. [Mary Austin, *Earth Horizon* (Sunstone
   Press, 2007), p.370, Google Book]

1855, Moved to the town of Atlanta, in Logan County, Ill., and became
   a member of the mercantile firm Gill & Co. [Lawrence Beaumont
   Stringer, *History of Logan County, Illinois* (Logan County, Ill.: Pioneer Publishing Co., 1911), p.482, Google Book]

1856, formed a law partnership with Mark Delahay and William Gallagher. [Henry Miles Moore, *Early History of Leavenworth City and
   County*, (Sam'l Dodsworth Book Co., 1906), p.267, Google Book]

1858, Mar. 18, In Illinois, Abraham Lincoln represented defendant Jefferson Dugger in a lawsuit relating to a breach of contract involving a sale of hogs. [The Lincoln Log website (lincolnlog.org)]

1859, Mar. 22, Lincoln and Dugger worked together representing the
   defendant in *Bell v. McPheeter.* [Earl Schneck Miers ed., *Lincoln*

Day by Day, A Chronology, 1809–1865, Vol. 2 (Washington, 1960), p.245]

1859, Dugger lived in Stranger Township, Leavenworth County, Kansas Territory. [*Kansas Compiled Census Index 1850–1890* (Ancestry. com) database]

1859, August, Jefferson Dugger became the editor of the *Kansas Daily State Register.* [Daniel Webster Wilder, *The Annals of Kansas* (1875), p.256, Google Book]

1859, December, *Kansas Daily State Register* first to publish Lincoln's speech in Leavenworth. [Fred Brinkerhoff, "The Kansas Tour of Lincoln the Candidate," *Kansas History,* Vol. 31, No. 4, p.289]

1861, April, He was a member of the Frontier Guard.

1862, Dugger was employed as clerk in the First Auditor's Office of the Treasury Department. [James Albert Winberger, *Department Directory and Register of Officers in the Service of the United States in the City of Washington* (1862), p.28, Google Book]

1863, Mar. 11, He was appointed Assistant Adjutant-General, rank of Captain. [Thomas O'Brien and Oliver Diefendork, *General Orders of the War Department 1861, 1862, 1863, Vol. II* (1864), p.474]

1863, July 16, Jefferson Lewis Dugger died; buried in Dugger Cemetery in Carlinville, Ill.

William Snow Dyer (1826–1882)

1826, Dec. 21, William Snow Dyer was born in Eastport, Maine, son of Charles Dyer and Hannah Snow. [Jonah Dyer, *The Journal of a Civil War Surgeon* (Univ. of Neb. Press, 2003), p.xv]

1848, William Dyer moved to Milwaukee. [Michael Chesson, "Civil War Surgeon and Union Hero–Dr. Franklin Dyer" (mslawmedia. org/2011/08/civil-war-surgeon-and-union-hero/)]

1858, He was in the Class of 1858 at the Medical School of Bowdoin College in Maine and attended lectures at Harvard. [*U.S. School Catalogs, 1765–1935* (Ancestry.com) database]

1860 June, William S. Dyer, M.D., lived in St. Louis. [*1860 U.S. Census, St. Louis, Mo.*]

1861, April, He was a member of the Frontier Guard.

1861, August, Assistant surgeon for the U.S. Army at Benton Barracks, St. Louis, Mo., in charge of the hospital. [Thomas Harrington, *The Harvard Medical School,* Vol. 2 (Lewis Publishing Co., 1905), p.974]

1864, He was discharged. [Ibid.]

1870, William S. Dyer lived in Jefferson County, Missouri, with his wife, Eugenia, and two children. [*1870 U.S. Federal Census, Valle Township, Jefferson, Mo.*]

1882, Aug. 14, He died in Chicago, Ill. [*Illinois, Cook County Deaths, 1878–1922* (Family Search)]

1882, Aug. 15, He was buried in St. Louis. [Ibid.] There is a tombstone at Hillside Cemetery in Eastport, Maine, with his name and the information "7th Enrolled Missouri Militia." [www.findagrave.com]

James Ward Eddy (1832–1916)

1832, May 30, James W. Eddy was born in Java, New York. [James Miller Guinn, *A History of California and an Extended History of Los Angeles and Environs,* Vol. 3 (Historic Record Co., 1915), p.584] He was the son of John Eddy and Caroline Ward. [Public Member Trees (www.ancestry.com)]

Ca. 1850, Educated at Genesee Wesleyan Seminary and Genesee College in Lima, N.Y. [Guinn, p.584.]

1855, He was admitted to the bar in Chicago, Ill. [Ibid.]

1857, Feb. 19, Married Belle A. Worsley in Kane County, Ill. [*Illinois Marriages, 1851–1900*]

1861, April, He was a member of the Frontier Guard.

1865, He became one of the officers of the Illinois & Fox River Railroad; incorporated by an act of legislature. [Rodolphus Waite Joslyn and Frank Wilbur Joslyn, *History of Kane County, Ill.,* Vol. 1 (Pioneer Publishing Co., 1908), p.158, Google Book]

1866, A member of the House Legislature from Kane County, he obtained a charter for the Millington Canal & Water Power Co. [Newton Bateman and Paul Selby, *Historical Encyclopedia of Illinois,* Vol. 2 (Munsell Publishing Co., 1914), p.900, Google Book]

1867, Eddy was a member of the Illinois State House of Representatives. [D. W. Lusk, *Politicians of Illinois, Anecdotes and Incidents. 1809– 1886* (Springfield, Ill.: H. W. Rokker, 1886), p.222, Google Book]

1869, Oct. 2, He spoke at the Reunion of the 124th Illinois Regiment held at Batavia. [*Sacramento Daily Union,* Vol. 38, No. 5777, Oct. 2, 1869 (California Digital Newspapers), p.3]

1871–1872, He was state senator in Illinois. [Newton Bateman and Paul Selby, *Historical Encyclopedia of Illinois* (Brookhaven Press, 1904), p.667, Google Book]

1881, He became President of the Arizona Mineral Belt Railroad. [Tim Ehrhardt, *Payson Roundup* (paysonroundup.com), March 6, 2013]

1896, March, He moved to California. [Wellington C. Wolfe, *Men of California* (Pacific Art Co., 1902), p.420, Google Book]

1896, October, His wife, Isabelle, died in Los Angeles. [Kane County, Ill. obituaries]

1900, He married Jane Fisher Wisewell. [Guinn, p.584]

1901, Constructed "Angel's Flight," an inclined cable railway in Los Angeles. It opened the same year. [No author, *Historic Spots in California* (Stanford Univ. Press), p.166, Google Book]

1903, December, Eddy was named president of the Griffith Park Railway, another inclined railway in Los Angeles. ["Griffith Park Railway Officers," *Los Angeles Herald,* Dec. 29, 1903]

1916, Apr. 13, He died in Los Angeles and was buried in Hollywood Forever Cemetery.

Thomas Ewing, Jr. (1829–1896)

1829, Aug. 7, Thomas Ewing, Jr. was born in Lancaster, Ohio. He was the son of Maria Wills (Boyle) Ewing and Thomas Ewing. His father was a U.S. Senator, Secretary of the Treasury, and Secretary of the Interior. [*Thomas Ewing, Jr. Papers,* Kansas State Historical Society (kshs.org)]

1849, Thomas Ewing, Jr. was appointed private secretary to President Zachary Taylor for a year. [Ibid.]

1854, He graduated from Brown University and went to law school in Cincinnati. [Ibid.]

1856, Jan. 8, He married Ellen Ewing Cox of Piqua, Ohio. [Ibid.]

1856–1857, Settled in Leavenworth, Kans., where he invested in real estate. After the Panic of 1857, he focused on railroad development. [David G. Taylor, "Thomas Ewing, Jr. and the Origins of the Kansas Pacific Railway Company," *Kansas Historical Quarterly* (Summer 1976)]

1858, Jan. 14, He asked the territorial government for an investigation of voter fraud after the election. [George W. Brown and Thomas Ewing, *Reminiscences of Gov. R. J. Walker* (1902), pp.165–67, Google Book]

1859, He went into a law partnership with his brother-in-law, William T. Sherman, and Daniel McCook in Leavenworth. [*Thomas Ewing, Jr. Papers*]

1861, February, Both Thomas Ewing, Sr. and Jr. attended the Washington Peace Conference. [Nicole Etcheson, "Tom Ewing's Dirty War," *N.Y. Times,* Aug. 23, 2003]

1861, April, He was a member of the Frontier Guard.

1861, He was appointed justice of the Kansas Supreme Court, but resigned in the summer of 1862 to join the Union Army. [*Thomas Ewing, Jr. Papers*]

1862, Sept. 15, He became the Colonel of the 11th Kansas Cavalry. [*Heitman's Register and Directory of the U.S. Army,* p.411]

1863, March, He was promoted to Brigadier General of Volunteers and placed in command of the District of the Border, made up of Kansas and the western Missouri counties. [*Thomas Ewing, Jr. Papers*]

1863, August, Ewing pursued Quantrill after the raid in Lawrence, but unsuccessfully. [Etcheson]

1863, Aug. 25, Ewing issued Order No. 11. [Etcheson]

1864, March, Ewing was made the Commander of the District of St. Louis. [Thomas Ewing, Jr. Papers]

1865, Feb. 23, He resigned from the Army. [*Heitman's Register,* p.411]

1865, Mar. 13, He was made a brevet Major General of Volunteers for his meritorious service at the Battle of Pilot Knob. [*Heitman's Register,* p.411]

1865, May, Ewing represented three of the conspirators at Lincoln's assassination trial. [Edward Steers, *Blood on the Moon: The Assassination of Abraham Lincoln* (Univ. Press of Ky. 2005), p.221]

1866–1870, He practiced law in Washington, D.C. [*Thomas Ewing, Jr. Papers*]

1870, Moved back to Lancaster, Ohio, and became active in the Democratic Party. [Ibid.]

1877–1881, Served as a Democrat from Ohio in the U.S. House of Representatives. [Ibid.]

1881, Moved to New York City and practiced law. [Ibid.]

1896, Jan. 21, He died from injuries in a streetcar accident. [Ibid.]

George Lea Febiger (1822–1891)

1822, Dec. 8, George Febiger was born in Philadelphia, Pa. ["Death of Col. Febiger," *New Haven Register,* Jan. 23, 1891.] He was the son of Christian Carson Febiger and Hannah Lea. [James Henry Lea, *The Ancestry and Posterity of John Lea, of Christian Malford* (New York: Lea Brothers & Co., 1906), p.97.]

    His grandfather, Christian Febiger, had been a colonel in the Revolutionary War and was one of Washington's most trusted officers. [Alexander M. Bielakowski, *Ethnic and Racial Minorities in the U.S. Military: An Encyclopedia* (ABC-CLIO, 2013), p.612, Google Book]

ca. 1840, He was educated at William and Mary College in Virginia. ["Death of Col. Febiger"]

1850, Lived as a grocery merchant in Cincinnati, Ohio, with his wife, Caroline, and his mother, Hannah F. Jones. [*1850 U.S. Federal Census, Cincinnati Ward 2, Hamilton, Ohio*]

1860, He was a boot manufacturer in Cincinnati, Ohio. [*1860 U.S. Census, Cincinnati Ward 1, Ohio*]

1861, April, He was a member of the Frontier Guard.

1861, May 3, He enlisted in the Army with the rank of Major and commissioned as an officer in the Regular Army Paymaster Department. [*U.S. Civil War Records and Profiles, 1861–1865* (Ancestry. com)]

1865, Mar. 13, He was promoted to Brevet Lieutenant Colonel. [Ibid.]

1886, Moved to New Haven, Conn. [*New Haven Register,* Jan. 23, 1891]

1886, Dec. 9, Retired from active service. [*N.Y. Times,* Dec. 10, 1886]

1891, Jan. 22, George L. Febiger died and was buried in Grove Street Cemetery, New Haven, Conn.

Henry C. Fields (1831–1903)

1831, February, Henry C. Fields was most likely born in Harrison County, Virginia (now W.Va.), where his father and mother, John Fields and Margaret Jarvis Fields, were living before moving to Indiana. [Don Norman, "Descendants of John Jarvis," *Hacker's Creek Pioneer Descendants* (www.hackerscreek.com)]

1850, Worked as a clerk at the collector's office in Fountain County, Ind., at age 19. [*1850 U.S. Federal Census,* Covington Township, Fountain County, Ind.]

1855, Oct. 9, Henry C. Fields was on the voter list in Leavenworth, Kansas Territory. [Graden, Debra, ed. *Kansas Voter Registration Lists, 1854–1856,* p.700 (Ancestry.com) database]

1858, Jan. 4, He went to the polls in the Kickapoo District to take a list of voters at the election, but was threatened with death. [*Reports of Committees of the House of Representatives, During the First Session of the Thirty-Fifth Congress* (Washington, James B. Steedman, Printer, 1858), pp.268–69.

1858, He was Clerk of the Court of Leavenworth County. [Henry C. Field, "Act of Incorporation," June 8, 1858, *Territorial Kansas Online* (www.territorialkansasonline.org)]

1861, April, He was a member of the Frontier Guard. ["Frontier Guard. An Interesting Reminiscence of that Historic Organization," *Winfield Courier,* Dec. 7, 1882]

ca. 1862, Married Laura Belle Embry. [*Michigan, Death Certificates* (www.familysearch.org) for daughter Catherine E. Fields Gregory]

1863, He worked as a clerk at the Pension Office in Washington, D.C. [*U.S. Civil War Draft Registration Records, 1863–1865.* (Ancestry. com) database]

1865–1867, Chief Clerk at the office of the Surveyor General of Kansas and Nebraska. [*Annual Reports of the Department of the Interior* (U.S. Gov't Printing Office, 1867), p.314, Google Book]

1870, June, He was a U.S. Mail agent living in Leavenworth County, Kans., with wife, Laura, and two daughters. [*1870 U.S. Federal Census, Delaware, Leavenworth, Kans.*]

1873, He was a member of the Kansas House of Representatives, Dist. 24, Leavenworth County. [*Kansas Legislators: Past and Present, Kansas State Library* (kslib.info/BusinessDirectoryii.aspx)]

1880–1900, He worked as a bookkeeper. [*1880 and 1900 U.S. Census, Leavenworth, Kans.*]

1903, Nov. 10, Henry C. Fields died in Chicago, Ill. He was buried in Downers Grove Cemetery in DuPage County, Ill. [*Illinois, Cook County Deaths, 1878–1922* (www.familysearch.org)]

James Fishback (1829–1895)

1829, Feb. 4, James Fishback was born in Fayette County, Kentucky, the son of Charles Fishback and Elizabeth Cosby Overton Fishback. [Public Member Trees, Ancestry.com]

1851, Sept. 11, He married Elizabeth Beattie in Macoupin County, Illinois. [*Illinois Statewide Marriage Index, 1763–1900,* Illinois State Archives database]

1852–1853, He was Postmaster of Macoupin County, Ill. [Charles A. Walker, *History of Macoupin County* (S. J. Clarke Publishing Co., 1911), p.426, Google Book]

1861, April, He was a member of the Frontier Guard.

1861, Aug. 10, James Fishback letter to Gov. Richard Yates of Illinois: "I send you by express today 74 linen havelocks, which you will please present to some of the companies of Illinois soldiers. Mrs. J. L. Dugger made them." ["Chronicling Illinois," Abraham Lincoln Presidential Library & Museum]

1861, Sept. 5, Fishback wrote a letter to Provost Marshal Porter informing on Ms. Bell, a "violent secessionist" who said she intended to poison the President, and she was sending information to Jefferson Davis. He wrote that Mr. Dugger could confirm, and the address he gave for the Duggers was the same as his. [Union Provost Marshal's File, NARA Catalog 2133278 (Fold3)]

1862–1865, Clerk in Treasury Department. [*U.S. City Directories, 1821–1989* (Ancestry.com) database]

1867, April, The Senate confirmed his nomination as Assessor of Internal Revenue for the 10th District of Illinois. ["From Washington," *Dubuque Daily Herald,* April 15, 1867, p.1]

1870, James Fishback, U.S. Revenue Office, lived in Jacksonville, Ill. [*1870 U.S. Census, Jacksonville, Ill.*]

1879, Clerk, Internal Revenue Office. [*U.S. City Directories, 1821–1989* (Ancestry.com) database]

1895, June 4, James Fishback died and was buried in Rock Creek Cemetery in Washington, D.C. with his wife, Elizabeth Beattie Fishback. [www.findagrave.com]

George W. Fisher (1798–1873)

1798, Aug. 6, George W. Fisher was born. [www.findagrave.com]

1850, George W. Fisher, shoemaker, lived in Ithaca, New York, with his wife, Catherine, and daughter Mary. [*1850 U.S. Federal Census, Ithaca, Tompkins, N.Y.*]

1860, He was listed on the census as a jailor living in Urbana, Ohio, with his wife and daughter and three inmates. [*1860 U.S. Federal Census, Urbana, Champaign County, Ohio*]

1861, April, He was a member of the Frontier Guard.

1867, June 26, "Council elected George W. Fisher Marshal. He formerly held the office." ["New Marshal," *Urbana Union,* June 26, 1867, p.3.]

1870, Geo. W. Fisher, a shoemaker, lived in Bath, Ohio. [*1870 U.S. Federal Census, Bath, Greene County, Ohio*]

1873, June 4, Fisher died and was buried in Mitman Cemetery in Fairborn, Greene County, Ohio. I.O.O.F. flag and Masonic emblem is on tombstone. [www.findagrave.com]

Charles Forster (1826–)

1826, August, Forster was born in Berlin, Prussia. [*Passport Applications, 1795–1905, NARA,* Catalog #566612 (www.fold3.com)]

1856, He immigrated to the United States. ["Consul-General Forster," *Indianapolis News,* Oct. 14, 1885, p.1]

1861, April, He was a member of the Frontier Guard.

1864–1871, He worked as a clerk at the Internal Revenue office in Washington. [*U.S. City Directories, 1821–1989* (Ancestry.com) database]

1872, He joined the Liberal Republican Party. He was the editor of several German newspapers in Indiana and some other states. ["Consul-General Forster," *Indianapolis News,* Oct. 14, 1885, p.1]

1880, Forster was a newspaper editor living in Evansville, Indiana, with his wife, Eliza, and children Irma and Herm. [*1880 U.S. Federal Census, Evansville, Vanderburgh, Ind.*]

1883–1884, He was assistant clerk at the Bureau of Statistics in Indiana and was commended by the chief of the Bureau for his "superior education and aptness." [Indiana Dep't of Statistics and Geology, *Annual Report of the Department of Statistics* (Indiana, 1884), p.8, Google Book]

1885, October, Forster was offered a position as U.S. consul in Calcutta. He asked to be transferred to a German city. ["Consul-General Forster," *Indianapolis News,* Oct. 14, p.1]

1885, Oct. 15, He was appointed by President Cleveland to U.S. Consul in Elberfeld, Germany. [*Memorial of Charles Forster, Late United States Consul, in Relation to the Discontinuance of the United States Consulate at Elberfeld, Germany,* U.S. Congressional Ed., Issue 2698 (U.S.G.P.O., 1890), pp.1–6.]

1889, The American consulate in Elberfeld was discontinued. [*Memorial of Charles Foster*]

1891–1894, He returned to his former job at the Bureau of Statistics. [Indiana Dep't of Statistics, various annual and biennial reports, 1891–1894]

Ira Freeman, Jr. (1829–1878)

1829, May 29, Ira Freeman, Jr. was born in New York, the son of Ira Freeman, Sr., and Abigail. [*Maryland Births and Christenings Index, 1662–1911* (ancestry.com) database]

1840, The Freemans lived in Kingsbury, N.Y. [*1840 U.S. Census, Kingsbury, N.Y.*]

1855, Ira Freeman, Jr. attended Union College in Schenectady, N.Y. [*U.S. School Catalogs, 1765–1935*]

1860, May 17, He was admitted to the bar in Washington, D.C. [*Evening Star*, May 17, 1860, p.3]

1860, June 8, He testified before the Covode Committee, investigating corruption in the Buchanan administration. [U.S. Congress, *The Covode Investigation* (Washington: The Committee, 1860), p.269.]

1861, April, He was a member of the Frontier Guard.

1863, Lived in Baltimore, Md. [*U.S. City Directories, 1821–1989* (Ancestry.com) database]

1863, He married Augusta Mary Johnson in Fulton, N.Y. [Edmund West, *Family Data Collection–Marriages* (Ancestry.com) database]

1864, Worked as a clerk at the Custom House in Baltimore. [*U.S. City Directories, 1821–1989* (Ancestry.com) database]

1870, He was listed in the census as a farmer living in Baltimore County, Md., with his wife, Augusta, and young son, Frank. [*1870 U.S. Federal Census, 11th Dist., Baltimore County, Md.*]

1876, He was an officer and lecturer of the Baltimore County Grange. [*The American Farmer, Devoted to Agriculture, Horticulture, and Rural Life*, Vol. 5, Issue 6 (S. Sands & Co., 1876) p.207, Google Book]

1878, July 2, He died and was buried in Saint John's Episcopal Church Cemetery, Kingsville, Md.

John A. Gareis (1831?–1884)

ca. 1831, John Gareis was born in Bavaria, Germany. [*1860 U.S. Census, 19th Ward, Baltimore, Md.*]

1860, He was a cabinetmaker in Baltimore. [Ibid.]

1861, April, He was a member of the Frontier Guard.

1861, Sept. 28, He enlisted in the 1st Regiment Maryland Cavalry as a Sergeant in Captain Wetschky's Company B, then was promoted to Quartermaster Sergeant. [NARA, *Compiled Service Records of Volunteer Soldiers Who Served in Organizations from Maryland*, Catalog ID 300398 (Fold3)]

1862, December, He was promoted to 2nd Lieutenant of Co. D. [Ibid.]

1863, January, Promoted to 1st Lieutenant and Regimental Adjutant. [Ibid.]

1863, June 9, He was reported wounded and missing at Brandy Station. He was first confined at Richmond, Va. [Ibid.]

1864, May, Sent to Macon, Ga., then confined at Camp Asylum in Columbia, S.C. [Ibid.]

1865, March, Paroled at N.E. Ferry, N.C., and admitted to Officer's Hospital in Annapolis, Md. on March 5. [Ibid.]

1865, Apr. 13, His certificate for sick leave said, "He is suffering from extreme debility . . . during which he was a Prisoner of War . . . unfit for duty and unable to travel," signed by the army surgeon. [Ibid.]

1865, Aug. 8, Discharged. [Ibid.]

1870, Lived in Baltimore with his wife, Sophia Gareis. [*1870 U.S. Census, 4th Ward Baltimore, Md.*]

1880, He worked as a postal clerk in Baltimore and lived with his wife, son, Otto, and daughter, Harmina. [*1880 Federal Census, Baltimore, Md.*]

1884, At the National Home for Disabled Volunteer Soldiers, his widow Sophia Gareis's application for his effects was granted. [*National Home for Disabled Volunteer Soldiers, Report of the Board of Managers* (U.S. Gov't Printing Office, 1886), p.21 (Ancestry.com) database]

Mark N. Garton (1834–1900)

1834, Mark N. Garton was born in N.J. and was the son of John and Mary H. Garton. [*U.S. Federal Census, Cohansey, Cumberland, N.J.*]

1860, The Garton family had moved to Fairfax County, Va. [*1860 U.S. Federal Census, South Orange & Alexandria Railroad, Fairfax, Va.*]

1861, April, He was a member of the Frontier Guard.

ca. 1861, He married Mary Mackley. [Marriages Records (www.familysearch.org)]

1863, July 1, Garton was a married farmer living in the District of Columbia. [*U.S. Civil War Draft Registration Records, 1863–1865.*]

1877–1900, He worked as a laborer in the Treasury Department at the Bureau of Engraving and Printing. [*U.S. Register of Civil, Military, and Naval Service. 1863–1959* (Ancestry.com) database]

1880, Mark N. Garton was a widower and lived in Washington, D.C. with the occupation of messenger. He could read but not write. [*U.S. Federal Census, Washington, D.C.*]

1900, Apr. 18, Garton died and was buried in the Congressional Cemetery in Washington, D.C.

Alfred M. Gibbons (1837–1899)

1837, A. M. Gibbons was born in Chillicothe, Ohio, the son of James H. Gibbons and Elizabeth Meads Gibbons. [Parker McCobb Read, *Bench and Bar of Wisconsin: History and Biography, with Portrait Illustrations* (Milwaukee: P. M. Read, 1882), pp.327–28, Google Book.] His family moved to Illinois when he was young. He went to an academy at Granville, Ill. [Ibid.]

1857, Gibbons was admitted to the bar in Ottawa, Ill. [Ibid.]

1859, Fall, Moved to Portland, Ore. He was appointed state's attorney for northern Oregon. [Ibid.]

1861, February, Moved to Washington, D.C. [Ibid.]

1861, April, He was a member of the Frontier Guard.

1863, Alfred M. Gibbons, age 27, lawyer, born in Ohio, unmarried. Residence: Peoria, Chillicothe, Ill. [*U.S., Civil War Draft Registration Records, 1863–1865,* (Ancestry.com) database]

1866, Aug. 11, He was elected delegate to the National Convention held in Philadelphia. ["Proceedings of the Illinois State Conservative Convention," *Ottawa Free Trader,* Aug. 11, 1866, 1]

1870, Alfred Gibbons, attorney, lived in Peoria, Illinois, with his wife, Martha, daughter, Josephine, and son, James. [*1870 U.S. Federal Census, Peoria, Chillicothe, Ill.*]

1870–1872, Ran the newspaper *Democrat* in Chillicothe, Ill. [Frank W. Scott, *Newspapers and Periodicals of Illinois, 1814–1879* (Springfield, Ill.: Illinois State Historical Library, 1910), p.150]

1878, Moved to Eau Claire, Wisconsin. [Read, p.328]

1882, Sept. 22, He was the delegate at the Republican County Convention from the city of Eau Claire. ["Republican County Convention," *Eau Claire Daily Free Press,* Sept. 22, 1882, p.4]

1884, Sept. 1, He was chairman of the county delegate committee. ["Republican County Convention," *Eau Claire Daily Free Press,* Sept. 1, 1884, p.3]

ca. 1885, He moved to Winona, Logan County, Kans. and became chairman of the board of county commissioners. [*Peoria Star* (Peoria County, Ill.), Feb. 7, 1899 (peoriacountyillinois.info/obits)]

1899, Feb. 6, Gibbons died in Winona, Logan County, Kans. [Ibid.]

Samuel Gilson (1820–)

1860, Samuel Gilson was listed as a road contractor living in Weston, Missouri, with his wife, Sophia, and two children, Albert and Kansas. He was born in New York. [1860 Census, Weston, Platte, Mo.]

1861, April, He was a member of the Frontier Guard.

1861, November, Gilson enlisted in Leavenworth, Kans., as a farrier in Company C of the 2nd Regiment, Kansas Cavalry. [Soldiers and Sailors Database (www.nps.gov)]

1862, April, He transferred from Company C to Company K and was discharged due to disability at Nashville. [Ibid.]

David Stuart Gordon [Gen.] (1832–1930)

1832, May 23, David S. Gordon born near Greencastle, Franklin County, Pa. ["Lieut. Colonel David Stewart Gordon, 2d U.S. Cavalry," *Nevada State Journal*, Dec. 15, 1889, p.3 (Newspaper. com)]; son of Alexander Gordon and Hanna Domb Ely [Source: www.ancestry.com]

ca. 1838–1847, Attended school [Ibid.]

ca. 1847, Started mercantile career at Hagerstown, Md., first as clerk and then with own business. [Ibid.]

ca. 1853, "Abandoned his business in Maryland" and attended medical lectures in Philadelphia. [Ibid.]

1857, Spring, Moved to Leavenworth, Kansas Territory and "engaged in general merchandise" business. [Ibid.]

1858, Business was "burned out." [Ibid.] Married Nanny Hughes. [[Ibid.] and www.ancestry.com]

1858–1861, Gordon elected auditor of Leavenworth City, Kans. [Ibid.]

1860, D.S. Gordon, enumerated in census, 2nd Ward, Leavenworth Co., Kansas Territory [Source: U.S. Census, Kansas Territory]

1861, April, Entered the Frontier Guard, Washington, D.C. "Elected First Sargeant." [op. cit.]

1861, Apr. 26, Enlisted as 2nd Lieutenant commissioned into 2nd Cavalry, 2nd Dragoons, reported to Ricker Barracks near the Capital. [*Nevada State Journal*, Reno, Nev., Dec. 15, 1889]

1861, May 31, David S. Gordon accompanied Lt. Charles Tompkins and his company on a raid to Fairfax Courthouse. [Blog (by "Don"): "Fidler's Green: David S. Gordon," *Crossed Sabers*: http://crossedsabers.blogspot.com/2011/03/fiddlers-green-david-s-gordon.html1862]

1861, June 1, Promoted 1st Lieutenant on June 1, 1861. [*American Civil War Research Database*]

1861, July 18, Skirmish "credited as having been the first pitched battle between the confederates and our troups of the late rebellion." [*Nevada State Journal*, op. cit., p.3]

1861, July 21, Captured, was POW at Bull Run, Va. [Civil War Database, op. cit.]

1861, July 23, Confined on July 23, 1861, at Richmond, Va. (Liggon Tobacco factory) [Ibid.] "Initially sent to Libby Prison in Richmond, he was subsequently incarcerated at Castle Pinckney, Charleston, S.C.; Columbia jail, S.C.; and Salisbury, N.C. He was not exchanged until August 1862." [Crossed Sabers, op. cit.]

1861, Sept. 21, Exchanged at Aiken's Landing, Va. [Civil War Database, op. cit.]

1863, Gordon served as an acting assistant adjutant general to General Schenk through the Gettysburg campaign. [Op. cit., Blog, *Crossed Sabers*]

1863, Apr. 25, Gordon promoted to captain (full, Army). [Civil War Database, op. cit.]

ca. 1864 David S. Gordon received a brevet to major, U.S. Army, for gallant and meritorious service at the battle of Gettysburg. [*Crossed Sabers, op. cit.*]

1864, August to October, Gordon "commanded regiment through the battle of Deep Bottom on July 27–28, 1864, and during the majority of the Shenandoah campaign from August to October 1864." [Ibid.]

1864, October, Gordon was assigned to Carlisle Barrack, Pa., for recruit duty and then to Cincinnati, Ohiohio, where he recruited for his regiment from to October 1864 to January 1865. [Ibid.]

1865, Gordon, back to commanding Company D, "regiment was assigned to duty on the frontier in November, and began the long march to Fort Leavenworth, Kans." [Ibid.]

1865, November–October 1866, Gordon and his men assigned to Fort Lyon, Colo., where they remained until October 1866 [Ibid.]

1866, Gordon with "2nd U.S. Cavalry was reassigned to the Department of the Platte under pre-war commander Philip St. George Cooke at the end of the year, and the regiment's companies were reassigned to forts in what is today Wyoming, South Dakota and Nebraska." [Ibid]

1867, "[A] column of infantry and cavalry was dispatched to the relief of Fort Kearney in January 1867. Gordon commanded a squadron of his own company and Company L in support of four companies of the 10th Infantry." [Ibid.]

1868–1869, Stationed at "Fort D.A. Russell, Wyoming Territory, where he [Gordon] and his company served from August 1868 to May 1869" [*Crossed Sabers, op. cit.*]

1870, May 4, Gordon and company "moving to Fort Bridger, Wyoming Territory in October. They were engaged in the affair at Miner's Delight, Wyoming Territory on May 4, 1870." [Ibid]

1877, Gordon "was promoted in the regiment to major on June 25, 1877." [Ibid.]

1889, Promoted to Lt. Colonel in same regiment where he became 2nd Lt. in 1861. [*Nevada State Journal*, Dec. 15, 1889, p.3]

1892, Gordon was assigned to command Fort Myer, Washington, D.C. [Crossed Sabers, op. cit.]

1896, Gordon was promoted to Brigadier General upon his retirement on May 23, 1896. [Ibid.]

1896, Promoted to colonel and command of the 6th U.S. Cavalry. [Ibid.]

1900, David S. Gordon, age 68, retired Col. U.S.A. enumerated with wife, Ann E. and two children in District of Columbia, Wash. [ED 44] [1900 U.S. Federal Census, Washington, D.C.]

1910, David S. Gordon, age 77, living with wife, Annie, married 50 years, had 5 children, [3 living], Alameda County, Cal. [1910 U.S. Federal Census, Alameda County, Cal.]

1911, David S. Gordon published an article in *Journal of the Military Service of the United States* titled "The Relief of Fort Phil Kearny." [*Crossed Sabers, op. cit.*]

1912, January, Married in New York to Belle Vedder Fleming, "a descendant of Nancy Hanks—Lincoln's mother—and the widow of Colonel Robert I. Fleming." [*San Francisco Chronicle*, May 30, 1919, p.11.]

1930, Jan. 30, Died Takoma Park, Md.

1930, Burial: Arlington National Cemetery, Arlington County, Va., Sec: E, Site: 984.

Samuel Wylie Greer [Capt.] (1826–1882)

1826, June 2, born Alleghany County, Pennsylvaniaa. ["Death of a Valued Citizen," *Winfield Courier*, Oct. 5, 1882, Winfield, Kans. [submitted to www.findagrave.com by Judy Mayfield]

ca. 1845, completed education at Oberlin College. [*Chronicles of Oklahoma*, Vol. 14, No. 3, Sept. 1936, "Frank H. Greer," by Joseph B. Thoburn, p.265, http://digital.library.okstate.edu/chronicles/v014/v014p265.html]

1853, Moved to Oskaloosa, Iowa. [*Winfield Courier, op. cit.*]

1855, Married Clotilda Hilton in Oskaloosa, Iowa. [Ibid.]

1856, October, Came to Leavenworth, Kansas Territory [Ibid.]

1858, October, Elected Territorial Superintendent; served 1858, Dec. 2–1861, Jan. 7. [Ibid.]

1861, Apr. 14, "Entered Army" in Washington City as private in the Frontier Guard. [Ibid.]

1861, Returned to Kansas, was enrolling officer at Ft. Leavenworth—later Governor Carney gave him commission as 2nd Lt. as recruiting officer. Recruited for Co. I, 15th Kans. Vol. Cav. Elected Captain and served until Oct. 1865. [Ibid.]

1865, October, Mustered out of service. [Ibid.]

1870, Listed as farmer, living Delaware Township, Leavenworth, County, Kans., with wife and three children: Edwin, Frank, and Albert. [1870 U.S. Federal Census, Delaware Twp., Leavenworth County, Kans.]

1871, January, Came to Cowley County, Kans., from Leavenworth County, Kans. [*Winfield Courier*, op. cit.]

1880, Samuel W. Greer, farmer, wife and six children listed in Cowley County, Kans. [1880 U.S. Census.]

1882, Sept. 30, Died of consumption, age 57 [*Winfield Courier*, op.cit.]

1882, Buried *Union Cemetery*, Winfield, Kans. [*Findagrave*]

Oscar Adrian Hale (1837–1868)

1837, July 21, He was born in Troy, Orleans County, Vt., the son of Raymond and Sarah F. (Currier) Hale. His great-grandfather was Col. Nathan Hale of the Revolutionary War. [Linda M. Welch, *Vermont in the Civil War* (vermontcivilwar.org) Cemetery Database]

1849, He inherited a good sum of money and entered Thetford Hill Academy. [Ibid]

1860, Graduated from Dartmouth College, then taught school at Ellicott's Mills, Md. [Ibid.]

1861, April, He was a member of the Frontier Guard.

1861, May, Took a position in the Post Office Dep't in Washington, D.C. [Ibid.]

1861, Oct. 8, He was commissioned Captain of Company D, 6th Regiment Vermont Volunteers. [E. D. Redington, comp., *Military Record of the Sons of Dartmouth in the Union Army and Navy, 1861–1865* (Boston: 1907) p.76, Archive.org (https://archive.org/details/militaryrecordof01redi)]

1863, Jan. 12, He was promoted to Major. [Ibid.]

1863, Mar. 18, Promoted to Lieutenant Colonel of the Regiment. [Ibid.]

1864, Aug. 21, He was wounded by a bullet in the right thigh at the Battle of Charles Town, but before this he had participated in all the battles of his regiment——"Warwick Creek, Lee's Mills, Williamsburg, Savage's Station, White Oak Swamp, Antietam,

Fredericksburg, Marye's Heights, and all the battles of the Army of the Potomac." [Ibid.]

1864, Oct. 28, Mustered out of his company. [Ibid.]

1864, December, He left America and settled in Rosario, Buenos Aires, South America. [Welch]

1868, Jan. 13, Oscar A. Hale died from pulmonary afflictions. He was buried in South America. [Ibid.]

Clark J. Hanks [Capt.] (1835–1904)

1835, Nov. 23, Clark Joshua Hanks was born in Greene County, Ill. He was the son of Joshua Hanks and Amelia Rape. [*Kansas City Times*, Kansas City, Mo., Dec. 31, 1883, p.26, cols. 2, 3]

1850, Clark J. Hanks, age 15, living in Scott County, Ill. with parents, Joshua, age 66, b. N.C., and mother Amelia, 46, b. S.C. [1850 U.S. Federal Census, Scott County, Ill.]

1855, July 18–Dec. 31, Clark J. Hanks, laborer. [Dept. of Interior], appointed from Illinois [Report: H. Exec. Doc. 55; March 17, 1856, Serial Set Vol. No. 853]

1860, July 21, Clark J. Hanks, 23, clerk, born Ill., living in the 3rd Ward of Leavenworth City, Leavenworth County, Kansas Territory in household of Robert and Mary Davis and family. [1860 U.S. Census Leavenworth, Kans.Terr.]

1861, April, In Frontier Guard at Washington, D.C.

1861, Oct. 1–1862, Feb 3, Copyist, office of Surveyor General of Kansas and Nebraska. ["Message of the President of the U.S. to the two Houses of Congress at the third session of the Thirty-seventh Congress." Dec. 1, 1862.–Serial Set Vol. No. 1157; Report: H. Exec. Doc. 1 pt. 2; p.102 (*Genealogybank*.com)]

ca. 1862, Clark J. Hanks married Mary A. Latta, daughter of Judge Samuel N. Latta.

1863, Jan. 1–1863, Sept. 30, Hanks was employed in office of Surveyor General of Kansas and Nebraska.

1863–1865, Hanks succeeded F.G. Adams as U.S. District Clerk in 1863. [Kansas Supreme Court Reports]

1863, Apr. 5, Clark J. Hanks #831, appointed Provost Marshall of the Military District, Dist. 1 [northern], Kans., non-dishonorable

discharge Aug. 21, 1865. [*The War of the Rebellion: A Compilation of the Official Records of the Union and Confederate Armies*]
[Correspondence, orders, reports, and returns of the Union
authorities from May 1, 1865, to the end; Series 3, Vol. 5, p.909
(Genealogybank)]

1865, in Secret Service, Treasury Dep't. [*Kansas City Times,* Dec. 31,
1883]

1865, C.J. Hanks, age 27, Provost Marshall, living in 3rd Ward, Leavenworth, Kans., with wife and son. [1865 Kansas State Census
Leavenworth, Leavenworth County, Kans.]

ca. 1868, Appointed Mail agent, served until 1871 ["A Most Valued Citizen," op. cit.]

1873–1877, Deputy Warden of Penitentiary, Leavenworth, Kans.

1875, C.H. Hanks, age 39, Dept. Warden R.S.P., with family, Delaware
Twp., Leavenworth, Leavenworth County, Kans.] [1875 Kansas
State Census, Leavenworth County, Kans.-Ancestry.com]

1880, C.J. Hanks, laborer in P.O., living with wife, Mary, and children
Samuel, age 17, born Kans.; Clark M., age 12, b. Kans.; Bessie H.,
age 5, born Kans.; and Edward, age 3, born Kans. in 3rd Ward of
Leavenworth City, Leavenworth County, Kans. [1880 U.S Federal
census—Leavenworth, Kans.]

1885, C.J. Hanks, age 49, Commissioner, came to Kansas from District
of Columbia, living with wife and three children, Leavenworth,
Kans. Attained rank of Captain and Provost Marshall. [1885 Kansas State Census, Leavenworth, Kans.—Ancestry.com]

1887, Clark J. Hanks, Pullman conductor. [Muster Roll G.A R., Burn-
side Post 28, Wyandotte County, Kans.]

1903, Judge, Kansas City, Kans. [Source: www.lattabranch.org]

1904, May 29, Died in Lansing, Kans. [*Kansas City Star,* May 30, 1904
(burial place unknown)].

Roswell Hart (1824–1883)

1824, Aug. 4, Roswell Hart was born, Rochester, Monroe County, N.Y.
[*Findagrave*]

1843, Graduated from Yale. [Hon. Roswell Hart Obituary, *New York
Times,* April 21, 1883, p.2]

ca. 1840s, Studied law. [Ibid.]

1847, Admitted to the bar. [Ibid.]

1850, He was a coal dealer in Rochester, Monroe County, N.Y. [1850 U.S. Federal Census, Monroe County, N.Y.]

1856, Delegate to Republican National Convention from New York. [Political Graveyard.com, http://politicalgraveyard.com/bio/hart. html]

1860, Sept., Spoke at meeting in Corinthian Hall, Rochester, N.Y., in favor of Lincoln. [Obit, op. cit.]

1861, Frontier Guard.

1863, July, Roswell Hart, Esq. appointed Provost Marshall for Monroe and Orleans districts. [*Albany Evening Journal*, Albany, N.Y., July 6, 1863, p.2, col. 8]

1865, March, Elected as a Republican to represent New York's 28th District in U.S. House of Representatives. [*Findagrave*]

1869–1876, Hart was placed in charge of Railway Mail service for New York and Pennsylvania. [*Info Please, congressional biographies*, N.Y., http://www.infoplease.com/biography/us/congress/hart-roswell .html]

1870, He was living in 3rd Ward, Rochester, Monroe County, N.Y., with his wife and children. Occupation, Asst. Superintendent Railroad Mail. [1870 U.S. Federal Census Rochester, Monroe County, N.Y.]

1883, Jan. 27, Died Rochester, Monroe County, N.Y. [*Findagrave*] of pneumonia. [Obit., op. cit. 2]

1883, Buried Mount Hope Cemetery, Rochester, Monroe County, N.Y. [*Findagrave*, op. cit.]

Samuel Leidy Hartman (1832–1913)

1823, Nov. 23, Hartman was born in Lancaster County, Pennsylvania. [Lancaster Historical Society, *Historical Papers and Addresses of the Lancaster Historical Society*, Vol. 18 (1914) p.15, Google Book]

1832, He worked as a clerk at Hager's store in Lancaster. [Ibid.]

1855, Took a position as express messenger on the Missouri River. [Ibid.]

1860–61, Worked as a Pony Express Rider in Kansas. [Ronald C. Young, *Lancaster County, Pennsylvania in the Civil War* (2002) p.138, Google Book]

1861, April, He was a member of the Frontier Guard.

1861, Oct. 1, Hartman enlisted in the 79th Pennsylvania Volunteers as a 2nd Lieutenant in Co. E. [Franklin Ellis, *History of Lancaster, Pennsylvania* (Everts & Peck, 1883) p.118, Google Book]

1862, Oct. 8, He was at the Battle of Perryville. [Lancaster Historical Society, p.15]

1863, February, He was an officer on the staff of General Lovell H. Rousseau, and accompanied him from Tennessee to Washington. ["Gen. Rousseau Visits Lancaster," *Lancaster at War* (lancasteratwar.com), February, 2013]

1864, Feb. 2, He was promoted to 1st Lieutenant. [Ellis, p.118]

1864, May 9, Promoted to Captain. [Ibid.]

1865, May 18, Discharged on Surgeon Certificate. [Ibid.] [*U.S. City Directories, 1821–1989*]

1876, June, Ulysses S. Grant was interviewed by Hartman. [Lancaster County Historical Society, "Grant Not Here," *Papers Read Before the Lancaster County Historical Society,* Vol. 19 (1915), p.114]

1903, Aug. 13, His letter describing the Battle of Perryville was published in the *National Tribune*. ["Battle of Perryville," *National Tribune,* Aug. 13, 1903, p.3]

1913, Jan. 23, Samuel L. Hartman died and was buried in Lancaster at Greenwood Cemetery.

John P. Hatterscheidt (1828?–1874)

ca. 1828, Hatterscheidt was born. [*Petition of John P. Hatterscheidt to Abraham Lincoln,* 1861, Document # 260301, *Papers of Abraham Lincoln*] (http://lincolnpapers2.dataformat.com/images/1861/00/260301.pdf)] He was born in Cologne, Prussia. [Norman E. Saul, *Concord and Conflict: the United States and Russia, 1867–1914* (Univ. of Kans. Press, 1996) p.14, Google Book]

1855, He married Eliza P. Pettit. [John P. Hatterscheidt, Jr.'s September 1855, Campbell County, Ky., birth record in index, *Kentucky Births and Christenings, 1839–1860* (Ancestry.com) database]

1857, **Spring,** He moved to Leavenworth and worked as an engineer and surveyor. [KSHS, *Transactions of the Kansas Historical Society,* 1908–1907, Vol. X (Topeka: State Printing Office, 1908) p.211]

1857–1858, A member of the territorial legislature, he attended the Leavenworth Convention. [Ibid.]

1858, **Jan. 4,** Attended the third session of the Territorial Legislature at Lecompton. [Daniel Webster Wilder, *Annals of Kansas* (G. W. Martin, 1875) p.158, Google Book]

1858, **July 5,** In Leavenworth, "the Turners listened to an oration by J. P. Hatterscheidt and addresses by J. C. Vaughn and Chas. F. Kob." [Cora Dolbee, "The Fourth of July in Early Kansas 1858–1861," *Kansas Historical Quarterly,* May 1942 (Vol. 11, No. 2), p.138]

1859, **May 18,** He represented Leavenworth at the Osawatomie Convention. [Frank Baron, *Abraham Lincoln and the German Immigrants: Turners and Forty Eighters,* (Lawrence, Kans.: The Society for German-American Studies, 2012), p.56.]

1859–60, President of the German Turner Society. [Baron, p.45]

1859, **Dec. 1,** He rode with Lincoln from Troy to Doniphan. [Baron, p.56]

1860, **Apr. 11,** He was selected as one of the delegates to the Chicago Republican National Convention. ["The Lawrence Convention," *Emporia Gazette,* April 21, 1860, p.1]

1860, **Apr. 28,** "Hatterscheidt is now at the head of the German paper in Leavenworth." [*Freedom's Champion,* April 28, 1860, *Kansas Newspapers Database* (www.kansasnewspapers.org)]

1860, John P. Hatterscheidt, architect, lived in Leavenworth with his wife, Eliza, and young son, John. [*1860 Federal Census, 1st Ward, Leavenworth City, Kansas Territory*]

1860, **September,** He was recruited to campaign for Lincoln in southern Indiana. [Baron, p.141]

1861, **March,** Hatterscheidt wrote Lincoln asking for the position of Consul in Antwerp, Belgium. Lincoln recommended him for the post on April 1. [*Collected Works of Abraham Lincoln,* Vol. 4 (Wildside Press, 2008) p.312, Google Book]

1861, **April,** He was designated 1st Corporal of the Frontier Guard. [*Emporia News,* May 4, 1861, p.2]

1861–65, Served as the U.S. Consul at Moscow. [*Official Roster of Kansas, 1854–1925,* KSHS, p.714.]

1874, Hatterscheidt died in Kazan, Russia. [Ibid.]

Cunningham Hazlett (1835–1873)

1835, Cunningham Hazlett was born in Ohio. [*Civil War Draft Registration Records, 1863–1865*] He was the son of Isaac Hazlett and Hettie Stillwell Hazlett.

1852, His mother married Robert S. Clark in Belmont County. [*Ohio Marriages, 1803–1900*]

1860, He was listed on the 1860 census as a trader. He lived with his mother, stepfather, and his Hazlett and Clark siblings in Morristown, Ohio. [*1860 U.S. Federal Census, Union, Belmont, Ohio*]

1861, April, He was a member of the Frontier Guard.

1861, May, Hazlett was appointed 2nd-class clerk in the Sixth Auditor's Office. ["Departmental," *National Republican* (Washington, D.C.), May 17, 1861, p.2]

1863, June, C. H. Hazlet, 28, clerk in Post Office Dep't, Washington, D.C. [*Civil War Draft Registration Records, 1863–1865*]

1869, Cunningham Hazlett was questioned by Clifford Arick at the Court of Inquiry of Gen. A. B. Dyer. Hazlett acknowledged that he and Arick were long-time friends. [A. B. Dyer, *Proceedings of a Court Inquiry Convened at Washington . . . ,* Vol. 2 (Washington: U.S. Gov't Printing Office), pp.260–65.]

1873, Feb. 25, Hazlett died in Washington, D.C. He was buried in Union Cemetery in Morristown, Belmont County, Ohio. [www .findagrave.com]

Joseph Heimer (1831–1899)

1831, Joseph Heimer was born. [*Civil War Draft Registration Records, 1863–1865* (Ancestry.com)

He was the son of Joseph and Sara Maria Heimer. [*Newspapers: Philadelphia Public Ledger Death Notices 1857–1864* (http://files. usgwarchives.net/pa/philadelphia/newspapers/publed20.txt)]

1850, He was a brick maker living in Philadelphia with his widowed mother, Maria Heimer, and two sisters. [*1850 U.S. Federal Census, North Liberties Ward 6, Phila., Pa.*]

1861, April, He was a member of the Frontier Guard.

1863, Joseph Heimer, occupation brick maker, was unmarried and living in the District of Columbia, with former military service of three months with the District of Columbia Volunteers. [*Civil War Draft Registration Records, 1863–1865,* (Ancestry.com) database]

1865, Jan. 11, He married Sarah M. Bean. [*District of Columbia Marriages, 1811–1950 databa*se]

1870–1880, He was a brick manufacturer and merchant. [*1870, 1880 U.S. Census, Washington, DC*]

1899, Jan. 4, A bill was introduced in the House by Mr. Adams to grant Joseph Heimer, late a private in Capt. James H. Lanes' company, District of Columbia Volunteers, a pension. It went to the Committee on Invalid Pensions. [*Journal of the House of Representatives of the United States being the Third Session of Fifty Fifth Congress* (U.S. Government Printing Office, 1899), 58]

1899, Apr. 14, Joseph Heimer died at age 68 and was buried in Congressional Cemetery in Washington.

Charles Hendley (1822–1895)

1822, Aug. 7, Charles Hendley was born. [*Bytes of History* (bytesofhistory.org/Cemeteries/DC_Congressional/Obits/H/Hendley.pdf)] He was born in Boston, Mass. [*District of Columbia, Select Deaths and Burials, 1840–1964* (Ancestry.com) database]

1856–1857, He was listed as a boot manufacturer in Newport, Ky. [*1856–57 Newport City Directory,* Campbell County, Ky. Gen Web (www.rootsweb.ancestry.com/~kycampbe/)]

1860, Hendley was a delegate to the Republican National Convention from Newport, Campbell County, Ky. [*PoliticalGraveyard.com, Index to Politicians*]

1860, November, "Republicans at Newport had a grand jollification over the election of Lincoln Thursday evening. . . . Speeches were made by Charles Hendley, one of the Lincoln Electors. . . ." ["Lincoln Vote in Kentucky," *Cleveland Morning Leader,* Nov. 12, p.2]

1861, Hendley moved to Washington, D.C., according to his son's 1927 obituary. ["C. M. Hendley, 75, Dies in Baltimore," *Evening Star*, Feb. 22, 1927] (bytesofhistory.org/Cemeteries/ DC_Congressional/Obits)]

1861, April, He was a member of the Frontier Guard.

1862–1885, He was a clerk at the Treasury Dep't in Washington. [*U.S. City Directories, 1821–1989* (Ancestry.com) database]

1895, Jan. 21, He died. [*District of Columbia, Select Deaths and Burials, 1840–1964* (Ancestry.com)]

Joseph J. Henry (1834–1862)

1834, Dec. 14, Joseph J. Henry was born. [www.findagrave.com] He was the son of William Henry III and Mary B. Albright. [Scott Paul Gordon, *A Henry Family Genealogy* (http://www.jacobsburghis tory.com/wp-content/uploads/2013/03/Henry-family-genealogy -JHS.pdf)]

    The Henry family of gunsmiths worked in Pennsylvania for nearly 200 years. J. J. Henry's father, William Henry, founded Boulten gun works in 1812. [Scott Paul Gordon, *AmericanLongrifles.com* (http://www.americanlongrifles.org/forum/index .php?topic=22490.0)]

April, 1861, He was a member of the Frontier Guard. "Captain Henry, the first officer from N.J. to fall in battle, was also the first volunteer from N.J. for the defense of Washington. He enlisted in Captain Lane's command to defend Washington. This company held Washington secure till the arrival of troops." [Madison Drake, *History of the Ninth N.J. Volunteers* (Elizabeth, N.J.: Journal Printing House, 1889), p.411]

1861, Nov. 11, Became Captain of Company H in the 9th N.J. Volunteers. [Drake, p.457]

1862, Feb. 8, He was killed at Roanoke Island, N.C. [Ibid.]

1862, Buried at Belvidere Cemetery, Belvidere, Warren County, N.J. [www.findagrave.com] "Captain Henry was killed by a round shot, was an accomplished gentleman, and a gallant officer of great promise. He fell, as he would have chosen to fall, at the head of his division." [Drake, p.452]

Frederick Godfried Hesse (1826–1911)

1826, Mar. 28, Hesse was born in Treves, Prussia. ["Famous Inventor Called by Death," *San Francisco Call*, Jan. 28, 1911 (*California Digital Newspaper Collection*), p.15]

1836–1841, He began his education at the Gymnasium in Saarbrucker, Germany. [*University of California Chronicle* (Univ. of Cal. Press, 1911), p.117, Google Book]

1841–1845, He attended the Realschule in Saarbrucker, where he qualified for the Royal Polytechnic School in Berlin. [Ibid.]

1847, He served a year in the Prussian army. He took part in the Revolution. ["Famous Inventor Called by Death"]

1849, Hesse immigrated to the United States. [*Univ. of Cal. Chronicle*, 117]

1850, He worked as an assistant in an architect's office in Providence, R.I. [Ibid.]

1851, He taught engineering at Brown University. [Ibid.]

Ca. 1854, He was a topographical and construction engineer for the railroad in Pennsylvania. [Ibid.]

1857, A consulting engineer in Washington, D.C., he edited the Patent Office Report. [Ibid.]

1858, He was an astronomer for the Chile Astronomical Exposition. [William C. James, *Illustrated History of the University of California, 1868–1895* (San Francisco: F. H. Dukesmith, 1895), p.114]

1861, April, Member of the Frontier Guard.

1862, Professor of mathematics of the U.S. Navy, and worked at the National Observatory in Washington, D.C. [*Univ. of Cal. Chronicle*, p.117]

1864, Served on the commission that settled the boundary dispute between Oregon and Washington. [Ibid.]

ca. 1868, Moved to San Francisco, where he was a consulting engineer. [Ibid.]

1875, He became Professor of Industrial Mechanics at the University of California. [Ibid.]

1876, His title was changed to Professor of Mechanical Engineering. [Ibid.]

1880, Hesse, at age 54, lived in Oakland, Cal., with his wife, Camella. [*1880 U.S. Census, Oakland, Cal.*]

1901, He became Professor of Hydraulics. [*Univ. of Cal. Chronicle*, p.117]

1904, He retired and was made Professor Emeritus. [Ibid.]

1911, Jan. 27, He died after having a stroke. ["Famous Inventor Called by Death"]

Phineas Warren Hitchcock (1831–1881)

1831, Nov. 30, Phineas Hitchcock was born in New Lebanon, Columbia County, New York. He was the son of Gad and Nancy (Prime) Hitchcock. [Dwight Whitney Marsh, *Genealogy of the Hitchcock Family* (Amherst, Mass.: Carpenter & Morehouse, 1894), p.459, Google Book]

1855, Hitchcock graduated from Williams College in Massachusetts. [Ibid.]

1855–1857, He studied law while supporting himself by writing for the newspaper in Rochester, N.Y. [*Transactions and Reports of the Nebraska State Historical Society* (Nebraska: Nebraska State Historical Society, 1885), pp.102–03, Google Book]

1857, Moved to Omaha, Nebraska Territory, and started his law practice. [Ibid.]

1858, Dec. 27, Married Ann M. Monell. [Marsh, loc. cit.]

1860, Went to the Republican Convention in Chicago as a delegate from the Nebraska Territory. [Nebraska State Historical Society, loc. cit.]

1861, April, He was a member of the Frontier Guard.

1861, May, Hitchcock was appointed to Marshal of the Nebraska Territory by Lincoln. [Ibid.]

1864, He was elected the Nebraska Territorial Delegate to the 39th Congress. [Ibid.]

1867–1869, Served as Surveyor General of Iowa and Nebraska. [Ibid.]

1870–1877, U.S. Senator from Nebraska. [Ibid.]

1873, He was instrumental in passing the Timber Culture Act. [Wilmon Henry Droze, *Trees, Prairies, and People* (Denton, Texas: Texas Women's Univ. Press, 1977), p.24, Google Book]

1881, July 10, Phineas W. Hitchcock died and was buried in Prospect Hill Cemetery in Omaha.

William G. Hoben (1829–)

1829, William G. Hoben was born in Maine. [*1860 Federal U.S. Census, Yarmouth, Cumberland, Maine*]

1851, Sept. 2, He married Lucretia Estey in New Brunswick. [*Brunswick Courier,* Sept. 6, 1851, Provincial Archives of New Brunswick (archives.gnb.ca)]

1855–1857, Hoben was pastor of the Dover First Baptist Church in Dover, New York. [Bacino, *Dover First Baptist* (doverfirstbaptist.org) 2007, from N. R. Feagles, *History of Dover First Baptist Church* (1932)]

1860, Hoben lived in Yarmouth, Maine, with his wife, Lucretia; son, Frank; and daughter, Isabel. [*1860 Federal U.S. Census, Yarmouth, Cumberland, Maine*]

1860, Nov. 10, He resigned as pastor in Yarmouth. ["Baptists," *New York Weekly News,* Nov. 10, 1860, *Old Fulton New York Postcards* (fultonhistory.com)]

1860, Hoben was the editor of the Portland newspaper *The Maine Son of Temperance.* [*Bangor Daily Whig and Courier,* 1860, *Old Fulton New York Postcards* (fultonhistory.com)]

1861, March, Went to Washington to apply for a chaplaincy in the Navy. [*Letters received by the Adjutant General, 1861–1870,* NARA Catalog ID 300368, (Fold3)]

1861, April, He was a member of the Frontier Guard.

1861, June, Hoben traveled from Washington into Virginia. Returning later that month, he met with Benjamin F. Butler and told him about the number of rebel forces gathering behind enemy lines. He stated that "he had been employed by the Commander in Chief as a spy." [*Letters received by the Adjt. General, 1861–1870,* NARA Catalog ID 300368 (Fold 3)]

1861, August, Hoben informed Seward about two contractors of supplies to the rebel army staying in Yarmouth. Cyrus F. Sargent and Octavius Hill were arrested a few days later. [*U.S. Congressional Serial Set,* Issue 3788 (1897), pp.673–77, Google Book]

1863, January, Hoben informed on Captain John H. Boyle and offered a plan for his arrest. [*Case Files of Investigations by Levi C. Turner* *and Lafayette C. Baker, 1861–1866,* NARA Catalog ID 656620 (Fold 3)]

1861–1865, "Army and Navy Record," Hoben served from North Yarmouth, Maine. [Corliss, p.831]

James H. Holmes [Capt.] (ca. 1833–1907)

ca. 1833, James H. Holmes was born in New York.

Prior to 1856, He was in the dray business in the store of Judge Schuyler at Ithaca, N.Y. [Testimony of James H. Holmes, Creator: Hyatt, Thaddeus Item No.: 2593, Thaddeus Hyatt Collection, #401 Box 1 Folder 5, KSHS Identifier: DaRT ID: 2593, Kansas Historical Society, *Kansas Memory* (http://www.kansasmemory.org/item/2593, http://www.kansasmemory.org/item/2593/text)

1856, James H. Holmes came to Osawatomie, Kans.Terr., and "joined the radical wing of the Free-State party under John Brown." [Ibid.]

1856, Aug. 30, James H. Holmes "fired first shot at Battle of Osawatomie," Kansas Territory ["John Brown Reburial Plan," *New York Times,* Aug. 26, 1899, p.6]

1856, November? Settled on Washington Creek, Douglas County, Kansas Territory [Op. cit.]

1857, Apr. 30, Letter to John Brown from James Holmes. [Kansas State Historical Society, John Brown Collection, #299, Box 1, Folder 22, Item # 102607, www.territorialkansasonline.org]

1857, Oct. 9, Married Julia Archibald, born Nova Scotia.

1858, James H. Holmes and his wife and her brother, Albert, traveled to Pike's Peak [*Kansas Historical Quarterly,* "Gold Fever in Kansas Territory Migration to the Pike's Peak Gold Fields, 1858–1860," Calvin W. Gower, Spring 1973 (Vol. 39, No. 1), pp.58–74.

1859–1862, Lived in Santa Fe, N.M.

1861, April, James H. Holmes served in Frontier Guard, Washington, D.C.

1870, June 14, James H. Holmes, 38, b. NY, "Clerk Interior," wife Julia, 33, b. Nova Scotia, and their two children, 10 and 6, both born New Mexico, were living with Archibald relatives in 5th Ward Washington, D.C. [U S. Fed. Census 1870, 5th Ward, Washington, D.C., https://www.familysearch.org]

Sometime between 1870 and 1880, Julia and James H. Holmes were divorced.

Lorenzo Pierce Holtslander (1820–1904)

1820, Dec. 16, He was born in Orange County, N.Y. [*District of Columbia, Select Deaths and Burials, 1840–1964* (Ancestry.com) database] He was the son of Lewis and Jane (McEwen) Holtslander. [www.findagrave.com] His father ran the stagecoach between Oberlin and Cleveland. [Guide to Westwood Cemetery, Oberlin Heritage Center (http://www.oberlinheritagecenter.org/researchlearn/gravestone)]

1838, He was a student at the preparatory school in Oberlin, Ohio. [Oberlin Collegiate Institute, *Catalog of the Trustees, Officers, and Students* (Cuyahoga Falls, 1838), p.18, Student Name Index Project]

1841–1844, Served in the U.S. Navy. [James Henry Lane Collection, Kenneth Spencer Research Library, University of Kansas (RH MS 28, Box 1, Folder XV)]

1847, May 27, Married Electra F. Parsons in Lorain County, Ohio. [*Ohio Marriages, 1800–1958* (Family Search) database]

1859, He was granted a patent for a marine hydraulic propeller. [Google Patents]

1860, Lived in Oberlin with his wife, Electra. [*1860 U.S. Federal Census, Oberlin, Lorain, Ohio*]

1861, Mar. 4, He attended Lincoln's inauguration. [James Henry Lane Collection]

1861, April, He was a member of the Frontier Guard.

1861, December, Employed in the civil service. [James Henry Lane Collection]

1864, He was a Freemason. [*Proceedings of the Grand Lodge of Free and Accepted Masons of the District of Columbia* (1864), p.99]

1865, Employed as a clerk at the Pension Office in Washington. [*Official Register of the United States* (1865) p.141 (Internet Archive)]

1870–1900, Lived in Washington as a Pension Examiner. [*1870, 1880, and 1900 U.S. Census, D.C.*]

1904, Apr. 7, He died in Washington, D.C. ["Died," *Evening Star,* Aug. 8, 1904, p.5]

1904, Apr. 11, He was buried in Westwood Cemetery in Oberlin, Ohio. [www.findagrave.com]

John Hopkins Houston (1796–1870)

1796, June 1, Houston was born in Gap, Lancaster County, Pa. [www.findagrave.com]

1825, June 3, His cousin, Sam Houston, wrote to tell him of his reasons for not marrying and his political plans. [Houston, Sam (1793–1863) to John H. Houston, Gilder Lehrman Institute of American History]

1825, Oct. 18, He married Gertrude P. Truxton in Washington, D.C. [*District of Columbia Marriages, 1811–1950* (Family Search) database]

1829, He was a clerk in the Auditor's Office of the Treasury Department. [*Official Register of the United States* (Washington: U.S. Gov't Printing Office, 1830) p.22, Internet Archive (archive.org)]

1850, John H. Houston lived in Washington with his wife, Gertrude, and his seven children. [*1850 Census, Washington Ward 5, Washington, D.C.*]

1861, April, He was a member of the Frontier Guard.

1863, Apr. 21, Lincoln appointed Houston as 2nd Comptroller of the Treasury ad interim. [*Abraham Lincoln Papers: Images from the National Archives and the Library of Congress* (Image 232403)]

1870, Feb. 18, He died and was buried at Oak Hill Cemetery in Washington, D.C. [www.findagrave.com]

Joseph Charles Howells (1823–1906)

1823, Jan. 27, Howells was born in England, the son of Henry Charles Howells and Mary (Best) Howells. [*Howells/Jordan Family Tree,* Public Member Trees (Ancestry.com)]

1831, October, His family came to the United States. [*New York, Passenger and Immigration Lists, 1820–1850* (Ancestry.com) database]

1831–1836, He first lived in Ohio. ["The McFarland Trial," *New York Times,* April 30, 1870]

1846, Learned the daguerreotype business in New York City. ["The McFarland Trial"]

1847, Feb. 12, Enlisted in the 1st Regiment of Massachusetts Volunteers and was a soldier in the Mexican War. [NARA, *Index to Compiled Service Records of Volunteers Who Served during the Mexican War,* Catalog ID # 654518 (Fold3)]

1849, Mar. 10, Married Louisa Odlin in Montgomery County, Ohio. [*Ohio County Marriages, 1789–2013* (Family Search) database]

1850, He was a dentist in Lewiston, Ill.. [*1850 U.S. Federal Census, Lewiston, Fulton, Ill.*]

1854, Continued dentistry and moved to Wisconsin. ["The McFarland Trial"]

1859, June, He received a patent for an improved omnibus register. [*U.S. Patent Office, Annual Report of the Commissioner of Patents* (U.S. Gov't Printing Office, 1860), p.437, Google Book]

1861, April, He was a member of the Frontier Guard.

1862, Listed as a clerk in Washington, D.C. [*U.S. City Directories, 1821–1989* (Ancestry.com database)]

1863, June, Joseph L. Howells, age 40, born England, clerk, Interior Dep't, Washington, D.C. [*U.S. Civil War Draft Registration Records, 1863–1865*]

1863, August, Received a patent for an improvement in secret pockets of wearing apparel. [*Collected Works of Sir Humphry Davy, U.S. Patent Office* (Smith, Elder & Co., 1866), p.585]

1863, He was a clerk at the Indian Office of the Dep't of the Interior. [*Register of Employees of the Indian Office Associated with the Nez Perce, 1861–1869* (www.lib.uidaho.edu)]

1865, Worked as a Customs inspector in New York. [*Officers and Agents, Civil, Military, and Naval, 1865* (Washington: U.S. Gov't Printing Office, 1866), p.121, Google Book]

1880, He was listed as a machinist living in Springfield, N.J., with wife, Louisa, and his four children, Ramona, Charles, Grace, and Joseph. [*1880 U.S. Federal Census, Springfield, Union, N.J.*]

1890, Received a pension for the Mexican War. [*United States Mexican War Pension Index, 1887–1826*]

1906, Feb. 16, Howells died after an operation at Roosevelt Hospital in New York. ["Joseph C. Howells," *New York Tribune,* Feb. 17, 1906 ("Chronicling America"), p.7]

Daniel Webster Hughes (1841–1883)

1841, Daniel W. Hughes was born in Philadelphia, Pa. [*District of Columbia, Select Deaths and Burials, 1840–1964* (Ancestry.com) database]

ca. 1855, He was a young employee of several newspaper offices in Philadelphia. ["Capt. Daniel H. [*sic*] Hughes," *National Republican,* March 22, 1883, p.3 ("Chronicling America")]

1858–1860, Worked as a page in the U.S. Senate; appointed by Senator Simon Cameron. [Ibid.]

1861, April, He was a member of the Frontier Guard. [Ibid.]

1861, May, Simon Cameron appointed him to the Regular Army with the rank of 1st Lieutenant. [Ibid.]

1862, May 15, Promoted to full Captain, commissioned an officer in the U.S. Volunteers Aide-de-Camp Infantry Regiment. [*U.S., Civil War Soldiers Records and Profiles, 1861–1865* (Ancestry.com) database]

1865, May 31, Mustered out. [Ibid.]

ca. 1866, He became a manager for Howe's Circus and theatrical combination. ["Capt. Daniel H. Hughes"]

1872, Nov. 23, He married Mary E. Douglas. [*District of Columbia Select Marriages, 1830–1921*]

ca. 1874, He took a government job with the War Department. ["Capt. Daniel H. Hughes"]

1880, Hughes was employed at the Surgeon General's Office. [*1880 Census, Washington, D.C.*]

1883, Mar. 3, Died in Washington, D.C. [*District of Columbia, Select Deaths and Burials, 1840–1964*]

1883, He was buried at Arlington Cemetery. [www.findagrave.com]

William Hutchinson (1823–1904)

1823, Jan. 24, William Hutchinson was born in Randolph, Orange County, Vt. [William Hutchinson Papers, Kansas State Historical Society, Topeka, Kans.]

Prior to 1847, Was teacher, farmer, and newspaper editor and publisher. [Ibid.]

1847, Married Helen Fish [ibid.] and had a farm in Orange County, Vt. ["William Hutchinson," by Kristina Gaylord, *Kansapedia*, Kansas Historical Society, Topeka, Kans., 2011]

1852 Hutchinson "became editor and publisher of the *Green Mountain Herald*, Randolph, Vt." [Ibid.]

ca. 1854, Correspondent re: Kansas situation for the *Boston Journal* and the *New York Times.* [Ibid.]

1855, April, Moved with family to Lawrence, Kansas Territory [Ibid.]

1850s, Formed partnership with G.W. Hutchinson and was secretary of the Big Springs Convention. ["William Hutchinson Dead," *Lawrence Daily Journal*, Lawrence, Kans., May 20, 1904, p.2].

1856, Present when Free State Hotel in Lawrence, Kansas Territory, was destroyed. ["William Hutchinson Dead," *ibid.*]

1856, Hutchinson was at the Battle of Fort Titus, Battle of Franklin, Bull Creek, and Washington Creek, etc. [William Hutchinson papers, KSHS]

1859, Lawrence delegate to the 1859 Wyandotte Constitutional Convention. [Ibid.]

1860s, Went to Washington, D.C. but maintained a home in Lawrence, Kans. [Ibid.]

1861, Joined James H. Lane's Frontier Guard, Washington, D.C. [Ibid.]

Prior to 1904, Employed in the Interior Dep't, Washington, D.C., until his death. [Ibid.]

1904, May 18, Death of William Hutchinson in Washington, D.C. [*Lawrence Daily Journal*, May 20, 1904]

Thaddeus Hyatt (1816–1901)

1816, July 21, He was born in Rahway, Union County, N.J. [Joseph W. Snell, *Thaddeus Hyatt Papers*, 1843–1898, Kansas Historical Society (www.kshs.org)]

1845, He patented the "illuminating vault cover," designed to cover cellars under city sidewalks in order to allow light. He made a fortune on this and continued experimenting with reinforced concrete over several decades. [Sara E. Wermiel, *California Concrete, 1876–1916* (academic paper, 2009)]

1854, Hyatt was one of the directors of the New York Kansas League, which promoted emigration to the Kansas Territory. [Letter, New York Kansas League to the Public, *Territorial Kansas Online*]

1856, July, He was appointed president of the Kansas National Committee. [William H. Isley, "The Sharps Rifle Episode in Kansas," *American Historical Review, Vol. XII, No. 1,* April 1907, p.562]

1856, He began giving money to John Brown for Underground Railroad activities. [Richard J. Hinton, "He Helped John Brown," *New York, NY World,* April 7, 1895, *Old Fulton NY Postcards* (fulton-history.com)]

1857, Hyatt advanced the money for the Kansas National Committee's distribution of goods to the settlers. [Richard Hinton, *John Brown and His Men* (New York and London: Funk & Wagnalls, 1894), p.125]

1859, December, He started a relief fund for the family of John Brown. [Snell]

1860, January, The Senate summoned Hyatt for its investigation of John Brown's raid. It was thought he was one of John Brown's backers. He protested the summons on the grounds that the Senate had no power to compel testimony of witnesses, but was charged with contempt and sent to jail for three months. [Edgar Langsdorf, "Thaddeus Hyatt in Washington Jail," *Kansas Historical Quarterly,* August 1940 (Vol. 9, No. 3), pp.225–39]

1860, July 4, He spoke at the gathering over John Brown's grave. [*Times-Picayune,* July 13, 1860, p.2]

1861, April, He was a member of the Frontier Guard at the White House.

1861, August, He was appointed U.S. Consul at La Rochelle, France, where he served until 1865. [Snell]

1873, Hyatt built a factory in New York to manufacture pavement lenses. [Peter Collins, *Concrete: The Vision of a New Architecture* (McGill-Queen's Press, 2004), p.58]

ca. 1878, He built a factory in London similar to the one in New York. [Ibid.]

1901, July 25, He died at his summer home at Sandown, Isle of Wight, England. [Snell]

1901, July, He was buried in Christ Church Cemetery in Isle of Wight, England. (www.finda grave.com)

Guido Ilges (1835–1918)

1835, Nov. 10, Guido Joseph Julius Ilges, born at Ahrweiler, Coblenz, Prussia. [Blog—*Historical Fort Benton, Major Guido Ilges 1835–1918* by Ken Robison for the *River Press,* Feb. 27, 2013]

1855, Immigration to U.S. [1900 U.S. Federal Census, Cincinnati, Ohio], departed from Port of Liverpool [Folder ON-78-1, Archives and Rare Book Library, Univ. of Cincinnati (Ohio)]

1860, June 25, Guido Ilges, age 22[?], born Prussia, Attorney at Law, living in Vincennes, Knox County, Ind. [1860 U.S. Federal Census, Vincennes, Knox County, Ind.]

1861, April, In Frontier Guard, White House, Washington, D.C. [Op. cit.]

1861, April or May, Appointed Captain by President Lincoln. [Ibid.]

1861, May 14, Guido Ilges left the Frontier Guard to accept his commission as Captain in the 14th U.S. Infantry Regiment. [*American Civil War Research Database*]

1864, Aug. 1, Promoted to Lieutenant Colonel (Brevet, Army) on Aug. 1, 1864 (Spottsylvania, Va.). [Ibid.]

1870, Guido Ilges, Captain, living at Fort Thompson garrison, Dakota Terr. [1870 U.S. Census]

1873, Dec. 10, He was promoted to Major in the 7th U.S. Infantry Dec. 10, 1873. [Blog: Behind AotW, U.S. Regular Infantry in Maryland, 1862, Feb. 24, 2009, http://behind.aotw.org/2009/02/24/us-regular-infantry-in-maryland-1862/]

1879, December, Transferred to the 6th Infantry. [Ibid.]

1881, Jan. 2, fought Gall's Dakota Indians in Poplar River, Mont. [Guido Ilges Death Record, www.findagrave.com]

1881, Sept. 25, fought Nez Perce Indians in Cow Creek Canyon, Mont. on Sept. 25, 1877.

1882, Feb. 6, Appointed Lieutenant Colonel of the 18th U.S. [Ibid.]

1908, Guido Ilges, hay weigher (never married). ["Old Indian Fighter Now Cincinnati Hay Weigher," *Cincinnati Post* (Ohio), OhioJan. 20, 1908, p.7—*GenealogyBank*]

1918, Jan. 14, Died at his home in Cincinnati, Ohio. [*Cincinnati Post,* Jan. 14, 1918]

Merritt Hitt Insley [Capt.] (1830 –1909)

1830, May 20, Merritt Hitt Insley was born in Ohio.

1855, May 24, Married Eliza P. Kiser, Tippecanoe County, Ind. [www .worldconnect.com]

1858, Spring, Came to Kansas and engaged in hotel business until 1861. [William G. Cutler, *History of the State of Kansas,* 1883, by A. T. Andreas, Chicago, Ill. "The hotel was at one time headquarters for Senator Lane and other well-known politicians." [*Leavenworth Weekly Times*, Oct. 9, 1913, p.6.]

1861 April, Insley served in the Frontier Guard.

1861, Aug 6, Lived in Lafayette, Ind., at time of enlistment as a Captain, commissioned into Quartermaster's Dep't. (U.S. Volunteers) [American Civil War Research database]

1863, Mar 13, Commissioned into Quartermaster's Dep't [headquartered at Ft. Leavenworth]. (Regular Army) [Cutler, op. cit.]

1863, Aug 13, Discharged from Quartermaster's Dep't (U.S. Volunteers). [Civil War Research database]

1865, May 26 Resigned from Quartermaster's Dep't (Regular Army). [Ibid.]

Between 1865 and 1870, Engaged in freighting. [Cutler, op. cit.]

1870, Lived in Leavenworth, Kans. [1870 U.S. Federal Census]. He was in the banking business with Daniel Shire and E. F. Kellogg. (The business was later known as Insley, Shire & Co). [Ibid.]

1880s, Insley was raising stock on his 1,200-acre farm in Leavenworth County. [Cutler, op. cit.]

1900, Lived in Denver, Colo.; was the manager of the Keeley Institute. [1900 U.S. Census, Denver, Colo.]

1909, Mar. 6, Merritt H. Insley died at his home in Leavenworth, Kans. [*Lawrence Daily World*, Lawrence, Kans., Mar 6, 1909, p.4]

John B. Irvin (1815–1867)

1815, Aug. 25, Irvin was born in Campbelltown, McKean County, Pa. [www.findagrave.com]

1858, February, He was one of the incorporators of the town of Kennekuk in Kansas. [*Private Laws of Kansas* (S. W. Driggs, 1858), p.348]

1859, Jan. 3, He was a member of the House and was elected Speaker *pro tem.* [Daniel Wilder, *Annals of Kansas* (G. W. Martin, 1875), 195–96]

1860, John Irvin was living in Grasshopper Falls with his wife, Eleanora, his son, George, and two daughters, Mary and Cate; listed as a medical doctor. [*1860 Census, Grasshopper, Kansas Territory*]

1861, April, He was a member of the Frontier Guard.

1867, Sept. 2, He died in Jonesboro, Ill., and was buried in Hiawatha, Kans.

Orsamus Hylus Irish (1830–1883)

1830, O. H. Irish was born in Malone County, N.Y. [*District of Columbia Select Deaths and Burials, 1840–1964*]. He was raised in New York City and educated in Erie, Pa. [*New York Times*, Jan. 28, 1883]

1857, Moved to Nebraska Territory. [Ibid.]

1860, He was a delegate to the Republican Convention in Chicago. [Ibid.]

1861, April, He was a member of the Frontier Guard.

1861, July, Lincoln nominated Irish for agent of the Indians of the Omaha Agency. [*Journal of the Executive Proceedings of the Senate of the United States*, Vol. 2 (1887), p.327]

1864, He was appointed Superintendent of Indian Affairs in Utah. ["O. H. Henry," *New York Times*, January 28, 1883.]

1867, "O. H. Irish, of Nebraska City, was elected Grand Master." ["Nebraska, 1867," *Freemasons, Grand Lodge of Ancient Free and Accepted Masons of the State of Connecticut*, p.320]

1869, Appointed U.S. Consul at Dresden, Germany. ["O. H. Henry"]

1877, He was made assistant chief of the Bureau of Engraving and Printing in Washington. [Ibid.]

1878–1883, Chief of Bureau of Engraving and Printing. [Ibid.]

1883, Jan. 27, Died in Washington, D.C. and buried at Oak Hill Cemetery. [www.findagrave.com]

James Allison Jenkins (1814–1873)

1814, James Allison Jenkins was born in Hardin County, Ky., the son of Jehu Jenkins and Hannah Buzon. [Warren Y. Jenkins, *The Jenkins, Boone, and Lincoln Family Records* (1925), pp.8–9]

1826, The Jenkins family moved to Montgomery County, Ill. [Ibid.]

1845, July 22, James A. Jenkins married Bathalia Jane Smith in Montgomery County, Ill. [*Illinois Marriages, 1790–1860* (Ancestry. com)]

1850, He was listed as a physician living in Montgomery County, Ill., with his wife, Jane. [*1850 U.S. Federal Census, South Part of Dist. 22, Montgomery County, Ill.*]

1856, May 16, Jenkins and Lincoln both signed a petition printed in the *Springfield Journal* calling for delegates to be elected at a convention in Bloomington, Ill., in opposition to the present administration and for the repeal of the Missouri Compromise. [Jesse W. Weik, *The Real Lincoln, A Portrait* (Boston and New York: Houghton Mifflin Co., 1923), pp.253–55 Google Book]

1861, He was a clerk in the Treasury Dep't. [*Official Register of the United States* (Washington, U.S. Gov't Printing Office, 1861), p.20, Google Book]

1861, April, He was a member of the Frontier Guard.

1862–1873, He was a clerk/auditor for the Treasury Dep't. [*U.S. City Directories 1821–1989*]

1873, July, Jenkins died and was buried in Glenwood Cemetery in Washington, D.C.

John W. Jenkins (1836–1887)

1836, John W. Jenkins was born in Virginia, the son of John and Frances C. (Smith) Jenkins. [Public Member Trees (Ancestry.com)]

1850, He and his family lived in Randolph County, Indiana. [*1850 U.S. Census, Randolph County, Ind.*]

1858, July 8, Jenkins arrived in Lawrence, Kansas Territory [*Randolph County Journal,* July 29, 1858, p.2]

1860, January, He was chosen as an assistant clerk of the Kansas legislature. ["Kansas Legislature," *White Cloud Kansas Chief* (White Cloud, Kans.), Jan. 12, 1860, p.2]

1861, April, He was a member of the Frontier Guard.

1864, Advertised his services as an attorney having association with S. C. Pomeroy and others in high positions in both Kansas and Indiana. [*1864 Washington D.C. City Directory,* p.10]

1866, He lived in Frederick County, Va. [IRS Tax Assessment Lists (Ancestry.com) database]

ca. 1869, Jenkins was Commonwealth Attorney for the City of Richmond under military appointment. [Robert R. Nuckols, *History of the Government of the City of Richmond, Virginia, and a Sketch of Those Who Administer Its Affairs* (Richmond: Williams Printing Co., 1899), p.79]

1872, October, Jenkins was elector for the Republican Party for the state at large in Virginia. [*Daily State Journal* (Alexandria, Va.) Oct. 1, 1872, p.2]

1873, April, Jenkins moved from Virginia to Washington, D.C. [*Daily State Journal* (Alexandria, Va.), p.1]

1874, He was appointed by President Grant to be secretary of the Territory of Colorado. Edward McCook's appointment as governor was made at the same time. When that was contested, Jenkins became acting governor and served the greater part of McCook's term. [Hubert Bancroft, *History of Nevada, Colorado, and Wyoming: 1540–1888* (San Francisco: History Co., 1890), p.653.]

1876, Jenkins was Special Assistant U.S. Attorney for the Territory of Colorado. [*Index to Reports of Committees of the House of Representatives,* 1876]

1881–1882, He was the prosecuting attorney in Lake County, Colo.. [Bancroft, p.653]

1887, Feb. 21, John W. Jenkins died in Denver. He was buried there in Riverside Cemetery.

John Wisner Jennings (1833–1907)

1833, Dec. 4, J. W. Jennings was born in Allen, Allegany County, N.Y. He was the son of Hector Jennings and Delina M. Cummings. [Public Member Trees (Ancestry.com)]

1854, He married Amelia Robinson. [Clarence Bagley, *History of Seattle from the Earliest Settlement to the Present Time,* Vol. III (Chicago: S. J. Clarke Publishing Co., 1916), p.921 (www.ebooksread.com)]

1858, Moved to Indiana. [Ibid.]

1860, Express messenger in Indianapolis. [*1860 Census, Indianapolis, Marion, Ind.*]

1861, April, He was a member of the Frontier Guard.

1861, Jenkins was Postmaster of the U.S. Senate. [Ibid.]

1870, He was an agent for the railroad in St. Louis. [*1870 Census, Saint Louis, Mo.*]

1907, Apr. 3, He died in Ramapo, N.Y. ["J. W. Jennings," *New York Tribune,* April 4, 1907, p.5]

John Wesley Jones (1825–1905)

1825, May 3, John W. Jones was born in Philadelphia, the son of William Patterson Jones and Ursula (Lindeman) Jones. [Peter E. Palmquist, *Pioneer Photographers from the Mississippi to the Continental Divide: A Biographical Dictionary 1839–1865* (Stanford Univ. Press, 2005), p.360]

1836, He attended McKendree College at the age of 11 in Alton, Ill. He later taught school. [Ibid.]

1847, He studied law in Quincy, Ill. with Archibald Williams, an associate of Abraham Lincoln's. [Ibid.]

1850, Jones went west for the gold rush before opening a store in Calaveras County. He got the idea of making a moving panorama of the overland trail to California with daguerreotypes and drawings, formed a company, and found backing. [Palmquist, loc. cit.]

1851, July, His crew left California and headed east. [Ibid.]

1851, October, The group arrived in St. Louis. [Ibid.]

1851, Fall, Jones settled in Melrose, Mass., and began supervising the painting of his "Great Pantoscope of California, the Rocky Mountains, Salt Lake City, Nebraska & Kansas." [Ibid.]

1853, The Pantoscope went on exhibit in New York. [Ibid.]

1861, April, He was a member of the Frontier Guard at the White House.

1861, May, He was commissioned as a 1st Lieutenant in the 12th U.S. Infantry. [Palmquist, loc. cit.]

1863, May 4, He was dismissed from military service. [Ibid.]

1863, June, He took command of the Curtain Horse Guards, an emergency volunteer company. [Ibid.]

1890, He ran as an Independent from the 3rd District of New York for U.S. Congress. [Ibid.]

1890, He founded the U.S. Volunteer Live Saving Corps. [Ibid.]

1905, Dec. 15, He died in Brooklyn. [Ibid.]

George H. Keller (1801–1876)

1801, Feb. 22, George Horine Keller ["Uncle George"] was born in Harrodsburg, Mercer County, Ky. [*Lawrence Daily World,* Nov. 25, 1907, p.3, col. 3] and [*A Standard History of Kansas and Kansans,* William E. Connelley, Lewis Publishing Co., 1918, Vol. 3, p.1209]

ca. 1812, He enlisted in the army for the War of 1812, but was refused by the mustering agent because of his [young] age. [*United States Biographical Dictionary, Kansas, and Portrait Gallery of Eminent and Self-Made Men.* Chicago and Kansas City: S. Lewis, 1879, p.53]

ca. 1820s, He moved to Terre Haute, Ind., and raised stock. [Connelley]

ca. 1835, Keller moved to Platte County, Mo., engaged in farming and manufacturing. [Ibid.]

ca 1850, Equipped a large train of merchandise and moved to "Sonoma Valley and the gold fields of California," where he founded the Town of Petaluma. [Ibid.]

1852, He returned to Weston, Mo., and farmed. [*United States Biographical Dictionary,* p.52]

1854, With other citizens he founded the City of Leavenworth, Kansas Territory [Connelley, op. cit., p.1209]

1854, In the fall, he completed the Leavenworth Hotel, Leavenworth, Kansas Territory [Ibid., pp.1209–1210]

1855, He built the Mansion House, Leavenworth, which he ran until it was sold in 1857 [Ibid., p.1210]

1856, Keller was "was branded a rank abolitionist and marked for assassination." [Ibid.]

1857–58, Elected member of the House of Representatives of the Free-State Territorial Legislature. [Ibid.]

1861, Private in Frontier Guard, Washington, D.C. [Source: "The Frontier Guard at the White House," *Genealogy Trails,* http://genealogytrails.com/kan/frontierguards.html]

ca. 1865, Keller became the first warden of the Kansas State Penitentiary. [Ibid.]

1866, Retired to his farm in Leavenworth County. [*A Standard History of Kansas and Kansans,* Connelley]

1876, Nov. 13, George H. Keller died, Leavenworth County, Kans. [Ibid.]

David Merriam Kelsey (1820–1884)

1820, May 1, David M. Kelsey was born in Vermont, the son of David Kelsey and Betsey Merriam. [Public Member Trees (Ancestry.com)]

1840s, He settled west of Chicago, taught school, and co-edited a village newspaper. [Robert R. Dykstra, *Bright Radical Star: Black Freedom and White Supremacy* (Harvard Univ. Press, 1993), p.80]

ca. 1845, He was on the antislavery lecture circuit. [Ibid.]

1848, He became editor of the *Iowa Freeman* in Fort Madison, Iowa. [Ibid.]

1849, Apr. 16, He married A. M. Mason in Lee County, Iowa. [*Iowa County Marriages, 1838–1934*]

1857, He was an Illinois House of Representatives member from DeKalb County. [David W. Lusk, *Politics and Politicians: A Succinct History of the Politics of Illinois* (Springfield, Ill.: D. W. Lusk, 1884), p.37]

1858, He attended the Illinois Republican convention as a delegate. [Republican Party, *Proceedings of the Republican State Convention, June 16, 1858* (Springfield: Bailhache & Baker, Printers) p.5]

1860, D. M. Kelsey lived in Nebraska. [*1860 U.S. Federal Census, Cass County, Neb.*]

1860, First auditor in the Treasury Dep't in Washington, D.C. [John Disturnell, *Register of Officers and Agents in the Service of the United States* (New York: J. H. Colton, 1863), p.34]

1861, March, He was considered for secretary of one of the territories. [Memorandum on Appointments to Territories, *Collected Works of Abraham Lincoln, Vol. 4* (quod.lib.umich.edu)]

1861, April, He was a member of the Frontier Guard.

1870, He was a clerk at the Treasury Office and living with his wife, Arabella, in Washington. [*1870 U.S. Federal Census, Washington Ward 2, Washington, D.C.*]

1880, Kelsey was listed on the census living at the Cleveland Asylum. [*1880 U.S. Census, Cleveland, Ohio*]

1884, July 14, Kelsey died and was buried at Ridgelawn Cemetery in Elyria, Ohio. [www.findagrave.com]

George W. Lee (1830–1882)

1830, George W. Lee was born in New York. [*1850 and 1870 U.S. Federal Census*]

1850, Geo. W. Lee lived in New York City and worked as a printer. [*1850 U.S. Census, New York, N.Y.*]

1851, He went to Oregon to start a lumber business. [*Evidence for the United States in the Matter of the Claim of the Puget's Sound Agricultural Co.* (Washington: M'Gill & Witherow, 1867), pp.287–96.]

1853, January, He moved to Steilacoom in Wash. Terr.; was involved in lumber business. [Ibid.]

1858, March, He and partner, Charles Prosch, first published the *Puget Sound Herald*. [Hubert Howe Bancroft, *History of Washington*, Vol. 31 (San Francisco: The History Co., 1890), p.378]

1858, May, Lee left Steilacoom. [*Evidence for the U.S.* op. cit.]

1860, Feb. 14, He married Ruth A. White in Washington, D.C. [*D.C. Marriages, 1811–1950*]

1861, April, He was a member of the Frontier Guard.

1870, Lee lived in Washington; his occupation was printer. [*1870 U.S. Census, Washington, D.C.*]

1876–1881, Lee lived in San Francisco. [*U.S. City Directories 1821–1989* (Ancestry.com) database]

1882, Lee died. [*Sacramento Daily Record Union*, April 18, 1882]

Samuel D. Leib (1809–1883)

1809, July 21, Leib was born in Schuylkill County, Pa. [*Baltimore Sun*, Nov. 3, 1883]

1831, He married Eliza Good. [*Pennsylvania Church and Town Records, 1708–1985*]

1838–1843, Associate judge in Schuylkill County. [*Births, Marriages & Deaths from the Carbon Advocate, 1882–1883*, Vol. II, No. 51, p.150]

1843–1858, Clerk in the Indian Department of the War Dep't. [*Official Register of the U.S.* (U.S. Gov't Printing Office, 1843), p.162, Google Book]

1860, Moved to Frederick County, Md. ["Death of Judge Samuel D. Leib," *Baltimore Sun*, November 3, 1882]

1861, April, He was a member of the Frontier Guard.

1861, He was a temporary clerk at the Patent Office. [House Documents, Vol. 186, p.54, Google Book]

1864, Clerk at the House of Representatives. [*House Documents*, Vol. 211; Vol. 214 (1865), p.2]

1867–1869, He was a messenger for the House of Representatives. [*U.S. City Directories 1821–1989*]

1879, Moved back to Washington, D.C. ["Death of Judge Samuel D. Leib"]

1880, Clerk in the War Dep't, widowed. [*1880 U.S. Census, Washington, D.C.*]

1883, Nov. 1, Died in Washington, D.C.; buried at Pottsville, Pa. ["Death of Judge Samuel D. Leib"]

William Marsh (1826–1913)

1826, Feb. 24, Marsh was born in Yorkshire, England, the son John and Hannah Marsh. [Alison, "William Marsh, Friend of a President," *Bentley Village, A History* (http://bentvillhistory.blogspot.com/2014/04/william-marsh-son-of-miller-friend-of.html)]

1853, Feb. 24, He married Charlotte Jennings Dawson in Thorne, Yorkshire. [Ibid.]

1855, April, They moved to the United States. [Ibid.]

ca. 1858, Moved to Springfield, Ill. His political articles published in the *Springfield Journal* brought him to the attention of Lincoln. His wife, Charlotte, taught music to the Lincoln children. [Ibid.]

1860, Organized a club of English, Irish, and Scottish naturalized citizens to aid Lincoln's campaign. [Ibid.]

1860, May, He took five ambrotype photographs of Lincoln after his nomination. [Ibid.]

1860, Became agent and correspondent for the *Chicago Tribune* during the election. [Ibid.]

1861, April, He was a member of the Frontier Guard.

1861–1862, Worked as a clerk at the Census Bureau in Washington, D.C. [Ibid.]

1862, Appointed U.S. Consul at Altona, a borough of Hamburg, Germany. [Ibid.]

1863–1867, He was in Altona through the war between Denmark and Prussia. [Ibid.]

1867, His book, *Songs and Poems,* was published. [www.worldcat.org]

1869, Returned to Bentley, Yorkshire. [Alison]

1870–1882, He was the agent for Sir William Ridley Charles Cooke. [Ibid.]

1882, He became estate steward for John Rylands of Manchester, large textile manufacturer. [Ibid.]

1886–1895, Moved to Dumfries, Scotland, where he managed the Hoddam Castle estate. [Ibid.]

1900, The Marshes moved back to Bentley. [Ibid.]

1913, Apr. 5, Marsh died and was buried in the Arksey Church Cemetery. [Ibid.]

Robert McBratney (1818–1881)

1818, Jan. 1, Robert McBratney was born in Columbus, Ohio. He was the son of Robert and Margaret (Hoskins) McBratney. [*U.S. Biographical Dictionary, Kansas* (S. Stewart & Co., 1879), pp.262–64]

1834, Began an apprenticeship at a printing office in Ohio. [Ibid.]

1838, Became editor of the *Union County Star* in Marysville, Ohio, and advocated the election of William Henry Harrison for president.

Superintended the building of the first log cabin; used the "Log Cabin Campaign," an emblem of the Whig party. [Ibid.]

1840, He studied law. [Ibid.]

1841, He became a proponent of abolitionism after a trip to New Orleans and Texas. [Ibid.]

1842–1848, Ran the *Xenia Torchlight* in Ohio. [Ibid.]

1848, Mar. 28, He married Mary Palmer. [Ibid.]

1849, Established the *Peninsular Freeman* in Detroit. [Ibid.]

1852, He returned to Ohio and resumed as editor of the *Xenia Torchlight.* [Ibid.]

1856, He was a delegate to the National Republican Convention and decided to move to Kansas. [Ibid.]

1857, Became a partner with Samuel Pomeroy in Atchison. They purchased the *Squatter Sovereign* and changed it from a pro-slavery to a free-state newspaper, *Freedom's Champion.* [Ibid.]

1860, Apr. 8, He married Mary E. Harbinson after wife Mary Palmer died in 1859. [Ibid.]

1861, Apr. 13, McBratney took part in organizing the Frontier Guard. [Ibid.]

1861, July 5, Lincoln appointed McBratney Register of the Land Office at Junction City, Kans. [*Journal of the Executive Proceedings of the Senate* (D. Green, 1887), p.370, Google Book]

1864, He was the presidential elector of the Republican Party. [*U.S. Biographical Dictionary,* loc. cit.]

1869, Member of an exploratory trip to the Solomon River Valley. [Martha B. Caldwell, "Exploring the Solomon River Valley in 1869," *Kansas Historical Quarterly,* Feb. 1937, Vol. 6, No. 1, pp.60–76]

1881, Feb. 6, He died in Santa Fe, N.M. [*Kansas Daily Tribune,* Feb. 8, 1881, p.1]

Daniel McCook, Sr. [Maj.] (1798–1863)

1798, June 20, Daniel McCook, Sr. was born in Canonsburg, Washington County, Pa. He was the son of Irish Revolutionary George McCook and Mary (McCormack). ["Daniel McCook," *The National Cyclopaedia of American Biography,* J.T. White Co., 1895, United States, p.130 (Google eBook)

ca. 1815 Educated at Jefferson College, Canonsburg, Pa. [Ibid.]

1817, Aug. 28, Daniel McCook married Martha Latimer. [*The Scotch-Irish in America: Proceedings and Addresses,* The Scotch-Irish Society of America, Nashville, Tenn., p.161] McCook family moved to New Lisbon, Ohio. [Ibid]

After 1826 McCook family moved to Carrolton, Ohio. [Ibid]

1840, McCook family living in Carrolton, Carroll County, Ohio. [1840 U.S. Federal Census]

1850, Sept 5, Daniel McCook[Sr.] living in Hardin County, Ill. [1850 U.S. Census, Hardin County, Ill.]

After 1857, son, Daniel McCook, Jr., moved to Leavenworth, Kansas, and became a law partner of William Tecumseh Sherman and Thomas Ewing, Jr. Daniel McCook, Jr. "organized militia company called Shield Grays and entered them into Federal service with the 1st Kansas." [*Biographical Dictionary of the Union: Northern Leaders of the Civil War,* John T. Hubbell, ed., Greenwood Publishing Group, 1995]

1861, April, Daniel McCook, Sr. served in Frontier Guard at Washington, D.C.

1862, Feb 24, Commissioned into Paymaster's Dep't. (U.S. Volunteers) [*American Civil War Database*]

1862, Mar. 24 Enlisted as Major at age 64. [Ibid.]

1863, Jul 19 Wounded at Buffington Island, Ohio. [Ibid]

1863, July 21 Died Portland, Meigs County, Ohio, from wounds in skirmish. [Ibid.]

1863, July 23, Buried Spring Grove Cemetery, Cincinnati, Hamilton County, Ohio. [*"The Fighting McCooks,"* http://www.carroll countyohio.mccook]

Edward M. McCook (Brig. Gen./Gov.) (1833–1909)

1833, June 15, Edward Moody McCook born in Steubenville, Ohio.

ca. 1859, Went to Colorado, early settler at Pike's Peak. Practiced law in that area. [Florida Memory, http://www.floridamemory.com/items/show/1595 and American Civil War Research database through University of Kansas]

1859, Representative in Kansas Legislature [ibid., Florida Memory]

1860, Sept. 23, E.M. McCook, age 26, Lake Gulch, Arapahoe, Kansas Territory

1860, Living Arapahoe County, Kansas Territory [1860 U.S. Census, Kansas Territory, p.487] [Heritage Quest Online by Proquest]

1861, April Served in Frontier Guard, Washington, D.C.

1861, May 8, Residing in Indianapolis, Ind., enlisted as 2nd Lieutenant, commissioned into 1st Cavalry.

1861, Promoted 1st Lieutenant effective May 8, 1861 (1st U.S. Army Cavalry).

1861, Aug 3, Transferred from 1st Cavalry (Regular Army) to 4th Cavalry (Regular Army). [Ibid.]

1861, Sept. 29, Discharged due to promotion from 4th Cavalry (Regular Army) and commissioned into Field and Staff, 2nd Cavalry (Ind.). [Ibid.]

1861, Promoted to Major (Full, Vol.) effective Sept. 29, 1861 (2nd Ind. Cavalry). [Ibid.]

1862, Promoted to Lieutenant Colonel (Full, Vol.) effective Feb. 11, 1862. [Ibid.]

1862, Promoted to Colonel (Full, Vol.) effective Apr. 30, 1862. [Ibid.]

1862, Promoted to First Lieutenant (Full, Army) on July 17, 1862. [Ibid.]

1864, Promoted to Brigadier General (Full, Vol.) effective Apr. 27, 1864. [Ibid.]

1865, Promoted to Major General (Brevet, Vol.) effective Mar. 13, 1865. [Ibid.]

1865, Promoted to Brigadier General (Brevet, Army) effective Mar. 13, 1865. [Ibid.]

1865, May, Took formal possession of Tallahassee, Fla. and raised the U.S. flag over the capitol.

1865, Married [1st wife] Mary G. Thompson. [James B. Thompson Collection, Denver Public Library]

1866, May 9, Resigned from General Staff. (U.S. Volunteers) [American Civil War Research Database]

1866–1869, Served as Minister to Hawaii. [Ibid.]

1869–1875, Served as Territorial Governor of Colorado under appointment from President Grant. [Ibid.]

1870, June 17, Edward McCook, age 38, b. Ohio, Governor of Territory, enumerated with Mary G., age 22, Edward M. McCook, age 2, b. Sandwich Island. [1870 U.S. Census, Denver, Colo.]

post 1870, Married second wife, Mary McKenna.

1880, June 2, Edward M. McCook, age 53, b. Ohio, living at New York, N.Y.

1890, Edward M. McCook was living at Ft. Hamilton, N.Y. [Biographies, Denver Public Library]

1903, Sept. 14, Edward McCook filed for Invalid pension, application #1303917, from Colorado. [U.S. General Index to Pension Files, 1861–1934, FamilySearch.org]

1909, Sept. 9, Edward McCook died Chicago, Ill. [*Wilmington Morning Star*, Sept. 10, 1909, p.5]

1909, Buried Union Cemetery, Steubenville, Jefferson County, Ohio [Ibid. and www.findagrave.com]

George R. McIntyre (1835–1863)

1835, Mar. 8, George R. McIntyre was born in Warren, Maine. [Andover Newton Theological School, *Andover Newton Bulletin* (1912), p.92, Google Book]

1855–1858, He attended Bowdoin College and graduated in 1858. [Ibid.]

1858, Went to the Newton Theological Institute. [Ibid.]

1859–1861, Studied law in Thomaston, Maine. [Ibid.]

1860, McIntyre was listed as a college student living with his mother, Sarah R. McIntyre, in Warren, Maine. [*1860 Federal United States Census, Warren, Knox, Maine*]

1861, Admitted to the bar in Rockland, Maine. [Andover Newton Theological School]

1861, April, He was a member of the Frontier Guard.

1861–1862, Clerk in Washington, D.C. [Andover Newton Theological School]

1861, Oct. 8, Married Abby L. Hart in Washington, D.C. [*Portland Transcript*, Oct. 12, 1861]

1863, Nov. 16, He died in Warren, Maine. [Andover Newton Theological School]

Crawford Gilbert McLaren (1836–1884)

1836, Jan. 21, Crawford G. McLaren was born in Morristown, Belmont, Ohio, the son of George and Mary (Birch) McLaren. [Public Member Trees (Ancestry.com)]

1860, He was a clerk living in Washington, D.C. [*1860 Federal Census, Washington Ward 2*]

1861, April, He was a member of the Frontier Guard.

1861, May 21, Married Sarah Josephine Marr. [*District of Columbia Marriages, 1811–1950*]

1863, Clerk for the P.O. Dep't living in Washington, D.C. [*Civil War Draft Records, 1863–1865.*]

1865–1875, Clerk at the Auditor's Office of the Treasury Department. [*U.S. Register of Civil, Military, and Naval Service* (Ancestry.com) database]

1867, Graduated from the Columbian College Law Dep't in Washington. [*U.S. School Catalogs, 1765–1935* (Ancestry.com) database]

1870, Lived in Washington with his wife, Josephine, and sons, John and James. [*1870 Census*]

1880, Lived in Washington with wife and four children. [*1880 Federal Census, Washington, D.C.*]

1883, Deputy Collector for the Customs Dep't in Pensacola, Fla. [*U.S. Register of Civil, Military, and Naval Service* (Ancestry.com) database]

1884, He died in Washington, D.C. [*District of Columbia Select Deaths and Burials 1840–1964*]

James Edward Mendenhall (1836–1889)

1836, July 17, James E. Mendenhall was born in Richmond, Wayne County, Ind. He was the son of James Rich Mendenhall and Sarah Terrell Williams. [www.findagrave.com]

1855–1856, Attended Antioch College in Ohio. [*U.S., School Catalogs, 1765–1935* (Ancestry.com database]

1861, April, He was a member of the Frontier Guard.

1863, June, James E. Mendenhall, 26, Wayne County, Ind. Previous military service: 75th Volunteer Infantry. [*U.S. Civil War Draft Registration Records, 1863–65* (Ancestry.com database]

1865, He was a farmer in Richmond, Ind. [J. C. Power, *Directory and Soldier's Register of Wayne County, Indiana* (W. H. Lantham & Co., 1865), p.138, Google Book]

1870, Mendenhall, no occupation, lived in Richmond with his mother and sister. [*1870 Census*]

1889, Oct. 2, Mendenhall died and was buried in Earlham Cemetery in Richmond, Ind.

John R. Meredith (1820–1880)

1820, Apr. 15, John Reid Meredith, born in Gettysburg, Pa. [A.T. Andreas, History of the State of Nebraska, compiled by Raymond Dale Western Historical Co., Chicago, Ill., 1882)

1832, Moved with parents to Pittsburgh, Pa. [Ibid.]

ca. 1838, Became store clerk and went to school. [Ibid.]

ca. 1840s, Became principal of the Academy at Steubenville, Ohio. [Ibid.] Studied law with Daniel L. Collier. [Ibid.]

1849, Admitted to the bar; practiced law in Steubenville, Ohio; and later served as District Attorney. [Ibid.]

1852, Married to Annie M. Collier. [Ibid.]

1856, Moved to Cincinnati. [Ibid.]

1857, Spring, Came to Omaha, Neb. [Ibid.]

Date unknown, Was a Democrat who later joined the Free Soil and Republican parties. [Ibid.]

ca. 1857–1865, Practiced law alone. [Ibid.]

1861, "Enlisted as a private soldier in the Guards at Washington City." [Ibid.]

1865–1871, Became associated with the firm of George W. Doane. [Ibid.]

1871, Sept. 5, Suffered a paralytic stroke [unable to take active part in work of the courts]. [Ibid.]

1880, Oct. 21, Died. [*Omaha, the Gate City and Douglas County, Nebraska*, Vol. 1, S.J. 1917, p.326]

Zenus Ferry Moody (1832–1917)

1832, May 27, Z. F. Moody was born in Granby, Mass., the son of Thomas H. and Hannah M. (Ferry) Moody. [Frank E. Hodgin and J. J. Galvin, *Pen Pictures of Representative Men of Oregon*

(Portland, Ore.: Farmer and Dairyman Pub. Co., 1882), Archive .org]

1851, He moved to Oregon City, Ore. Terr., and worked on the U.S. surveys. [Ibid.]

1853, Moved to Brownsville, Ore., where he opened a mercantile business. [Ibid.]

1856, He was appointed inspector of U.S. surveys in California. [Ibid.]

1857–1861, Continued work as a surveyor in Morgan County, Ill. [Ibid.]

1861, April, Enrolled in one of the companies formed to protect the city. [Ibid.]

1862–1865, Moved back to Oregon and continued in the mercantile business in The Dalles, Ore., and engaged in the development of mines in Umatilla County. [Ibid.]

1865–1867, Operated a transportation company in Eastern Oregon, Washington, and Idaho. [Ibid.]

1867–1869, Mercantile business in Boise City, Idaho. [Ibid.]

1869, He returned to The Dalles and became a Wells Fargo agent. [Ibid.]

1880, He was elected to the State Legislature. [Ibid.]

1882–1887, Governor of Oregon. [Ibid.]

1887, He retired and lived in Salem, Ore. [Ibid.]

1917, Mar. 14, Moody died in Salem and was buried there at City View Cemetery.

William D. Nichols (1826–1891)

1826, Nichols was born in New York. [www.findagrave.com]

1847, He was a graduate of New York State University at Albany, and then taught for seven years. [State University of New York (SUNY) at Albany, *An Historical Sketch of the State Normal College at Albany, New York, and a History of its Graduates for Fifty Years, 1844–1894* (Albany: Brandow Printing Co., 1894), p.115.]

1854, He married Margaret A. Uline, another graduate of SUNY at Albany.

1860, Nichols, a farmer, lived in Iowa with wife Margaret. [*1860 Census, Davenport, Iowa*]

1861, April, He was a member of the Frontier Guard. [www.findagrave .com]

1861, May, He received a patent for a device for milking cows. [*National Republican,* May 24, 1861, p.1]

1866, He began manufacturing windmills of his own design in Chicago. [E. C. Alft, *Elgin: An American History* (www.elginhistory.com)]

1870–1877, Four patents for improvements in windmills. [Google Patents]

1880, Windmill manufacturer in Batavia, Ill. [*1880 Federal Census, Batavia, Kane County, Ill.*]

1882–1887, His company, Nichols, Murphy & Geister, manufactured and marketed the Nichols Centennial Windmill in Elgin, Ill. [T. Lindsay Baker, *Field Guide to American Windmills* (Univ. of Okla. Press, 1985), p.202, Google Book]

1891, May 10, Died in Elgin and buried in Bluff City Cemetery; tombstone inscribed "Frontier Guards."

James Chester Normile (1844–1892)

1844, James C. Normile was born in Ireland. [*Daily Argus,* Mt. Vernon, N.Y., Aug. 10, 1892, p.1.] He was the son of William Normile, an Irish farmer who lived in Doniphan County, Kansas. ["Startling," *Parsons Daily Sun,* Aug. 10, 1892, p.1.]

1859, Normile went to Atchison, Kansas Territory, and worked as a waiter at the Massasoit House. [Ibid.]

1860, He entered Lowry Academy, a primary and preparatory school in Washington, D.C. [Ibid.]

1861, April, He was a member of the Frontier Guard.

1863, District of Columbia, James E. Normile, age 20, single, born Ireland, watchman at Treasury Building. [*U.S. Civil War Draft Registration Records, 1863–1865* (Ancestry.com) database]

1864–1867, He attended Georgetown College, where he was a class officer and a participant in several dramatic plays. [*U.S. School Catalogs 1765–1935* (Ancestry.com) database]

1867, Received an M.A. from Georgetown. [*Catalog of the Officers and Students of Georgetown University* (Baltimore: John Murphey & Co., 1886), p.110 (Archive.org)]

1869, Moved to St. Louis. [L. U. Reavis, Saint Louis (St. Louis: C. R. Barns, 1876), p.545, Google Book.]

1872, Elected Circuit Attorney of St. Louis. [*Daily Argus,* loc. cit.]

1876, Elected Judge of the Criminal Court in St. Louis. [Ibid.]

1880, He was listed on the census as being age 32, single, a lawyer, born in Louisiana, father born France, mother born Ireland. [*1880 U.S. Federal Census, St. Louis, Mo.*]

1890, Re-elected Judge of the Criminal Court in St. Louis for six years. [Ibid.]

1892, He filed a lawsuit against the *St. Louis Post-Dispatch* for libel. It came out at the trial that Normile had lied about his genteel Louisiana family and came from humble Irish immigrant roots. He went home and poisoned himself. [Thomas M. Spencer, *The St. Louis Veiled Prophet Celebration: Power on Parade, 1877–1995* (Univ. of Mo. Press, 2000), pp.21–22, Google Book]

1892, Aug. 9, James C. Normile died. ["Startling"]

1892, Aug. 11, He was buried in Calvary Cemetery in St. Louis. [www .findagrave.com]

James H. Northcott (1809–1878)

1809, James H. Northcott was born in Kentucky.

1850, He was a teacher in Sangamon County, Ill. [1850 U.S. Federal Census]; Married Catherine Hersey.

1860, James Northcott lived with wife, Catherine, and six children in Sangamon County, Ill. [1860 U.S. Federal Census]

1861, Mar. 14, Arrival at Brown's Hotel, Washington, D.C., "J.H. North-cutt, [of] Kan," *Evening Star* (Washington, D.C., p.4.)

1862, Jan 10, He enlisted as Private, 1st Cavalry (Wisconsin). Wounded nine times in one battle. [U.S. Census of Union Veterans and Widows of the Civil War, 1890, Chemung, N.Y.; Familysearch. org]

1862, Dec. 18, Discharged 1st Cavalry, Wis., from effects of wounds. [Ibid.]

1870, Claim Agent, Sangamon County, Ill. [1870 U.S. Federal Census]

1878, James H. Northcott died; buried in Mechanicsburg Cemetery, Mechanicsburg, Sangamon Co., Ill.

Algernon Sidney Paddock (1830–1897)

1830, Nov. 9, A. S. Paddock was born at Glens Falls, N.Y. [Jim McKee: "A.S. Paddock, the Senator and his Hotel," Journalstar.com, http://journalstar.com/lifestyles/misc/jim-mckee-a-s-paddock-the-senator-and-his-hotel/article_c36ea77a-df19-5ec6-9d26-d3d6d3559604.html]

ca. 1843, Entered Glens Falls Academy [Ibid.]

ca. 1848, Enrolled at Union College, Schenectady, NY [Ibid.]

ca. 1852, Left Union College because of financial problems; went to Detroit, Mich., to read law. [Ibid.]

1856, Admitted to the New York Bar and worked on the "Fremont for President" campaign. [Ibid.]

1857, May, Went to Omaha, Neb., and preempted land at Fort Calhoun.

1858, Became "a writer with strong anti-slavery voice for *Omaha Republican.*"

1860, "Delegate to the 1860 Republican Convention in Chicago." "On hand for Abraham Lincoln's nomination." [Ibid.]

1861, In Frontier Guard, Washington, D.C.

ca. 1861, President Lincoln appointed Paddock Secretary of State for the Nebraska Territory. [Ibid.]

1864, Delegate to the Republican National Convention in Baltimore, Maryland. [McKee, Ibid.]

1867, Unanimously nominated for Governor of Nebraska but declined. [Ibid.] Instead, "remained in Omaha, Nebraska working for Republican & Missouri Railroad." [Ibid.]

1869, Married Emma Mack.

1872, Moved to Beatrice, Neb., and purchased a house.

1875, Elected to U.S. Senate.

ca. 1881, Appointed by President Chester Arthur to the Utah commission. [Ibid.]

1887, Elected to second Senate term. Introduced Food and Drug Act. [Ibid.]

1897, Oct. 17, Died in Beatrice, Neb. [*Findagrave*, http://www.findagrave.com/cgi-bin/fg.cgi?page=gr&GRid=13056]

1897, Buried Prospect Hill Cemetery, Omaha, Douglas County, Neb.

Marcus Junius Parrott (1828–1879)

1828, Oct. 27, Marcus J. Parrott was born in Hamburg, Aiken County, South Carolina, but raised in Dayton, Ohio. His father was a Quaker who moved to Ohio to escape the influences of slavery. [Frank W. Blackmar, *Kansas: A Cyclopedia of the State, Vol. II* (Chicago: Standard Publishing Co., 1912), p.444. His father was Thomas Parrott and his mother Sarah R. Sullivane. [Public Member Trees, Ancestry.com]

1849, Graduate of Dickenson College in Carlisle, Pa. [Ibid.]

1851, He attended Harvard. [*U.S. School Catalogs 1765–1935* (Ancestry.com) database]

1853–1854, Served as a representative in the Ohio state legislature as a Democrat. [Blackmar, loc. cit.]

1855, Moved to Leavenworth and began a law practice. [Ibid.]

1855, Sept. 5, Attended the Big Springs Convention. [Kansas State Historical Society, "Centennial at Pike's Pawnee Village," *Transactions of the Kansas State Historical Society,* Vol. 10 (1908), p.133]

1855, October, He was a delegate to the Topeka Constitutional Convention. [Territorial Kansas Online]

1857, Delegate to the Free State conventions at Topeka, Centropolis, and Grasshopper Falls.

1857, He was elected the Kansas territorial delegate to the U.S. Congress and reelected in 1859. [Ibid.]

1859, December, Parrott met Lincoln in Leavenworth. [Kansas State Historical Society, "Lincoln in Kansas," *Transactions of the KSHS,* Vol. 7 (1902), p.541]

1861, April, He lost his bid for the U.S. Senate. [Blackmar, 445]

1861, April, He was a member of the Frontier Guard.

1861, Aug. 3, Enlisted as Captain in the Adjutant General Department. [American Civil War Database]

1862, Aug. 22, He resigned. [Ibid.]

1862, 1864, and **1874,** Ran for U.S. Congress but was defeated. [Blackmar, 445]

1879, Oct. 4, He died in Dayton, Ohio, and is buried at Woodland Cemetery there.

William Young Patch (1818–1884)

1818, William Y. Patch was born in New York. [*1860 Federal Census, 10th District, San Francisco, Cal.*]

1841, June, He married Clarissa Williams in St. Louis. [California Library, *Pioneer Index File (1906–1934)*]

1851, He was a produce merchant in St. Louis. [*Times-Picayune*, April 10, 1851]

1852, Patch and his wife sailed around the Horn to San Francisco. [*San Mateo Times*, March 10, 1944]

1853, He worked as a produce merchant in San Francisco. [*Sacramento Daily Union*, Jan. 3, 1853]

1857–1858, Tax Collector for the City and County of San Francisco and member of the People's Reform Party. [Internal Revenue Service, *History of the San Francisco District: Challenge and Change, 1862–1990* (1991), pp.17–18 Archive.org]

1861, Jan. 1, He and John C. Fremont left San Francisco on a steamship headed for the East Coast. ["Later from the Pacific," *New York Times*, Jan. 19, 1861, p.5]

1861, April, He was a member of the Frontier Guard.

1862, Lincoln appointed Patch as Collector and Assessor of Taxes for the 1st District in California. ["The Appointment of Collectors," *Dubuque Herald*, Aug. 2, 1863, p.1]

1880, Worked as farmer in Solano, Cal., with his wife. [*1880 Census, Fairfield, Solano, Cal.*]

1881, Aug. 13, Patch applied for a pension for his service in Lane's Company, Frontier Guards, D.C. Volunteers. [NARA, *Index to Pension Files* (Fold3)]

1884, Feb. 20, He died in Oakland, Cal., and was buried in Laurel Hill Cemetery in San Francisco. ["Died," *Daily Alta California*, Feb. 22, 1884, p.8]

John W. Perkinson (1806–)

1806, John W. Perkinson was born in Virginia. [*1870 Federal Census, Baltimore, Maryland*]

1851, He was listed as a botanic physician living in Baltimore. [*Matchett's Baltimore Directory*, 1851.]

1854, His botanic medicine laboratory was damaged in a fire. [*The Sun* (Baltimore), Aug. 15, 1854, p.1.]

1861, April, He was a member of the Frontier Guard.

1870, J. W. Perkinson, physician, lived with his family in Baltimore. [*1870 Census, Baltimore, Maryland*]

Jared Phillips (1828–1862)

1828, Oct 5, Jared Phillips was born in Massachusetts, son of Samuel Phillips and second wife Mary McCollum. ["A Sketch of the Samuel Phillips Family" by Levi Beebe of Great Barrington, Mass., Berkshire Book, Vol. 1. Berkshire Historical and Scientific Society (Pittsfield, Mass.), Press of the Sun Printing Co., Berkshire County (Mass.), 1892, p.217]. Phillips attended Lenox Academy in Lenox, Mass.]

1850, Jared Phillips was living with parents, Great Barrington, Mass. [1850 U.S. Census, Berkshire County, Mass.].

1855, Mar. 13, Jared Phillips, age 24, married Eliza P. Perry, Lee, Mass. [www.Familysearch.org]

1855, Jared Phillips and family settled in Leavenworth, Kansas Territory Jared was taken prisoner by a drunken mob. They called him an "abolitionist" and threatened him with hanging, but he escaped. [Beebe, p.226]

1855, May, Jared Phillips' brother, William Phillips, a Leavenworth attorney, was taken to Weston, Mo. by a pro-slavery mob. He was tarred, feathered, and ridden on a rail. [Beebe, pp.222–23.]

1856, September, Jared's brother, William Phillips, was murdered In Leavenworth "by pro-slave ruffians"; Jared Phillips was shot and wounded in arm, requiring amputation. [*Kansas Claims—U.S. Congressional Serial Set,* Vol. 1106, U.S. Gov't Printing Office (1861), pp.49, 231–35 and 509–12.]

1859, Arthur Phillips, son, born in Leavenworth County. [1860 U.S. Census, Kansas Territory]

1860, July, Phillips was a "trader" at South Park, Kansas Territory [1860 U.S. Census, Arapahoe County, Kansas Territory]

1860, July, Eliza Phillips, wife, and son, Arthur Phillips, were living in Leavenworth, Kansas Territory [1860 U.S. Census]

1861 Apr. 18–May 3, Member of Frontier Guard in Washington, D.C. [Beebe, op. cit., p.227]

1861, Apr. 20, Jared Phillips wrote a letter to his wife while he was in Frontier Guard. [Ibid., p.228]

1861, May 3, Honorable discharge of Jared Phillips by J.H. Lane, Capt. [Ibid., p.227]

1862, Aug. 9, He was working on a wagon train en route west when he was taken prisoner by the Snake Indians about 50 miles from Fort Hall [Idaho] and murdered. [Ibid., p.230]

Samuel Clarke Pomeroy (1816–1891)

1816, Jan. 3, Samuel C. Pomeroy was born in Southampton, Mass., son of Samuel and Dorcas (Burt) Pomeroy. [Burt, Henry M. and Silas W., *Early Days in New England, Life and Times of Henry Burt of Springfield,* (Springfield, Mass.: Clark W. Bryan Co.,1893, p.447]

ca. 1831, Entered Amherst College [Class of 1835]. [Ibid., p.448]

1837, Went to Onondaga County, N.Y., to teach and engage in mercantile business. [Ibid, p.448]

1840, Removed to South Butler, Wayne County, N.Y., aiding in the election of Hon. William H. Seward to governor. [Ibid., p.448]

1841, Organized the Free Soil Party. [Ibid., p.448]

1842, Moved back home to take care of his father. [Ibid., p.448]

1844, Wife, Anna Pomeroy, died.

1846, Married to second wife, Lucy Ann Gaylord. [*House Divided, The Civil War Research Engine at Davidson* College, http://hd.housedivided.dickinson.edu/node/12955]

1852, Elected to the Legislature over both the Whig and Democratic nominees. [Burt, op. cit., p.448]

1854, Chosen financial agent for New England Emigrant Aid Co. [Burt, ibid., p.448]

1854, Aug. 27, Conducted a party of settlers to Kansas and, upon arrival in Kansas Territory, selected the town site of Lawrence. [Burt, ibid., p.448]

ca. 1856, Moved to Atchison, Kansas Territory, where he was elected the first mayor and secured the pro-slavery sheet [paper] called

"Squatter Sovereign" and made it a Free State paper. [Burt, ibid., p.449]

ca. 1861, James H. Lane and Pomeroy chosen "first senators from the new state."[Burt, ibid., p.449]

1861, Apr. 13, Pomeroy reached Washington as Senator-elect. [Burt, ibid., p.449]

1861, Apr. 16, Enlisted as a private in the Frontier Guard. [Ibid., p.449]

1861[?], July 4 Sworn into office, "drew the term of six years and took the seat lately vacated by Jefferson Davis." [Burt, ibid., p.450]

1861–1873, Served as U.S. Senator from Kansas for 12 years. [Ibid., p.450 and *Findagrave*]

1863, Death of "Mrs. Senator Pomeroy" aboard the vessel *Armenia*. [*The Liberator*, Boston, July 31, 1863]

1865, Sept. 20, Pomeroy was married to third wife, Mrs. Martha S. Whiting of Boston. [*The Junction City Union*, Junction City, Kans., Oct. 7, 1865, p.2]

1873, Pomeroy "sought reelection in 1873 but was opposed by a Republican faction." ["Samuel Clarke Pomeroy, 1816–1891," Territorial Kansas Heritage Alliance, *Territorial Kansas*; *Online*, http://www2.ku.edu/~imlskto/cgibin/index.php?SCREEN=bio_sketches/pomeroy_samuel]

1891, Aug. 27, Died at Whitinsville, Mass. [Burt, op. cit., p.450.] Buried in Forest Hills Cemetery, Boston, Mass. [*Biographical Directory of the United States Congress, 1774–present*]

Robert L. Ream (1809–1885)

1809, Oct. 16, Robert L. Ream, born Center County, Pa. [1880 U.S. Census, Washington, D.C.]; father born Germany, mother born Germany.

1832, Lived in Canton, Ohio, several years and worked in mercantile business. [Death notice, "A Pioneer to Madison, to Rest," *Wis. State Journal*, Nov. 27, 1885]

1835, October, Married to Lavinia (McDonald), Massillon, Ohio. [Ibid.]

1836, Brought family to Wisconsin. [www.Wisconsin.org]

1838, April, Robert L. Ream and family moved to Madison, Wis., and became landlord in first log hotel in Madison. [*"A Pioneer to Madison,"* op. cit.]

1839, Elected Register of Deeds. [Ibid.]

1840–1842, Appointed and served as County Clerk. [Ibid]

1849, Chief Clerk of the Assembly. ["A Pioneer to Madison," op. cit.]

1852, Ream moved his family to Washington, where he worked for the U.S. General Land Office. [Ibid.]

1854, The Ream family moved to Kansas. [Ibid.] Ream was Chief Clerk, Surveyor General's Office, Kansas and Nebraska [*Daily Commonwealth*, Topeka, Kans., Nov. 15, 1885, p.2]

1856, Ream was dismissed by Surveyor General Calhoun for being too friendly with the Free-State men.

1856, Sept. 29, Letter sent to Robert L. Reams, Chief Clerk, Surveyor General's Office, by Surveyor General Calhoun accusing Reams of being abolitionist and a friend of Lane, Robinson, and Reeder, etc. ["Affairs in Kansas, Proceedings of the New Governor," *New York Herald*, Oct. 26, 1856, p.8]

1860, Some of the Ream family moved back to Washington, D.C. [www.Wisconsin History.org]

1862, Daughter Lavinia (Vinnie) Ream went to work in the U.S. Post Office to help the family financially. Became a protégé of Clark Mills and learned to model portrait medallions and busts. [*Vinnie Ream: An American Sculptor*, Edward Cooper (Academy Chicago Publishing, 2004)]

1864, Daughter Vinnie Ream worked on a bust of President Lincoln. [*An American Sculptor, ibid.*, and Glenn Sherwood, *Labors of Love: The Life and Art of Vinnie Ream* (Sun Shine Press Publications, 1997)]

1870, June, Robert L. Ream, living in Washington, D.C. with wife and daughters. [1870 U.S. Census]

1870–1885, Draftsman at Land Dep't, Washington, D.C. [*Wis. State Journal*, op. cit.]

1870, January, Statue of President Abraham Lincoln by daughter Lavinia Ream-Hoxie was unveiled in the Capitol at Washington, D.C. in Jan. 1870. [*Vinnie Ream: An American Sculptor*, op. cit.]

1880, Clerk in the Interior Dep't, Washington, D.C. [1880 U.S. Federal Census, Washington, D.C.]

1883, Appointment special agent of General Land Office. [*Courier-Journal*, Louisville, Ky., July 10, 1883]

1885, Nov. 21, Death of Robert L. Ream. [*Findagrave* and *Wis. State Journal*, Nov. 27, 1885]

1885, Robert L. Ream buried Glenwood Cemetery, Washington, D.C. [*Findagrave*].

William Wallace Ross (1828–1889)

1828, Dec. 25, W. W. Ross was born in Huron County, Ohio. He was the son of Sylvester F. and Cynthia (Rice) Ross, from New England. [*United States Biographical Dictionary, Kansas Vol.* (Chicago and Kansas City: S. Stewart & Co., 1879), p.601, Google Book]

1839, His family moved to Noble County, Ind., where he was educated by his father. [Ibid.]

1846, His family moved to the Wisconsin Territory. [Ibid.]

ca. 1852, Ross learned the trade of printing and worked for the *Free Democrat* in Milwaukee. There, he participated in the first rescue of a fugitive slave from jail in defiance of the fugitive slave law. [Ibid.]

1855, March, He married Mary Berry in Milwaukee and moved to Lawrence, Kansas Territory [Ibid.]

1855, October, He worked with John Speer in Topeka, printing for the Topeka Constitutional Convention. He and Speer became partners and moved the *Kansas Tribune* to Topeka. [Ibid.]

1857, His brother, Edmund G. Ross, bought out Speer's interest in the *Kansas Tribune*. [Ibid.]

1857, He was a member of the Leavenworth Constitutional Convention. [*U.S. Biographical Dictionary*, p.602]

1858, Wife, Mary, died. [Ibid.]

1859, September, The Ross brothers began publishing *The Kansas State Record*. [*Ibid.* at p.601]

1860, He was a delegate from Kansas Territory to the Republican National Convention in Chicago that nominated Lincoln. [*Ibid.* at p.602]

1860, Aug. 13, He married Julia Whiting in Topeka. [*Kansas Vital Record Abstracts, 1854–2009*]

1861, April, He was a member of the Frontier Guard.

1861, He was appointed agent for the Pottawatomie Indians. [*U.S. Biographical Dictionary,* p.602]

1865, He was mayor of Topeka. [Ibid.]

1866, Jan. 24, His wife Julia died. [*Topeka Weekly Leader,* Jan. 25, 1866]

1870, He married Sara S. Betts. She died the next year. [*U.S. Biographical Dictionary,* p.602]

1878–1879, He practiced law in Washington, D.C. [*U.S. City Directories 1821–1989* (Ancestry.com)]

1878–1882, Ross built six Italianate row houses in Topeka, which are now on the National Register of Historic Places. [Topeka Landmarks Commission, *Topeka Landmarks Registry* (2014)]

1880, He was involved in mining in Colorado. [*1880 Federal Census, Silverton, San Juan, Colo.*]

1889, June 5, He died in Los Angeles, Cal., and was buried in the Hollywood Forever Cemetery.

William H. Russell (Col.) (1802–1873)

1802, Oct 9, William Henry Russell, ["Owl" Russell], born in "Poplar Hill," Fayette County, Ky. Son of Robert S. [Anna Russell des Cognets, *William Russell and His Descendants* (Lexington, Kentucky, 1884), p.83–85; Biography, William Henry Russell, *Dictionary of American Biography* (New York, 1935); Obituary, *Daily National Republican*, Washington, D.C., Oct. 14, 1873][Grandnephew of Patrick Henry?]

1824, Mar. 11, Married Zaenett Freeland in Calvert County, Maryland.

ca. 1830, Practiced law in Nicholas County, Ky. [and Fayette Co?]

1830, Member of Kentucky Legislature.

1831, Instrumental in securing the election of Henry Clay to the U.S. Senate. [*Daily National Republican*, Oct. 14, 1873]

1831, Emigrated to Callaway County, Mo.

1832, Judge Advocate of a regiment in the Black Hawk War.

1838–40, Member of the legislature from Calloway County, Mo.

1841 or 1844 [?], Appointed U.S. Marshal of the District of Missouri [included Missouri, Iowa, Minnesota, Kansas, and Nebraska] by President Harrison.

1846, Went to California. Appointed Secretary of State by Commodore Stockton.

1849, Returned to California and practiced law at San Jose.

1850, William Henry Russell, age 45, listed as lawyer in 1850 Census for Blue [Springs?] Twp., Jackson County, Mo. with wife, Zaenett, age 44, born, Maryland.; Eugene, 26, b. Md.; Frederic, 20, b. Ky.; Thomas, 18, b. Ky.; Josephine, 17, b. Mo.; Harry, 15, b. Mo.; and George, 12, b. Mo. [U.S. Census, 1850, Jackson County, Mo.]

1851, Appointed Collector of Customs at Monterey, Cal.

1851, ". . . [a] gold-headed ebony cane was presented by Hon. Henry Clay to his personal friend Col. William H. Russell of California but native of Kentucky." [*New York Herald*, Apr 17, 1861, p.5, col. D]

ca. 1858, Divorced from wife [Zaenette Russell] by Kansas Territorial Legislature. [Genealogical query by descendant of W.H. Russell, William LaBach, Mar. 25, 2007, www.genforum.com]

1860, A key witness in the court-martial of Lt. Col. John Fremont. [*Colonel William H. Russell, Sir*, by Henry Clay Simpson [a descendant], Publisher: Ashland Museum Bookstore, 1st ed. (2011)]

1861, [March or April?], Russell presented a gold-headed ebony cane to Cassius M. Clay. The cane had been given to Russell in 1851 by Hon. Henry Clay. [*New York Herald,* op. cit.]

1861, Apr. 17, Cassius M. Clay presented the gold-headed ebony cane he had received from Col. Russell to Abraham Lincoln, "knowing that he was always a personal friend and admirer of Henry Clay." [Ibid.]

1861, April, In Lincoln Guards.

1861–1865, Appointed U.S. Consul at Trinidad, Cuba. Served until after the Lincoln assassination.

1862, June 25, Married Mary J. Dyer in Washington, D.C.

1867, May 9, Col. William Henry Russell recommended by Robert J. Walker to President Andrew Johnson for appointment to post of Consul-General at Havana. [Anna Russell des Cognets, *William Russell and His Descendants* (Lexington, Ky., 1884), pp.83–84]

1873, Oct. 13, He died in Washington, D.C. [Obituary, *Daily National Republican*, Oct. 14, 1873]

1873, Interred in Oak Lawn Cemetery, Georgetown, Washington, D.C.

James T. Sample (1821–ca. 1909)

1821, July 12, James T. Sample was born in Allegheny, Pa. [*Canonsburg Weekly Notes* (Canonsburg, Pa.), June 21, 1889, p.1] Sample was known as "Admirable" Sample. ["Personal," *Butler Citizen*, Butler County, Pa., May 23, 1890, image 3]

1846, Dec. 21, James T. Sample enlisted 2nd Reg. Pennsylvaniaa. Vols., Co. F. (Mexican-American War) [L.H. Everts, *History of Allegheny Co., Pennsylvania*]

1847, September, James T. Sample, wounded Battle of Mexico, lost leg.

1848, Feb. 29, Discharged from 2nd Reg. Pennsylvaniaa. Vols., Co. F. [Ibid.]

1861, in Frontier Guard, Washington, D.C.

1864, James T. Sample, of Allegheny, Pa., was Assistant Sergeant at Arms ["The Legislature," *American Citizen*, Butler, Butler County, Pa., Jan. 13, 1864, p.2]

1870, James Sample, age 49, real estate agent, in Sewickley Borough, Allegheny County, Pa., with wife, Hannah, age 42, and three children. [1870 U.S. Federal Census, Sewickley Borough, Allegheny County, Pa.]

1897, Married to Mrs. Eugenia Emerson Kauffman after deeding all his property to his children. ["Sample Finally Gets His Bride," *Canonsburg Weekly Notes* (Canonsburg, Pa.), April 13, 1897, p.1]

ca. 1898, Sample, living in Southampton, England, receiving U.S. military pension for loss of right leg at Chapultepec, Mexico. [Ann. Rpt., Military Pensions, p.42, U.S. Pension Bureau, U.S. Gov't Printing Off., 1898]

1900, June, James T. Sample, age 78, living with wife, Eugenia, age 43, b. SC, in Allegheny, Allegheny County, Pa. [1900 U.S. Federal Census, Allegheny, Allegheny County, Pa.]

ca. 1909, James T. Sample died?

Turner Sampson [Maj.] (1814–1880)

1814, Dec. 1, Turner Sampson, born Londonderry, N.H. [*Lawrence Journal World*, Jan. 22, 1880]

ca. 1832, "As young man, went to Andover, Mass., and learned the trade of a dyer." [Ibid.]

1840, Jan. 21, Turner Sampson married Eliza W. Holly, Andover, Mass. [*Vital Records of Andover, Mass.*, Vol. II, Topsoil, Mass., 1912, p.294]

ca. 1840s, Two children born and died in Mass. [Ibid.] Moved to Virginia for three years; worked as dyer.

pre-1854, Moved to Farmington Falls, Maine; worked as hotel keeper.

1854, Dec. 19, Arrived in Lawrence, Kansas Territory

ca. 1859, Wife died, remains taken back to Massachusetts for burial.

1860, T. Sampson, age 31, b. New Hampshire, living in Douglas County, Kansas Territory [1860 U.S. Federal Census, Kansas Territory]

ca. 1860, Laid out the town of Lexington, Johnson County, Kansas Territory

1861, April, In Frontier Guard in Washington, D.C.

1861, Married Mrs. S[ybil]. A. Taylor [Turner Sampson obituary, op. cit.]

ca. 1862, Son, H. Turner Sampson, born.

after 1862, Adopted two children, Julia F. and Florence P. [Obit., op. cit. and 1865 Kansas State Census]

1863 or 1864, Turner Sampson and his family returned to Lawrence, Kans.

1865, Turner Sampson, livery stable keeper, living with wife, Sybil. [1865 Kansas Census, Douglas County]

1870, Turner Sampson, living with wife, Sybil. [U.S. 1870 Census, City of Lawrence, Douglas County, Kans.]

1880, Jan. 21, [Maj.] Turner Sampson died. [Death notice, *Springfield Republican*, Jan. 27, 1880, Springfield, Mass., p.6 and *Lawrence Journal World*, Jan. 22, 1880]

1880, January, Sampson Turner was buried in Oak Hill Cemetery, Lawrence, Kans.

Phillip Church Schuyler (1805–1872)

1805, Schuyler was born in Stillwater-on-the-Hudson into a prominent old New York family. [Charles Clark, *Kansas Bogus Legislature* (kansasboguslegislature.org)]

1832, Jan. 12, He married Lucy Dix in Seneca Falls, N.Y. [Public Member Trees, Ancestry.com]

1855, He moved to Kansas Territory in the spring with a group of settlers backed by the Emigrant Aid Society. He settled on land that is now Burlingame, Kans. He ran a sawmill. [Clark, op. cit.]

1855, October, Schuyler was a delegate to the Topeka Convention. He was part of the radical group calling for immediate statehood with a Free-State constitution. [Ibid.]

1856, January, He was elected Secretary of State. [Ibid.]

1859, Elected Probate Judge of Osage County. [Ibid.]

1860, Apr. 16, Married Louisa Bigelow. [G. Howe, *Genealogy of the Bigelows* (Hamilton, 1890), p.235]

1861, April, He was a member of the Frontier Guard. [*Collections of the KSHS,* Vol. 10 (1908), p.419]

1872, July 16, Schuyler died in Burlington, Kans., and was buried there in the Burlington City Cemetery.

Thomas Shankland (1810–)

1810, Thomas Shankland was born in New York. [*1850 Federal Census, Van Horst, Hudson, N.J.*]

1835, Nov. 4, He married Laura Degen in Wash., D.C. [*D.C. Marriages, 1826–50* (Ancestry.com)]

1844, January, Was appointed Commissioner of Deeds in New York. [*New York Herald,* Jan. 23, 1844]

1850, Shankland, a lawyer, was living in Van Horst, N.J., with his wife, Laura, and four children. [*1850 Federal Census, Van Horst, Hudson, N.J.*]

1855, October, Thomas Shankland's name appears on the poll list for Leavenworth signed by J. H. Lane. [*Report of the Special Committee Appointed to Investigate the Troubles in Kansas* (Washington: Cornelius Wendell, 1856), p.698, Google Book]

1855, December, Shankland and Samuel Pomeroy both left the Kansas Territory with identical sets of a memorial to the President and the Senate. Pomeroy was arrested, but Shankland made it through. ["From Kansas," *Red Wing Sentinel,* Jan. 5, 1856, p.2]

1856, April, "Communications were received . . . from Thos. Shankland, Kansas, in regard to Bible distribution in that Territory." [American Bible Society, *Bible Society Record* (1856), p.62]

1856, Apr. 23, "A large and enthusiastic Kansas Meeting was held at Concert Hall, Utica, on Wednesday evening last, at which Generals Shankland and Pomeroy made speeches." ["Kansas Meeting," *Oneida Sachem,* April 26, 1856]

1856, June, He was chosen as a substitute delegate to the Republican Convention in Philadelphia. ["Kansas Affairs," *New York Times,* June 19, 1856]

1856, August, Judge Shankland, of Kansas, and Rev. Henry Ward Beecher spoke at the Young Men's Republican Club in Brooklyn. ["Republican Movements in Brooklyn," *New York Times, Aug.* 29, 1856]

1860, Working as a lawyer. [*1860 Federal Census, New York, Ward 22, District 2*]

1861, December, His wife, Laura, died. [www.findagrave.com]

1861, Dec. 12, Lincoln nominated Thomas Shankland as American Consul at Port Louis, Isle of France. [*Journal of Executive Proceedings of the Senate* (D. Green, 1887), p.3, Google Book]

1863, Jan. 16, Lincoln replaced Shankland as consul. [*Journal of the Senate* (M. Glazier, 1887), p.32]

1864, Oct. 9, Shankland wrote Lincoln asking for another position. [Abraham Lincoln Papers at the Library of Congress, Series 1, General Correspondence]

1865, He testified at the trial for the assassination of Lincoln when a friend of his, Thomas Green, was questioned about his connection with the Surratts. Green was exonerated. [William C. Edwards, *The Lincoln Assassination: The Evidence* (Univ. of Illinois, 2008)]

1869, September, He resigned his position as Assistant U.S. Treasurer at New York. [*Philadelphia Inquirer,* Sept. 7, 1869]

Silas Sisson (1802–1863)

1802, Feb. 26, Silas Sisson was born in Middletown, Rhode Island, the son of David Sisson and Rebecca (Cornell) Sisson. [William Richard Cutter, *New England Families, Genealogical and Memorial, Vol. 4* (Lewis Historical Publishing Co., 1915), p.2314, Google Book]

1825–1828, He attended Brown University in Providence. [*U.S. School Catalogs, 1765–1935*]

1832, May 7, Sisson was a delegate from Newark, N.J. at the Republican Convention in Washington, D.C. [*Washington National Intelligencer,* May 8, 1832, p.3]

1832, Sept. 5, Simon Sisson, of Newark, N.J., married Lydia B. Davis of Northborough, Mass. [*Massachusetts, Town and Vital Records, 1620–1988* (Ancestry.com) database]

1834, He moved to Louisville, Ky. [*Papers of Abraham Lincoln,* Images from the National Archives and the Library of Congress, Doc. No. 262221]

1846–1849, He was Superintendent of Schools in Louisville. [Jefferson County Public School History (http://media.jefferson.k12.ky.us/groups/jcpshistory/wiki/2f797/Silas_Sisson.html)]

1844, President Tyler appointed Sisson Surveyor and Inspector of Revenue for the port of Pawcatuck, Rhode Island. [*Brooklyn Daily Eagle,* June 20, 1844, p.2]

1850, A lawyer, living with his wife, Lydia, and two daughters. [*1850 Census, Louisville, Ky.*]

1856, He was a city councilman in Louisville. [Jefferson County Public School History]

1861, Apr. 17, Cassius M. Clay wrote Lincoln and recommended Sisson for a consulate. [*Papers of Abraham Lincoln,* Images from the National Archives and the Library of Congress, Doc. No. 262220]

1861, Apr. 19, Sisson wrote Lincoln from Washington, D.C. asking for a consulship in Glasgow, Scotland. [*Papers of Abraham Lincoln,* Images from the National Archives and the Library of Congress, Doc. No. 262221]

1861, April, He was a member of the Frontier Guard.

1863, Oct. 2, He died in Louisville. He was buried at Laurel Hill Cemetery in Philadelphia, Pa.

Delano T. Smith (1830–1905)

1830, Nov. 6, Delano T. Smith was born in Litchfield, Herkimer County, N.Y. [William Battan, *Past and Present of Marshall County, Iowa,* Vol. 1 (Marshall County, Iowa: Brookhaven Press, 1912), p.513]

ca. 1848, He received his education at Clinton Liberal Institute in Oneida County, New York. [Ibid.]

1851, Admitted to the Bar in Albany when 21 years old. [Ibid.]

1852, Moved to Dixon, Ill., and practiced law. [Ibid.]

1855, Moved to Minneapolis, Minn. [Ibid.]

1857–1858, He was a member of the Territorial House of Representatives and the first Minnesota State Senate. [William Murray, *Minnesota in Three Centuries, 1655–1908,* Vol. 3 (Pub. Soc. Minn., 1908), p.60]

1861, He was a member of the Frontier Guard. [Battan, p.514]

1861, Nov. 12, Lincoln appointed Smith to Third Auditor of the Treasury. [Abraham Lincoln, *Collected Works of Abraham Lincoln,* Vol. 5 (Wildside Press LLC, 2008), p.21, Google Book]

1863–1864, He was U.S. Tax Commissioner of the state of Tennessee. [Battan, p.514]

1865, He moved to New York City and opened a real estate office. [*New York Times,* Jan. 13, 1898, p.7]

1865, He promoted building a railway under Broadway. ["Subway Idea Author, Delano T. Smith, Dead," *Evening Telegram* (New York), May 10, 1905, p.3]

1869, He settled in Marshalltown, Iowa, dealing in real estate and livestock. [Battan, p.515]

1905, May 10, Delano T. Smith died and was buried in Marshalltown, Iowa, at Riverside Cemetery.

George Washington Smith (1836–1881)

1836, Oct. 16, G. W. Smith was born in Butler County, Pa. He was the son of Judge George Washington Smith, Sr. and Catherine H.

Smith. [Frederick Phisterer, *Army of the Cumberland* (Columbus, Ohio: John L. Trauger, 1898), p.124 (Archive.org)]

ca. 1854, He attended medical school at Ann Arbor, Mich. [Ibid.]

1855, Smith was Sergeant Major in the Free State Militia during the Wakarusa War; his father was a member of Gen. Lane's staff. [List of Companies, November-December, 1855, Territorial Kansas Online]

1856, He was wounded at the Battle of Franklin. [U.S. Congress, *Reports of Committees* (1878), p.1]

1861, April, He was a member of the Frontier Guard.

1861, Summer, He enlisted as a Lieutenant in the 13th Pennsylvania Infantry, but resigned in August. [Mark W. Johnson, *That Body of Brave Men* (Da Capo Press, 2003), p.609, Google Book]

1861, August, Smith joined the 18th U.S. Infantry stationed at Camp Thomas near Columbus, Ohio. As captain, he commanded eight companies of the regiment. [U.S. Congress, *Reports of Committees,* p.1]

ca. 1862, He met and married Jennie T. Ridgway in Ohio. [Phisterer, p.124]

1863, Smith fought in the Battle of Chickamauga. [Johnson, p.609]

1865, Fought in the Battles of Averysborough and Bentonville. [Ibid.]

1866, April, Smith resigned his commission with the 18th Infantry, disappointed because though he had been recommended for three brevets, he received only one for Chickamauga. [Johnson, p.609–10]

1870, He worked as a grain merchant and lived with his wife, Jennie; daughter, Kate; and young son, George in Douglas County, Kans. [*1870 Federal Census, Wakarusa, Douglas, Kansas*]

1873, June, He reenlisted as Second Lieutenant in the 9th Cavalry, famous for its regiments of Buffalo Soldiers. [Johnson, p.610]

1873–1881, He saw action with the Apaches and was peripherally involved with the Lincoln County War in policing and peacemaking activities. [Dan L. Thrapp, *Encyclopedia of Frontier Biography,* Vol. 3 (Univ. of Nebraska Press, 1991), p.1320]

1881, Aug. 19, he was killed in a battle with Apache Indians in the Membres Mountains, New Mexico. His remains were brought back to

Lawrence and he was buried in Oak Hill Cemetery. [Johnson,
p.610]

Joseph Vial (Victor) Smith (1826–1865)

1826, Sept. 29, Joseph Vial (Victor) Smith was born. He was the son of
George Knight Smith and Prudence (Drown) Smith. [*Global Find
a Grave Index for Burials at Sea and Other Select Burial Locations,
1300s–Current* (Ancestry.com) database]

1848, He was publisher of the *Cincinnati Globe* and a friend and supporter of Salmon P. Chase. [John Niven, *Salmon P. Chase Papers*
(Kent State Univ. Press, 1993), p.205, Google Book]

1854, Mar. 23, He married Caroline Rogers in Ohio. [*Ohio Marriages
1800–1858* (Family Search)]

1861, April, He was a member of the Frontier Guard.

1861, July, Lincoln appointed Victor Smith the Customs Collector for
the District of Puget Sound. [Frederick J. Blue, *Salmon P. Chase:
A Life in Politics* (Kent State Press, 1987), p.142, Google Book]

1861, August, Smith arrived in the Puget Sound. Being an abolitionist
and having the power to decide how government money would be
disbursed, he was immediately disliked. [Hubert Howe Bancroft,
History of Washington, Idaho, and Montana (History Co., 1890),
pp.219–20, Google Book]

1861, December, He recommended that the Customs House at Port
Townsend be moved to Port Angeles, which made him even more
unpopular. [Bancroft, pp.220–21]

1862, June, Secretary of Treasury Salmon P. Chase used his influence to
have a bill passed to move the Customs House to Port Angeles.
[Bancroft, pp.220–21]

1863, December, A landslide near Port Angeles caused the dam to break
and a wall of water crushed the new Customs House and the
Smith residence beside it. [Bancroft, p.224]

1865, The Customs House was returned to Port Townsend.

1865, July, Victor Smith drowned when the steamer *Brother Jonathan*,
bound from San Francisco to Portland, hit a reef during a storm
and sank. [Noah Brooks, *Washington in Lincoln's Time* (Century
Co., 1895), p.123, Google Book]

Edward Spicer (1832–1901)

1832, Edward Spicer was born in [Barrington], Yates County, N.Y. He was the son of John and Mary (Decker) Spicer. [Julie A. Milan, *Descendants of Gregory Spicer* (familytreemaker.genealogy.com)]

1830–1850, The Spicer family lived in Barrington, N.Y. In 1850, John Spicer and his son, Edward, age 18, were listed as farmers. [1830, 1840, and 1850 Federal Census]

1856–57, Edward Spicer worked as a messenger for the House of Representatives in Washington, D.C. [*Clerks and Other Employees, House of Representatives*, Google Books]

1856, March, Edward Spicer's father, John Spicer, settled in Kansas Territory [1859 Kansas State Census]

1856, September, Edward Spicer's father, John, was appointed justice of the peace in Lecompton Township. [David E. Meerse, "No Propriety in the Late Course of the Governor—The Geary-Sherrard Affair Reexamined," *Kansas Historical Quarterly*, Autumn 1976]

1858, November, Spicer with his family in Lawrence. [Kansas State Census Collection, 1855–1925.]

1859, July 16, "U.S. vs Edward Spicer for contempt," 27-02-07-05, Folder 68. [Joseph P. Laframboise, *Finding Aid for the Kansas Territorial Records*, Kansas Historical Society]

1860, Edward, age 27, farmer, born New York, living in Wakarusa township (Lawrence P. O.), with his father, John Spicer, two brothers, and three sisters. [1860 U.S. Federal Census, Wakarusa, Douglas, Kansas Territory]

1863, November, On payroll in Folder Room. [House of Representatives, Miscellaneous Documents]

1864–1869, Edward Spicer listed as a clerk and Supervisor of the Folding Room in Washington. [Washington, D.C. City Directories]

1870, August, E. Spicer, clerk, in Washington, D.C. [1870 U.S. Federal Census, Washington, D.C.]

Job B. Stockton [Capt.] (1837–1910)

1837, July 12, Job B. Stockton, born Clermont County, Ohio, son of Job Stockton, born New Jersey, and Catherine Posey, born Maryland.

[U.S. Passport Applications 1795–1925, Ancestry.com, and 1900 U.S. Federal Census, Ballona Twp., Los Angeles County, Cal.]

1857, Stockton's Hall, built in 1857 in Leavenworth, Kansas Territory, was named after Job B. Stockton of Leavenworth.

1859, Dec. 3, Abraham Lincoln spoke at Stockton's Hall on Dec. 3, 1859, when he came to Leavenworth. [Article, *Kansas History*, Winter 2008, Vol. 31, Issue 4, p.289]

1861, April, Job B. Stockton in Frontier Guard, Washington, D.C.

1861, May, Job B. Stockton brought arms used by the Lincoln Guard to Leavenworth for use by two Infantry companies. [*Milwaukee Morning Sentinel*, Thursday, May 16, 1861, p.1, col. 1]

1861, May, Job B. Stockton, living in Leavenworth, Kans., enlistment as Captain.

1861, May 29, Commissioned into Co. G, 1st Kans. [Vol.] Inf. [American Civil War Research Database, *Report of the Adjutant General of the State of Kansas*, Hudson, 1896]

1862, July 15, Resigned from 1st Infantry (Kans.) on July 15, 1862. [Ibid.]

1863, Sept. 16, Letter from J.B. Stockton, Leavenworth, Kans., to James H. Lane awaiting orders regarding "mountain horitzers" sent at Lane's solicitation, " to be used by the citizens of Kansas in defense of the State." Wanted to drill Lawrence, Kans., citizens [after Quantrill Raid]. [http://www.pddoc.com/skedaddle/010/0127 .htm]

1863, Oct. 1, Capt. Job B. Stockton, Commanding Battery, in camp near Sarcoxie, Mo., sent report to Capt. A. Blocki, Asst. Adjt. Gen., First Brigade, Army of Kans., regarding the [first] Battle of Newtonia [Newton County, Mo.]. [American Civil War Research Database]

1886, Job B. Stockton married Lettie/Leddie Ann Hall, Cal. She was born in Kans. in Sept. 1870.

1900, Job Stockton, farmer, living in Ballona Twp., Los Angeles, Cal.,with wife, Leddie, born Kans. and three sons, ages 10, 8, and 5, all b. Kans. [1900 U.S. Federal Census, Ballona Twp., Los Angeles County, Cal.]

1910, Apr. 19, Stockton died in Sawtell, Cal. [*Findagrave*], at soldier's home, Los Angeles. "He is said to have been a favorite of the martyred President." ["Served as White House Guard Under Lincoln," *San Francisco Chronicle* (Cal.), Apr. 21, 1910, p.2]

1910, Stockton was buried in Los Angeles National Cemetery, Los Angeles, Cal. [*Findagrave*]

Thomas H. Sypherd (1831–1916)

1831, Mar. 3, Thomas H. Sypherd was born in Virginia. [www.find agrave.com]

prior to 1850s, Resident of southern Ohio.

ca. 1850s, Established a newspaper at Des Moines, Iowa, called *The Iowa Citizen*. [*The Valley and the Shadow: Comprising the Experiences of a Blind Ex-editor*, J. M. Dixon, 1868] [Google Books]

ca. 1857, Sypherd and family went to Kansas City, Mo., where he "accumulated wealth." [*Ibid.*]

1860, T.H. Sypherd, age 28, b. Va., Editor, lived with wife and daughter in Kansas City, Jackson County, Mo. [1860 U.S. Federal Census, Kansas City, Jackson County, Mo.]

1861, April, Was in Frontier Guard.

1861, Sypherd accepted a clerkship in the Patent Office in Washington, D.C.

1870, F. H. Sypherd lived Arlington Township, Alexandria, Va., with wife and child, Clerk, U.S. Treasury [Washington, D.C.]. [1870 U.S. Federal Census, Arlington Township, Alexandria, Va.]

ca. 1876, Sypherd was "40 years an Auditor for Post Office Department." [*Washington Post*, Oct. 12, 1916]

1880, Thomas H. Sypherd, 49, farmer, living Arlington, Va., with wife, a printer. [1880 U.S. Federal Census]

1893, Oct. 10, Marriage to Annie Walker.

1900, Thomas Sypherd, b. Va., clerk, Treasury, living in Washington, D.C. with wife, Annie. [1900 U.S. Census, Washington, D.C.]

1910, Thomas H. Sypherd, age 79, Gov't Auditing clerk, Treasury Dept., living with wife in Washington, D.C. [1910 U.S. Federal Census, Washington, D.C.]

1916, Oct. 11, Sypherd died. [*Washington Post* (Washington, D.C.), Oct. 12, 1916, p.3]

Samuel F. Tappan [Col.] (1831–1913)

1831, June 29, Samuel Forster Tappan, b. Manchester by the Sea, Essex County, Mass. ["Col. Samuel Forster Tappan memorial," www .findagrave.com]

ca. 1840s, Received a common education, later worked in cabinet maker's trade making chairs in his hometown and subsequently worked in Boston, Mass. [*Tappan-Toppan Genealogy: Ancestors and Descendants of Abraham Toppan of Newbury, MA 1606–1672*, D. L. Toppan, Arlington, Mass., 1915, p.52]

1854, August, Samuel Tappan, reporter, was in the first party of the New England Emigrant Aid Company to Lawrence, Kansas Territory in company of other abolitionists, including Daniel Anthony and Dr. John Doy. ["The Emigrant Aid Company Parties of 1854," Louise Barry, *Kansas Historical Quarterly,* May 1943, Vol. 12, No. 2, p.118, transcribed by lhn; digitized with permission of the Kansas Historical Society]

ca. 1855, Tappan was correspondent for the *New York Tribune.* [*Kansas: A cyclopedia of state history,* Standard Pub. Co., Chicago, 1912. [Vols. I & II edited by Frank W. Blackmar; Vol II, pp.231, 412, 796]

1855, Traveled with Martin Conway in Kansas Territory speaking in favor of the Free-State movement. [Ibid.]

1855, November, Samuel Tappan was a participant in the rescue of Jacob Branson during the Wakarusa War. ["Branson Rescue" (recollections of S.C. Smith), *Lawrence Daily Journal,* Aug. 3, 1895, 2]

1856, Clerk of the Topeka Constitutional convention and the House of Representatives [Ibid]

1856, Tappan went East and brought arms and ammunition to Kansas Territory by way of Iowa and Nebraska. [Ibid.]

1857, Speaker of the Topeka House of Representatives. [Ibid.]

1858, Secretary of the Leavenworth Constitutional Convention. [ibid.]

1859, Clerk of the Wyandotte Convention. [Ibid.]

1860, settled in area later to become Denver, Colorado; became active in city and state activities. [Ibid.]

1861, April, in Frontier Guard, Washington, D.C. [*Kansas, A Cyclopedia of State History,* Blackmar, p, 701]

1861, Aug 26, Enlisted and Commissioned into Field and Staff, 1st Cavalry, Colorado. [American Civil War Research Database]

1862, Mar. 28, Samuel F. Tappan was on the field at the Battle of Glorieta Pass [New Mexico]. "In Memoriam, Samuel F. Tappan," *Veterans of the New Mexico Campaign. (*http://www.pgnagle.com/memorial/tappan.html)

1865, In response to public outrage about the Nov. 29–30, 1864, Sand Creek massacre in which 150 Indians, many of them women and children, were reportedly massacred and mutilated, Samuel F. Tappan was appointed to head the military commission in Denver to investigate Col. Chivington's role in the massacre. [*A Wild West History of Frontier Colorado: Pioneers, Gunslingers and Cattle . . .* , Jolie Anderson Gallagher, History Press, Charleston, South Carolina, 2011, 90–91]

1865, Mar. 13, Promoted to Colonel (Brevet, Vol.) [American Civil War Research Database]

1865, Nov 1, Mustered out of 1st Cavalry (Colorado). [Ibid.]

ca. 1867, Adopted a Cheyenne Indian girl whom he named Minnie Tappan. She was a "survivor of the Chivington massacre in Wyoming." [Death notice, *Evening Star,* Washington, D.C., Nov 25, 1873, 4]

1869, Apr. 21, Samuel Tappan married Cora L.V. Daniels, District of Columbia. She was the leading spiritualist, Cora L.V. (Scott) Hatch Daniels (later known as Cora L.V. Richmond) and moved to Washington, D.C., [Ibid]. In 1859, at the urging of Mrs. Lincoln, President Lincoln was said to have attended Cora's lectures in Washington, D.C., ["*Cora L.V. Richmond*: The Most Amazing Medium You've Never Heard Of." http://theunobstructeduniverse.com/TUU_Blog/cora-l-v-richmond-the-most-amazing-medium-youve-never-heard-of/]

1913, Jan. 6, Samuel Tappan died in Washington, D.C. [www.findagrave.com]

1913, Tappan was buried at Arlington National Cemetery, Arlington, Va. [Ibid.]

Chester Thomas, Sr. [Capt.] (1810–1891)

1810, July 18, Chester Thomas, [Sr.], "Uncle Chet," was born in Troy, Bradford County, Pennsylvania, son of Jacob and Susannah (Rowley) Thomas. ["Chester Thomas: A Tribute to his Memory" written by Hon. Sidney Clarke, April 16, 1891, *Topeka Weekly Capital*, Topeka, Kans., p.6, cols. 1 and 2, and *Findagrave*]

1832, Elected Constable in Pennsylvania. [Ibid., p.207]

1833, Feb. 7, Chester Thomas married first wife, Thankful Sophia Stevens. [Ibid.]

1855, Sept. 21, Wife, Thankful Thomas, died. [Ibid.]

1856, Oct. 9, Married second wife, Lydia L. Stevens. [Ibid.]

1858, April, Chester Thomas, drawn by "his devotion to the anti-slavery clause," moved with his family from Pennsylvania to Shawnee County, Kansas Territory [Ibid.]

1858, October, Thomas Chester, Sr. and Lydia Chester [wife] with five minor children settled in Auburn, Shawnee County, Kansas Territory [1859 Kansas Territory census-FamilySearch.org]

1859, Elected to the Territorial Council representing Shawnee, Osage, and Lyon counties. [Kansas Territory]

1860, March, Chester Thomas, Shawnee County, age 48, oldest on Territorial Legislative Council.

1860, June, Chester Thomas, Sr., age 48, farmer, b. Pennsylvania, living in Auburn Township, Shawnee County, Kansas Territory, with Lydia Thomas, age 25, wife and five children, all b. Pennsylvania. [1860 U.S. Federal Census, Shawnee County, Kansas Territory]

1861, April, In Frontier Guard, White House, Washington, D.C.

1861, President Lincoln appointed him Special Mail agent for Kansas, Nebraska, Dakota, Colorado, and Utah.

1861, Mr. Thomas's "persistent endeavors in behalf of Topeka" were instrumental in securing the vote to make Topeka the Kansas state capital. [*United States Biographical Dictionary*–Kansas Vol., p.207]

1862, Entered the army as Captain and Assistant Quartermaster, relinquished position two years later because of ill health. [*Atchison Daily Globe*, Atchison, Kans., April 29, 1891, p.181, col. E]

1864, Dec. 2, Wife Lydia died. [*U.S. Biographical Directory*–Kansas Vol., 1879, p.207]

1864, Chosen presidential elector for Kansas and cast his vote for Lincoln.

1865, May, Living in Topeka, Kans. with his children and domestic servants. [1865 Kansas State Census]

1870, June, Chester Thomas, [Sr.], age 59, farmer, real estate, Topeka, Shawnee County, Kans., with three children. [1870 *U.S. Federal Census,* Shawnee County, Kans.]

1872, July 7, Married Mary E. McComb. [*U.S. Biographical Directory*–Kansas Vol., 1879, p.207]

1880, June, Chester Thomas [Sr.], age 69, b. Pennsylvania, Police Judge, living in Topeka, Shawnee County, Kans., with wife Mary E., b. Pennsylvania, age 34 and son, Sidney, age 3, b. Kans. [1880 U.S. Federal Census, Shawnee County, Kans.]

1891, April, Chester Thomas, Sr., died. ["A Politician Who Was Active, yet Well Liked," op. cit.]

1891, Apr. 3, Chester Thomas, [Sr.] interred in Topeka Cemetery, Topeka, Kans.

Patrick Henry Townsend (1823–1864)

1823, Oct. 20, P. H. Townsend was born in Salisbury, New Hampshire. He was the son of John Townsend and Anne (Baker) Townsend. [John Jacob Dearborn, *History of Salisbury, NHa* (W. E. Moore, 1890), p.812]

ca. 1845, Townsend attended Phillips Exeter Academy in Exeter, N.H. [Dearborn, p.813]

1850, Graduated from Bowdoin College in Brunswick, Maine. [Ibid.]

1850, Townsend worked at the Treasury Department in Washington and studied law. [Ibid.]

1853–1854, He moved to Exeter, N.H., then moved to Galena, Ill., worked in the office of Elihu Benjamin Washburn and completed his law studies. [Ibid.]

1855, Townsend moved to the Kansas Territory. [Dearborn, p.814]

1856, May 21, He was in Lawrence the night the Free State Hotel was burned. [Ibid.]

1857, Townsend was a correspondent from Kansas for the *Independent Democrat* in Concord, N.H. [Letters of Julia Louisa Lovejoy, 1856–1864, Pt. 2 (www.kshs.org), p.277]

1858, Sept., He attended the first meeting of the Free State Party in Lawrence. [Minutes, First Meeting of the Territorial Central Committee of the Free State Party in Lawrence, Territorial Kansas Online]

1859, July, Townsend was a delegate to the Wyandotte Constitution representing Douglas County. [James Levi King, *Kansas Constitution Convention* (Kans. State Printing Plant, 1920), p.16, Google Book]

1860, Oct. 3, He wrote Abraham Lincoln about the drought and the poor economic situation in Kansas, coupled with armed invaders and federal troops. [Abraham Lincoln Papers, Library of Congress]

1861, April, P.H. Townsend was appointed first-class clerk in the Pension Office. ["Departmental," *National Republican,* April 5, 1861, p.2]

1861, April, He was a member of the Frontier Guard.

1861–1864, Townsend held the clerkship in the Department of the Interior for three years. [Nehemiah Cleaveland, *History of Bowdoin College* (J. R. Osgood & Co., 1882), p.664, Google Book]

1864, May 21, Patrick Henry Townsend died. He was buried in Exeter Cemetery, Exeter, N.H.

John C. Vaughn [Col./Judge] (1806–1892)

1806, John C. Vaughn born South Carolina, son of Sarah and Willie [?] Vaughn. [www.findagrave.com]

1829, Feb, John C. Vaughn, "Court of Appeals . . . admitted to practice in the courts of Law and Equity, in this state. . ." [*Charleston Courier,* Charleston, S.C., Feb. 7, 1829, p.2]

1837, John C. Vaughn came to Ohio from South Carolina and "commenced the study of law." ["It was Governor Vance. . ." *Cleveland Leader,* Cleveland, Ohio, Dec. 15, 1884, p.4]

ca. 1840, Admitted to the bar. Volunteered to defend a Quaker man indicted in Kentucky but a resident of Ohio for sheltering a runaway slave. [*Cleveland Leader,* Cleveland, Ohio, Dec. 15, 1884]

1848, John C. Vaughn was defeated as candidate for election to the U.S. senate— "received within two votes of as many as Salmon P. Chase, who was then elected." [*Plain Dealer,* Cleveland, Sept. 27, 1892, p.2]

1850, Col. John C. Vaughn, in connection with Thomas Brown, established the newspaper *True Democrat,* "the free-soil organ of northern Ohio." In 1853 Brown withdrew from that paper. [Virtualology website, http://virtualology.com/apthomasbrown1/]

1850, John C. Vaughn, editor and proprietor of the *True Democrat,* pioneer anti-slavery newspaper of Cleveland. Founder of the *Cleveland Leader.* [*Plain Dealer,* Cleveland, Ohio, Aug. 2, 1881, p.1] Also formerly of *Louisville Examiner* [*Anti-Slavery Bugle,* New Lisbon, Ohio, May 11, 1849, Image 3]

1850, John C. Vaughn, age 44, editor and lawyer, was living with wife, Sarah, and their four children in Cleveland, Cuyahoga County, Ohio. [1850 U.S. Federal Census]

1853, Joe Medill and J.C. Vaughn went to Chicago and purchased the *Chicago Tribune.* In 1857, John C. Vaughn retired from editorial management of the *Chicago Tribune* to resume practice of law. [*Anti-slavery Bugle,* April 4, 1857, Image 3]

1857, John C. Vaughn was editor in chief of *Leavenworth Times* for 17 or 18 years.

1858, Feb. 25, John C. Vaughn, one of the secretaries of the convention that organized the *National Republican Party* at Pittsburg, Pa. ["A Portrait Received," op. cit.]

1860, July, J.C. Vaughn, living in Leavenworth City, Leavenworth County, Kansas Territory [1860 U.S. Federal Census]

1861, April, Served in Frontier Guard, Washington, D.C. ["The Kansas Men Who were Ready to Protect President Lincoln," *Kansas Semi-Weekly Capital,* Topeka, Kans., Aug. 4, 1896, p.5]

1875, Vaughn was a member of the Kansas House of Representatives. ["A Portrait Received," op. cit.]

1880, June, J.C. Vaughn, Police Judge, living in Leavenworth City, Kans.. [1880 U.S. Federal Census]

1892, Sept. 25, John C. Vaughn, age 86, died in an "old men's home" at Walnut Hills, Cincinnati, Ohio.

1892, Sept. 26, The body of John C. Vaughn was cremated at the Cincinnati, Ohio, crematory.

Norton J. Vedder (1847–1883)

1847, Dec. 11, Norton Vedder was born in Illinois. His father was Nicholas Vedder and his mother was Indiana (Hanks) Vedder. [www.findagrave.com] His mother was a cousin of Nancy Hanks Lincoln. [Richard Hanks, *Hanks Historical Review,* Vol. 6, Issue 3]

1861, Apr. 15, "Col. Delahay (who was a candidate for the U.S. Senate) and daughter are stopping with N. Vedder, Esq. at 362 Massachusetts St." ["Personal," *National Republican,* April 15, 1861, p.3]

1861, April, He was a member of the Frontier Guard.

1861, September, His father, Nicholas Vedder, was made paymaster of U.S. Volunteers. ["Paymasters of Volunteers," *New York Times,* Sept. 6, 1861, p.1]

1865, Norton J. Vedder worked for the Pay Department, and was employed in Washington. [*U.S. Register of Civil, Military, and Naval Service, 1863–1959* (Ancestry.com) database]

1874, Norton J. Vedder was a paymaster's clerk in the War Department employed in Atlanta. [*Official Register of the United States* (U.S. Gov't Printing Office, 1878), p.212, Google Book]

1883, Sept. 30, "September 30 at New Orleans, La., of bilious fever, Norton J. Vedder, only son of Colonel Nicholas Vedder, United States Army, retired." ["Died," *Washington Post,* Oct. 5, 1883] He was buried at Rock Creek Cemetery in Washington, D.C. [www.findagrave.com]

George W. Walker (1836–1878)

1836, George W. Walker, b. Pennsylvania, son of [Dr.] Thomas and Harriett (Coskery) Walker, Waynesboro, Adams County, Pa. [www.ancestry.com]

1860, George W. Walker, merchant at Waynesboro, Pa. [1860 U.S. Federal Census, Waynesboro,Pa.]

1861, In Frontier guard, age 24.

1861, Walker and William Brotherton "started for Martinsburg, West Virginia, to follow after the army with a two-horse wagon laden with sundry supplies useful to the troops." [*Waynesboro: The history of a settlement in the county formerly called Cumberland, but later Franklin, in the Commonwealth of Pennsylvania, in its beginnings, through its growth into a village and borough, to its centennial period, and to the close of the present century: including a relation of pertinent topics of general state and county history*, Benjamin Matthias Nead, 1900] [https://archive.org/stream/waynesborohisto00assogoog#page/n0/mode/2up Internet Archive]

1861, July 16, Walker and Brotherton were captured by Confederate scouts and charged with furnishing goods to federal troops. [Ibid.]

1861, July 22, George W. Walker was held in the Winchester, Va., jail as a POW [ibid.]; "Spent seven months in Libby Prison." [Obit. of George W. Walker, *The Herald and Torch*, Hagerstown, Md., Aug. 28, 1878]

1862, Feb. 19, Released as POW, left for home (Waynesboro,Pa.). [*Richmond Enquirer,* Feb. 19, 1862]

1862, Aug. 10, Enlisted as First Lieutenant. Commissioned into E Company, 126th Infantry, Pennsylvania. [American Civil War Research Database]

1863, May 20, George W. Walker mustered out of 126th Infantry at Harrisburg, Pa. [Ibid.]

1863, June 5, Lt. George W. Walker accepted appointment as the enrollment officer for Washington Twp., Waynesboro, Pa. [www.ancestry.com]

1863, Dec. 24, Married to Maggie S. Funk in Waynesboro, Pa. [Ibid.]

1870, George W. Walker, 34, grocer, wholesale and retail, living with wife, Margaret, age 23. [1870 U.S. Federal Census, Hagerstown, Washington County, Md.]

1878, Aug. 24, George W. Walker died in Hagerstown, Md. [Obit. of George W. Walker, op. cit.]

1878, George W. Walker was buried in Rose Hill Cemetery, Hagerstown, Washington County, Md. [Ibid.]

Leicester Walker (1836–1916)

1836, Sept. 3, Walker was born in Sandusky, Ohio. [Will. H. McDonald, *Illustrated History of Lincoln County, Nebraska* (American

Historical Society, 1920), p.17, Google Book] He was the son of Leicester Walker, Sr. and Juliet (Andrews) Walker. [*The Firelands Pioneer*, Vols. 12–13 (The Society, 1876), p.120, Google Book]

1858–60, Walker was involved in merchandizing in Lawrence, Kans., and then returned to Ohio. [Major Leicester Walker, Civil War Soldier, Rancher (http://lincoln.negenealogy.org/l_walker.html)]

1861, April, He was a member of the Frontier Guard.

1861, May, He was appointed secondnd lieutenant of the 2nd U.S. Cavalry and joined his company in Washington, D.C. [McDonald, p.17]

1861, July, He fought in the first Battle of Bull Run. [Ibid.]

1862, January, Walker was made first lieutenant of Company C of the 5th U.S. Cavalry. [Ibid.]

1862, He fought in the Second Battle of Bull Run, the Battle of Antietam, and the Battle of Fredericksburg. [Ibid.]

1863, Fought in the Battle of Gettysburg and served on the staff of General Meade. [Ibid.]

1864, Walker was transferred to General Sheridan's staff as chief of ordnance. [Ibid.]

1865, Spring, Walker was sent to Washington suffering from an attack of pneumonia and was unable to join his command until the end of the war. [Ibid.]

1865, December, He was ordered to Charleston with four companies of his regiment. [Ibid.]

1866, Placed in the command of the post at Aiken, S.C. There he was the head of the Freedman's Bureau and had charge of all elections. [Ibid.] While he was stationed at Aiken, he married Georgia S. Warren. [McDonald, p.18]

1868, Campaign in Kansas, Colorado, New Mexico, and Texas under General Sheridan. [McDonald, p.17]

1869, Walker marched with 400 men from Fort Harker, Kans., to Fort McPherson, Neb., fighting Indians. He was recommended for brevet lieutenant colonel for the Battle of Summit Springs, in which Chief Toll Boll was killed. [McDonald, pp.17–18]

1870, He was stationed in North Platte, commanding the post there, with a company from the 9th Infantry protecting the settlers and the Union Pacific Railroad. [McDonald, p.18]

1870, Dec. 30, He resigned from the army and spent the rest of his life in North Platte. [Ibid.]

1916, Apr. 9, Leicester Walker died and was buried in North Platte, Lincoln County, Neb.

Elisha Fuller Wallace (1792–1870)

1792, Mar. 30, Elisha F. Wallace was born in Milford, New Hampshire, the son of James and Betsey (Kimball) Wallace. [George Thomas Chapman, *Sketches of the Alumni of Dartmouth College* (Riverside Press, 1867), p.158, Google Book]

1806, Read law in Salem, Mass. [Ibid.]

1811, Graduated from Dartmouth College. [U.S. School Catalogs 1765–1935 (Ancestry.com) database]

1812, Received a B.A. degree from Yale. [Ibid.]

1815–1819, Practiced law at Marblehead, Mass. [Chapman, p.158]

1820, Moved to Amherst, Mass., and married Lydia Wheelwright in Boston. [Ibid.]

1825, Moved to Syracuse, N.Y. [Roger Hiemstra, Articles, May Memorial Universalist Society, p.131]

1861, April, He was a member of the Frontier Guard.

1861, Dec. 23, Abraham Lincoln nominated Elisha F. Wallace of New York to be U.S. Consul at St. Iago, Cuba. [*Journal of the Senate,* Vol. 37, Issue 2 (M. Glazier, 1887), p.27, Google Book]

1870, Aug. 15, Died in Syracuse, N.Y. and buried there in Oakwood Cemetery.

Elias Wampole (ca. 1808–1863)

ca. 1808, He was born in Pennsylvania. [1850 U.S. Federal Census, Trenton, Mercer County, N.J.]

1829, Feb. 3, Wampole married Catharine Laboucherie in Huntington, N.J. [*New Jersey Marriages, 1678–1985* (Family Search) database]

1850, Elias Wampole was nominated for Indian Agent in the Oregon Territory. [*Journal of the Senate* (M. Glazier, 1887), p.222, Google Book]

1859, Wampole campaigned for Lincoln in Illinois. [Allen C. Guelzo, *Abraham Lincoln: Redeemer President* (Wm. B. Eerdmans, 2002), p.279, Google Book]

1860, Elias Wampole, farmer in Menard County, Ill., lived with wife, Catherine, and four children. [1860 U.S. Federal Census, Menard, Ill.]

1861, April, He was a member of the Frontier Guard.

1862, Feb. 10, Wampole was nominated as Consul at Laguayra, Venezuela, and confirmed Mar. 6, 1862. [*Journal of the Senate,* Vol. 37, Issue 2 (M. Glazier, 1887), p.115, Google Book]

1864, Wampole's death in Venezuela. ["General News," *New York Times,* Jan. 26, 1864]

George F. Warren (1822–)

1822, George F. Warren was born in Maine. [Wyandotte Constitution List, KSHS]

1852, November, He moved west and worked as a carpenter on a steamboat on the Mississippi. [William Anderson Howard, *Report of the Special Committee Appointed to Investigate the Troubles in Kansas* (Washington: Cornelius Wendell, 1856), p.395]

1855, March, Moved to Leavenworth, Kans. and worked as a clerk at the Leavenworth Hotel. He witnessed heavily armed Missourians arriving to vote at the March 30 election. [Ibid.]

1855, April, Warren joined the secret "Kansas Legion" of Free-State men formed and was authorized to form a regiment. [Horace Greeley, *History of the Struggle for Slavery Extension* (Dix, Edwards & Co., 1856), p.104, Google Book]

1855, He attended the Sand Bank meeting and the Big Springs Convention. [Charles Clark, *Kansas Bogus Legislature.Org* (kansasboguslegislature.org)]

1855, December, Taken prisoner by pro-slavery men and held by Sheriff Jones in Lecompton; later released in Lawrence, Kans. [Howard, pp.1097–1101]

1856, He was a delegate to the Republican National Convention from Leavenworth, Leavenworth County, Kansas. [politicalgraveyard. com]

1857–1858, Warren was sergeant-at-arms for the House in Lecompton and the Leavenworth Constitutional Convention. [Clark, op. cit.]

1859, Warren was sergeant-at-arms for the Wyandotte Convention. [Wyandotte Constitution List, KSHS]

1860, He attended the Railroad Convention in Topeka, representing Douglas County. [Clark, op. cit.]

1861, **April,** He was a member of the Frontier Guard.

1862, **July,** He was appointed assistant quartermaster with rank of captain. [Oliver Diefendorf, *General Orders of the War Department* (1864), p.440, Google Book]

Cooper Kinderdine Watson [Hon.] (1810–1880)

1810, **June 18,** Cooper Kinderdine Watson, b. Jefferson County, Kentucky. [*Bench and Bar of Ohio: a Compendium of History and Biography*, Century Publishing & Engraving Co., Chicago (1897), pp.321 –24]

1830, Married Caroline Durkee of Zanesville, Ohio. [Ibid.]

ca. 1838, Apprenticed and later employed as a tailor in Newark, Ohio. [*Newark Advocate* (Newark, Ohio), June 5, 1868; Issue 23; col. B] and [Ibid.]

ca. 1840s, Studied law, Marion, Ohio. [*Bench and Bar,* Op. Cit.]

1842, **January,** Cooper K. Watson admitted as attorney in Chancery, Late Term of U.S. Circuit Court, District of Ohio. [*Ohio Statesman*, Columbus, Ohio, Jan. 7, 1842]

1842, **Feb. 17,** Cooper K. Watson declined appointment as county Whig delegate to Convention. [Letter from Cooper K. Watson in *Ohio Statesman*, Columbus, Ohio, Feb. 25, 1842, p.3, www.genealogy bank.com]

1850, Cooper K. Watson, age 39, residing Tiffin City, Clinton Twp., Seneca County, Ohio, with wife, Caroline, b. Ohio and 7 children b. Ohio. [1850 U.S. Federal Census, Seneca County, Ohio]

1854, Elected to Congress as a "Free Soiler."

1855–57, U.S. Representative from Ohio, 9th District. [*Bench and Bar*, op. cit.]

1856, Article regarding "Judge Douglas' letter to Cooper K. Watson." [Article Mentions James Lane.] [*Daily Ohio Statesman*, Columbus, Ohio, Apr. 30, 1856, p.2]

1860, July 27, C. K. Watson, attorney, residing in Tiffin City, Seneca County, Ohio, with wife, Caroline, and three children. [1860 U.S. Federal Census, Seneca County, Ohio]

1861, April, In Frontier Guard, Washington, D.C. [*Perrysburg Journal*, Perrysburg, Ohio, June 20, 1861, p.3]

1870, Cooper K. Watson, attorney at law, age 57, residing Tiffin, Seneca County, Ohio, with wife, Caroline, age 56, and one adult daughter. [1870 U.S. Federal Census]

1873, Delegate to Ohio State Constitutional Convention from Huron County, Ohio. [*Bench and Bar*, op. cit.]

ca. 1880, Judge of the Court of Common Pleas. [*Decatur Daily Republican*, Decatur, Ill., May 21, 1880, p.2]

1880, May 20, Died, Sandusky, Erie County, Ohio. Buried Greenlawn Cemetery, Tiffin, Seneca County, Ohio.

William B. Waugh (1817–1877)

1817, Sept. 3, William B. Waugh born in Maryland, son of Bishop Beverly Waugh of the Protestant Episcopal Church and Catherine Bushby. [*Waugh Family Notes*, Donald Gradeless, http://family.gradeless.com/waugh.htm, and *A Waugh family history: John of Litchfield, Connecticut, Milo and Elizabeth (Kious) Waugh of Ohio and Indiana* : allied lines of Bowers, Butcher, Hamilton, Hopkins, Kious, Minor & Ward, P.L. Waugh, 1986, GoogleBooks.org and *Philadelphia Inquirer*, Philadelphia, Pa., May 19, 1877, p.1]

ca. 1830–40s, William B. Waugh married Caroline M. Kettlehume and had four children. [*A Waugh Family History*, op. cit.]

1839, Apr. 16, William B. Waugh, appointed clerk, employed in service of Indian Office in Washington, D.C. during 1839. [*Public Documents printed by order of Senate of the United States, During the First Session of the Twenty-sixth Congress, Begun and Held at the City of Washington*, Dec. 2, 1839 (1840), Google eBook]

1840, Waugh, Democrat, Office of Indian Affairs. [*Extra Globe*, Francis Preston Blair, 1841, p.15]

1850, Apr. 1, William B. Waugh, "Secretary," one of signers of treaty with Wyandot Indians. Washington, D.C. [*Indian Affairs Laws and Treaties*, p.588, Google eBook]

1850, July 30, Wm. Waugh, 35, Clerk Dept., living in Washington, D.C. [1850 U.S. Census, Washington, D.C.]

1857, Resigned from Indian Bureau. [Op. cit.]

1857, April, Waugh settled in Leavenworth, Kansas Territory [1859 census of Stranger Township, Leavenworth County, Kansas Territory, Ancestry.com]

1859, Wm. B. Waugh, living Stranger Creek Township, Leavenworth County, Kansas Territory [Ibid.]

1860, William B. Waugh, age 42, merchant, in Leavenworth, Kansas Territory [1860 U.S. Census, Leavenworth, Kansas Territory]

1861, April, William B. Waugh in Frontier Guard, Washington, D.C.

1865, Reentered into Indian Bureau.

1869, William B. Waugh succeeded Maj. Charles Mix, Chief Clerk and Acting Commissioner of Indian Affairs, who was removed [Mix retired May 1, 1869]. [*Cleveland Leader*, Cleveland, Ohio, Apr. 24, 1869, p.1]

1877, May 18, William Waugh, Chief of the Civilization Division of Indian Affairs ["the oldest and one of the most faithful clerks in the bureau"] died in Washington, D.C. [*New York Herald*, May 18, 1877, p.10]

1877, Buried in Historic Congressional Cemetery, Washington, D.C.

George Brevitt Way [Maj.] (1811–1873)

1811, May 5, George B. Way born, Maryland. [American Civil War Research Database]

1835, George B. Way was hired by a group of Toledo businessmen to be editor of *Toledo Blade*. [http://www.toledolibrary.org/images/docwidget/toledo_profile/Chapter02.pdf]

1844–1845, Served as mayor of Toledo, Ohio. [*Findagrave*]

1851, The Whig State Convention for Ohio nominated George B. Way a "Supreme Judge" [*Daily Illinois State Register*, Springfield, Ill., July

12, 1851, p.2; *Huron Reflector* (Norwalk, Ohio), Aug. 5, 1851, p.3]
[see attachment to email].

1861, June 1, Enlisted as major, Paymaster's Department, U.S. Volunteers. [American Civil War Research Database]

1861, June 25, Acceptance as additional paymaster in the Army of the
U.S., Washington, D.C. [Fold3.com]

1861, August, Appointment as additional paymaster in the Army of the
U.S., Washington, D.C. [Ibid.]

1868, July 8, Death notice [*Daily National Intelligencer*, July 19, 1868] *or*

1868, Aug. 8 [*Findagrave*] George B. Way died Urbana, Champaign
County, Ohio. [Ibid.]

Franklin Webster (1824–1865)

1824, June 27, Franklin Webster was born in Haverhill, Massachusetts.
[*General Catalogue of Dartmouth College* (1900), pp.200–01
Google Book]. He was the son of David and Betsey (Kimball)
Webster. [*Massachusetts, Town and Vital Records, 1620–1988*
(Ancestry.com) database]

1845, He graduated from Dartmouth. [*The Dartmouth* (1867), p.120,
Google Book]

1850, Webster was a teacher in Cambridge, Mass. [1850 U.S. Census,
Cambridge, Mass.]

1854, He received a degree at Harvard. [*U.S. School Catalogs 1765–1935*.
(Ancestry.com) database]

1861, April, He was a member of the Frontier Guard.

1861–1862, he practiced law in Chicago. [*U.S. City Directories, 1821–
1989* (Ancestry.com) database]

1861, Aug. 24, Lincoln appointed him as American consul in Munich,
Germany. [Papers of Abraham Lincoln: Images from the National
Archives and the Library of Congress]

1865, May 4, Webster died and was buried in Munich. [*General Catalogue of Dartmouth College*] [G. Henry Horstman, *Consular Reminiscences* (J. B. Lippincott, 1886), p.134, Google Book]

Addison A. Wheelock (1832–)

1832, A. A. Wheelock was born in New York, the son of Otis and Hannah Wheelock. [*1850 U.S. Federal Census*, Vienna, Oneida County, N.Y.]

1857, Wheelock was a delegate to the California Republican State Convention from the county of El Dorado. [*Sacramento Daily Union*, July 9, 1857, p.2]

1858, He was editor of the *True Republican* published in Coloma, Cal. [*Sacramento Daily Union*, June 15, 1858] In August, he began publishing the *Daily Evening Republican*. [*Sacramento Daily Union*, Aug. 23, 1858]

1861, March, The Republicans of the California State Central Committee wrote Lincoln to recommend Addison A. Wheelock for a position in the new administration. [Ira P. Rankin and Others to Abraham Lincoln, *The Lincoln Papers*, Images from the National Archives and the Library of Congress]

1861, April, He was a member of the Frontier Guard.

1861, September, Nicholas Vedder wrote Lincoln to recommend Wheelock. [Nicholas Vedder to Abraham Lincoln, *The Lincoln Papers*, Images from the National Archives and the Library of Congress]

1865, June 1, Wheelock married Sarah E. Brunson in St. Johns, Clinton County, Mich. [*Michigan Marriages, 1822–1995* (Family Search) database]

1867, Wheelock went on a tour through Kansas and spoke at women's suffrage meetings with Elizabeth Cady Stanton and Samuel Pomeroy. [*Daily Kansas Tribune*, Aug. 27, 1867, p.2]

1868, He was a lecturer living in Toledo, Ohio. [U.S. City Directories 1821–1989 (Ancestry.com) database]

1870, Wheelock, editor of the *American Spiritualist,* lived in Cleveland, Ohio, with his wife Sarah and daughter Helen. [1870 Federal Census, Cleveland, Cuyahoga County, Ohio]

1872, Wheelock, editor, lived in New York City. [*U.S. City Directories 1821–1898* (Ancestry.com) database]

1908, Feb. 10, A pension application was filed for Addison Wheelock, Frontier Guard, D.C. Infantry from the state of Washington. [*General Index to Pension Files, 1861–1834* (Ancestry.com) database]

Ebenezer White [? – ?]

1861, April, He was a member of the Frontier Guard.

1861, July, Ebenezer White was placed on the staff of James H. Lane with rank of second lieutenant. ["Gen. Fremont's Staff," *Janesville Daily Gazette,* July 7, 1861, p.3]

1861, Oct. 30, Ebenezer White wrote Lyman Tumble asking for assistance in getting authorization for recruiting "a Company of Mounted Sappers, Miners & Engineers" for General Lane's Kansas Brigade. The letter had Lincoln's endorsement on it. [*Collected Works of Abraham Lincoln, Vol. 5* (Wildside Press, LLC, 2008), p.9]

1862, April, The 10th Regiment Kansas Infantry was organized, and Ebenezer White was listed as a second lieutenant in Companies F and S. The regiment was discharged at Fort Leavenworth, September 1865. [National Park Service, Civil War Soldiers and Sailors database]

1871, Sept. 20, Invalid pension for Ebenezer White, 2nd Lt. Co. F and S, Kansas Infantry. [U.S. Civil War Pension Index 1861–1934 (Ancestry.com) database]

1885, Mar. 3, Pension approved for Sarah A. White of Abington, Mass., widow of Ebenezer White, late a lieutenant in the Kansas Cavalry Volunteers. [Richard Peters, *United States Statutes at Large* (U.S. Gov't Printing Office, 1885), p.672, Google Book]

Nathaniel Greene Wilcox (1805–1876)

1805, Feb. 22, Nathaniel Greene Wilcox was born in Connecticut. [Letter from Nathaniel G. Wilcox to Gov. Yates, Apr 28, 1861, Washington, D.C.] ["Nathaniel G. Wilcox to Richard Yates," *Chronicling Illinois,* http://alplm-cdi.com/chroniclingillinois/items/show/993] [Yates Family Papers, Box 2, Folder 3 (Mar. 1–Apr. 19, 1861), Abraham Lincoln Presidential Library and Museum]

1833, Nathaniel Wilcox went to Illinois. [Ibid., p.2] Later went to Louisiana and Pike County, Mo. Received staff appointment from Gov. Boggs.

1844, Served as a delegate to Baltimore Convention. [Ibid., p.2]

1848, In Philadelphia at the time of the meeting of the National Whig convention. Elected to fill vacancy over A. Lincoln, Dr. Rouse of Peoria, John Tilson of Quincy, and others. [Ibid., p.3]

1849, Appointed receiver of the law office at Stillwater, Minn., by General Taylor. [Ibid., p.3]

1850, Reappointed by President [Millard]. Fillmore [Ibid., p.3]

1852, Elected to Minnesota Legislature for one year. [Ibid., p.3]

1856, Member of Republican state convention at Bloomington, Ill., and appointed to the Republican National Convention in Philadelphia. "First member there [?] to suggest and put in nomination the Hon. A. Lincoln as a candidate for the Vice President." [Ibid., p.3]

1860, Delegate from county to the Republican State Convention at Decatur in 1860 and was appointed alternate delegate to the Hon. O.H. Browning for the state at large to the National Convention at Chicago. [Letter, Wilcox to Yates, April 28, 1861, op. cit., p.3]

1861, April, Served in Frontier Guard. [Ibid., p.3]

1861, Apr. 14, Letter to Gov. Richard Yates from Nathaniel G. Wilcox dated April 14, 1861, in which Wilcox requests his recommendation for an appointment for the office of "Agent for Chippewa Indians of Lake Superior." [http://alplm-cdi.com/chroniclingillinois/items/show/881] [*Chronicling Illinois*]

["Nathaniel G. Wilcox to Richard Yates," *Chronicling Illinois*, Yates Family Papers, Box 2, Folder 3 (Mar. 1–Apr. 19, 1861), Abraham Lincoln Presidential Library and Museum.]

1861, Apr. 28, Letter from [Col.] Nathaniel G. Wilcox. Washington, D.C. to Yates, Governor, State of Illinois. He asked for recommendation for appointment of brigadier general. He writes of being a Frontier Guard with Lane. "High private in the ranks of Genl. Jim Lane's company of Frontier Rangers" raised to guard the President's house. . . ." [http://alplm-cdi.com/chroniclingillinois/items/show/993] [Yates Family Papers, Box 2, Folder 3 (March 1–April 19, 1861), Abraham Lincoln Presidential Library and Museum.]

1861, May 10, Letter from Gov. Richard Yates offering Wilcox a post as one of the aides to the governor. http://alplm-cdi.com/chroniclin-gillinois/items/show/1065 [Yates Family Papers, Box 2, Folder 3 (March 1–April 19, 1861), Abraham Lincoln Presidential Library and Museum.]

1861, Aug. 5, Enlisted as major, commissioned into Paymaster's Department, U.S. Vols. [American Civil War Research Database]

1863, Feb. 21, Resigned from Paymaster's Department. [American Civil War Database]

1865, Living in Frederick, Schuyler County, Ill. [1865 Illinois State Census, Schuyler County, Illinois, Familysearch.org]

1870 N.G. Wilcox, farmer, living in South Dixon Twp., Lee County, Ill. [1870 U.S. Federal Census, South Dixon Township, Lee County, Ill.]

1876, Aug. 9, Died Green County, Iowa, buried Paton Cemetery. [Nathaniel Green Wilcox, *Findagrave.com*]

Abel Carter Wilder (1828–1875)

1828, Mar. 18, A. Carter Wilder was born in Mendon, Worcester, Mass. [Frank W. Blackmar, *Kansas: A Cyclopedia of State History*, Vol. 2 (Chicago: Standard Publishing Co., 1912), p.917]

1849, He moved to Rochester, N.Y., where two of his brothers were living, and became active with the Whig and Free Soil parties. [Ibid.]

1857, He moved to Leavenworth, Kansas Territory [Ibid.]

1859, He was made secretary of the Kansas Republican State Central Committee. [Ibid.]

1859, Dec. 1, Along with Marcus J. Parrott, Wilder heard Lincoln speak in Troy, Doniphan County, Kans. [Linus Pierpont Brockett, *Life and Times of Abraham Lincoln* (Bradley & Co., 1865), 121]

1860, He was chairman of the Kansas delegation at the Republican National Convention in Chicago and voted for Seward. [Blackmar, p.917]

1860–1861, Chairman of the Republican Central Committee. [Ibid.]

1861, Jan. 28, M. J. Parrott telegraphed A. Carter Wilder when the Kansas bill passed the house. D. W. Wilder's two-day-old newspaper, the Leavenworth *Conservative,* was first to get the news. ["When

Kansas Became a State," *Kansas Historical Quarterly,* Vol. 7, No. 1, Spring 1861]

1861, Apr. 16, He arrived at the Willard Hotel in Washington, D.C. ["Arrivals at the Hotels," *Evening Star,* April 16, 1861, p.4]

1861, April, He was a member of the Frontier Guard.

1861, Aug. 7, Wilder was appointed by Lincoln as a brigade commissary in Kansas and was stationed at Ft. Scott. [Blackmar, p.917]

1863–1865, Member of the 38th Congress. [William G. Cutler, *History of the State of Kansas* (Chicago: A. T. Andreas, 1883), p.236]

1865, Moved back to Rochester and became publisher of the *Evening Express.* [Blackmar, pp.917–18]

1872–1873, Became mayor of Rochester but resigned in 1873 because of his health. [Blackmar, p.918]

1875, Dec. 22, He died in San Francisco, buried at Mt. Hope Cemetery in Rochester, N.Y. [Ibid.]

William Parker Wright (1823–1905)

1823, Jan. 6, W. Parker Wright was born in Nelson, New Hampshire. He was the son of Oliver Wright and Rhonda Taylor. [Samuel Dunster, *Henry Dunster and His Descendants* (Central Falls, R.I.: E. L. Freeman & Co., 1876), p.240]

1835, His family moved to Nunda (Livingston County), New York, where he and his father and brothers ran the first furnace. [H. Wells Hand, *1808–1908 Centennial History of the Town of Nunda* (Rochester, N.Y.: Rochester Herald Press, 1908), p.269]

1852–1859, W. Parker Wright and his brother Charles B. Wright were in business building fire engines in Rochester, N.Y. [Samuel Dunster, p.240]

1861, April, He was a member of the Frontier Guard.

1861, He was employed at the Navy Yard in Washington. As a skilled mechanic, he worked for the government on the mounting of the Dalgren guns for the protection of the city. [Hand, p.269]

1862, September, Worked as a volunteer at the hospital near the Navy Yard. ["Correspondence," *Nunda News,* Oct. 11, 1862, p.1]

1866, June 14, Married Gertrude E. Simonson in Port Byron, Ill. [Samuel Dunster, p.241]

1872, He was employed by Rock Island Engine Works as a machinist in Chicago. [Ibid.]

1900, Wright living in Cook County, Ill. [*1900 Federal Census,* Proviso, Cook County, Ill.]

1904, Nov. 21, Admitted to Home for Disabled Soldiers in Sawtelle, Cal. Military History: April 18, 1861 to May 3, 1861, Frontier Guard, Washington, D.C. [*U.S. National Homes for Disabled Soldiers,* 1866–1938 (Ancestry.com) database]

1905, Jan. 28, William Parker Wright died. Buried at Evergreen Cemetery in Los Angeles, Cal.

William M. Zearing (1824–1899)

1824, Nov. 30, William M. Zearing was born in Harrisburg, Pennsylvania, son of John Zearing. ["Death of William M. Zearing," *Chicago Daily Tribune,* Chicago, Ill., Aug 11, 1899, p.2]

1842, Zearing family settled in Bureau County, Ill. in 1842. [Ibid.]

1844, William Zearing began study of Law at Dickinson College, Carlisle, Pa. [Ibid.]

Date unknown, Graduated Law College of Harvard. [*Sun,* Baltimore, Md., Aug. 12, 1899, p.1]

1861, April, William Zearing was in the Frontier Guard, Washington, D.C.

1861, Apr. 16, He enlisted as a private. [American Civil War Research Database]

1861, Apr. 25, William Zearing enlisted in Company B, 8th Inf. (Ill.). [Ibid.]

1861 July 25, Mustered out Company B, 8th Ill Inf. [Ibid.]

1864, July 24, William Zearing married Annie Cannon of Louisville, Ky. [Louisville, Ky. newspaper]

1871, William Zearing retired from law and went into real estate. ["Death of William Zearing," op. cit.]

n.d. Lived on his farms in Minnesota but spent most winters in Washington, D.C. [Ibid.]

1899, Aug. 10, William M. Zearing died on Mackinac Island, Mich. ["Death of William Zearing," op. cit.]

Endnotes

Prologue

1. Michael J. Klein, *The Baltimore Plot: The First Assassination Conspiracy, 1860–1861* (Yardley, Pa.: Westholme Publishing, 2008), 1–2.

2. Abraham Lincoln Message to Congress, July 4, 1861.

3. Harold Holzer, *Abraham Lincoln As I Knew Him: Gossip, Tributes and Revelations from His Best Friends and Worst Enemies* (Chapel Hill, N.C.: Algonquin, 1999), 110.

4. Adam Goodheart, *1861: The Civil War Awakening* (New York: Vintage Books, 2011), 273.

5. John Lockwood & Charles Lockwood, *Siege of Washington: The Untold Story of the Twelve Days That Shook the Union* (New York: Oxford University Press, 2011), xii, 3.

6. Doris Kearns Goodwin, *Team of Rivals: The Political Genius of Abraham Lincoln* (New York: Simon & Schuster, 2005), 298–99; James M. McPherson, *Battle Cry of Freedom: The Civil War Era* (New York: Oxford University Press, 1988), 285; Edward D. Mansfield, *The Life and Services of Lieut. General Scott* (New York: N.C. Miller, 1862), 532.

7. Lockwood, *supra* note 5, at xiii.

8. Frank W. Blackmar, *Kansas: A Cyclopedia of State History, Embracing Events, Institutions, Industries, Counties, Cities, Towns, Prominent Persons, Etc.*, Vol. I (Chicago: Standard Publishing Company, 1912), 701; Wendell Holmes Stephenson, *The Political Career of General James H. Lane*, Vol. III (Topeka: Kansas State Historical Society, 1930), 104, n. 3; Erich Langsdorf, "Jim Lane and the Frontier Guard," *Kansas Historical Quarterly*, Vol. IX, No. 1 (February 1940), 15; Stephen B. Oates, *The Whirlwind of War: Voices of the Storm, 1861–1865* (New York: Harpers Collins, 1998), 12.

9. The history and events that propel the story are true. Most of the dialogue and thoughts of the men are my own.

10. Theodore B. Gates, *The War of the Rebellion* (New York: P.F. McBreen, 1884), 16.

Chapter 1

1. James M. McPherson, *The War That Forged a Nation: Why the Civil War Still Matters* (New York: Oxford University Press, 2015), 2; Michael J. Klein, *The Baltimore Plot: The First Assassination Conspiracy, 1860–1861* (Yardley, Pa.: Westholme Publishing, 2008), 324–26.

2. Charles P. Stone, "Washington on the Eve of the War," *Century Illustrated* 26:3 (July 1883), 458–59; Goodwin, *Team of Rivals*, 327.

3. Goodwin, *id.*

4. *Id.*, 328. "The New Administration," *N.Y. Times*, March 4, 1861.

5. Goodwin, *supra* note 6, at 329; Goodheart, *supra*, at 18.

6. Craig Miner, *Seeding Civil War: Kansas in the National News*, 1854–58 (Lawrence: Univ. Press of Kans., 2008), 4–5.

7. "Arrivals at the Hotels," *Evening Star* (Washington), April 15, 1861; Samuel C. Pomeroy, "The Times of War and Reconstruction: Reminiscences of Hon. S. C. Pomeroy," *Kansas Biographical Scrapbook*, P, Vol. VI, 145; Earnest B. Ferguson, *Freedom Rising: Washington in the Civil War* (New York: Vintage Books, 2004), 45–47.

8. Goodwin, *Team of Rivals*, 347–48; Elizabeth Keckley, *Behind the Scenes: or, Thirty Years a Slave, and Four Years in the White House* (G. W. Carlton & Co.: 1868), 81.

9. Erich Langsdorf, "Jim Lane and the Frontier Guard," *Kansas Historical Quarterly* Vol. 9, No. 1 (February 1940), 15.

10. Carol Dark Ayers, *Lincoln and Kansas* (Manhattan: Sunflower Univ. Press 2001), 12; Langsdorf, "Jim Lane and the Frontier Guard," 15; "Serenade," *Evening Star* (Washington), April 16, 1861.

11. Lockwood, *Siege of Washington*, 6.

12. Goodheart, *1861: The Civil War Awakening*, 139.

13. Lockwood, *Siege of Washington*, 7.

14. Klein, *supra* note 1, at 10.

15. Don E. Fehrenbacher, ed., *Collected Works of Abraham Lincoln*, (Stanford: Stanford University Press, 1996), 210; David Von Drehl, *Rise To Greatness: Abraham Lincoln and America's Most Perilous Year* (New York: Henry Holt, 2012), 90.

16. Lockwood, *Siege of Washington*, 8.

17. *The New York Times*, April 15, 1861, 1.

18. Alexander Kelly McClure, *Abraham Lincoln and Men of War-Times: Some Personal Recollections of War and Politics during the Lincoln Administration* (New York: Times Publishing Co., 1892), 59–61.

19. Lockwood, *Siege of Washington*, 10, 26–27.

20. *Harper's Weekly*, April 27, 1861; "The Union and Free Speech Meeting on Tuesday Night," *The National Republican* (Washington), April 18, 1860.

21. Lockwood, *Siege of Washington*, 25; Von Drehl, *supra* note 5, at 4.

22. Richard McGowan Lee, *Mr. Lincoln's City: An Illustrated Guide to the Civil War Sites of Washington* (n.p.: EPM Publications, 1981), 58.

23. William Howard Russell, *My Diary North and South* (Boston: H.P. Burnham, 1863), 32, 56.

24. Goodheart, *supra*, at 61. Typhoid fever is a deadly bacterial infection spread through drinking water contaminated by human waste. Even at the White House, the pipes that fed the faucets drew from the unclean Potomac River. Lockwood, *Siege of Washington*, 33.

25. Lee, *Mr. Lincoln's City*, at 58; Goodheart, *1861: The Civil War Awakening*, 61.

26. James Henderson to Abraham Lincoln, April 16, 1861, *Abraham Lincoln Papers*, Library of Congress; Lockwood, *Siege of Washington*, 59–60.

27. Job Stockton to Abraham Lincoln, April 8, 1861, *Abraham Lincoln Papers*, Library of Congress.

28. Pomeroy, *Reminiscences*, 145.

29. *Id.*; *New York Tribune*, April 18, 1861, 5; Heber S. Thompson, *The First Defenders* (n.p.; First Defenders Ass'n, 1910), 14.

30. Von Drehl, *supra* note 5, at 6.

31. "Frontier Guards," *Winfield Courier*, Dec. 7, 1882; Pomeroy, *Reminiscences*. Pomeroy attributed this conversation with Lincoln to himself in his 1886 "Reminiscences," but I find it unlikely. There is no evidence Pomeroy met privately with Lincoln to discuss such sensitive matters. Pomeroy was not the leader of the Frontier Guard, nor was he even an officer. Pomeroy's 1856 surrender of Lawrence to its destruction by pro-slavery soldiers was well known, and Lincoln would have never put his life and the lives of his family members in Pomeroy's hands. This conversation sounds much more like one that Lane, as captain of the company, had with Lincoln. Lane likely recounted the conversation to Pomeroy and Pomeroy inserted himself into it. Lane was dead by 1886, and so was unable to correct the record. Pomeroy's unscrupulousness eventually destroyed his career.

32. Roy Bird, "Jim Lane's Misnamed Frontier Guard," *America's Civil War*, Vol. 12, Issue 1 (March 1999), 8; "Rumors of the Invasion of Washington Tonight Have Excited Much War Feeling," *Daily Post* (Providence, R.I.), April 19, 1861.

33. "Old Frontier Guard," Nov. 6, 1906, unidentified newspaper article, Nat'l Union Catalog of Manuscript Collections.

34. John Hay, *Inside Lincoln's White House: The Complete Civil War Diary of John Hay*, Michael Burlingame, John R. Turner Ettlinger eds. (Carbondale: Southern Illinois Univ. Press, 1997), 8, 17.

Chapter 2

1. J. C. Furnas, *The Americans: A Social History of the United States, 1587–1914* (New York: G. P. Putnam's Sons, 1969), 115; U.S. Const., art. 1, sec. 2, cl. 3; Mason's "judgment of heaven" speech to the Constitutional Convention, Aug. 22, 1787, *Notes of Debates in the Federal Convention of 1787, Reported by James Madison* (New York: W.W. Norton, 1966).

2. Craig Miner, *Seeding Civil War: Kansas in the National News 1854–58* (Lawrence, Kans.: Univ. Press of Kans. 2002), 8–9, 190; James M. McPherson, *The War That Forged a Nation: Why the Civil War Still Matters* (New York: Oxford Univ. Press, 2015).

3. Goodheart, *supra*, at 18.

4. In describing slavery and the Missouri Compromise, Thomas Jefferson wrote: "[W]e have the wolf by the ear, and we can neither hold him, nor safely let him go. Justice is on one scale, and self-preservation on the other." Paul Leicester Ford, ed., *The Works of Thomas Jefferson*, Vol. 12 (New York: G. P. Putnam's Sons, 1905), 159.

5. H. Douglas Hurt, *Agriculture and Slavery in Missouri's Little Dixie* (Columbia: Univ. of Missouri Press, 1992), 170–71; Diane Mutti Burke, *On Slavery's Border: Missouri's Small Slave-Holding Households, 1815–1865* (Athens, Ga.: Univ. of Georgia Press, 2010), 24–25, 50, 98, 200.

6. The Fugitive Slave Act of 1850 mandated that states to which escaped slaves fled were obligated to return them to their masters upon their discovery and subjected persons who helped runaways to imprisonment. The passage of the Act stoked fears among Northern abolitionists that the "needle on the country's moral compass was turning south." Many Northern states enacted laws to nullify the Act's effects. Jan Biles, "Free or Slave Kansas? A Decision That Split the Nation," *Topeka Capital-Journal*, March 9, 2015.

7. Jan Biles, *id.*

8. David M. Potter, *The Impending Crisis: America Before the Civil War, 1848–1861* (New York: Harper Perennial, 2011), 160; Jay Monaghan, *Civil War on the Western Border, 1854–1865* (Lincoln, Neb.: Univ. of Nebraska Press, 1955), 3–4.

9. Miner, *supra*, at xiii, 1.

10. Monahan, *Civil War on the Western Border*, 5, 7–8; Nicole Etcheson, *Bleeding Kansas: Contested Liberty in the Civil War Era* (Lawrence, Kans.: Univ. Press of Kans., 2004), 19.

11. Abraham Lincoln to Joshua Speed, Aug. 24, 1855, *Abraham Lincoln Papers*, Library of Congress.

12. Etcheson, *Bleeding Kansas, id.* at 29; Joshua M. Zeitz, *Lincoln's Boys: John Hay, John Nicolay, and the War for Lincoln's Image* (New York: Penguin Group, 2014), 41.

13. James M. McPherson, *Battle Cry of Freedom: The Civil War Era* (New York: Oxford Univ. Press, 1988), 146–47.

14. Richard White, *It's Your Misfortune and None of My Own* (Univ. of Okla. Press, 1993), 160; Goodwin, *Team of Rivals*, 184; John Speer, *Life of Gen. James H. Lane: The Liberator of Kansas* (Garden City, Kans.: John Speer, Printer, 1896), 18; James P. Muehlberger, *Reflections on Lincoln's Kansas Campaign*, 78 Kansas Bar Ass'n 24 (November/December 2009), 25.

15. "Early Days of a War Eagle," *Kansas City Star*, Feb. 23, 1902. Anthony later served in the Frontier Guard.

16. *Id.*; Frank W. Blackmar, *The Life of Charles Robinson* (Topeka, Kans.: Crane & Co., 1902), 111.

17. Lewis C. Hunter, *Steamboats on the Western Rivers: An Economic and Technological History* (New York: Dover, 1949), 226–28; Gary E. Moulton, ed., *The Definitive Journals of Lewis & Clark*, Vol. 2, Gary E. Moulton ed. (Lincoln, Neb.: Univ. of Nebraska Press, 1986), 312.

18. "Early Days of a War Eagle," *Kansas City Star*, Feb. 23, 1902.

19. Patricia A. Duncan, *Tallgrass Prairie: The Inland Sea* (Kansas City, Mo.: Lowell Press, 1978), 5–8.

20. "Early Days of a War Eagle," *Kansas City Star*, Feb. 23, 1902. The Delaware Indians soon became friends of the settlers and taught some of them which plants were edible, which were medicinal, and where to find nuts, berries, and edible roots.

21. N. Richard Cordley, *A History of Lawrence, Kansas* (Lawrence, Kans.: Lawrence Journal Press, 1895), 3–5. The newcomers called the town Wakarusa, Yankee Town, and New Boston before they settled on Lawrence.

22. Etcheson, *Bleeding Kansas*, at 40.

23. Speer, *supra*, at 49; Ian Michael Spurgeon, *Man of Douglas, Man of Lincoln: The Political Odyssey of James H. Lane* (Columbia, Mo.: Univ. of Missouri Press, 2008), 159.

24. "Early Days of a War Eagle," *Kansas City Star*, Feb. 23, 1902.

25. *Id.*

26. S.C. Gwynne, *Empire of the Summer Moon: Quanah Parker and the Rise and Fall of the Comanches, The Most Powerful Indian Tribe in American History* (New York: Scribner, 2010), 149–50.

27. Robert Collins, *Jim Lane: Scoundrel, Statesman, Kansan* (Gretna, La.: Pelican Publishing Co., 2007), 14. Some of the Western men in the territory may have worked as drovers for the cattle drives up the Military Road from Texas to Fort Leavenworth to supply the soldiers with beef, horses, and mules. Others may have worked the cattle drives from Westport and Independence to the Oregon and California territories to supply the growing population with beef cattle. Louise Barry, *Beginning of the West: Annals of the Kansas Gateway to the American West* (Topeka: Kans. Historical Soc'y, 1972), 1150–52, 1157–58.

28. Robert A. Carter, *Buffalo Bill Cody: The Man Behind the Legend* (New York: John Wiley & Sons, 2000), 15–16; Etcheson, *Bleeding Kansas*, at 50.

29. Carter, *id.* at 16–18; David S. Reynolds, *John Brown, Abolitionist: The Man Who Killed Slavery, Sparked the Civil War, and Seeded Civil Rights* (New York: Vintage Books, 2005), 162.

30. Carter, *id.* at 18–19.

31. *Id.* at 19–23.

32. *Id.* at 23. William's mother, Mary, took in lodgers to support her family, including James Butler Hickok, who befriended young William. Hickok was later known as "Wild Bill" Hickok. Joseph G. Rosa, *Wild Bill Hickok: Sharpshooter and U.S. Marshal of the Wild West* (New York: Rosen Publishing Group, 2004), 24.

33. Cecil Howes, "Pistol-Packing Pencil Pushers," *Kansas Historical Quarterly*, Vol. 13 no. 2 (May 1944), 116.

34. Etcheson, *Bleeding Kansas*, 58.

35. *Id.* Lawyers in the Kansas Territory quickly learned that they needed to be as skilled with a pistol as with a pen—if they wanted to survive.

36. Roy P. Bassler, *The Collected Works of Abraham Lincoln*, Vol. 2 (New Brunswick: Rutgers Univ. Press 1953), 247 (Abraham Lincoln to Joshua Speed, Oct. 16, 1854).

Chapter 3

1. Kendall E. Bailes, *Rider on the Wind: Jim Lane and Kansas* (Shawnee Mission: Wagon Wheel Press, 1962), 3–4.

2. Frank W. Blackmar, *Kansas: A Cyclopedia of the State,* Vol. II (Chicago: Standard Publishing Co., 1912), 444; "One of the Old Guards, Death of Major Turner Sampson," *Lawrence Daily Journal*, Lawrence, Kans., Jan. 22, 1880; List of Companies, Item No. 102910, Kansas State Historical Society, Territorial Kansas Online; *Wyandotte County and Kansas City, Kansas Historical and Biographical* (Chicago: Goodspeed Publishing Co., 1890), 500. Parrott, Sampson, Smith, and Bancroft later served in the Frontier Guard.

3. Bailes, *Rider on the Wind*, 5–9. One of Lane's political mentors, Stephen A. Douglas, was also known to discard articles of clothing during his speeches. In the midst of speaking, Douglas would "cast away his cravat and undo the buttons on his coat, captivating his audience with the air and aspect of a half-naked pugilist"; Goodwin, *Team of Rivals,* 165.

4. Robert Collins, *Jim Lane: Scoundrel, Statesman, Kansan* (Gretna, La.: Pelican Publishing Co., 2007), 19.

5. Wendell Holmes Stephenson, *The Political Career of General James H. Lane* (Topeka, Kans.: Kansas State Historical Soc'y, 1930), 22–23; Collins, *Jim Lane*, 18–19.

6. Spurgeon, *supra*, at 30.

7. *Kansas Free State*, April 30, 1855; Stephenson, *supra* note 58, at 22–27. Lane was 40, no youngster by frontier standards, where the average male did not live to see his 40th birthday, and so he was often called "Old Jim." Lane soon discovered that, in the KT, it was an accomplishment to grow old.

8. Etchison, *Bleeding Kansas,* 53.

9. *Herald of Freedom*, Sept. 8, 1855.

10. Douglas L. Wilson, *Herndon's Informants* (Carbondale: Univ. of Illinois Press, 1998), 52–53.

11. A slave was worth big money. They were loaned out, borrowed against, and used as collateral.

12. Etcheson, *Bleeding Kansas,* 78; Speer, *supra*, at 91.

13. Stephenson, *supra*, at 46.

14. Etcheson, *Bleeding Kansas,* 71.

15. Speer, *supra*, at 37.

16. W.M. Paxton, *Annals of Platte County, Missouri* (Kansas City, Mo.: Ramfre Press, 1965, *reprint*), 209.

17. Frank W. Blackmar, ed., *Kansas: A Cyclopedia of State History, Embracing Events, Institutions, Industries, Counties, Cities, Towns, Prominent Persons, Etc.* (Chicago: Standard Publishing Company, 1912), 938–39.

18. John Speer, *supra*, at 52, 70.

19. Wendell Holmes Stephenson, *supra*, at 55–56; Speer, *supra*, at 53.

20. Lloyd Lewis, "The Man the Historians Forgot," *Kansas Historical Quarterly* 8 (Feb. 1939), 188–89.

21. Stephenson, *supra*, at 56–57.

22. Speer, *supra*, at 61–63.

23. Charles Robinson, *The Kansas Conflict* (New York: Harper & Brothers, 1892), 205–06.

24. "No War in Kansas: Missourians Turned Home," *Red Wing Sentinel*, Dec. 4, 1855 (Lawrence, K.T.)

25. Stephenson, *supra*, at 56–57; Speer, *supra*, at 64. The day before, a detachment of Missouri soldiers had captured Free State Lieutenant Colonel Marc Parrott as he was taking a load of gunpowder into Lawrence and took him back to their camp. He got wet swimming his horse across the river and feared he would either be hung or freeze to death during the horrible night, but he was released the next day as the Slavers broke camp; Dec. 13, 1855, Marc Parrott letter to Thomas Parrott, Territorial Kansas Online, Item No. 101946.

26. Stephenson, *supra*, at 57–58; Speer, *supra*, at 67–70.

27. William Anderson, *Report of the Special Committee Appointed to Investigate the Troubles in Kansas: With Views of the Minority of Said Committee* (United States Congress), 395, 1097–1101.

28. Stephenson, *The Political Career of General James H. Lane*, 60–61.

29. Stephenson, *The Political Career of General James H. Lane*, 68–69; Baron, *Abraham Lincoln and the German Immigrants*, 35; Richard Josiah Hinton, *John Brown and His Men* (Harpers Ferry: Funk & Wagner Co., 1894), 90–91.

Chapter 4

1. Transactions and Reports of the Nebraska State Historical Society (Nebraska: Nebraska State Historical Soc'y, 1885), 102–03; Alan L. Shepherd, "Gentile in Zion: Algernon Sidney Paddock and the Utah Commission, 1882-1886," *Nebraska History* 57 (Fall 1976): 359–77; A. T. Andreas, *History of the State of Nebraska* (Chicago: Western Historical Co., 1882), 326; Grant Lee Shumway, *History of Western Nebraska and Its People* (Western Publishing & Engraving Co., 1918), 432. The Lane Trail was also used by abolitionists as an Underground Railroad to lead African-American freedom-seekers north to escape

slavery. "Delivering Ann Clark to Freedom," *Reflections,* Kansas State Historical Soc'y (Spring 2014), 10–11.

2. Etcheson, *Bleeding Kansas,* 42–43.

3. *Id.*

4. *Id.,* at 61.

5. Daniel R. Wilder, *The Annals of Kansas* (Topeka, Kans.: Kansas Publishing House, 1886), 100; Speer, *supra,* at 24–25; John Stauffer, *Giants: The Parallel Lives of Frederick Douglass and Abraham Lincoln* (New York: Twelve, 2009), 155; Edgar Langendorf, "S.C. Pomeroy and the New England Emigrant Aid Company, 1854–1858," *Kansas Historical Quarterly,* Vol. 7, No. 4 (Nov.1938), 381.

6. William Phillips, *The Conquest of Kansas, by Missouri and Her Allies* (Boston: Phillips, Sampson & Co., 1856), 292.

7. James O. Adams, ed., *The History of Salisbury, New Hampshire* (Manchester: William E Moore, 1890), 812–15; Stauffer, *Giants,* 152.

8. Michael Fellman, *Inside War: The Guerrilla Conflict in Missouri during the American Civil War* (New York: Oxford Univ. Press, 1989), 4–5.

9. Craig Miner, *Seeding Civil War: Kansas in the National News,* 1854–1858. (Lawrence Kans.: Univ. Press of Kansas, 2008), 83, 110, 185–86, 251; *Lawrence Republican,* Aug. 1, 1856.

10. *Id.*

11. The sexual imagery that occurred throughout the oration was neither accidental nor without precedent. Abolitionists routinely accused slaveholders of wanting slavery so that they could engage in forcible sexual relations with their slaves. William James Hoffer, *The Caning of Charles Sumner: Honor, Idealism and the Origins of the Civil War* (Baltimore: Johns Hopkins Univ. Press, 2010), 62.

12. William C. Davis, *Brother against Brother: The War Begins* (Alexandria, Va.: Time Life Books, 1983), 78.

13. Stephen Puelo, *The Caning: The Assault That Drove America to Civil War* (Yardley, Penn.: Westholme Publishing, 2012); Stauffer, *Giants,* 155; Goodheart, *1861: The Civil War Awakening,* 38.

14. Autobiography of August Bondi; N.B. Blanton, "Letter from Kansas," *The Ripley Bee* (Ripley, Ohio), Oct. 4, 1856; Baron, *Abraham Lincoln and the German Immigrants,* 191.

15. Lewis, *supra,* at 99.

16. Speer, *supra,* at 106; Oswald Garrison Villard, *John Brown 1800–1859: A Biography Fifty Years After* (Boston: Riverside Press, 1910), 225. Lane was a master of rhetorical devices such as alliteration, the repetition of consonant

sounds to bring out a rhythm and make words echo: "The Missourians poured over the border, with bowie knives in boots, their belts bristling with revolvers."

17. David Herbert Donald, *Lincoln* (New York: Simon & Schuster, 1995), 191–92.

18. One of those in the audience was Nathaniel Green Wilcox, a member of the Republican state convention, who was the "first member there to suggest and put in nomination the Hon. A. Lincoln as a candidate for the Vice President." April 28, 1861 letter from Nathaniel G. Wilcox to Richard Yates, *Chronicling Illinois*, accessed Nov. 26, 2014. Wilcox later served in the Frontier Guard; Henry Clay Whitney, "Lincoln's Last Speech, Now First Published from the Unique Report," *McClure's Magazine* (September 1896), 319–31.

19. Lewis, *supra*, at 100.

20. *Id.*, 99–100.

21. *Id.*, 100; Speer, *supra*, at 111.

22. Durwood Ball, "Scapegoat? Col. Edwin B. Sumner and the Topeka Dispersal," *Kansas History: A Journal of the Central Plains*, Vol. 33 (Autumn 2010), 65, 69–74; "Topeka Movement," Collection of Kansas State Historical Soc'y (1915), 235.

23. "Kansas Reminiscences," *Chariton (Iowa) Herald*, April 12, 1894.

24. "Memorable Ride," *Topeka Daily Capital*, Sept. 25, 1883, at 6; "President Arthur: Experiences in Kansas in 1857," *Leavenworth Times*, July 29, 1883, at 2. Arthur decided to return to New York City and engage in Republican politics; James Patrick Morgans, *John Todd and the Underground Railroad: Biography of an Iowa Abolitionist* (McFarland, 2006), 112.

25. "Kansas Reminiscences," *Chariton (Iowa) Herald*, April 5, 1894; Baron, *Abraham Lincoln and the German Immigrants*, 29; "William Hutchison Dead," *Lawrence Daily Journal*, May 20, 1904.

26. Speer, *supra*, at 235.

27. *Id.* at 114–15.

28. *Id.* at 112.

29. Sept. 3, 1856, Daniel Woodson letter to William Hutchison.

30. Speer, *supra*, at 52; Stephenson, *The Political Career of Gen. James H. Lane*, 162.

31. *Missouri Republican*, Aug. 31, 1856; Speer, *id.* at 113.

32. Stephenson, *supra*, at 78–79, 130; Reeder M. Fish, *The Grim Chieftain of Kansas* (Clarion Book Print, 1885), 86. The legend of Jim Lane survived long after his death. In the 1950s, a researcher traveled the rural Ozarks, recording

the folk songs of the elderly. "Old Jim Lane" was sung by one elderly woman. Bryce Benedict, *Jayhawkers: The Civil War Brigade of James Henry Lane* (Norman: Univ. of Okla. Press, 2009), 12.

33. Craig Miner, "Lane and Lincoln: A Mysterious Connection," in *Kansas History: A Journal of the Central Plains*, Vol. 24 (Autumn 2001), 186, 190; Speer, *supra*, at 153.

34. Bondi, *Autobiography*, 144. Holmes was a political leader as well as a fighter. On April 30, 1857, he wrote a letter to John Brown that the Free State men refused to pay taxes to the Bogus KT Government to support enforcement of the Slave Code and would set up their own government. Territory of Kansas online.org., accessed March 25, 2015.

35. Rita G. Napier, "Origin Stories and Bleeding Kansas," *Kansas History: A Journal of the Central Plains,* Vol. 34, No. 1 (Spring 2011), 32–35.

36. "Murder of William Phillips," *Springfield Republican,* Oct. 22, 1856; Kansas Claims—U.S. Congressional Serial Set, Vol. 1106 (U.S. Gov't Printing Office, 1861), 49, 231–35, 509–12.

37. P. J. Strasdenraus, "Immigrants or Invaders," *Kansas Historical Quarterly*, Vol. 24, No. 4 (Winter 1958), 394–97. Shortly before traveling to Iowa, Daniels and Thaddeus Hyatt, a wealthy New York merchant who was chairman of the National Kansas Committee and a friend of President Pierce, called upon the President seeking protection for Kansas settlers. The President rebuked them, saying that "Bibles, rather than Sharps rifles" should be sent to Kansas. W. H. Isley, "The Sharps Rifle Episode in Kansas History," *American Historical Review,* Vol. 12, No. 3 (April 1907), 546–47. Daniels and Hyatt later served in the Frontier Guard.

38. Strasdenraus, *supra*, at 397.

39. *Id.* Geary was unpopular with both sides. Pro-Slavers plotted to goad the governor into a gunfight, a frontier-style assassination. Ronald D. Smith, *Thomas Ewing Jr.: Frontier Lawyer and Civil War General* (Columbia: Univ. of Mo. Press, 2008), 41.

40. *New York Herald,* Oct 26, 1856, 8. When Ream was asked to assist one of the pro-slavery men in the "execution of the pro-slavery laws," Ream refused, saying, "God damn the laws, and the men that made them." *Id.* (Ream would soon serve under Lane as a Frontier Guard); N.B. Blanton, "Letter from Kansas," *The Ripley Bee,* Oct. 4, 1856 (Ripley, Ohio).

41. William Phillips, *A Conquest of Kansas, by Missouri and Her Allies* (Boston: Phillips, Sampole & Co., 1856).

Chapter 5

1. Spurgeon, *supra*, at 83; Eleanor L. Turk, "The Germans of Atchison, 1854–1859: Development of an Ethnic Community," *Kansas History: A Journal of the Central Plains*, Vol. 2, No. 3 (Autumn 1979), 146.

2. Goodheart, *1861: The Civil War Awakening, supra*, at 238. At the time, 39 independent states constituted the German Confederation, including the Austrian Empire, which inherited the German territories of the former Holy Roman Empire. There was no "Germany" as such until its many regions were unified by Otto Von Bismarck in 1871. Turk, *supra*, at 147.

3. Baron, *Abraham Lincoln and the German Immigrants*, 44.

4. Frank Baron, "Abraham Lincoln and the German Immigrants: Turners and Forty-Eighters," *Yearbook of German-American Studies*, Vol. 4 (Topeka: Soc'y for German-American Studies, 2012), 35.

5. *Id.*, at 35–36, 153, 155.

6. *Id.* at 45.

7. *Id.* at 37–38.

8. Stauffer, *supra*, at 157.

9. *Id.* at 42–43.

10. S. C. Gwynne, *Empire of the Summer Moon: Quannah Parker and the Rise and Fall of the Comanches, The Most Powerful Indian Tribe in American History* (New York: Scribner, 2010), 149–50.

11. *Smoky Hill and Republican Union* (Junction City, Kansas), Nov. 21, 1861; Baron, "Abraham Lincoln and the German Immigrants," 46.

12. Baron, *supra*, at 44.

13. Doris Kearns Goodwin, *Team of Rivals* (New York: Simon & Schuster, 1995), 196. Lane also ordered the ferry boats in Doniphan to be cut loose the night before the election so that they could not be used by Missourians to cross the river onto Kansas soil to vote; Wilder, *Annals of Kansas*, 197.

14. *Leavenworth Times*, Nov. 21, 1857.

15. Bassler, Vol. 2, 448; *Leavenworth Times*, Nov. 21, 1857. The only book many frontiersmen had brought West was the Bible, which was often the only book those who could read had read.

16. Baron, *supra*, at 49.

17. Frank Baron, "James H. Lane and the Origins of the Kansas Jayhawks," *Kansas History: A Journal of the Central Plains*, 34, no. 2 (Summer 2011), 115–17. The leader of the 7th Kansas Calvary, Charles Jenison, gave his regiment the unofficial title of the "mounted Kansas Jayhawkers"; *Id.* at 124. In 1886, the University of Kansas, located in Lawrence, selected the Jayhawk as its mascot. In

the 1880s, the Civil War was still a fresh wound for Missourians who had lived during the border war and the Civil War, and they carried a gut-level dislike, even hatred, for Jayhawks. Four years later, the University of Missouri, located in Columbia, reciprocated by choosing the Tiger as its mascot. For nearly 25 years, former Confederate officer and newspaperman John Newman Edwards had praised the Missouri guerrillas fighting during the Civil War as "tigers"; Edwards, "Terrible Quintet," *Kansas City Star,* Feb. 25, 2012.

18. Baron, *James H. Lane and the Origins of the Kansas Jayhawks, supra,* at 121.

19. Baron, *supra,* at 194, 196.

20. *Id.* at 195.

21. *Id.* at 195–96.

22. Smith, *supra,* at 58. Kickapoo was named after a local band of Kickapoo Indians. The Kickapoo people had originally lived near the Fox and Wisconsin rivers near Lake Michigan. Many of their warriors fought in the Battle of Tippecanoe and the War of 1812. The government then forced the tribe to relocate to the Kansas Territory.

23. *Id.* at 59–60. Ewing later served in the Frontier Guard.

24. *Id.* at 51.

25. *Id.* at 52–53.

26. *Id.* at 53–54.

27. *Id.* at 54–55.

28. Speer, *supra,* at 93–94.

29. *Id.* at 214.

30. *Id.* at 188–90, 203–04, 209.

31. Smith, *supra,* at 74.

32. *Id.* at 203–04, 215.

33. *Id.* at 205.

34. Republican Party, Proceedings of the Republican State Convention, Held at Springfield, Illinois, June 16, 1858 (Springfield: Bailhache & Baker, 1858), 5.

35. Stauffer, *supra,* at 199; Miner, 4–5.

Chapter 6

1. Margaret Solomon, "A Bloomer Girl Conquers Pike's Peak," *American History Illustrated* (Jan. 1984), 45. Gold was also reported as being found at Ralston Creek, near Pikes Peak. Soon-to-be Frontier Guard James Holmes led an expedition from Lawrence to Pikes Peak. The group's Delaware Indian guide backed out of his agreement to lead the party because Indians threatened his life if he

led white men west, so the group was forced to follow the Arkansas River, for none knew where water could be found in the vast plains. Holmes found no gold but his wife, Julia Archibald Holmes, became famous for being the first woman on record to hike to the top of Pikes Peak. *Id.*

2. Charles Whalen & Barbara Whalen, *The Fighting McCooks* (Bethesda: Westmoreland Press, 2006), 290–91.

3. Martha B. Caldwell, "When Horace Greeley Visited Kansas in 1859," *Kansas Historical Quarterly*, vol. 9, no. 2 (May 1940), 118.

4. By the time they neared Denver City, most had eaten their load to half its size.

5. Caldwell, *supra* note 189 at 134–36.

6. "The Battle of Solomon Fork," *Journal of Lieutenant Eli Long,* 1857 (Carlisle, Pa.: U.S. Army Military History Inst.); Caldwell, *supra* at 138–40.

7. Speer, *supra*, at 250.

8. Caldwell, *supra*, at 133.

9. Calvin W. Gallagher, "Gold Fever in Kansas Territory: Migration to the Pike's Peak Gold Fields, 1858–1860," *Kansas Historical Quarterly*, Vol. 39, No. 1 (Spring 1973), 58–74; Whalen, *supra* note 188 at 291; Edward McCook to Mary Sheldon, May 10, 1861, *Butler-McCook Papers*, Library of Congress.

10. Historical Papers and Addresses of the Lancaster Historical Society, Vol. 18 (1914), 15. Another rider for the Pony Express was Buffalo Bill Cody, Frontier Guard Joseph Cody's nephew.

11. The 1860 U.S. Census reflected 143,643 Kansas inhabitants, of whom 34,242 were in the vicinity of Denver City and Pike's Peak. Noble L. Prentice, *History of Kansas* (Topeka: 1899), 96.

Chapter 7

1. Roy P. Bassler, ed., "James Quay Howard's Notes on Lincoln," *Abraham Lincoln Quarterly*, Vol. IV, No. 8 (Dec. 1947), 396.

2. Richard W. Etulain, "Abraham Lincoln Looks West," *Wild West* (April 2009), 26–28.

3. *Id.* at 30.

4. Fred H. Brinkerhoff, "The Kansas Tour of Lincoln the Candidate," *Kansas History: A Journal of the Central Plains* 31 (Winter 2008–2009), 275.

5. Carol Dark Ayres, *Lincoln and Kansas: Partnership for Freedom* (Manhattan, Kans. Sunflower Univ. Press, 2001), 67–68. On March 4, 1859, Lincoln wrote

to Martin F. Conway, a lawyer living in Lawrence, who was the KT representative of the 25-member Republican National Committee, which would make the crucial decision nine months later on where to hold the May 1860 Republican National Presidential Convention. Lincoln asked Conway whether he thought the Kansas Republicans would welcome Lincoln at the May 1859 KT Republican convention. Library of Congress, March 16, 1859, letter from M.F. Conway to Abraham Lincoln. Was Lincoln also attempting to ascertain whether Conway supported Lincoln, such that Conway might be willing later that year to steer the national convention to Lincoln's home state of Illinois? Conway would also soon serve in the Frontier Guard.

6. Jefferson L. Dugger to Abraham Lincoln, May 4, 1859. Lincoln later used the term "wide-awake" in a speech, which inspired the formation of many "wide-awake" clubs of young men campaigning for his nomination for president in 1860. Jon Grinspan, "Young Men for War: The Wide Awakes and Lincoln's 1860 Presidential Campaign," *Journal of American History* (Sept. 2009), 357, 361.

7. *U.S. Biographical Dictionary* (S. Lewis & Co., 1879), 601–02.

8. "Lieut. Colonel David Stewart Gordon, 2d U.S. Cavalry," *Nevada State Journal,* Dec. 15, 1889; William G. Cutler, *History of the State of Kansas* (Chicago: A. T. Andreas, 1883); Hubert Howe Bancroft, *History of Nevada, Colorado and Wyoming: 1540–1888* (San Francisco: History Co., 1890), 653.

9. Ayres, *supra,* at 73.

10. James P. Muehlberger, "Reflections on Lincoln's Kansas Campaign," *J. Kans. B. Ass'n* (November 2009), 25. Growing up on farms, many frontiersmen had gone to school sporadically, only a few months at a time.

11. Douglas L. Wilson, *Lincoln's Sword: The Presidency and the Power of Words* (New York: Alfred A. Knopf, 2006), 30, 90. Lincoln attended less than one year of primitive schooling on the frontier. When he set his sights on becoming a "public man," he needed to learn grammar and try to soften his frontier dialect. Around the age of 22, he began working with a New Salem, Illinois, schoolteacher, Mentor Graham, to learn grammar. 30 years after his grammar lessons, when it came time to be sworn in as president, the only New Salem friend he invited to sit with him on the platform at his inauguration was Mentor Graham. C.A. Tripp, *The Intimate World of Abraham Lincoln* (New York: Free Press, 2005), 52.

12. Fred H. Brinkerhoff, "The Kansas Tour of Lincoln the Candidate," *Kansas Historical Quarterly,* (1945): 294–307, reprinted in *Kansas History: A Journal of the Central Plains* 31 (Winter 2008–2009), 275–93.

13. The Hannibal to St. Joseph Railroad line had opened for traffic on February 15, 1859. The 260-mile-long railroad line was traversed in just over four hours; the route had taken 12 days by horse. Poorly laid tracks gave a bruising bump-bump-bump to the cars as they chugged along. *History of Daviess County, Missouri* (1984), 11.

14. Ayres, *supra*, at 74.

15. Doris Kearns Goodwin, *Team of Rivals*, (New York, Simon & Schuster, 2005), 231; Earl S. Miers, ed. *Lincoln Day by Day*. U.S. Government Publication, Washington DC. Vol. III, (1969), 48; David Herbert Donald, *Lincoln* (New York: Simon & Schuster, 1995), 46.

16. Tripp, *The Intimate World of Abraham Lincoln*, 50–51. It would be another ten years before a bridge spanned the mighty Missouri River.

17. *Lincoln in Kansas*, Kansas Historical Collections, 1901–1902 (1902), 536–52; Patrick Leopold, *Gray's Doniphan County History: A Record of the Happenings of Half a Hundred Years* (Roycroft Press, 1905), 166.

18. *Lincoln in Kansas*, *supra*, at 537.

19. Elwood Free Press, Dec. 3, 1859: The local newspaper reported Lincoln's words as "the fathers" but I believe this to be an aural error by the reporter. Two months later, at Cooper Union, Lincoln used the phrase "our fathers" at least five times. Harold Holzer, *Lincoln at Cooper Union: The Speech That Made Abraham Lincoln President* (New York: Simon & Schuster, 2004), 122–23.

20. Holzer, *id.* at 122.

21. *Lincoln in Kansas*, *supra*, note 214 at 538–39; Theodore C. Sorensen, "A Man of His Words," *Smithsonian* (Winter 2009), 60.

22. *Lincoln in Kansas*, *supra*, at 539; Rufus Rockwell Wilson, "Intimate Memories of Lincoln, Franklin G. Adams," *Proceedings of the Kansas Historical Society,* Vol. VII, 213–14.

23. Ayres, *supra*, at 88–90. Speeches in 1859 America were typically much longer than they are today, and a speech of only an hour and a half would have been considered short by 1859 standards. Many of those in the audience probably traveled quite a distance by horse or wagon to hear Lincoln's address, and they would have felt shortchanged by a speech of less than an hour and a half in duration.

24. Fred Kaplan, *Lincoln: The Biography of a Writer* (New York: Harper Collins, 2008), 67. Once a farmer asked Lincoln why he did not put his stories in a book. Lincoln replied, "Such a book would stink like a thousand privies." *Id.*

25. Edgar Lee Masters, *Lincoln, the Man* (New York: Dodd, Mead, 1931), 145.

26. *The Daily Argus* (Mt. Vernon, N.Y.), Aug. 10, 1892; "J. C. Normile lived in Atchison," *Atchison Daily Globe,* Aug. 10, 1892, 1; Thomas M. Spencer, *Power on Parade,* 1877–1995 (Columbia: Univ. of Mo. Press, 2000), 22.

27. Ayres, *supra*, at 95.

28. *Id.* at 99–101.

29. Holzer, *supra*, at 131–32.

30. Burlingame, *Abraham Lincoln: A Life,* 576; *Lincoln in Kansas,* 540–44.

31. Sheridan Baker, *The Complete Stylist* (New York: Crowell Co., 1972), 4.

32. Ayres, *supra*, at 119. Anthony, Wilder, and Parrott would soon serve in the Frontier Guard.

33. *Id.* at 127–29.

34. Mary E. Delahay, Judge Mark W. Delahay, *Kansas Historical Collection, X* (1907), 640; Daniel W. Wilder letter to William Herndon, Nov. 24, 1866 ("Mr. Lincoln knew Lane well even when I first saw him ('59)"); Wilson, *Herndon Informants,* 418–19. Lane later included a note in a Feb. 17, 1860, letter to Delahay in which Lane goes out of his way to say that he and Lincoln had never met. Ayres, *Lincoln and Kansas,* 142. This is a curious denial, refuted by two firsthand accounts of unbiased witnesses at the Delahay dinner. Why would Lane have made an effort to create a misleading record? Plausible deniability is one possible explanation. Lincoln notes in his letter to Delahay, prior to visiting Leavenworth, that Lane was a controversial figure who might damage Lincoln's reputation as a moderate Republican. Lincoln was running for president and did not want to be associated with the controversial Lane. Ever cautious, ever ambitious, Lincoln (and Delahay) would have wanted Lincoln to escape the outcast status to which abolitionists were relegated in national politics. Lincoln and/or Delahay may have had second thoughts about Lincoln's meeting with Lane, and they may have wanted something that Lincoln could later use to refute any damaging allegations about the meeting. Delahay may have asked Lane to send him the letter.

35. Baron, *supra*, at 57.

36. *"Lincoln Day by Day," New York Tribune,* Aug. 30, 1860; *Collected Works of Abraham Lincoln, Second Speech at Leavenworth, Kansas* (Roy B. Bassler ed.), Dec. 5, 1859, Vol. III, 502–04.

37. *Collected Works, supra* at 306; Ayres, *supra*, at 123; Lincoln to James W. Somers, Springfield, March 17, 1860.

38. "The Lincoln Convention," *Emporia Gazette,* April 21, 1860.

Chapter 8

1. Von Drehl, *supra*, at 237.

2. Circular of the Republican Nat'l Committee, Emporia Weekly News (Emporia, Kans.), Sept. 17, 1859; Martin F. Conway letter; Goodwin, *supra* note 212, at 228. Republican leaders later concluded: "Had the Convention been held at any other place, Lincoln would not have been nominated." Goodwin, *Team of Rivals*, 229, 254.

3. Goodwin, *supra* at 229; Reinhard H. Luthin, *The First Lincoln Campaign* (Gloucester, Mass.: P. Smith, 1964), 20–21.

4. Richard W. Etulain, *Lincoln Looks West: From the Mississippi to the Pacific* (Carbondale: Southern Illinois Univ. Press, 2010), 90.

5. Ayres, *supra* note 202, at 105.

6. Holzer, *supra* note 216, at 219, 234–35.

7. Baron, "Abraham Lincoln and the German Immigrants," *supra*, at 66; Abraham Lincoln letter to Joshua Speed, Aug. 24, 1855.

8. Baron, *supra*, at 77.

9. *Id.* at 96–98.

10. *Id.* at 94, 101.

11. *Id.* at 117–19.

12. David Herbert Donald, *Lincoln* (New York: Simon & Schuster, 1996), 244–45.

13. Goodheart, *supra*, at 35–36.

14. *Id.* at 40.

15. *Id.*

16. Goodwin, *supra*, note 212, at 252; Baron, *supra*, note 152, at 133; *Lincoln's Journalist: John Hay's Anonymous Writings for the Press, 1860–65* (Michael Burlingame ed.) (Carbondale: Southern Illinois Univ. Press, 1998), 1. Other delegates to the convention included William Ross and A.C. Wilder from the Kansas Territory, O. H. Irish, Phineas Hitchcock, and Algernon Paddock from the Nebraska Territory; Charles Hendley from Kentucky; and John B. Brown from Virginia. These men later served in the Frontier Guard. Brown was a farmer and dairyman who lived in Alexandria. Rebel authorities arrested Brown after he returned home from the convention on the trumped-up charge of "circulating incendiary documents" because he had a copy of the pro-Union *Washington Star* newspaper. *New York Times,* June 12, 1860.

17. Goodheart, *supra*, at 32–33.

18. "William Marsh, Son of a Miller, Friend of a President," http://bentvill history.blogspot.com (acquired August 26, 2014). In May 1860, William Marsh took five beautiful, now famous, photographs of the candidate.

19. Baron, *supra*, at 141.

20. *Id.* at 151, 154, n.3; Henry Villard, *New York Herald*, Dec. 9, 1860.

21. Klein, *supra*, at 18–19.

22. *Id.* at 37–38.

23. *Id.* at 42.

24. *Id.* at 30–31.

25. *Id.* at 10, 29–31.

26. *Id.*

27. *Id.* at 16.

28. *Id.* at 120–21.

29. *Id.*; "Harold Holzer, Lincoln's Tough Guy," *Civil War Times* (June 2014), 72, 77.

30. Goodheart, *supra*, at 25; Isaac H. Arnold, "The Baltimore Plot to Assassinate Abraham Lincoln," *Harper's New Monthly Magazine*, Vol. 37 (New York: Harper & Brothers, 1868), 123–28.

31. David G. Taylor, "Business and Political Career of Thomas Ewing Jr.: A Study of Frustrated Ambition," PhD Thesis, University of Kansas (1970), 159.

32. *Id.* at 276–77.

33. Klein, *supra*, at 323, 328.

34. Ernest Mettendorf, *Between Triumph and Disaster: The History of the 46th New York Infantry, 1861 to 1865* (Eden, N.Y.: self-published, 2012), 5; Frank H. Pierce III, *The Washington Saengerbund, A History of German Song and German Culture in the Nation's Capital* (Washington: The Washington Saengerbund, 1981), 11. The German-Americans constituted Company B, Turner's Rifles, District of Columbia Militia, and were commanded by Captain Wladimir Krzyzanowski. That night, at his Inaugural Ball, Lincoln visited with Tom Bancroft, who had fought in the Kansas Territory under Lane, and George Bassett, the vice president of the Washington Republican Association, both of whom later served in the Frontier Guard.

35. Goodheart, *supra*, at 287.

Chapter 9

1. John G. Nicolay & John Hay, *Abraham Lincoln: A History, Vol. 4* (New York: Century Co., 1890), 104–05; Lucius Crittenden, *Invisible Siege: The Journal of Lucius E. Crittenden,* April 15, 1861–July 14, 1861 (San Diego: Americana Exchange Press, 1969), 3.

2. *The National Republican* (Washington, D.C.), April 17, 1861.

3. Ida Tarbell, *Life of Lincoln,* Vol. 2 (New York: Doubleday & McClure, 1903), 44–45.

4. Lockwood, *supra,* at 82.

5. Goodwin, *supra,* at 349–50.

6. Lockwood, *supra,* at 84, 86.

7. *Id.* at 88; Stanley Kimmel, *Mr. Lincoln's Washington,* 172. Just four years earlier, ten people died after trainloads of Baltimore gang members came to Washington to influence the city's municipal elections. President Buchanan was forced to order the U.S. Marines at the Navy Yard into the city to maintain order.

8. "Gen. James H. Lane's Company," *The Nat'l Republican,* April 20, 24, 1861; *Frontier Guard Roll & Other Proceedings,* April 18, 1861, Frontier Guard Records, Library of Congress ("Roll"). The 116 men who served the entire time of the Frontier Guard's service were included in the Roll, which I discovered in the Library of Congress. The Roll states that it was prepared by Clifford Arick, Secretary of the Frontier Guard, and states: "This is to certify that the foregoing are the substantial memoranda of facts and incidents connected with the organization, service and discharge of the Frontier Guard." It authorizes a certificate of discharge for each man, to be signed by Lane. In the same file folder with the Roll was a December 20, 1908, letter from Clifford Arick's son (Cliff) to his sister, Lucy, who may have been employed at the Library of Congress. The letter refers to Ida Tarbell's 1903 *Life of Lincoln,* in which Tarbell references the Frontier Guard and Lincoln's speech to them when they "muster[ed] out." Arick tells his sister he believes that Lincoln's speech is in "that roll book you have." Library of Congress records indicate that the Roll was donated by Ms. Arick in 1927 (who spelled her surname "Arrick" at the time). In a January 22, 1907, letter to David Gordon, Frontier Guard Prentice Clark refers to a list of Frontier Guard soldiers "as certified to by General Lane." The Roll appears to be the official Roll approved by Lane. Based upon its formal, elegant, and bound appearance, it appears the Roll was prepared by Arick sometime after the Guard left the White House, apparently based in part upon his handwritten day-by-day (although some days are missing), loose page accounts. I also discovered in the Library of Congress a list of the names of an additional 48 men. The list states it was prepared by Frontier Guard George L. Febiger, and appears to be a list of men who spent only a night or two with the

Guard and who were not included in the Roll. I have included information about these additional men throughout this book.

9. *Frontier Guard Roll & Other Proceedings*, April 18, 1861, Frontier Guard Records, Library of Congress. Delahay was staying with Nicholas Vedder in Washington. Vedder's wife was Indiana Hanks, the sister of Delahay's wife, Mary. Both of the Hanks daughters were second cousins to Abraham Lincoln's mother, Nancy Hanks. Frontier Guard member Clark Hanks was brother to Indiana and Mary. 15-year-old Norton Vedder was Nicholas's son, and one of the youngest members of the Frontier Guard. "Personal," *Nat'l Republican* (Washington, D.C.), April 15, 1861.

10. *Nat'l Republican* (Washington, D.C.), April 20, 24, 1861.

11. *Willmer Tribune* (Minnesota), Sept. 24, 1902, Clay's men patrolled the downtown streets near Willard's Hotel. Lockwood, *supra*, at 94.

12. Goodwin, *supra* note 212, at 359; Goodheart, *supra*, at 78; John Speer, *supra*, at 238.

13. On the east side of the second floor, accessible through a central corridor that ran past the library, were the presidential offices. Adjacent to the reception room was the president's office, with an adjoining room to Nicolay's office. All three rooms had windows facing the south lawn. Across the narrow corridor were Hay's office and a large bedroom that the two secretaries shared for the next four years.

14. Erich Langsdorf, "Jim Lane and the Frontier Guard," *Kansas Historical Quarterly*, Vol. 9 (1940), 16.

15. *Frontier Guard Roll & Other Proceedings*, April 18, 1861, Library of Congress.

16. See Chapter 7, *supra*; Warren Y. Jenkins, *The Jenkins, Boone, and Lincoln Family Records* (no pub. listed, 1925), 8.

17. Langsdorf, *supra*, at 13, 15–17.

18. *Id.* at 15–17.

19. "Frontier Guards," *Winfield Courier*, Dec. 7, 1882.

20. John Hay, *Inside Lincoln's White House: The Complete Civil War Diary of John Hay* (Michael Burlingame and John R. T. Ettlinger eds.) (Carbondale: South. Ill. Univ. Press 1997), 1–2; *Proceedings of the Frontier Guard*, April 18, 1861.

21. *Id.* at 1; *Frontier Guard Roll & Other Proceedings*, April 18, 1861.

22. "When Kansas Soldiers Camped on Velvet Carpets," *Kansas City Star*, Dec. 15, 1907.

Chapter 10

1. Lockwood, *supra*, at 33, 107; *Charleston Mercury,* April 26, 1861.

2. Goodheart, *1861: The Civil War Awakening,* 173; *Charleston Mercury,* April 26, 1861, p.1, col. 4.

3. "The Union and Free Speech Meeting on Tuesday Night," *Nat'l Republican* (Washington, D.C.), April 18, 1861; "An Epoch in Our History," *Nat'l Republican* (Washington, D.C.), May 1, 1861.

4. "Noise Keeps an Army Out," *Cincinnati Inquirer,* July 6, 1907.

5. John Hay, *Inside Lincoln's White House: The Complete Civil War Diary of John Hay* (April 20, 1861), Michael Burlingame & John R. T. Ettinger eds. (Carbondale: Southern Ill. Univ. Press, 1999), 4.

6. George Wilson Brown to Abraham Lincoln, April 19, 1861, *Abraham Lincoln Papers,* Library of Congress; Lockwood, *supra* note 5, at 122.

7. "Maryland As of Yore!" *Charleston Mercury,* April 26, 1861, p.1, col. 7.

8. Hay, *supra,* at 2–3.

9. *Nat'l Republican* (Washington), April 20, 1861; *Proceedings of the Frontier Guard,* April 19, 1861, Frontier Guard Records, Library of Congress.

10. John Hay, *Inside Lincoln's White House* (diary entry, April 19, 1861), *supra,* at 3; John Nicolay to Therena Bates, April 19, 1861, in Nicolay, *With Lincoln in the White House,* 34–35; Lockwood, *The Siege of Washington,* 135.

11. George Brown to Abraham Lincoln, April 19, 1861, *Abraham Lincoln Papers,* Library of Congress; Lockwood, *The Siege of Washington,* 137.

12. Lockwood, *supra,* at 138.

13. *Id.* at 139; Hay, *Inside Lincoln's White House* (April 20, 1861), *supra,* at 4.

14. John Nicolay, *The Outbreak of the Rebellion* (New York: Scribner's, 1882), 98; *Frontier Guard Roll & Other Proceedings,* April 20, 1861, Library of Congress.

15. *Frontier Guard Roll & Other Proceedings,* April 20, 1861; Jan. 22, 1909, letter from P. M. Clark to David S. Gordon, Washington Historical Society.

16. Hay, *supra,* at 9; April 20, 1861, James Lane letter to Abraham Lincoln.

17. Whalen, *supra,* at 2.

18. Wiley Sword, *The Historic Henry Rifle: Oliver Winchester's Famous Civil War Repeater* (Lincoln, R.I.: Andrew Mowbray, 2002), 30; Minutes of Shenandoah County (Va.) Court, Sept. 11, 1837; *Baltimore Sun,* July 12, 1856; *Proceedings,* Frontier Guard Records, Library of Congress. One of the members of the Frontier Guard may have been a light-skinned African-American. Constant Freeman Smith, a 26-year-old from Washington, was one of the men on the list whom I was unable to conclusively identify. However, Baltimore census records

state that the father of Constant Freeman Smith was born in Barbados, an island where slavery was legal until 1834. After emancipation, many freed slaves took on the name "Freeman" to indicate their emancipated status. If Smith was African-American, he may have been one of the first African-Americans to enlist in the Union cause. 1880 Census, Baltimore, Md., 2d Election Dist., June 8–9, 1880, line 49.

19. April 20, 1861, Jared Phillips letter, quoted in Levi Beebe, *A Sketch of the Samuel Phillips Family*, *Berkshire Book*, Vol. 1, Berkshire Historical Society (Pittsfield, Mass.: Sun Printing Co., 1892), 228.

20. *Frontier Guard Roll & Other Proceedings*, April 20, 1861, Library of Congress.

21. Abraham Lincoln, Message to Congress, May 27, 1862, and *Rebellion Record,* Frank Moore ed,, Vol. 5 (New York: G. P. Putnam, 1863), 145; Whalen & Whalen, *supra*, at 10.

22. John G. Nicolay & John Hay, *Abraham Lincoln: A History,* Vol. 4 (New York: Century Co., 1890), 137; Helen Nicolay, *Lincoln's Secretary: A Biography of John G. Nicolay* (New York: Longmans, Green, 1949), 80; *New York Tribune*, April 24, 1861.

23. *Frontier Guard Proceedings*, April 21, 1861; "An Epoch in Our History," *Nat'l Republican,* May 1, 1861.

24. Roy Bird, "Jim Lane's Misnamed Frontier Guards Had a Lofty Charge to Protect the President of the United States," *America's Civil War,* Vol. 12, Issue 1 (March 1999), 8–9.

25. Henry Villard, *Memories of Henry Villard, Journalist and Financier, 1835–1900,* Vol. 1 (Boston: Houghton Mifflin, 1904), 166; Frederick Douglass, *Hope and Despair in Cowardly Times*, in the Frederick Douglass Papers, Ser. 1, "Speeches, Debates and Interviews," John W. Blessingame, Vol. 3 (New Haven: Yale Univ. Press, 1985), 101; Winfield Scott to Abraham Lincoln, April 22, 1861, *Abraham Lincoln Papers*, Library of Congress; Lockwood, *supra*, at 190.

26. John G. Nicolay & John Hay, *Abraham Lincoln: A History,* Vol. 4, 107 (New York: Century Co. 1890); *Frontier Guard Roll & Other Proceedings*, April 22, 1861.

27. *Abraham Lincoln: The Observations of John G. Nicolay and John Hay* (Michael Burlingame ed.), 55.

28. *Frontier Guard Roll & Other Proceedings*, April 22, 1861; "A Religious Martyr," *Kansas City Star*, Oct. 18, 2009.

29. *Frontier Guard Roll & Other Proceedings*, April 22, 1861.

30. Lockwood, *supra*, at 182.

31. *Id.* at 193; Whalen, *supra*, at 10, 291–92.

32. Lockwood, *supra,* at 193.

33. Whalen, *supra*, at 291–92.

34. Report No. 337, 51st Congress, 1st Session, Cong. Ed., Vol. 2704 (Feb. 20, 1890).

35. *Id.*; "The Times of War and Reconstruction: Reminiscences of Honorable S.C. Pomeroy," in *Kansas Biographical Scrapbook,* P, Vol. VI, 143.

36. *Frontier Guard Roll & Other Proceedings*, April 23, 1861; Ayres, *supra*, at 18–19.

37. Ayres, *supra* at 17.

38. *Frontier Guard Roll & Other Proceedings*, April 24, 1861.

39. Henry Villard, *Memoirs of Henry Villard, Journalist and Financier,* 1835–1900, Vol. 1 (Boston: Houghton Mifflin, 1904), 169; Chittenden, *Recollections*, 130; John Hay, diary entry, April 24, 1861, and *Inside Lincoln's White House*, 11.

40. Lockwood, *Siege of Washington,* 218; *Frontier Guard Roll & Other Proceedings*, April 24, 1861. On April 24, Marcus Parrot left Washington on the steamer *Keystone State* and arrived in New York on April 26 on his way back to Kansas. Perhaps for this reason, Lane did not list Parrott on the official roll of the Frontier Guard.

41. Philip St. George Cocke to Robert E. Lee, April 24, 1861, OR, ser. 1, vol. 2, 777–779.

42. *New York World,* April 30, 1861, at 4; Hay diary, April 25, 1861.

43. *New York Tribune,* April, 27, 1861, 5.

44. *Frontier Guard Roll & Other Proceedings*, April 25, 1861; Jan. 22, 1909, letter from P. M. Clark to David S. Gordon, Washington Historical Society. Henry Villard, writing a half-century later, believed that the taking of Washington might have ended the war in April 1861. Henry Villard, *supra*, at 167.

45. *Frontier Guard Roll & Other Proceedings*, April 26, 1861.

46. "Noise Keeps an Army Out," *Cincinnati Inquirer,* July 6, 1907; *Willmer Tribune* (Minn.), Sept. 24, 1902; Levi Beebe, *A Sketch of the Samuel Phillips Family* (Pittsfield, Mass.: Sun Printing Co., 1892).

47. *Frontier Guard Roll & Other Proceedings*, April 26, 1861.

48. Hay, *supra*, at 4–10; Jan. 22, 1907, letter from Prentice Clark to David Gordon, Washington Historical Society. The Frontier Guard were never enrolled in the Union army. Several bills were introduced in Congress to do so. The last bill passed the Senate in 1894 and was sent to the House, where the record ends. Cong. Rec., Vol. XXVII, Pt. 3, 2086, 2176.

49. *Frontier Guard Roll & Other Proceedings*, April 27, 1861.

50. *Id.*

51. Abraham Lincoln, "Message to Congress," May 27 1862, in *Rebellion Record,* Frank Moore ed., Vol. 5 (New York: G. P. Putnam, 1863), 146.

52. May 4, 1861, Daniel McCook letter to Richard Phelps, Library of Congress; Speer, *supra*, at 238; "Dr. Bancroft to Talk of Lincoln," *Quincy Daily Whig,* Aug. 8, 1908, at 8; "Saved the Capital," *Daily News Democrat* (Huntington, Ind.), Sept. 6, 1902, at 7.

53. *Nicolay Journal,* Feb. 17, 1862; Von Drehl, *supra*, at 75; "Noise Keeps an Army Out," *Cincinnati Inquirer,* July 6, 1907.

54. Bird, *supra*, at 9; Ayres, *supra*, at 23.

55. Hay, *supra*, at 13.

56. *Frontier Guard Roll & Other Proceedings*, April 27, 1861.

Chapter 11

1. Gary R. Kremer, "The Abraham Lincoln Legacy in Missouri," *Missouri Historical Review,* Vol. 103, No. 2 (Jan. 2009), 108.

2. Wilder, "The Annals of Kansas," 45; *Kansas City Star,* July 24, 2011; Goodheart, *supra* note 4, at 234. Warring factions at the time referred to themselves as either "federals" or "secessionists"—and the latter was shortened to "secesh."

3. "No person holding any office under the United States shall be a member of either house during his continuance in office." Const., art. 1, § 6.

4. Abraham Lincoln to Simon Cameron, June 20, 1861, in *The Collected Works of Abraham Lincoln,* Roy Bassler ed., Vol. 4 (New Brunswick: Rutgers Univ. Press, 1953), 414. Lincoln apparently did not want to create documents that could later be used against him if objections were raised to Lane's illegal appointment. Lincoln's concerns soon proved to be valid.

5. Ronald D. Smith, *Thomas Ewing Jr.: Frontier Lawyer and Civil War General* (Columbia: Univ. of Missouri Press, 2008), 150. Lane retaliated against Robinson by encouraging the Kansas legislature to charge Robinson with participating in a bond scandal. Although Robinson was acquitted, his reputation was permanently damaged; *Id.* at 150.

6. "Military Movements in Kansas," *Milw. Morning Sentinel,* May 16, 1861, 1; Pomeroy, *supra*, at 145.

7. American Civil War Research Database, First Infantry Kansas.

8. James M. McPherson, *Battle Cry of Freedom: The Civil War Era* (New York: Oxford University Press, 1988), 351–52; William Garrett Piston, *Wilson's Creek*

(Charlotte: North Carolina Univ. Press, 2000), 45, 307; Shelby Foote, *The Civil War: A Narrative, Fort Sumter to Perryville* (New York: Random House, 1958), 94; W. S. Burke, *Official Military History of Kansas Regiments during War for the Suppression of the Great Rebellion* (Leavenworth, Kansas, 1870), 3; Michael E. Banasik, ed., *Reluctant Cannoneer: The Diary of Robert T. McMahon of the 25th Independent Ohio Light Artillery* (Iowa City: Press of the Camp Pope, 2000), 57.

9. Collins, *supra*, at 189.

10. *Lawrence Republican*, Oct. 3, 1861; Spurgeon, *supra*, at 184, 223. One African-American freed by Lane's command was asked how he came to be free. His quick response was, "God sent Jim Lane and his army for me—I don't care what anybody says." Speer, *supra*, at viii.

11. Bryce Benedict, *Jayhawkers: The Civil War Brigade of James Henry Lane* (Norman, Okla.: Univ. of Oklahoma Press, 2009), 4; Speer, *supra*, at 263.

12. Collins, *supra*, at 189.

13. At least one author has recently claimed that Lane's men executed nine Osceola civilians. No authority is provided for this allegation, nor is a single one of the alleged victims identified. Richard F. Sunderwirth, *The Burning of Osceola, Missouri* (Independence, Mo.: Two Trails Publ'g, 2007), 137. The sole support for this claim is that a place exists in the local cemetery where some believe unmarked graves exist that could date to the 1860s. This is too slender a reed on which to base a charge of murder. Even more compelling, a two-day investigation in 1899, including interviews of survivors of the event 37 years earlier, refutes this recent fabrication: whoever was killed died in the skirmish before Lane's men entered the town. John Speer, *The Burning of Osceola, Missouri by Lane, and the Quantrill Massacre Contrasted*, Transactions of the Kansas State Historical Society, Vol. VI (Topeka: W. Y. Morgan, 1900), 305–08.

14. Speer, *supra*, at 212.

15. Spurgeon, *supra*, at 108–09.

16. J. H. Lane, Feb. 26, 1862, on his return to the Senate, in "Kansas Historical Pamphlets," Vol. 6, Library and Archives Division, Kansas State Historical Society; James Lane to John Fremont, Sept. 24, 1861, in U.S. War Department, *The War of the Rebellion: A Compilation of the Official Records of the Union and Confederate Armies,* 1st ser., Vol. 3 (Washington, D.C.: Gov't Printing Office, 1893), 505.

17. Abraham Lincoln to David Hunter, Dec. 31, 1861, in *Collected Works* (Bassler ed.), *supra*, at Vol. 5, p.84.

18. Spurgeon, *supra*, at 121–22.

19. "An Early Kansas Character," *Kansas City Gazette*, June 2, 1892.

20. Von Drehl, *supra*, at 26.

21. Spurgeon, *supra*, at 220–23.

22. *Id.* at 223–25; *New York Herald*, Dec. 18, 1861.

23. Spurgeon, *supra*, at 229.

24. *Id.* at 230–31.

25. *Id.* at 234–36; John Speer, *supra*, at 261.

26. Ian Michael Spurgeon, *Soldiers in the Army of Freedom: The First Kansas Colored, the Civil War's First African-American Combat Unit* (Norman, Okla.: Univ. of Oklahoma Press, 2014), 3–5. The men were not mustered into U.S. military service until January 13, 1863, after Abraham Lincoln issued the Emancipation Proclamation.

27. This was nine months before the 54th Massachusetts Infantry (the black regiment in the movie "Glory") stormed Fort Wagner. In fact, the First Kansas Colored Infantry was marching victoriously off the field from Honey Springs, its fourth engagement, at the time the Massachusetts 54th attacked Fort Wagner. Spurgeon, *supra*, at 5.

28. *Id.* at 107.

29. Donald L. Scott, July 10, 2014, Island Mound, Mo., Presentation; Spurgeon, *supra*, at 97, 107.

30. Spurgeon, *supra*, at 235–37.

31. Ayers, *supra*, at 25; Spurgeon, *id.* at 115.

32. Smith, *supra*, at 163.

33. *Id.* at 183.

34. *Id.*

35. *Abraham Lincoln*, Nov. 19, 1863, Gettysburg Address; Smith, *supra*, at 188–89.

36. Michael Fellman, *Inside War: The Guerrilla Conflict in Missouri During the Civil War* (New York: Random House, 1995), 251, n.3.; Don E. Fehrenbacher, *Abraham Lincoln, Speeches and Writings,* Vol. 2 (Library of America, 1989), 523.

37. "Eyewitness Reports of Quantrill's Raid," in *Kansas History: A Journal of the Central Plains* 28 (Fred N. Six ed. Summer 2005), 101–02.

38. Albert Castel, *William Clark Quantrill: His Life and Times* (New York: Frederick Fell, 1962), 119–20, 122; Richard S. Brownlee, *Gray Ghosts of the Confederacy: Guerrilla Warfare in the West, 1861–1865* (Baton Rouge, La.: Louisiana State Univ. Press, 1958).

39. Jan Biles, "Quantrill's Raid: Abomination Against Civilians," *The Topeka Capital-Journal*, June 10, 2015; Only a single structure belonging to Lane sur-

vived the raid. It was a stable built on the highest point of Lane's property. Now the oldest building on the campus of the University of Kansas, it serves as the annex for the Max Cade Center for German Studies. Charles Robinson's home was spared by the guerrillas. Collins, *supra*, at 288–89.

40. Lane was outraged by the Lawrence Massacre and laid the blame on a lack of diligence by the Union military authorities. Others pointed out that, of all Quantrill's Kansas robberies and murders, not one of them occurred when Lane had any military command. When Lane's Brigade patrolled the border, Quantrill's band of murderers hid in the hills between Kansas City and Independence and confined themselves to murdering men in Missouri. Speer, *supra*, at 270.

41. Smith, *supra*, at 229.

42. *Id.*

43. *Id.* at 231; Edgar Langsdorf, "Price's Raid and the Battle of Mine Creek," *Kansas History: A Journal of the Central Plains*, Vol. 37, no. 2 (Summer 2014), 81; William Force Scott, *The Story of a Cavalry Regiment: The Career of the Fourth Iowa Veteran Volunteers; From Kansas to Georgia, 1861–1865* (New York: G. P. Putnam's Sons, 1893), 304–06.

44. Langsdorf, *supra*, at 83.

45. Spurgeon, *supra*, at 147.

46. Speer, *supra*, at 275.

47. *Abelard Guthrie Diary*, Jan. 18, 1862, Abelard Guthrie Collection, Library and Archives Division, Kansas State Historical Society.

48. Charles Robinson to A. A. Lawrence, June 27, 1863, University of Kansas, Charles and Sarah T. Robinson Collection, Library and Archives Division, Kansas State Historical Society; Miner, "Lane and Lincoln: A Mysterious Connection," 188. Lincoln told the Kansas governor who followed Robinson, Thomas Carney: "Lane knocks at my door every morning. You know he is a persistent fellow and hard to put off. I don't see you very often and have to pay attention to him." L.W. Spring, *Kansas* (Boston: Houghton Mifflin, 1890), 274.

49. Spurgeon, *supra*, at 142–43. The meeting of the Union League was significant, because two-thirds of the delegates were also members of the Republican National Convention. *Id.*

50. Speer, *supra*, at 262. Frontier Guard Chester Thomas was chosen presidential elector for Kansas and cast his vote for Lincoln.

51. John C. Waugh, *Reelecting Lincoln* (New York: Random House 1997), 197.

52. Mark Wells Johnson, *That Brave Body of Men: The U.S. Regular Infantry and the Civil War in the West* (Cambridge, Mass.: Da Capo Press, 2003), 609.

53. *Historical Papers of the Lancaster Historical Society,* Vol. 18 (1914), 15. Hartman later wrote that it was "very unfair" that the service of the Frontier Guard had been forgotten, since their service at the White House was "as noteworthy as any [service] subsequently rendered [in the Civil War]." "The Clay and Frontier Guards," *National Tribune* (Washington, D.C.), July 12, 1906. See Appendix II and Civil War records of Tom Bancroft, Sam Greer, Merritt Insley, Sam Tappan, and Ebenezer White.

Chapter 12

1. McPherson, *supra*, at 334.

2. *Id.* at 335–36.

3. Whalen & Whalen, *supra*, at 55. The Union and Confederates gave different names to several Civil War battles. In most cases, the Confederates named the battle after the town that served as their base, while the Union forces chose the landmark nearest to the fighting or to their own lines.

4. McPherson, *supra,* at 341–42.

5. Whalen & Whalen, *supra,* at 62.

6. *Id.* at 64–66; Letter from Daniel McCook to Steed, Oct. 10, 1861, *McCook Papers*, Library of Congress.

7. Will H. McDonald, *An Illustrated History of Lincoln County, Nebraska and Her People,* Vol. 2 (American Historical Soc'y, 1920), 17–18. At the battle of Gettysburg, Walker was ordered by General Pleasanton to report to General Mead for duty on Meade's staff during the battle, and he may have been the only member of Meade's staff to survive. *Id.*

8. "Late Col. David Stuart Gordon, 2d U.S. Cavalry," *Nevada State Journal* (Reno, Nevada), Dec. 15, 1889.

9. Whalen & Whalen, *The Fighting McCooks,* 81.

10. *Id.* at 213; July 23, 1863, *McCook Papers.* Daniel McCook had eight sons, seven of whom fought for the Union, and the oldest, Dr. Latimer McCook, tended to wounded Union soldiers on 38 battlefields. Daniel's brother John had five sons, all of whom fought for the Union. Overall, 17 McCooks fought for the North in the Civil War: three major generals, three brigadier generals, one naval lieutenant, two colonels, one major, one lieutenant, four surgeons, one private, and one chaplain. Four gave their lives to save the Union.

11. Whalen & Whalen, *supra*, at 292; Ed McCook to Mary Sheldon, May 10, 1861, *Butler–McCook Papers*, Library of Congress.

12. Whalen & Whalen, *supra*, at 293–94.

13. *Id.* at 299–300.

14. *Id.* at 300–04.

15. *Id.* at 304–05.

16. *Id.* at 307.

17. *Id.* at 306–08.

18. Id., at 308.

19. Fergus Bordewich, "The Election That Saved the United States," *Wall Street Journal,* Aug. 30, 2014.

20. Whalen & Whalen, *The Fighting McCooks,* 310.

21. *Id.* at 337–38.

22. *Id.* at 338.

23. *Id.* at 339.

24. *Wyandotte County and Kansas City, Kansas* (Chicago: The Goodspeed Publishing Co., 1890), 501; Several drops of Lincoln's blood fell on a theater program, which Bancroft picked up and later donated to the Kansas State Historical Society at Topeka, Kansas. "Dr. Bancroft to Talk of Lincoln," *Quincy Daily Whig,* Aug. 8, 1908.

25. William C. Edwards, *The Lincoln Assassination—The Rewards Files* (Google E-Book, 2012), 143–48.

26. Whalen & Whalen, *supra,* at 338–44. West Virginia had become a state in 1862.

27. Linda M. Welch, *Vermont in the Civil War* website; Madison J. Drake, *History of the Ninth New Jersey Volunteers* (Elizabeth, N.J.: Journal Printing House, 1889), 411; U.S. Civil War Soldier Records and Profiles, 1861–1865.

28. Jerald E. Podair, "Daniels, Edward Dwight," *Dictionary of Virginia Biography,* Vol. 3, edited by Sara B. Bearss, et al., (Richmond: Library of Virginia, 2006), 696–98; *Lawrence Daily Journal,* Lawrence, Kansas, November 6, 1901, 1; *Kansas Daily Tribune,* Lawrence Kansas, April 20, 1882, 3. See also Appendix II biographies for Denny Balch, John Carpenter, Charles and Thomas Champion, Henry Clinton, William Dyer, Daniel Webster Hughes, and William Parker Wright.

29. Dean B. Mahin, *The Blessed Place of Freedom: Europeans in Civil War America* (Dulles, Va.: Brassey's Inc., 2006), 16.

30. See Appendix II biographies for each man.

31. NARA, "Compiled Service Records of Volunteer Soldiers Who Served in Organizations from Maryland" (Catalog ID 300398); *Case Files of Investigations by Levi C. Turner and Lafayette C. Baker, 1861–1866,* NARA Catalog ID

656620; Paul Lanham, *Terror in the Dark—The Confederate Guerrilla Boyle,* Prince Georges County Historical Society, January 1975, Vol. III, no. 1. Boyle escaped and attacked Secretary Seward as part of John Wilkes Booth's assassination plot.

32. "Noise Keeps an Army Out," *Cincinnati Inquirer,* July 6, 1907.

Chapter 13

1. Spurgeon, *supra,* at 156–59.

2. Miner, *supra,* at 198–99. Ecclesiastes 12:6. Was Lane also thinking of when Lincoln broke Mary Delahay's pitcher, rendering it useless?

3. Miner, *id.* at 189; Charles Robinson to A.A. Lawrence, June 27, 1863, University of Kansas, Charles and Sarah T. Robinson Collection, Kansas State Historical Society; Old Testament, *Psalm 22,* suggests that a bull of Basham represented brutal strength.

4. Collins, *supra,* at 284.

5. *Id.* at 284, 288–89.

6. *Id.* at 289; Miner, *supra,* at 190.

7. Isaac Goodnow to Friend Sherman, April 1, 1858, Box 2, Isaac Goodnow Collection, Kansas State Historical Society.

8. Sidney Clarke, "Lane of Kansas," *Kansas City Journal,* Sept. 14, 1879, in "Kansas Reminiscences" clippings, Vol. 1, 161–200, Kansas State Historical Society; Leverett Spring, "The Career of a Kansas Politician," *American Historical Review* (1898), 101; William E. Connelly, James Henry Lane, The "Grim Chieftain" of Kansas, (Crane & Co., 1899), 7. The historiography on John Brown, whose reputation was eclipsed in much the same way as Lane's, and for some of the same reasons, is described in James Malin, *John Brown and the Legend of Fifty-Six* (Philadelphia: American Philadelphia Society, 1942).

9. Spurgeon, *supra,* at 141–42, 161, 164–65.

10. Lloyd Lewis, "The Man the Historians Forgot," *Kansas Historical Quarterly* 8 (February 1939), 85–87, 93; Michael Burlingame, *The Inner World of Abraham Lincoln* (Urbana, Ill.: Univ. of Illinois Press, 1994), 92–93.

11. Lewis, *supra* at 88; Prentice, *Jim Lane,* 117.

12. Craig Miner, *Lane and Lincoln: A Mysterious Connection,* 196.

13. "Lane Autobiography" in *Kansas Crusader of Freedom* (Doniphan City, KT), Feb. 3, 1858. Lane's enemies claimed that he was refused a divorce in Indiana and so moved to Kansas to obtain one, but was refused again. I found no facts to support either claim. It is true that Lane's wife left the Kansas Terri-

tory during her husband's absences during the Free State fight, returned to Indiana, and filed for divorce on grounds of abandonment. The couple remarried in 1859, however, when Lane returned to Indiana and campaigned for Lincoln; Spurgeon, *supra*, at 18.

14. Guthrie diary, Feb. 27, 1862, *St. Joseph (Mo.) Daily News*, Nov. 6, 1902, in Kansas Biographical Scrapbooks, Vol. 168:117, Kansas State Historical Society.

15. Gary Wills, *Lincoln at Gettysburg*, 74–76; Spring, *The Career of a Kansas Politician*, 87, 104; Miner, *Lane and Lincoln: A Mysterious Connection*, 198. In the 19th century, depression, particularly when it led to suicide, was considered a character flaw, not an illness.

16. James P. Muehlberger, *The Lost Cause: The Trials of Frank and Jesse James* (Yardley, Pa.: Westholme Publishing, LLC, 2015), x; Lewis, *The Man Historians Forgot*, 91; Sean Wilentz, "Who's Buried in the History Books?," *New York Times*, March 13, 2010. There was one reported incident of an unidentified female slapping Lane on a street in Washington, but this could have been a pro-slavery woman unhappy with Lane's opposition to slavery.

17. "Death of General E. M. McCook," *Nat'l Tribune* (Washington, D.C.), Sept. 16, 1907; "General Edward McCook Is Inmate of a Soldier's Home," *Fort Wayne News* (Fort Wayne, Ind.), March 9, 1900.

18. Smith, *Thomas Ewing, Jr.*, 297–98, 339.

19. *An Illustrated History of Lincoln County, Nebraska and Her People,* Vol. 2 (Will H. McDonald ed.), American Historical Soc'y, 1920, 17–18.

20. Mark Wells Johnson, *That Brave Body of Men: The U.S. Regular Infantry and the Civil War in the West* (Cambridge, Mass.: Da Capo Press, 2003), 609–10; Frederick Nolan, *The Lincoln County War: A Documentary History* (Sunstone Press, 2009), 660.

21. "Retirement of David S. Gordon," *Nat'l Tribune* (Washington, D.C.), May 30, 1922.

22. Thomas K. Tate, *Under the Iron Eyelids: A Biography of James Henry Burton, Armorer to the Nations* (Google E-Book), 329; A.T. Andreas, *History of the State of Kansas* (Chicago: Western Historical Co., 1883); *United States Biographical Dictionary,* Kansas Vol. (Chicago: S. Lewis & Com., 1879), 66–67.

23. Grant Lee Shumway, *History of Western Nebraska and Its People* (Western Publishing & Engraving Co., 1918), 432.

24. Edgar Langsdorf, "Thaddeus Hyatt in Washington Jail," *Kansas Historical Quarterly*, Vol. 9, No. 3 (August 1940), 225–39.

25. See Appendix II biographies.

26. Peter E. Palmquist, *Pioneer Photographers*, 360–62; "Death List of a Day," *New York Times*, Jan. 13, 1898, at 7; *Lawrence Daily Journal & Evening Tribune*, May 9, 1893; Adin Ballou, *An Elaborate History and Genealogy of the Ballous in America* (Providence, R.I.: E. L. Frederick & Son, 1888), 467.

27. William A. DuPuis, "When a Girl Sculpted Lincoln," *Sunday Star* (Washington, D.C.), Feb. 11, 1912.

28. *Id;* Lincoln was said to have never recovered from Willy's death—twice having Willy's body disinterred just to see him again. Goodwin, *Team of Rivals*, 80.

29. DuPuis, *supra.*

Epilogue

1. Lewis, "The Man History Forgot," 88; Speeches of Gen. J.H. Lane (Washington: McGill & Witherow, n.d.), 4, 8.

2. Collins, *Jim Lane*, 301–02.

3. Stephen B. Oates, *The Whirlwind of War: Voices of the Storm, 1861–1865* (New York: Harper Collins, 1998), 12.

4. *U.S. Biographical Dictionary* (Chicago: American Biographical Co., 1883), 66; E. D. Reddington, *Military Record of the Sons of Dartmouth in the Union Army and Navy, 1861–65*, 76; 39th Congress of the United States, April 13, 1866. See Appendix II biographies.

5. Herndon, *Life of Lincoln*, 101–02.

6. Jon Lauk, "The Silent Artillery of Time: Understanding Social Change in the Rural Midwest," *Great Plains Quarterly* 19 (Fall 1999), 246.

7. Miner, *Lane and Lincoln: A Mysterious Connection*, 199.

Acknowledgments

I was very fortunate to have some excellent historical researchers—Judy Sweets and Debby Lowery—who provided invaluable assistance and who spent countless hours researching the men in the Frontier Guard. Without them, this book would not exist. Thanks to Michelle Krowl, Library of Congress, for her assistance in identifying and obtaining some of the original Frontier Guard source materials located in the Library of Congress; Tim Rues, Kansas Historical Society, for his assistance regarding Kansas Territorial history and James H. Lane; Frank Baron, for his groundbreaking research and translation of Kansas Territorial German language newspapers as to the German-American role in Bleeding Kansas and for generously sharing that knowledge; Carol D. Ayres for kindly sharing her research regarding Abraham Lincoln's 1859 visit to the Kansas Territory; Ron Smith, who generously shared his research regarding Thomas Ewing, Jr.; and Ian Michael Spurgeon, who shared his research regarding Sidney Clarke. Thanks to Peter J. Casagrande, who patiently reviewed an early version of this manuscript and made many helpful suggestions. Thanks to the Freedom's Frontier National Heritage Area, which supports and makes available research on Bleeding Kansas and the Civil War along the Kansas/Missouri border. The staff of the Johnson County, Kansas and Kansas City, Missouri public libraries were also extremely helpful in obtaining source materials.

Last, but certainly not least, thanks to my publisher, Jon Malysiak, at Ankerwycke Books, who guided me through this process and made invaluable suggestions that made the book better, and to Kaitlyn Bitner, for her striking cover design. Any errors are mine.

Index